The Death Penalty
As Cruel Treatment
and Torture

Advisor in Criminal Justice to
Northeastern University Press
GIL GEIS

The Death Penalty
As Cruel Treatment
and Torture

CAPITAL PUNISHMENT CHALLENGED
IN THE WORLD'S COURTS

William A. Schabas

Northeastern University Press
BOSTON

Northeastern University Press

Copyright 1996 by William A. Schabas

Library of Congress Cataloging-in-Publication Data
Schabas, William, 1950–
    The death penalty as cruel treatment and torture :
capital punishment challenged in the world's courts /
William A. Schabas.
        p.   cm.
    Includes bibliographical references and index.
    ISBN 1-55553-268-3 (cl. : acid-free paper)
    1. Capital punishment.   2. Torture.   I. Title.
K5104.S335   1996
341.4'81—dc20   96-8241

Designed by Joyce C. Weston

Composed in Janson by Coghill Composition, Richmond, Virginia. Printed and bound by The Maple Press, York, Pennsylvania. The paper is Perfection Eggshell Recycled, an acid-free stock.

MANUFACTURED IN THE UNITED STATES OF AMERICA
00 99 98 97 96   5 4 3 2 1

To Marguerite and Louisa

CONTENTS

PREFACE

I thank the many colleagues and friends who have contributed directly or indirectly to this work, including Markus Schmidt, Katia Boustany, Georges Le Bel, Pierre Robert, Eric Prokosch, Hugo Adam Bedau, Peter Hodgkinson, Michael Radelet, Christopher Keith Hall, and Laurel Angus. My work was helped immensely by the important contribution of my research assistant, Yanick Charbonneau. I am also grateful for the research funding I received from my institution, the Université du Québec à Montréal. Thanks, once again, are also due to Penelope for her encouragement and support.

William A. Schabas
Université du Québec à Montréal
November 1995

ABBREVIATIONS

A.	Atlantic Reporter
A.C.	Appeal Cases
A.F.D.I.	Annuaire français de droit international
AI	Amnesty International
A.I.R.	All India Reporter
A.J.I.L.	American Journal of International Law
All E.R.	All England Reports
Ariz.	Arizona Reporter
B.F.S.P.	British Foreign and State Papers
B.Y.I.L.	British Yearbook of International Law
Cal.	California Reports
Cal.Rptr.	California Reporter
C.C.C.	Canadian Criminal Cases
C.H.R.	Commission on Human Rights
C.H.R.Y.	Canadian Human Rights Yearbook
C.L.R.	Commonwealth Law Reports
C. of E.	Council of Europe
Coll.	Collection of Decisions of the European Commission of Human Rights
Conn.	Connecticut Reporter
Cr.App.R.	Criminal Appeal Reports
Crim.L.R.	Criminal Law Review
C.R.N.S.	Criminal Reports New Series
C.R.R.	Canadian Rights Reporter
C.Y.I.L.	Canadian Yearbook of International Law
D.L.R.	Dominion Law Reports
Doc.	Document
D.R.	Decisions and Reports of the European Commission of Human Rights

E.H.R.R.	European Human Rights Reports
E.S.C.	Economic and Social Council
E.T.S.	European Treaty Series
F.	Federal Reporter
F.C.	Federal Court
F.C.R.	Federal Court Reports
F.C.T.D.	Federal Court Trial Division
G.A.	General Assembly
H.L.	House of Lords
H.R.J.	Human Rights Journal
H.R.L.J.	Human Rights Law Journal
H.R.Q.	Human Rights Quarterly
I.C.J.	International Court of Justice
I.C.L.Q.	International and Comparative Law Quarterly
I.C.R.C.	International Committee of the Red Cross
I.H.R.R.	International Human Rights Reports
I.L.M.	International Legal Materials
I.L.R.	International Law Reports
Iowa	Iowa Reporter
J.C.P.C.	Judicial Committee of the Privy Council
J.D.I.	Journal du droit international
L.Ed.	Lawyer's Edition
L.N.T.S.	League of Nations Treaty Series
L.R.C.	Law Reports of the Commonwealth
L.R.T.W.C.	Law Reports of the Trials of the War Criminals
Mass.	Massachusetts Reporter
Md.	Maryland Reporter
Minn.	Minnesota Reporter
N.E.	North Eastern Reporter
Nev.	Nevada Reporter
N.I.L.R.	Netherlands International Law Review
N.Q.H.R.	Netherlands Quarterly of Human Rights
N.R.	National Reporter
N.W.	North Western Reporter
N.Y.	New York Reporter
O.A.S.	Organization of American States
O.A.S.T.S.	Organization of American States Treaty Series
O.A.U.	Organization of African Unity
Ore.	Oregon Reporter
P.	Pacific Reporter

Pa.	Pennsylvania Reporter
R.C.A.D.I.	Recueil de cours de l'Académie du droit international de la Haye
Res.	Resolution
R.G.D.I.P.	Revue générale de droit international public
R.L.R.	Rhodesian Law Reports
R.S.C.	Revised Statutes of Canada
R.U.D.H.	Revue universelle des droits de l'homme
S.A.	South African Law Reports
S.A.L.J.	South African Law Journal
S.-C.H.R.	Sub-Commission on Prevention of Discrimination and Protection of Minorities
S.C.	Supreme Court
S.C.	South Carolina Reporter
S.C.R.	Supreme Court Reports
S.Ct.	Supreme Court
S.E.	South Eastern Reporter
So.	Southern Reporter
T.S.	Treaty Series
T.W.C.	Trials of the War Criminals
U.K.T.S.	United Kingdom Treaty Series
U.N.	United Nations
U.N.C.I.O.	United Nations Conference on International Organization
U.N.T.S.	United Nations Treaty Series
U.S.	United States
W.I.R.	West Indies Reports
W.L.R.	Weekly Law Reports
W.W.R.	Western Weekly Reports
Z.L.R.	Zimbabwe Law Reports
Z.S.C.	Zimbabwe Supreme Court

TABLE OF CASES

The chief and the worst pain is perhaps not inflicted by wounds, but by your certain knowledge that in an hour, in ten minutes, in half a minute, now, this moment your soul will fly out of your body, and that you will be a human being no longer, and that that's certain—the main thing is that it is certain. Just when you lay your head under the knife and you hear the swish of the knife as it slides down over your head—it is just that fraction of a second that is the most awful of all. . . . To kill for murder is an immeasurably greater evil than the crime itself. . . . [H]ere all . . . last hope, which makes it ten times easier to die, is taken away for certain; here you have been sentenced to death, and the whole terrible agony lies in the fact that you will most certainly not escape, and there is no agony greater than that. Take a soldier and put him in front of a cannon in battle and fire at him and he will still hope, but read the same soldier his death sentence for certain, and he will go mad or burst out crying. Who says that human nature is capable of bearing this without madness? Why this cruel, hideous, unnecessary, and useless mockery? . . . It was of agony like this and of such horror that Christ spoke. No, you can't treat a man like that!

DOSTOIEVSKY, *The Idiot*

INTRODUCTION

ON JUNE 6, 1995, the South African Constitutional Court abolished the death penalty.[1] The justices declared it to be incompatible with the country's interim constitution, which prohibits "torture of any kind, whether physical, mental or emotional" and "cruel, inhuman or degrading treatment or punishment."[2] This judgment was rendered unanimously by the newly created eleven-member tribunal, which had been sworn into office by President Nelson Mandela only hours before the hearings began. Slightly more than a year earlier, in January 1994, the United Nations Human Rights Committee concluded that capital punishment as practiced in the State of California,[3] using the gas chamber, violated the norm against "torture or . . . cruel, inhuman or degrading treatment or punishment" found in article 7 of the International Covenant on Civil and Political Rights.[4] And in November 1993 the Judicial Committee of the Privy Council[5] concluded that a wait of several years prior to execution following sentence of death—commonly known as the "death row phenomenon"—breached the Jamaican constitution's guarantee against "torture or . . . inhuman or degrading punishment or other treatment."[6] The Supreme Court of Zimbabwe had reached a similar conclusion in May 1993.[7] Both were inspired by a 1989 judgment of the European Court of Human Rights,[8] which declared that extraditing an individual to the United States, where he would probably wait six to eight years between a death sentence and execution, violated the prohibition of "inhuman and degrading punishment" set out in article 3 of the European Convention on Human Rights.[9]

These five cases are drawn from different tribunals, operating under different instruments and in different contexts. One is an anachronistic vestige of British colonialism. Two are constitutional courts of post-apartheid southern Africa. Two are international tribunals created by human rights treaties. The common thread running through these cases is the death penalty, and the application of the human rights norm prohibiting cruel punishment and torture. Although the precise constitutional or international law texts have minor differ-

3

ences, they essentially enunciate the same principles. The five cases are evidence of an increasing willingness by judges to limit or totally abolish the death penalty by relying on what is a universal rule of human rights law prohibiting cruel punishment or torture. Besides their significance for death penalty jurisprudence, they are a marvelous example of the synergy between national and international courts that has come to characterize contemporary human rights law.

Cruel treatment and torture are prohibited by virtually all contemporary international human rights instruments, and by most domestic bills of rights or constitutions. Article 5 of the Universal Declaration of Human Rights states: "No one shall be subjected to torture or to cruel, inhuman or degrading treatment or punishment."[10] With what are generally minor variations, this formula is repeated in the major international instruments: the four Geneva Conventions,[11] the International Covenant on Civil and Political Rights,[12] the European Convention on Human Rights,[13] the American Declaration of the Rights and Duties of Man,[14] the American Convention on Human Rights,[15] and the African Charter of Human and Peoples' Rights.[16] In this now classic formulation, "torture" is associated with "cruel, inhuman and degrading treatment or punishment." In fact, jurists have rarely attempted to draw nice legal distinctions between the two categories. To the extent that they can be distinguished, torture may contain a notion of intentional cruelty designed to obtain information or a confession, whereas "treatment or punishment" is more concerned with the alleged goals of criminal law sanctions: deterrence, retribution, the protection of society, and rehabilitation. Torture has sometimes been defined as "an aggravated and deliberate form of cruel, inhuman or degrading treatment or punishment."[17]

Like most of the international human rights norms, especially in the field of civil rights, the prohibition of torture derives from domestic constitutional instruments, notably those of the Enlightenment and the seventeenth- and eighteenth-century revolutions in England, the United States, and France. The English Bill of Rights of 1689 did not speak specifically of torture, but declared that "cruel and inhuman treatment or punishment" would not be allowed. The wording was emulated by the framers of the United States Constitution, who included it in the Eighth Amendment. The Americans, notably Thomas Jefferson, were not without influence in Parisian revolutionary circles, and they exported the norm back across the Atlantic. It appears in the French Déclaration des droits de l'homme et du citoyen as a requirement that "[l]a loi ne doit établir que des peines strictement et évidemment nécessaires" [Only punishment that is strictly and obviously necessary may be established by law].

During the nineteenth and twentieth centuries, the norm prohibiting cruel treatment and torture filtered into domestic constitutions throughout the world and, in 1948, into the universal human rights system. I shall develop this history of the principle in greater detail in a distinct part of this study. Suffice it to say, at this stage, that although there are some essentially minor differences between the formulation of the norm in different legal systems, the prohibition of cruel treatment and torture is a generally recognized human rights standard. While some instruments speak of "cruel and unusual" or "cruel *or* unusual" punishment, whereas others speak of "cruel, inhuman and degrading" or simply "inhuman and degrading" punishment, the principle is fundamentally the same everywhere. Some refer to "torture," and others only to "cruel" treatment and punishment, but the reality they describe is quite comparable. The notions are synonymous even if there are slight variations in the texts.

Perhaps the most compelling argument for this attempt at homogenizing such a human rights standard is that the prohibition of torture or other cruel, inhuman, and degrading treatment or punishment is deemed to be a customary norm.[18] The closest international law comes to an overlap between customary and conventional norms is in common article 3 to the four Geneva Conventions,[19] which operates as a kind of lowest common denominator of human treatment.[20] Common article 3 prohibits "cruel treatment and torture," a phrase that is close to the text in the Universal Declaration of Human Rights and the other instruments, although certainly not identical. But by its very nature, a customary norm does not lend itself to precise "black-letter" formulation. It is a concept, a notion, an idea, that is being prohibited. And jurists around the world seem to agree that this prohibition is universal, and that it exists even where it is difficult or impossible to identify a positive legal text that is clearly applicable.[21] For the purposes of this book, I shall describe the entire spectrum of similar provisions using the phrase employed in common article 3, the prohibition of "cruel treatment and torture."

But as a consequence of a whole range of factors, even seemingly identical norms receive different interpretations. Murder, for example, is a crime in all societies, but its definition, specifically as relates to such ancillary matters as the question of applicable defenses or parties to the infraction, varies considerably from jurisdiction to jurisdiction, even from judge to judge. Within the context of human rights law, these inevitable differences in interpretation have received enormous attention in recent years as they relate to cultural differences. The Vienna Conference on Human Rights proclaimed that "[a]ll human rights are universal, indivisible and interdependent and interrelated."[22] The significance of torture as it pertains to universal human rights norms was underscored in several paragraphs of the Vienna Declaration and Programme of Action.[23] But the human rights recognized in the Universal Declaration of

Human Rights and its derivatives are originally a Western creation, and as a whole they continue to be criticized as displaying a culturally biased and perhaps imperialistic conception.[24] As the Chinese delegate to the 1993 Vienna Conference on Human Rights put it:

> The concept of human rights is a product of historical development. It is closely associated with specific social, political and economic conditions and the specific history, culture and values of a particular country. Different historical stages have different human rights requirements. Countries at different development stages or with different historical traditions and cultural backgrounds also have different understanding and practice of human rights. Thus, one should not and cannot think [of] the human rights standard and model of certain countries as the only proper ones and demand all other countries to comply with them.[25]

The scholar Jack Donnelly has said of this problem that we now have a situation of "normative universality," but that we are still far from having attained "moral universality."[26]

Furious debates on the subject of cultural relativism have been provoked in international forums respecting women's or children's rights, where views on such matters as abortion, genital mutilation, and even dress codes are highly charged questions, deeply rooted in culture and religion. Yet some rights, particularly the core civil rights, are often felt to escape this debate. Murder is murder, goes the argument, and there is no question of the right to life being irrelevant to certain cultures yet fundamental to others. Human life is sacred, whatever the society, and it must be protected by law.[27]

Is the same true of the prohibition of torture, or other cruel, inhuman, and degrading treatment or punishment? It is true that this norm is as basic as the guarantee of the right to life. Yet its cultural dimension is inescapable. For while murder may have an objective aspect—there must, necessarily, be a dead victim—torture or cruel treatment are concepts inevitably bound up with culturally conditioned attitudes. What constitutes cruelty differs enormously from one society to another.[28] To take a rather banal example, when the European Court of Human Rights considered whether corporal punishment by "birching" went contrary to the European Convention's prohibition of "inhuman or degrading treatment or punishment," Judge Fitzmaurice, who sat on behalf of the United Kingdom, admitted that in his view the fact that there was no violation was undoubtedly conditioned by his own youthful experience in English public schools.[29] His views were not shared by the majority of the Court, perhaps because the other judges could not empathize with his nostalgia for such brutality and had not been culturally conditioned to appreciate its alleged benefits.

Somewhat more chilling is the debate during the 1994 session of the United Nations Commission on Human Rights, where the special rapporteur on the Sudan, Gaspar Biro, presented his comments on the so-called Islamic punishments.[30] According to Professor Biro, such practices as amputation for crimes of theft and stoning to death for the crime of adultery, allegedly dictated by Islamic law doctrines, run contrary to the prohibition of torture or cruel, inhuman, and degrading treatment or punishment found in article 7 of the International Covenant on Civil and Political Rights.[31] He was vehemently denounced by the Sudanese representative, Abdelaziz Shiddo, who accused him of insulting religious values in a "Satanic paragraph" of his report, adding that "he must assume the responsibility" for his comments. The report, continued Ambassador Shiddo, was "flagrant blasphemy and a deliberate insult to the Islamic religion."[32] Professor Biro was forced to leave Geneva under police escort. Later that year, during debate at the autumn session of the General Assembly, the Sudanese delegate affirmed that "capital punishment was a divine right according to some religions, in particular Islam. . . . [C]apital punishment was enshrined in the Koran and millions of inhabitants of the Muslim world believed that it was a teaching of God."[33] That Islamic culture will dictate interpretations of the terms "cruel, inhuman and degrading" that are "significantly, if not radically, different from perceptions of the meaning of this clause in other parts of the world" is evoked in the writings of Professor Abdullahi Ahmed An-Na'im.[34]

Most judicial interpretation of the norm prohibiting cruel treatment or torture has endeavored to take account of this element of "cultural relativism," construing the concept with regard to "evolving standards of decency"[35] or some equivalent notion in the particular culture involved. In other words, views prevalent in the general public are factors in determining the scope of what constitutes torture or other cruel, inhuman, and degrading treatment or punishment. Consequently, the norm not only varies from one society to another but also evolves over time. What was tolerated by society in 1945 may no longer be so in 1995. As Chief Justice Donald R. Wright of the Supreme Court of California wrote, "Judgments of the nineteenth century as to what constitutes cruelty cannot bind us in considering this question any more than eighteenth century concepts limit application of the Eighth Amendment."[36] Or, to cite a much earlier judgment of the United States Supreme Court, the prohibition of cruel and unusual punishment in the Eighth Amendment "may be therefore progressive, and is not fastened to the obsolete, but may acquire meaning as public opinion becomes enlightened by a human justice."[37]

But if the norm is universal, is it appropriate that its construction should vary depending on the culture of the society where it is being invoked? When, for example, the Human Rights Committee determines that execution by asphyxiation with poisonous gas is inhuman and degrading in the State of California, where more sophisticated techniques like injection with lethal drugs exist, does the same view hold for societies in other parts of the world? Although religious strictures may enter into this, as in the case of the Islamic punishments that are justified with textual references to sacred writing, other factors such as economic development may also be at work. Prison conditions would seem to be an excellent example of this problem. What is deemed a harsh carceral regime in a prosperous European state may be considered the lap of luxury in a developing country in central Africa. Very little consideration has been given in international law to the relativism of application of the norm prohibiting cruel treatment and torture, although it may be appropriate to refer to such doctrines as the "margin of appreciation" that has been developed within the European regional human rights system.[38]

This brings me to the death penalty. There is little or no doubt that when the various positive legal prohibitions of cruel treatment and torture were first set out in the seventeenth and eighteenth centuries, abolition of the death penalty was barely contemplated. The English revolutionaries who drafted the "cruel and unusual punishment" norm of the 1689 Bill of Rights sought, at best, to curb the worst excesses of Stuart executions—these might include disemboweling while the prisoner was still alive, followed by drawing and quartering.[39] But there are also quite recent examples. At the time of drafting of the Universal Declaration of Human Rights in 1948, the death penalty was widely practiced. It had been imposed by the international criminal tribunals at Nuremberg and Tokyo on most of the major war criminals. The General Assembly rejected attempts to add a call for abolition of capital punishment to the instrument, as this might alienate states not yet willing to envisage such a step.[40] Moreover, to the extent that the death penalty was contemplated in the international human rights instruments, the matter remained focused on another norm, the guarantee of the right to life. The amendment to the Universal Declaration proposing that the death penalty be abolished[41] was made to article 3, which protects the right to life, and not to article 5, dealing with cruel, inhuman, and degrading punishment. The death penalty, by its very definition, is a form of punishment, and it is surprising that the drafters of the Universal Declaration and the other early international human rights instruments did not consider that it might be deemed "cruel." Yet only a few decades later, judicial consideration of the death penalty has dwelt not so much on the right to life as on the prohibition of cruel treatment and torture. Sometimes, this is because the "right to life" provision in the legal instrument being considered actually allows the death penalty, as in the United States Bill of Rights,[42] the European Convention on Human Rights,[43] or the International Covenant on Civil and Political Rights.[44] Yet even where constitutional norms express the right to life in unqualified terms, many judges have puzzled over the scope of this enigmatic norm.[45] Quite simply, they seem to have found it easier to address the question of the death penalty from the standpoint of the prohibition of cruel treatment or torture.[46]

The value of a dynamic interpretation of the legal norm prohibiting cruel treatment or torture takes on its full importance in this context. As society has matured,[47] its attitude towards the death penalty has evolved considerably. This proposition hardly requires justification. Several new treaties have come into force that seek to bring up to date the right-to-life provisions of the international human rights treaties and to eliminate the death penalty as an exception to the right to life.[48] As a result, nearly fifty states are now bound, as a question of international law, to suppress the death penalty. More than half the world's states are now abolitionist either de jure or de facto, and almost all of them have taken this step since the end of World War II.[49]

It is certainly premature to suggest that the universal norm prohibiting cruel treatment and torture, whether this be in customary or conventional form, now compels abolition of the death penalty. Yet if it is understood that this norm must necessarily evolve as society matures, then we must already anticipate such a development. This has begun to take place, appropriately, on a regional level, where it is easier to draw such conclusions. In *Soering* v. *United Kingdom*, Judge Jan De Meyer of the European Court of Human Rights took such an approach in concluding that article 2§1 of the European Convention on Human Rights, to the extent that it allowed the death penalty as an exception to the right to life, was no longer operative.[50] This was because of the evolving standards in Europe, where, for all practical purposes, the death penalty no longer exists. In other words, article 3 of the Convention, prohibiting "inhuman or degrading treatment," conflicted, in its 1989 and not its 1950 interpretation, with article 2§1 of the Convention. The result, concluded Judge De Meyer, was the triumph of article 3. The majority of the Court was not prepared to go as far, and it felt that to the extent articles 2§1 and 3 were in contradiction, this was a matter for the states parties to resolve by amendment of the Convention and not something to be tackled by the judiciary.

The better view, in my opinion, is that taken in Judge De Meyer's individual opinion. Courts may not abdicate their duty to apply human rights norms because these appear to be in conflict. It is of the essence of legislation that conflicts exist, and of the essence of the judicial role that these be resolved. A view similar to that of Judge De Meyer was taken by the Supreme Court of Japan in a 1948 judgment, where it affirmed that the country's constitution

> should not be regarded as eternally approving the death penalty. The judgment of whether certain punishments are cruel is a question that should be decided according to the feelings of the people. However, because the feelings of the people cannot escape changing with the times, what at one time may be regarded as not being a cruel punishment may at a later period be judged the reverse. Accordingly, as a nation's culture develops to a high degree, and as a peaceful society is realized on the basis of justice and order, and if a time is reached when it is not felt to be necessary for the public welfare to prevent crime by the menace of the death penalty, then both the death penalty and cruel punishments will certainly be eliminated because of the feelings of the people.[51]

Conflict between courts and legislators is a recurring theme in this area. At first blush, of course, constitutions and international human rights treaties are designed to protect individuals against capricious and whimsical lawmakers. If legislators have the last word on what constitutes "cruel treatment," why bother attempting to give the norm any superlegislative status by including it in a constitution or international human rights instrument? Yet on the other hand, if what constitutes cruelty is to be assessed in light of evolving standards of a maturing society, what better judge of the matter is there than a democratically elected legislature? Surely elected lawmakers are closer to the pulse of society than appointed judges? And this, in effect, is the approach that the United States Supreme Court has taken. From its progressive abolitionist posture in the 1972 *Furman* v. *Georgia* decision,[52] it beat a dramatic retreat only four years later in *Gregg* v. *Georgia*,[53] in large measure due to a furious legislative reaction to *Furman* that apparently terrified the judiciary.

As noted above, the death penalty was deemed incompatible with the prohibition of cruel treatment or torture in the memorable 1995 judgment of the South African Constitutional Court.[54] Some other domestic courts will doubtless follow the example set by this remarkable new Court, created as part of the Mandela revolution. But it is unlikely, at least in the short term, that this development will lead to a wave of judicial abolitionism in states where the death penalty is not only still provided for by legislation but also continues to be applied. Yet in the case of retentionist countries, the norm prohibiting cruel treatment or torture is of paramount importance, because it serves to limit the scope of the death penalty. Indeed, most death penalty litigation is undertaken in states where that sentence continues to be pronounced and carried out. Although there are occasional valiant but rather frustrating attempts at abolishing the death penalty by judicial pronouncement, most litigants set their sights somewhat lower. Generally, they have focused on one or another aspect of capital punishment, attempting to chip away at the death penalty rather than confront it head on. Foremost among these ancillary issues are two subjects that this book will address in considerable detail, the "death row phenomenon" and the method of execution.

The "death row phenomenon" describes the period that the prisoner must wait between fixing of the sentence and execution. In some cases, this may involve not only the delay as such but also what are often appalling conditions of detention imposed upon those for whom all hope has been abandoned, the "walking dead." As for the method of execution, this has been a source of ongoing debate that never ceases to provoke difficulties; the proper way to kill a human being continues to perplex the courts, as a series of recent decisions by domestic and international tribunals has shown. These two themes have a common element. If the death penalty is to meet the test of cruel treatment or torture, then it must be devoid of suffering or, to be more accurate, of superfluous suffering.

Yet here it runs into trouble with respect to its basic justifications, which are rooted in criminal law theory. There are four principal aims of punishment: deterrence, retribution, protection of society, and rehabilitation. The latter two are largely irrelevant to the debate: if a prisoner is executed, clearly society has been protected from any chance of recidivism; moreover, rehabilitation is, for obvious reasons, out of the question. Thus, deterrence and retribution are the anchors of the debate. Both call for punishment that is visited with a certain amount of horror. How, then, do we take the horror out of the death penalty while preserving its horror? If retribution (or vengeance) is the goal, why not let the prisoner suffer in miserable conditions, all the while contemplating the eventual walk to the gallows? If the goal is deterrence, surely the association of death with other suffering, pain, and indignity can only help to further this objective.

But even those who favor the death penalty will balk at some of its more grotesque excesses. Courts continue to restrict the accoutrements that accompany capital execution. There is, to borrow the phrase used by the Judicial Committee of the Privy Council in a 1993 "death row phenomenon" case, an "instinctive revulsion" to such cruel, inhuman, and degrading treatment. What gives rise to such revulsion? asked their Lordships. "The answer can only be our humanity."[55]

This book addresses the application of the legal norm, found in domestic constitutional law and in customary and conventional international law, that prohibits cruel treatment and torture. As I have already explained, this norm is formulated in different ways but it describes essentially the same reality. The principal sources are judicial decisions of national and international tribunals—more specifically, the supreme or constitutional courts of the United States, India, South Africa, Canada, the United Kingdom, Zimbabwe, Tanzania, Trinidad and Tobago, Nigeria, and Hungary; the United Nations Human Rights Committee; and the European, American, and African Commissions and Courts of Human Rights. A debt must be acknowledged here to David Pannick's seminal study, *Judicial Review of the Death Penalty.*[56] Published in 1983, its focus was on comparative law, if for no other reason than because international caselaw was virtually non-existent at the time. A dozen years later this has all changed, and in recent years there has been a spate of international decisions accompanied by important developments in domestic courts.

These issues should fascinate jurists, irrespective of their own views on the supposed merits of the death penalty. In the first place, there is a rich and unique interplay of comparative and international law. Most of the recent judicial decisions make frequent reference to the judgments of courts in other jurisdictions that are based on other legal instruments and systems. This is in itself rather remarkable, because comparative law has traditionally been the preserve of academics rather than judges. In addition, there is much to be learned about the debate surrounding cultural relativism from this discussion, for here is a core civil rights norm, the prohibition of cruel punishment, that is conditioned by such a culturally loaded adjective. Then, there is the matter of the interplay between legislator and judge in the application of fundamental norms. Are constitutional or international norms designed to protect the individual from the lawmaker or, alternatively, does the lawmaker inject some kind of democratic content into the interpretation of the scope of human rights? There are, finally, important issues of legal interpretation that arise where two principles appear to conflict.

This book is not intended to be a polemic, but rather a study of the law as it has been, as it is now, and as it is developing. It must be borne in mind that there are fundamental moral and ethical issues lurking in the background of the legal debate. Nevertheless, it is beyond the scope of this work or the expertise of its author to address them. But if I may anticipate the conclusion in an introduction, the trend in both comparative and international law clearly favors the progressive limitation and ultimate abolition of the death penalty. Law makes an important, although not exclusive, contribution to this process.

THE PROHIBITION OF

CRUEL TREATMENT AND

TORTURE

THE NORM, which I have chosen to label the prohibition of cruel treatment and torture, borrowing the phrase used in common article 3 to the Geneva Conventions of 1949,[1] has been expressed, with relatively minor differences in terminology, in the modern human rights instruments and in the constitutions of most states.[2] Its origins can be traced to the documents of the sixteenth- and seventeenth-century Enlightenment and the revolutions that accompanied it, and to their common ancestor, the Magna Carta. To go much further back, one would need to leave the field of law and consider principles of philosophy, ethics, and religion.

Advocates of capital punishment, and notably those who insist on retribution as its fundamental justification, repeat the oft-quoted injunction "an eye for an eye, a tooth for a tooth." This statement of the *lex talionis* can be found in the Old Testament. In Genesis, it is stated: "Whoso sheddeth man's blood, by man shall his blood be shed: for in the image of God made he man."[3] Yet Cain, the son of Adam and Eve, was not punished in this way, but only condemned to exile, bearing a distinctive brand on his forehead. The principle also appears in several places in Exodus, in which Moses receives the laws from Yahweh, the Jewish God,[4] and is expressed more amply in Leviticus: "If a man injures his neighbor, what he has done must be done to him: broken limb for broken limb, eye for eye, tooth for tooth. As the injury inflicted, so must be the injury suffered."[5]

Although the *lex talionis* is now generally viewed as a mandate for vengeance and retribution, at its beginnings it was a progressive development reflecting early attempts to formulate a rule of proportionality in the determination of criminal sanctions. It may also be considered as a limitation on abusive or excessive punishment. The Latin *talio* means "equivalent to," and the *lex talionis* imposes a limit on punishment by prescribing that it may not exceed the scope of the original crime. The same notion of proportionate punishment is found in Aristotle's *Ethics.*[6]

In England, the *lex talionis* was codified under the Laws of King Alfred, and specific penalties fixed for all offenses.[7] However, this enlightened tradition came to an end following the Norman conquest of England in 1066. It was replaced with a discretionary "amercement," imposed as punishment for all types of crimes.[8] The excesses of the Norman kings and of their courts brought the first great manifestation of the rule of law whose direct lineage with our contemporary human rights instruments can be clearly demonstrated. The Magna Carta, imposed upon King John by the barons at Runnymede in 1215, stands for the principle that even the sovereign is not above the law. It is the source of several important human rights norms, including such concepts as due process. Punishment, and particularly the Norman system of "amercement," is addressed in three separate chapters of the Magna Carta.[9] Specifically, chapter 20 sets out the rule of proportionality: "A freeman shall not be amerced for a slight offense, except in accordance with the degree of the offense."

Over the years that followed proclamation of the Magna Carta, the principle of proportionality in punishment and the prohibition of excessive punishments became entrenched in the English common law.[10] But although the common law prohibited excessive punishments, it did not impose any limit on cruel punishments. In other words, if the crime was barbarous, the *lex talionis* implied that the punishment would be so as well. In the early years of the English judicial system, imposition of the death penalty, at least by our contemporary standards, was particularly barbaric. William Blackstone, writing of the early Stuart period, described punishment for treason as follows:

> The punishment of high treason in general is very solemn and terrible: (1) That the offender be drawn to the gallows, and not be carried or walk; though usually (by connivance, at length ripened by humanity into law) a sledge or hurdle is allowed, to preserve the offender from the extreme torment of being dragged on the ground or pavement. (2) That he be hanged by the neck and then cut down alive. (3) That his entrails be taken out and burned while he is yet alive. (4) That his head be cut off. (5) That his body be divided into four parts. (6) That his head and quarters be at the king's disposal.[11]

Note, however, the role Blackstone attributes, even at the time, to "humanity" in mitigating the most gruesome excesses of capital punishment. The penalty for standing mute, according to Blackstone, was

> that the prisoner be remanded to the prison from whence he came, and put into a low, dark chamber, and there be laid on his back on the bare floor, naked, unless where decency forbids; that there be placed upon his body as great a weight of iron as he could bear, and more;

that he have no sustenance, save only, on the first day, three morsels of the worst bread, and, on the second day, three draughts of standing water, that should be nearest to the prison door; and in this situation this should be alternately his diet till he died, or (as anciently the judgment ran) till he answered.[12]

Debate on the subject of these brutal methods of punishment arose during the sixteenth century. The archbishop of Canterbury's approval of torture in order to extract confessions was challenged by Puritan politicians, who invoked the Magna Carta in support of their arguments.[13] When Sir Robert Beale published *A Book against Oaths Ministered in the Court of Ecclesiastical Commission* in 1583, denouncing the use of torture by the church courts and arguing it violated the Magna Carta, he was in turn censured by the archbishop, John Whitgift, because "[h]e condemneth (without exception of any cause) the racking of grievous offenders as being cruel, barbarous, contrary to law, and unto the liberty of English subjects."[14] The Puritans took their more enlightened approach to punishment to America, where it appeared in a provision of the Massachusetts Body of Liberties, of 1641: "For bodily punishments we allow amongst us none that are inhumane, barbarous or cruel."[15]

The Puritan Revolution in England presents one of the early manifestations of abolitionism. After the defeat of Charles I, the Levellers attacked capital punishment, except in extreme cases of murder and treason. As Justice Peter D. Cory of the Supreme Court of Canada noted, "[T]he Levellers decried the imposition of capital punishment for property offences, observing that many of those arraigned were poor labourers who stole things of small value out of necessity."[16] A Puritan reformer, Gerrard Winstanley, considered the death penalty immoral: "It is not for one creature called man to kill another, for this is abominable to the Spirit, and it is the curse which hath made the Creation to groan under bondage; for if I kill you I am a murderer, if a third come, and hang or kill me for murdering you, he is a murderer of me; and so by the government of the first Adam, murder hath been called Justice when it is but the curse."[17] The idea, promoted by the Puritans during the English Revolution, that there were limits to the barbarity involved in inflicting the death penalty and other severe punishments took form, in 1689, with the adoption of the Bill of Rights.

ENGLISH BILL OF RIGHTS OF 1689

Enacted on December 16, 1689, following its adoption by the Commons and the House of Lords,[18] the Bill of Rights stands as one of the great tangible results of the democratic upheaval that rocked England throughout the seventeenth century. Specifically, it was the result of negotiations involving the succession to the throne following the end of Stuart rule. The new monarchs, William and Mary, were obliged to recognize the Bill of Rights as part of their accession. The document reads, in part:

> Whereas the late King James the Second, by the assistance of divers evil counsellors, judges, and ministers employed by him, did endeavor to subvert and extirpate the protestant religion, and the laws and liberties of this kingdom. . . .
>
> And whereas . . . excessive fines have been imposed; and illegal and cruel punishments inflicted . . . [a]ll which are utterly and directly contrary to the known laws and statutes and freedoms of this realm. . . .
>
> And thereupon the said lords spiritual and temporal, and commons . . . do in the first place (as their ancestors in like case have usually done) for the vindicating and asserting their ancient rights and liberties, declare. . . .
>
> 10. That excessive bail ought not to be required, nor excessive fines imposed; nor cruel and unusual punishments inflicted.[19]

There has been much academic debate about the context of the Bill, which may be quite germane to efforts at establishing the intent of Parliament at the time. The drafting of the "cruel and unusual punishment" clause has often been linked to public reaction to the Bloody Assizes of 1685, where (in the spirit of Blackstone's *Commentaries*) disembowelling while still alive, as well as drawing and quartering, was imposed upon the insurgents of the Monmouth Rebellion.[20] However, because such sanctions continued to be applied for many years after enactment of the Bill of Rights in 1689, some scholars have suggested that barbaric punishments are not what was contemplated by the drafters.[21] They argue that the "original meaning" of the clause was not conditioned by the Bloody Assizes, and probably derived from reaction to a severe sentence imposed upon Titus Oates, fabricator of the "Popish Plot" of 1678, for the crime of perjury (several innocent persons having been convicted as a result), which included life imprisonment, whipping, and periodic pillorying.

This interpretation suggests that the clause was not directed at ostensibly barbaric or torturous punishments, but rather to the issue of proportionality,[22] that is, to severe punishment not authorized by statute and not within the jurisdiction of the court.[23] Such a view would appear to be confirmed by the provision's drafting history. An earlier version of the cruel and unusual punishment clause, prepared by a Commons committee chaired by Sir George Treby, declared: "19. The requiring excessive bail of persons committed in criminal cases and imposing excessive fines, and illegal punishments, to be prevented."[24] As can be seen, the term "unusual" is a latecomer in the drafting process, and, as Anthony F. Granucci has quite convincingly explained, "[t]he final phraseology, especially the use of the word 'unusual,' must be laid simply to chance and sloppy draftsmanship."[25]

This argument relies not only on the context of the drafting but also on subsequent practice of the English government. It is not without its flaws. For while it may be accurate to state that post-1689 criminal sentences remained almost unspeakably barbaric, and largely unchanged from the times of the Stuarts, sentences also remained grossly disproportionate. During the late seventeenth and well into the eighteenth century, capital punishment was imposed for the most trivial of offenses, including petty theft.[26] If English penal policy in the eighteenth century is any guide, a strong case can actually be made that section 10 of the Bill of Rights had little or no practical consequence. The excesses of the common law in the American colonies during this period were particularly shocking. As recently as 1947, a justice of the United States Supreme Court was to note that "[p]reconstitutional American history reeked with cruel punishment."[27] The same was the case in New France following the English conquest in 1759; folk ballads sung to this day tell of the harsh penal regime "dipt in blood" that, for the common people, was possibly the most visible and detested manifestation of the regime that followed the Battle of Quebec.[28] Thus, subsequent practice seems a poor guide to assessment of the intent of the drafters of the Bill of Rights, and this leaves only one leg of the argument to support what is a relatively conservative interpretation of section 10 of the document.

The courts of the United States have shown some interest in the question of original intent, seeing in the distinctions I have just described some indication that its equivalent in the U.S. Bill of Rights and in several of the state constitutions does not contemplate the punishment in and of itself but only its disproportionality.[29] In the context of capital punishment, at least when imposed for murder, the argument of disproportionality is certainly not the strongest in the abolitionist arsenal. Courts in the United Kingdom and in other common-law jurisdictions have been relatively indifferent to this "original intent" argument, and seem to favor a more dynamic approach to the provision. The cruel and unusual punishment clause of the English Bill of Rights was cited by the members of the Judicial Committee of the Privy Council as recently as 1983. According to Lords Scarman and Brightman in *Riley v. Attorney-General of Jamaica*, which dealt with the death row phenomenon in Jamaica, "execution after inordinate delay would have infringed the prohibition against cruel and unusual punishments to be found in section 10 of the Bill of Rights of 1689."[30] Their Lordships continued: "It is no exaggeration, therefore, to say that the jurisprudence of the civilized world, much of which is derived from common law principles and the prohibition against cruel and unusual punishments in the English Bill of Rights, has recognized and acknowledged that prolonged delay in executing a sentence of death can make the punishment when it comes inhuman and degrading."[31]

Section 10 of the English Bill of Rights is the direct ancestor of constitutional provisions in other countries that remain applicable to this day. The Eighth Amendment to the Constitution of the United States borrows the phrase virtually word for word,[32] and it is included in many of the state constitutions as well. Cruel and unusual punishment is also prohibited by such recent instruments as the 1960 Canadian Bill of Rights[33] and the 1982 Canadian Charter of Rights and Freedoms.[34] Although the phrase was not adopted textually by the drafters of the Universal Declaration of Human Rights,[35] it had considerable influence on their deliberations, and there is little doubt that section 10 of the English Bill of Rights is a very legitimate ancestor of article 5 of the Universal Declaration.

Any attempt at a brief historical review of the norm prohibiting cruel treatment and torture would not be complete without mention of the influence of Cesare Beccaria, an Italian criminologist of the eighteenth century. His book *Dei delitti e delle pene*,[36] published in 1764, convinced such statesmen as Voltaire, Jefferson, Paine, Lafayette, and Robespierre of the uselessness and inhumanity of capital punishment.[37] This is important to keep in mind in considering the constitutional instruments that these men were involved in drafting, notably the American Bill of Rights (Jefferson and Paine) and the French Déclaration des droits de l'homme et du citoyen (Jefferson, Paine, Lafayette, and Robespierre). Beccaria's writings even led to ephemeral measures abolishing the death penalty in Austria and Tuscany.[38] To this day, they are cited by the courts in judgments examining the legality of the death penalty.[39]

UNITED STATES BILL OF RIGHTS

In early 1776, an assembly of revolutionary delegates in Virginia met to consider a declaration of independence. They agreed to instruct the colony's delegates to the Continental Congress to declare independence, and furthermore to draft a declaration of rights. A committee chaired by George Mason was entrusted with preparing the document that became the Virginia Bill of Rights.[40] Adopted on June 12, 1776, it was largely inspired by the English Bill of Rights of 1689. Section 9 dealt with cruel and unusual punishment: "That excessive bail ought not to be required, nor excessive fines imposed, nor cruel and unusual punishments inflicted."[41] The same provision was soon incorporated in the constitutions of eight other former colonies, and it was subsequently included by the federal government in the 1787 Northwest Ordinance.[42] As one author put it with perhaps unnecessary cynicism, the "cruel and unusual" clause had become constitutional "boilerplate."[43] The adoption of a series of state constitutions was only a prelude to the enactment of the United States Constitution, which came into force in 1789, following ratification by the various legislatures. The only difference between section 10 of the English Bill of Rights of 1689 and the "cruel and unusual punishment" clause adopted as the Eighth Amendment of the United States Constitution was replacement of the word "ought" by the word "shall," a distinction that does not ever seem to have been viewed as being of any legal significance.

Capital punishment was widely used in the United States at the time the Constitution was drafted, and there cannot be any serious suggestion that the framers sought indirectly to abolish it by proscribing cruel and unusual punishments with the Eighth Amendment. Clearly, they regarded the death penalty as a legitimate punishment, because they expressly allowed it in another provision, the Fifth Amendment: "nor shall any person . . . be deprived of life, liberty, or property, without due process of law."[44] The heart of the debate about the original intent of the framers is whether they felt that the cruel and unusual punishment clause was directed solely against torturous punishment—a construction that finds support in the drafting history of the English Bill of Rights—or whether they also sought to limit the legislative power to define forms of punishment.

The state conventions convened to ratify the draft United States Constitution generated some interesting debates about the scope of the "cruel and unusual punishment" clause. In Massachusetts, delegate Holmes objected to the clause because it apparently failed to impose limits on the methods of punishment, which might theoretically include such barbarous devices as "racks and gibbets."[45] In the Virginia convention, Patrick Henry complained that the draft constitution might allow "torture," and he expressed concern with current practice in continental Europe, where it was widely used to extract confessions.[46] George Mason answered that he considered the clause to prohibit torture.[47] But as Justice Brennan of the United States Supreme Court was to observe two centuries later, commenting on these rare suggestions of legislative intent:

> It does not follow, however, that the Framers were exclusively concerned with prohibiting torturous punishments. Holmes and Henry

were objecting to the absence of a Bill of Rights, and they cited to support their objections the unrestrained legislative power to prescribe punishments for crimes. Certainly we may suppose that they invoked the specter of the most drastic punishments a legislature might devise.[48]

During debate on the cruel and unusual punishment clause in the First Congress of the United States, only one exchange is recorded:

Mr Smith, of South Carolina, objected to the words 'nor cruel and unusual punishments;' the import of them being too indefinite.

Mr Livermore: The clause seems to express a great deal of humanity, on which account I have no objection to it; but, as it seems to have no meaning in it, I do not think it necessary. What is meant by the terms excessive bail? Who are to be the judges? What is understood by excessive fines? It lies with the court to determine. No cruel and unusual punishment is to be inflicted; it is sometimes necessary to hang a man, villains often deserve whipping, and perhaps having their ears cut off; but are we in future to be prevented from inflicting these punishments because they are cruel. If a more lenient mode of correcting vice and deterring others from the commission of it could be invented, it would be very prudent in the Legislature to adopt it; but until we have some security that this will be done, we ought not to be restrained from making necessary laws by any declaration of this kind.[49]

In his seminal article on the intent of the Eighth Amendment's framers, Anthony Granucci calls the notion that the provision contemplates not disproportionate but torturous or barbaric punishments the "American misinterpretation" of the "cruel and unusual punishment" clause derived from the 1689 Bill of Rights.[50] In other words, the American framers gave "cruel and unusual punishment" a broader scope than had the English parliamentarians a century earlier. Professor Granucci attributes this to the influence of the Massachusetts Body of Liberties. The legislative history of the provision, as Granucci argues compellingly, tends to show that the framers of the Constitution considered it to impose a limit upon the legislative power to prescribe punishments.[51] Justice Thurgood Marshall, citing Granucci's work, has written: "Whether the English Bill of Rights prohibition against cruel and unusual punishments is properly read as a response to excessive or illegal punishments, as a reaction to barbaric and objectionable modes of punishment, or both, there is no doubt whatever that in borrowing the language and in including it in the Eighth Amendment, our Founding Fathers intended to outlaw torture and other cruel punishments."[52]

The Eighth Amendment had very little immediate impact within the U.S. judicial system; the Supreme Court did not even refer to it until nearly eighty years after its enactment.[53] In *Wilkerson* v. *Utah*, decided in 1878, the Court rejected a challenge to the death penalty where execution by firing squad was alleged to be contrary to the Eighth Amendment.[54] A little more than a decade later, in *Kemmler*, it did the same in an attack directed against introduction of the electric chair in the State of New York.[55] In these early cases, the Supreme Court adopted a conservative assessment of the original intent of the framers: "Punishments are cruel when they involve torture or a lingering death: but the punishment of death is not cruel within the meaning of that word as used in the constitution. It implies that there is something inhuman and barbarous— something more than the mere extinguishment of life."[56] According to Professor Hugo Adam Bedau, referring primarily to the nineteenth-century authorities, "An unbroken line of interpreters has held that it was the original understanding and intent of the framers of the Eighth Amendment . . . to proscribe as 'cruel and unusual' *only* such modes of execution as compounded the simple infliction of death with added cruelties or indignities."[57]

In 1909, the Eighth Amendment was again argued before the Supreme Court in *Weems* v. *United States*. The appellant had been sentenced to fifteen years' imprisonment in chains at hard labor for making a false entry in a government payroll book. The offense was one of absolute liability, no proof of guilty intent being required by the applicable statute. A majority of the Court favored expanding the scope of the Eighth Amendment so as to cover all forms of disproportionate or excessive punishment, although two justices, White and Holmes, insisted that English history supported a narrower reading of the provision.[58] *Weems* is the first case in which the United States Supreme Court actually found a criminal sanction that had been duly enacted by the legislature to be unconstitutional because of conflict with the Eighth Amendment.[59] It represents a significant departure from the approach in *Wilkerson*[60] and *Kemmler*,[61] in that it abandons a deference for legislated sanctions and deems that "when we come to punishments, no latitude ought to be left, nor dependence put on the virtue of representatives."[62] As Justice William Brennan would later state the point, "Judicial enforcement of the Clause, then, cannot be evaded by invoking the obvious truth that legislatures have the power to prescribe punishments for crimes. That is precisely the reason the Clause appears in the Bill of Rights."[63]

Since *Weems*, there have been only a handful of other examples. In *Trop* v. *Dulles*, the Supreme Court held that denial of citizenship for desertion from the armed forces was "cruel and unusual punishment" contrary to the Constitution. It was in *Trop* that Chief Justice Earl Warren established a dynamic standard for application of the Eighth Amendment, declaring that its construction would vary as a function of "the evolving standards of decency that mark the progress of a maturing society."[64] With these words, the chief justice effectively impeded any attempt to freeze the interpretation of the Eighth Amendment to the norms applicable in 1791, when the amended Constitution was adopted.[65] By the time *Trop* was decided, in 1958, the death penalty was already being viewed as an anomaly in enlightened systems of criminal law. Chief Justice Warren, who was attempting to find some coherent framework for applying the Eighth Amendment in what was still, at the time, one of the rare examples of its consideration by the Supreme Court, evidently found it difficult to reconcile capital punishment with the prohibition of cruel and unusual punishment. If the death penalty were to be permitted by the Constitution, surely mere deprival of citizenship could not be found unconstitutional? Or to put it another way, if revoking citizenship for desertion was a breach of the Eighth Amendment, how could capital punishment ever be sustained? (At the time, desertion—Trop's offense—was also a capital crime.)[66] Chief Justice Warren was forced to make some inelegant distinctions:

> At the outset, let us put to one side the death penalty as an index of the constitutional limit on punishment. Whatever the argument may be against capital punishment, both on moral grounds and in terms of accomplishing the purposes of punishment—and they are forceful— the death penalty has been employed throughout our history, and, in a day when it is still widely accepted, it cannot be said to violate the constitutional concept of cruelty. But it is equally plain that the existence of the death penalty is not a license to the Government to devise any punishment short of death within the limit of its imagination.[67]

Capital punishment, then, at least according to Chief Justice Warren in 1958, was still "widely accepted" and therefore compatible with the "evolving standards of decency" test. But this left American jurists embroiled in controversy and confusion about how these "evolving standards" were to be determined.

In *Furman* v. *Georgia*,[68] decided in 1972, a majority of the United States Supreme Court struck down the death penalty legislation then in force within the country.[69] Although at the time several jurisdictions had abolished capital punishment, and in many others it had fallen into disuse, it was still on the statute books of a majority of the states, as well as being applicable in federal criminal law and military law. The judgment stands as a benchmark of United States Supreme Court death penalty jurisprudence, and it continues to be cited with approval in other jurisdictions.[70] A bare majority of the Court, five judges out of nine, relied on the Eighth and Fourteenth[71] Amendments in concluding that existing legislation whereby juries had virtually unfettered discretion to impose the death penalty was plagued by arbitrariness and caprice and therefore ran afoul of the Constitution. "The high service rendered by the 'cruel and unusual' punishment clause of the Eighth Amendment," wrote Justice William O. Douglas in his concurring reasons, "is to require legislatures to write penal laws that are evenhanded, nonselective, and nonarbitrary, and to require judges to see to it that general laws are not applied sparsely, selectively, and spottily to unpopular groups."[72] But only two members of the majority, Justices Marshall and Brennan, were unqualified abolitionists.[73] Following the reasoning of Earl Warren in *Trop* v. *Dulles,* they argued that "evolving standards of decency" had rendered the death penalty incompatible with the Eighth Amendment. Chief Justice Warren Burger sensed the ambiguity in the majority's position. His dissenting reasons literally invited the state legislatures to correct the consequences of *Furman* by adopting new death penalty statutes that would meet the criticisms of those of his brethren who found the previous legislation wanting but who were not prepared to condemn capital punishment outright:

> Since the two pivotal concurring opinions turn on the assumption that the punishment of death is now meted out in a random and unpredictable manner, legislative bodies may seek to bring their laws into compliance with the Court's ruling by providing standards for juries and judges to follow in determining the sentence in capital cases or by more narrowly defining the crimes for which the penalty is to be imposed. If such standards can be devised or the crimes more meticulously defined, the result cannot be detrimental.[74]

In effect, three members of the five-justice majority in *Furman* had left the door open to the legislatures to devise new statutes removing the defects. Specifically, this meant correcting the absence of guidelines for exercise of the jury's discretion that had been condemned in the judgment.[75]

Chief Justice Burger's invitation was quickly taken up. In the few years that followed *Furman,* more than thirty state legislatures enacted new death penalty legislation. A few states responded to the separate opinions in *Furman* by reintroducing mandatory sentencing;[76] most attempted to provide legislated guidelines for exercise of discretion by capital-sentencing juries. Four years later in 1976, five such statutes were challenged before the Supreme Court in a series of cases of which the lead decision is *Gregg* v. *Georgia.*[77] The finding in *Furman* was shunted aside, and a new majority upheld the new death penalty statutes as being compatible with the Constitution. Two principal grounds supported its reasoning: the death penalty had been considered permissible by the framers of the Eighth Amendment,[78] and it might serve "two principal social purposes: retribution and deterrence."[79] According to the majority, the legislative reaction to *Furman* was helpful evidence in fixing where "evolving standards of decency" ought to be positioned, a bizarre development whereby within a period of a few years aggressive state lawmakers, initially concentrated in the South, were in effect able to modify the Eighth Amendment.

The plurality in *Gregg* held that "the concerns expressed in *Furman* that the penalty of death not be imposed in an arbitrary or capricious manner can be met by a carefully drafted statute that ensures that the sentencing authority is given adequate information and guidance. As a general proposition these concerns are best met by a bifurcated proceeding at which the sentencing authority is apprised of the information relevant to the imposition of sentence and provided with standards to guide its use of the information."[80] Since *Gregg*, the Eighth Amendment has been a blunt weapon indeed in death penalty advocacy. It has been regularly invoked in a large number of cases challenging various aspects of capital punishment, including execution of individuals for crimes committed while under the age of eighteen,[81] imposition of the death penalty on the mentally retarded,[82] and racial bias in death sentencing.[83] Litigants have had little success in dislodging the effects of the *Gregg* precedent.

Many of the recent death penalty cases heard by the courts of the United States have been undertaken in the context of the various state constitutions, which generally echo the cruel and unusual punishment provisions of the federal Constitution. The early state constitutions provided models for the federal instrument, and it, in turn, inspired subsequent state constitutions. The federal Constitution is also applicable to state laws, including death penalty legislation, as has been held since 1962.[84] Because of this close relationship between the texts, caselaw under the federal Constitution is regularly used to construe the corresponding provisions in the state constitutions.[85] The state courts consider that in interpreting their own constitutions, even where the provisions are identical, they are not necessarily bound by the precedents set by the U.S. Supreme Court when it construes the federal Constitution.[86] Although such courts cannot restrict the protections afforded by the federal Constitution, they may expand them on the basis of a textually identical state constitutional provision.[87] Moreover, in some cases there are minor differences in wording. In the constitution of New York State, for example, the "cruel and unusual punishment" clause substitutes the word "ought" for the word "shall".[88] Probably the most important of these differences, and the one that has attracted significant judicial attention, is the provision in some state constitutions that punishment not be "cruel *or* unusual." This has suggested to their highest courts that the provision is disjunctive rather than conjunctive—that is, according to such a text punishment is unconstitutional if it is cruel, or if it is unusual.[89] Justice Liacos of the Massachusetts Supreme Judicial Court noted the disjunctive wording of the state provision, indicating that it might deserve "a separate and distinct meaning" from that of the Eighth Amendment.[90] He argued that under his state's constitution, unacceptable punishments needed only to be either cruel or unusual, and not both. Justice Quirico, in dissent, took issue with this position:

> [T]he total absence of any sound reason for the difference in interpretation gives cause to question the decision in this case. There is no historical reason to suppose that these words, first adopted as a part of the Massachusetts Constitution in 1780 and then adopted as part of the First through Tenth Amendments to the United States Constitution in 1790, were intended to have different meanings in substantially similar societal settings, both of which clearly recognized and sanctioned capital punishment for certain crimes. There is no other apparent reason why the nearly identical State and Federal constitutional provisions should not dictate identical results.[91]

The California Constitution also has a disjunctive formulation of the prohibition. In *People* v. *Anderson,* that state's supreme court noted that some commentators have considered the disjunctive form to be without significance.[92] Furthermore, earlier California decisions had treated "cruel and unusual" conjunctively.[93] However, observed the Court, most of the models examined by the framers, derived from various state constitutions, used the disjunctive form. It said that

> [t]he fact that the majority of constitutional models to which the delegates had access prohibited cruel or unusual punishment, and that many of these models reflected a concern on the part of their drafters not only that cruel punishments be prohibited, but that disproportionate and unusual punishments also be independently proscribed, persuades us that the delegates modified the California provision before adoption to substitute the disjunctive "or" for the conjunctive "and" in order to establish their intent that both cruel punishments and unusual punishments be outlawed in this state.[94]

DÉCLARATION DES DROITS DE L'HOMME ET DU CITOYEN

The close ties between the revolutionaries in the thirteen colonies and their comrades in France led to considerable synergy in the drafting of the respective bills of rights.[95] One of the important contributors to the French Déclaration des droits de l'homme et du citoyen of 1789 was the Marquis de Lafayette, who had not only participated in the American Revolution but was actually assisted in his work by the United States ambassador to Paris, Thomas Jefferson.[96] Article 8 of the Déclaration ensures protection against penalties that are not "strictement et évidemment nécessaires" [strictly and obviously necessary]). It was this provision, when applied to the French Code pénal of 1791, which resulted in a generous reduction in the length of sentences and the suppression of a range of grotesque corporal punishments indulged in by the ancien régime.[97] The context of the adoption of article 8 of the Déclaration indicates that there was concern both about the proportionality of sentences, as such, and about the method by which punishment was imposed.[98]

This provision of the Déclaration also provoked debate in the National Assembly about the necessity of retaining the death penalty.[99] The French revolutionaries, undoubtedly inspired by the writings of Cesare Beccaria and his followers, including Voltaire, clearly understood that the new human rights principles of the Enlightenment called into question the legitimacy of capital punishment. Initially, Robespierre argued vigorously for the abolition of the death penalty.[100] He failed to convince the majority of the National Assembly, and the death penalty was retained, although in the form proposed by his colleague, Dr. Guillotin. (He was not, however, the inventor of the guillotine, the device having been used for many years as an elite form of punishment reserved for aristocrats. It was introduced generally during the French Revolution to eliminate the suffering involved in executions and to ensure that imposition of the death penalty involved nothing but the extinction of life.) Although discouraged at the National Assembly's refusal to abolish capital punishment altogether, Robespierre later had a change of heart. He called for the execution of Louis XVI, whom he labelled a "criminal envers l'humanité."[101] His American colleague Thomas Paine considered this a betrayal.[102] Robespierre's failure to effect abolition of the death penalty and his subsequent support for it would, of course, have ironic personal consequences.

UNIVERSAL DECLARATION OF HUMAN RIGHTS

The twentieth century brought the emergence of international human rights law. Interestingly, several of the original draft declarations in this area did not include the prohibition of cruel treatment and torture. For example, an early attempt to draft a truly international and universal declaration of human rights, by the International Law Institute at its 1929 meeting at Briarcliff Manor, New York,[103] contained no such provision. Early on in World War II, it became clear that establishing international human rights norms would be an essential part of the postwar peace process.[104] Several organizations and individuals attempted to prepare texts. One of them, Professor Hersh Lauterpacht, in his important book of 1945, *An International Bill of the Rights of Man*, proposed the following provision: "The law shall provide . . . against inhuman and cruel punishment."[105] At the San Francisco Conference, which established the United Nations in June 1945, there were efforts to adopt an "international bill of rights" as part of the U.N. Charter or as an adjunct to it, and with this in mind drafts were submitted by Panama and Cuba.[106] But neither of these texts included clauses dealing with cruel treatment and torture.

The San Francisco Conference decided not to include a list of human rights norms in the Charter.[107] Subsequently, the Commission on Human Rights was created by the Economic and Social Council, in accordance with article 68 of the United Nations Charter; it was assigned responsibility for drafting the "International Bill of Rights."[108] The commission's secretariat, headed by John P. Humphrey, then prepared a general memorandum on the proposed bill of rights,[109] a comparative analysis of various drafts that had already been submitted to the organization by governments, nongovernmental organizations, and individuals,[110] and a study of the human rights provisions in trusteeship agreements endorsed by the General Assembly.[111] Subsequently, the secretariat prepared a draft outline bill consisting of a preamble and forty-eight articles,[112] one of which concerned the prohibition of cruel treatment and torture: "No one shall be subjected to torture, or to any unusual punishment or indignity."[113] A lengthy annotated text was also prepared by the Secretariat,[114] presenting the draft outline articles of the Universal Declaration, accompanied by the observations made by members of the Commission on Human Rights, equivalent articles in the draft international declarations or proposals submitted by Chile, Cuba, Panama, India, and the United States, and relevant texts from national constitutions. Once again, there were few proposals dealing with punishment or torture. Only the Inter-American Juridical Committee, in a draft submitted by Chile, urged adoption of a phrase prohibiting "cruel or unusual punishments." However, the review noted that provisions dealing with cruel treatment and torture could be found in the constitutions of Afghanistan, Argentina, Bolivia, Chile, Costa Rica, Ecuador, El Salvador, Greece, Guatemala, Haiti, Honduras, Iraq, Mexico, Nicaragua, Norway, Panama, Paraguay, Philippines, Poland, Syria, Turkey, the United States, and Uruguay.[115]

The secretariat draft was amended somewhat by the Commission on Human Rights. The text adopted by the commission for presentation to the General Assembly read: "No one shall be subjected to torture or to cruel, inhuman or degrading treatment or punishment." The provision approved by the commission was one of two paragraphs in a distinct article that dealt with both punishment and slavery.[116] The words "[n]o one shall be subjected" were used in order to indicate that this was an individual right. An alternative formulation, "It shall be unlawful to subject," was criticized because it tended to emphasize that this was an obligation of states.[117] The commission's draft provision on cruel treatment and torture was left unchanged by the Third Committee of the General Assembly. However, in the final version adopted by the General Assembly on December 10, 1948, the prohibition was placed in a distinct article.[118] Drafting of the Universal Declaration took nearly two years, and there were lengthy debates about many of its provisions in the Commission on Human Rights and the Third Committee. However, the torture and cruel punishment provision was astonishingly uncontroversial, and there is virtually no record of debate. As I have mentioned, until the last minute the provision was joined with the text prohibiting slavery, and most of the discussion dwelled on the latter question.[119]

It seems clear that the drafters of article 5 of the Universal Declaration saw their text at least in part as an answer to the inhuman treatments perpetrated by the Nazis. According to Albert Verdoodt, the *travaux préparatoires* suggest an interpretation of article 5 by which no person, even if guilty of a crime, shall be submitted to punishment or to practices that are cruel, inhuman, or degrading. He notes that this goes well beyond what was traditionally considered to constitute torture. Given the fact that the text of article 5 was subject to little or no discussion during the drafting, Verdoodt says that the provision should receive a very generous interpretation.[120] "Although Article 5 was a response to the atrocities committed by the Nazis during the Second World War, it was intended to provide protection from a full range of conduct that would threaten the dignity of the individual," another scholar has observed. "However, no indication was given as to the parameters of the protection or, indeed, how it would differentiate between two distinct types of conduct: that which definitely must be outlawed, and that which (while possibly leading to an equal amount of suffering) should not be prohibited."[121]

Article 5 was not, then, at its inception concerned with the death penalty. It seems indeed odd that the issue did not even arise, given the rather ominous reference to "punishment" in the text of the provision, and the fact that delegates to the Third Committee had been virtually preoccupied by the capital punishment debate (albeit within the context of article 3).[122] It is only subsequent interpretation of article 5 that suggests its relevance to the issue of the death penalty. It must be kept in mind that the Universal Declaration was not conceived of as a binding treaty. That mission was to be confided to the future International Covenant on Civil and Political Rights, whose drafting was already well under way in December 1948, although it would be another eighteen years before its final text would be adopted by the General Assembly,[123] and yet another ten years until it would come into force, in 1976.[124] The Universal Declaration of Human Rights was adopted as a "common standard of achievement," according to the terms of its preamble; it is not subject to ratification, nor may states indulge in such related procedures as reservation or objection. Yet many jurists have since argued that the Universal Declaration represents a codification of customary norms.[125] If such an argument stumbles on provisions like the right to free and fair elections, where state practice since 1948 can hardly be deemed to confirm the existence of a customary rule, the suggestion is somewhat more tenable with respect to the prohibition of torture or cruel, inhuman, or degrading treatment or punishment.

In the late 1960s, there were efforts to associate article 5, as well as article 3 (which enshrines the right to life), with the issue of limitation and eventual abolition of the death penalty. A draft resolution proposed in the 1968 session of the Commission on Human Rights[126] related abolition of the death penalty not only to article 3 of the Universal Declaration but also, apparently for the first time, to article 5. The resolution was adopted by the commission and subsequently by the General Assembly with virtual unanimity.[127] In an explanation of its vote, the United States said that the reference to articles 3 and 5 of the Universal Declaration of Human Rights in the resolution's preamble did not necessarily mean that respect for the Universal Declaration implied approval of abolition of the death penalty.[128] A second resolution adopted at the 1968 session of the General Assembly, "Capital Punishment in Southern Africa," also linked article 5 to the question of the death penalty.[129] Article 5 has also been associated with the death penalty in a resolution of the Economic and Social Council.[130]

Subsequent General Assembly and Economic and Social Council resolutions concerning the death penalty have frequently referred to article 3 of the Universal Declaration, but not to article 5.[131] In December 1989, when the General Assembly adopted the Second Optional Protocol to the International Covenant on Civil and Political Rights, which in effect amends that Covenant and formally prohibits capital punishment, the preamble mentioned article 3 but made no reference to article 5 of the Universal Declaration.[132] Thus, after the early 1970s, article 5 has had little formal connection with issues related to capital punishment. However, death penalty jurisprudence developed in the context of other international instruments, which are themselves derivative of the Universal Declaration, ought to be relevant to the latter's interpretation.

An association between article 5 and death penalty issues is also made by the special rapporteur on torture, who is appointed by the United Nations

Commission on Human Rights. When he met with the Committee Against Torture, the special rapporteur on torture suggested that "prolonged stays in death row" amounted to torture.[133]

INTERNATIONAL COVENANT ON CIVIL AND POLITICAL RIGHTS

The International Covenant on Civil and Political Rights[134] (the "Covenant") and the International Covenant on Economic, Social and Cultural Rights[135] are international treaties intended to transform the "common standard of achievement" found in the Universal Declaration of Human Rights into binding legal obligations. These three documents, together with the two optional protocols to the International Covenant on Civil and Political Rights,[136] constitute what is known as the "International Bill of Rights." The Covenant is considered to be a "universal" instrument because it is open for ratification or accession by all members of the United Nations and its subsidiary bodies, as well as non-members who may be invited to participate.[137] It creates the Human Rights Committee,[138] an eighteen-member expert body charged with examining periodic reports from states parties,[139] inter-state complaints,[140] and individual petitions.[141] The committee has developed a significant amount of jurisprudence that is extremely helpful to the interpretation of the Covenant's provisions. Moreover, the periodic reports filed by states parties provide a useful guide to their own practice and to their *opinio juris*, elements that are of use both in interpreting the Covenant[142] and in attempting to clarify the status of the customary legal norms that are reflected in its conventional provisions.[143]

Like the Universal Declaration of Human Rights, from which it is derived, the Covenant contains distinct provisions dealing with the right to life and with the protection against cruel treatment and torture, both of which are germane to the issue of the death penalty. Article 6 proclaims the right to life, affirming that it may not be taken "arbitrarily" and that a sentence of death may only be imposed for the most serious crimes. Furthermore, article 6 excludes the death penalty in the case of crimes committed by persons under the age of eighteen and for pregnant women. The Human Rights Committee has said that "article 6 provides a limited authorization to States to order capital punishment within their own jurisdiction."[144] In a final paragraph, article 6 stresses the Covenant's abolitionist orientation: "Nothing in this article shall be invoked to delay or to prevent the abolition of capital punishment by any State Party to the present Covenant."[145]

Article 7 concerns cruel treatment and torture. It states:

No one shall be subjected to torture or to cruel, inhuman or degrading treatment or punishment. In particular, no one shall be subjected without his free consent to medical or scientific experimentation.

The first sentence of the provision is identical to the text of article 5 of the Universal Declaration of Human Rights.[146] It was adopted by the Commission on Human Rights in 1949, very early in the drafting of the Covenant, upon a proposal by Lebanon that the provision "read exactly as article 5 of the Declaration of Human Rights."[147] In 1954, the commission submitted its final draft of the Covenant to the General Assembly, where it lingered in that body's Third Committee before eventually being adopted in 1966.[148] In the Third Committee, there were attempts to introduce the phrase "unusual punishment,"[149] but this was felt to be unacceptably vague and, furthermore, delegates considered the fact that punishment might be "unusual" did not necessarily make it reprehensible.[150] As in the case of the Universal Declaration of Human Rights, it seems clear from the *travaux préparatoires* that the drafters of the Covenant did not consider article 7 to be relevant to the issue of the death penalty. During their deliberations, that matter had been thoroughly canvassed in debate about the detailed provisions of article 6. Nevertheless, only a few years after adopting the Covenant in 1966, the General Assembly noted the importance of article 5 of the Universal Declaration—whose text is identical to the first sentence of article 7 of the Covenant—in a resolution dealing with the progressive limitation and eventual abolition of capital punishment.[151] Since then, however, the General Assembly resolutions concerning the death penalty have referred only to article 6 and not to article 7.[152] The Human Rights Committee has said that "in principle, lawful capital punishment under article 6 does not *per se* raise an issue under article 7."[153]

The Human Rights Committee has examined the scope of article 7 in two of its general comments. These are statements of several paragraphs issued periodically by the committee that address problems with the interpretation of various provisions of the Covenant. As such, they may be considered to constitute a form of "official interpretation" of the treaty. In 1982, in the first of the two general comments concerning torture and cruel, inhuman, and degrading punishment, the committee made no mention of the death penalty. On the other hand, the committee declared that it considered corporal punishment to be covered by article 7.[154] The second of the general comments on article 7, issued in 1992, "replaces General Comment no. 7(16) reflecting and further developing it."[155] When the two are compared, a significant evolution in the Human Rights Committee's attitude to the death penalty as a form of cruel treatment and torture becomes apparent. In this revised document, the committee addressed the death penalty by repeating several points that had initially been expressed in its general comment on article 6 and the right to life.[156] This strongly suggested, for the first time, that the committee contemplated a role for article 7 in the context of the debate about capital punishment:

> As the Committee has stated in its general comment No. 6(16), article 6 of the Covenant refers generally to abolition of the death penalty in terms that strongly suggest that abolition is desirable. Moreover, when the death penalty is applied by a State party for the most serious crimes, it must not only be strictly limited in accordance with article 6 but it must be carried out in such a way as to cause the least possible physical and mental suffering.[157]

Furthermore, in a reference that is clearly pertinent to the issue of the death row phenomenon, the committee observed that "the prohibition in article 7 relates not only to acts that cause physical pain but also to acts that cause mental suffering to the victim."[158] The second general comment on article 7 also implies that the committee is prepared to consider matters of penal policy as falling within the ambit of the provision. It makes specific reference to the Standard Minimum Rules for the Treatment of Prisoners,[159] adding that "[n]o penitentiary system should be only retributory; it should essentially seek the reformation and social rehabilitation of the prisoner."[160] A leading authority on the Covenant and the Human Rights Committee, Professor Manfred Nowak, writing in 1993, has noted that "it is a question of the *ordre public* as to how long the death penalty, and also life imprisonment or solitary confinement, can continue to be viewed as beyond the scope of Art. 7."[161] The second general comment on article 7 suggests that this reevaluation has already begun.

In a 1994 opinion in a contentious case filed under the Optional Protocol, the committee indeed found a violation of the Covenant in a death penalty matter. It considered that the method of execution—asphyxiation by poison gas—constituted cruel, inhuman, and degrading punishment contrary to article 7.[162] In its views in that case, the committee concluded: "In determining whether, in a particular case, the imposition of capital punishment constitutes a violation of article 7, the Committee will have regard to the relevant personal factors regarding the author, the specific conditions of detention on death row, and whether the proposed method of execution is particularly abhorrent."[163] However, in two other Canadian cases (involving extradition to Pennsylvania, where since 1990 execution has been carried out using another form of poisoning, the technique of lethal injection) the Human Rights Committee refused to condemn the practice.[164] Over the course of a long series of cases, the committee has resisted applying article 7 to the death row phenomenon, taking the view that prolonged detention while awaiting execution, absent any other aggravating factors, could not be considered to violate the Covenant.[165] Yet on one occasion it ruled that a delay of several hours in announcing a last-minute reprieve to two convicts ran afoul of article 7.[166] Recently, and likely due to the influence of decisions by such prominent international tribunals as the European Court of Human Rights[167] and the Judicial Committee of the Privy Council,[168] the committee appears to be modifying its rather conservative view on the death row phenomenon.[169]

The committee has noted that the purpose of article 7 "is to protect the integrity and dignity of the individual."[170] For many years, it did not feel that it was terribly important to draw sharp distinctions between the adjectives "cruel," "inhuman," and "degrading," which the Covenant uses to describe treatment and punishment,[171] although there have been suggestions that it is now tending to do this.[172] Professor Dominic McGoldrick has observed critically that "[t]he Human Rights Committee has failed to define or establish criteria for distinguishing between the terms in article 7."[173] He suggests that states could be very interested in the distinction, as they might, for example, be prepared to be condemned for cruel treatment under certain circumstances, but not for torture.[174]

The Human Rights Committee has stated that it considers the prohibition of torture or cruel, inhuman, and degrading treatment or punishment to constitute a customary norm.[175] As such, it takes the position that the provision is not subject to reservation, a technique whereby states ratify a multilateral treaty à la carte, choosing to exempt certain obligations. International law tolerates this procedure, but only to the extent that the reservations are not incompatible with the object and purpose of the treaty.[176] According to the committee, a reservation to a customary norm is necessarily in conflict with the object and purpose of the Covenant. Only one state party has ever dared to formulate a reservation to article 7. The United States of America, when it ratified the Covenant in 1992, declared: "The United States considers itself bound by Article 7 to the extent that 'cruel, inhuman or degrading treatment or punishment' means the cruel and unusual treatment or punishment prohibited by the Fifth, Eighth or Fourteenth Amendments to the Constitution of the United States."[177] The purpose of the reservation, according to the State Department's legal advisor, was to make it clear that the United States "do[es] not accept the 'death row phenomenon' as constituting 'cruel, unusual [*sic*] or degrading treatment or punishment,' as the European Court of Human Rights recently held."[178] This reservation was objected to by nine European states,[179] and the Human Rights Committee has declared that it considers the reservation to be incompatible with the Covenant's object and purpose and therefore invalid.[180]

The significance of article 7 as one of the "core" human rights enshrined in the Covenant is underscored by the fact that it is also not subject to derogation.[181] Derogation is allowed by several human rights treaties, including the Covenant,[182] and, occasionally, by domestic constitutions.[183] Derogation must normally meet conditions of both form and substance. Rights may be derogated in times of war or crisis, but any decision by the state to suspend fundamental rights must be notified to responsible international authorities.[184] However, in accordance with article 4 of the Covenant a handful of "core rights" are deemed to be nonderogable. This is the case with cruel treatment and torture. The prohibition of derogation by international instruments is a sign of the hierarchical importance of the prohibition in human rights law. It is also invoked as evidence that the norm is a customary principle, and moreover that it belongs to the category of peremptory norms (*jus cogens*)—that it is "a norm accepted and recognized by the international community of States as a whole, as a norm from which no derogation is permitted."[185] Referring to these provisions, Professor Manfred Nowak says the prohibition of torture "has taken on a special status in the protection of human rights under international law."[186] It is his view that torture is prohibited "by general international law."[187]

REGIONAL HUMAN RIGHTS INSTRUMENTS

Complementing the International Covenant on Civil and Political Rights are three regional human rights treaties, in Europe,[188] the Americas,[189] and Africa.[190] Generally, only states within a particular region may participate in such a treaty and in its implementation bodies. Regional treaties are close relations of the Covenant and the Universal Declaration of Human Rights. In fact, in its preamble each of the three regional instruments specifically acknowledges the role of the Universal Declaration.

The European Convention on Human Rights[191] was adopted by the Council of Europe on November 4, 1950, following a relatively brief drafting period, and came into force some three years later. It preceded the Covenant by sixteen years, and the latter's provisions are consequently, in some respects, somewhat more modern. The European Convention was influenced not only by the text of the Universal Declaration of Human Rights, to which reference is made in the first sentence of its preamble, but also by the early drafts of the International Covenant then being considered by the United Nations Commission on Human Rights.

Article 3 of the European Convention states: "No one shall be subjected to torture or to inhuman or degrading treatment or punishment."[192] There is, as can be seen, a minor difference between the text of article 3 of the Convention and that of article 5 of the Universal Declaration of Human Rights, upon which it is clearly based,[193] in that the adjective "cruel" has been dropped. The original proposal had called for an explicit reference to article 5 of the Declaration, and a subsequent proposal incorporated the text of article 5 without modification.[194] However, the final version of the European Convention on Human Rights did not include the word "cruel" because, according to one scholar, it was considered to be too subjective and moreover unnecessary, given reference to "inhuman" and "degrading" punishment.[195] Nor is the relationship between "torture" and "inhuman and degrading treatment or punishment" elucidated, suggesting to the scholar Frédéric Sudre that the latter phrase is merely redundant.[196] The only reported debate during drafting of article 3 of the Convention concerned whether the provision should mention particular forms of torture.[197] At one point, delegate Cocks of the United Kingdom reminded the drafters of the peremptory aspect of the norm:

> The Consultative Assembly takes this opportunity of declaring that all forms of physical torture, whether inflicted by the police, military authorities, members of private organizations or any other persons are inconsistent with civilized society, are offences against heaven and humanity and must be prohibited. It declares that this prohibition must be absolute and that torture cannot be permitted by any purpose whatsoever, for extracting evidence, for saving life or even for the safety of the State.[198]

The surprisingly slight attention given by the drafters to the text of article 3 only reinforces my view that there is little to be gained in dissecting the text, either in the European Convention or for that matter in any of the other instruments.

The richness of the European Convention is a consequence of its highly developed judicial system. States parties may make an optional declaration (which they now all do as a matter of course) recognizing the jurisdiction of the European Commission on Human Rights and the European Court of Human Rights to receive petitions from individuals alleging violation of the Convention.[199] The commission has initial jurisdiction, and, if it considers the matter to be admissible and not manifestly ill-founded or defective on some procedural ground, the matter may then be referred to the European Court by the commission itself, the state party concerned, or the individual petitioner.[200] Since the commission began operating in the late 1950s, the Strasbourg organs, as they are known, have built up an enormous resource of human rights caselaw, some of it dealing with article 3.

The scope of article 3 was first considered in some detail by the European

Commission in a petition lodged against the Greek dictatorship by Denmark, Norway, Sweden, and the Netherlands in 1969. The commission said degrading treatment or punishment was conduct that "grossly humiliates" persons before others or drives them to act against their will or conscience.[201] "Inhuman treatment" was conduct that "deliberately causes severe suffering, mental or physical, which, in the particular situation, is unjustifiable."[202] The commission considered "torture" to be an aggravated form of inhuman treatment, effected with a particular purpose, such as obtaining a confession or information.[203] By referring, in the *Greek case*, to conduct "which, in the particular situation[,] is unjustifiable," the European Commission introduced a notion of justifiability in application of the norm. It was an "apparent blunder"[204] that the commission endeavored to correct in *Ireland* v. *United Kingdom*, another inter-state application, which alleged torture and other ill-treatment in the detention centers of Northern Ireland. Admitting that its earlier decision had "given rise to some misunderstanding," the commission stated that "there can never be, under the Convention or under international law, a justification for acts in breach of that provision."[205] The European Court of Human Rights later endorsed this view: "The Convention prohibits in absolute terms torture and inhuman or degrading treatment or punishment, irrespective of the victim's conduct. Unlike most of the substantive clauses of the Convention and of Protocols Nos. 1 and 4, Article 3 makes no provision for exceptions and, under Article 15§2, there can be no derogation therefrom even in the event of a public emergency threatening the life of the nation."[206]

Like the International Covenant on Civil and Political Rights,[207] the European Convention expressly contemplates the death penalty as a permitted exception to the right to life.[208] The provision quickly became an anachronism, because since 1950 there have been few executions in states parties to the Convention, and most Council of Europe members are now also parties to Protocol No. 6 to the Convention, which outlaws the death penalty in time of peace.[209] Litigation has arisen, however, concerning extradition, where fugitives have been apprehended in a state party to the Convention on behalf of a requesting state that still applies the death penalty. The question posed was whether an individual could be extradited for a capital crime without breaching the Convention obligations of the extraditing state. In *Kirkwood* v. *United Kingdom*, the European Commission considered the nexus between article 2§1, which tolerates capital punishment, and article 3, which prohibits inhuman and degrading treatment. According to the commission's report:

> Whilst it acknowledges that the Convention must be read as one document, its respective provisions must be given appropriate weight

where there may be implicit overlap, and the Convention organs must be reluctant to draw inferences from one text which would restrict the express terms of another.

As both the Court and the Commission have recognized, Article 3 is not subject to any qualification. Its terms are bald and absolute. This fundamental aspect of Article 3 reflects its key position in the structure of the rights of the Convention, and is further illustrated by the terms of Article 15§2 which permit no derogation from it even in time of war or other public emergency threatening the life of the nation.

In these circumstances the Commission considers that notwithstanding the terms of article 2§1, it cannot be excluded that the circumstances surrounding the protection of one of the other rights contained in the Convention might give rise to an issue under article 3.[210]

Thus, the commission envisaged the possibility of article 3 overshadowing article 2§1, although in the specific facts of the case it considered that Kirkwood's application was inadmissible, because he had not demonstrated that detention on California's death row was inhuman and degrading treatment within the meaning of article 3. The same issue returned to the European Commission several years later in the case of Jens Soering, who had been arrested in the United Kingdom under an extradition warrant issued at the request of the United States. A national of the Federal Republic of Germany, Soering had helped to murder his girlfriend's parents while living in Virginia and had then fled to the United Kingdom.

The commission followed its caselaw in *Kirkwood* and dismissed the argument based on article 3 of the Convention, although it found that there had been a breach of article 13, which ensures the right to an effective remedy.[211] The matter was then taken before the European Court of Human Rights, which unanimously reversed the commission. In *Soering* v. *United Kingdom*,[212] the Court held that a lengthy wait on death row, to which an extradited fugitive would be subject in Virginia, constitutes an "inhuman or degrading punishment or treatment" within the meaning of article 3 of the Convention.[213] In Soering's favor were mitigating circumstances, including his young age (eighteen at the time of the crime), a severe psychological disorder, and the fact that he had been manipulated by his accomplice, who had received a life sentence. Furthermore, Germany, which intervened in the proceedings before the Court, also had jurisdiction over Soering and proposed to try him before its criminal courts. Germany abolished the death penalty in the late 1940s.

The United Kingdom was entitled to refuse Soering's extradition to the United States because of a condition in the extradition treaty between the two countries entitling either contracting party to insist upon an undertaking from the other that the death penalty would not be imposed.[214] The provision is drawn from article 11 of the European Convention on Extradition, which states that, when the offense is punishable by death under the law of the requesting party but not that of the requested party, or the death penalty is not normally carried out by the latter party, "extradition may be refused unless the requesting Party gives such assurance as the requested Party considers sufficient that the death-penalty will not be carried out."[215] The United Kingdom had obtained from the Virginia prosecutor a commitment to inform the trial judge that the United Kingdom hoped the death penalty would not be imposed, but Soering insisted that this was an inadequate assurance.[216]

The European Court of Human Rights considered that the enunciation of principles, such as that forbidding the execution of minors, in "other, later international instruments, the former of which [the International Covenant on Civil and Political Rights] has been ratified by a large number of States parties to the European Convention, at the very least indicates that as a general principle the youth of the person concerned is a circumstance which is liable, with others, to put in question the compatibility with article 3 of measures connected with the death sentence."[217] Other cases where violation of article 3 might arise could include a death penalty out of all proportion to the crime or public execution.[218] In his concurring opinion in *Soering*, Judge Jan De Meyer held that extradition of Jens Soering would breach not only article 3 but also article 2 of the Convention. Because article 2§1 permits imposition of the death penalty only where this "is provided by law," and because the death penalty is not "provided by law" in the United Kingdom, the fact that it is allowed in Virginia is irrelevant, he wrote.[219] "When a person's right to life is involved, no requested State can be entitled to allow a requesting State to do what the requested State is not itself allowed to do."[220] Judge De Meyer added that the unlawfulness of the death penalty in Europe was recognized by the Committee of Ministers when it adopted Protocol No. 6 to the Convention in December 1982:

> No State party to the Convention can in that context, even if it has not yet ratified the Sixth Protocol, be allowed to extradite any person if that person thereby incurs the risk of being put to death in the requesting State. Extraditing somebody in such circumstances would be repugnant to European standards of justice, and contrary to the public order of Europe.[221]

Because of the reference to the death penalty in article 2 of the Convention, the majority of the European Court of Human Rights refused to conclude that the death penalty per se constitutes inhuman treatment.[222] As the scholar Francis Jacobs observed ironically (many years before the judgment in *Soering*), punishment might be contrary to article 3 of the Convention "only if it did not involve the ultimate penalty."[223] The suggestion that the Convention's recognition of the death penalty as an exception to the right to life is now obsolete and incompatible with the legal conscience and practice of contemporary Europe, advanced by Judge De Meyer in his concurring opinion, was not followed by his colleagues on the Court.[224] The majority referred to the subsequent adoption of Protocol No. 6 as evidence that the states parties to the European Convention preferred the approach of an additional protocol to one of implicit abrogation of article 2§1.[225] In fact, in 1979, when the issue arose of amending article 2 of the Convention so as to bring it into step with the more advanced norms of the American Convention on Human Rights, the Steering Committee on Human Rights of the Council of Europe felt that any such amendment would imply acceptance of the death penalty at a time when there was a general trend towards abolition.[226] Amendment of the Convention might only legitimize the death penalty, and so the lawmakers of the Council of Europe chose the route of an optional protocol, updating the Convention and abolishing the death penalty. Consequently, the current inadequacies, indeed the obsolescence, of article 2§1 of the Covenant can only be properly appreciated in the light of Protocol No. 6.

Although the Court refused to rule that the death penalty was inhuman and degrading, it indirectly attacked capital punishment by deciding that extradition of Soering would violate article 3 because of his potential suffering on death row. The Court concluded that if extradited and subsequently sentenced to death, Soering might spend from six to eight years in Virginia's penitentiaries awaiting execution, and that this would constitute a violation of the Convention. *Soering* has had an enormous impact going well beyond the frontiers of Europe. Tribunals throughout the world have recognized the persuasive value of the European Court's conclusions concerning the death row phenomenon, precisely because the norm, set out in article 3 of the European Convention, corresponds in content if not in precise form to similar prohibitions in other international or domestic legal texts. In some situations, the provisions are virtually identical, because of the role the European Convention played in the drafting of modern constitutions. Specifically, when former British dependencies were decolonized, they often included the provisions of the Convention in their new constitutions so as to ensure that the same rights accruing to them prior to independence (by virtue of the United Kingdom's ratification of the Convention with application to such dependencies) would be maintained. As members of the Judicial Committee of the Privy Council noted in 1983, section

17(1) of the Constitution of Jamaica is "almost identical" to article 3 of the European Convention[227] and is one of a family of similar constitutions that includes those of Trinidad and Tobago, Bermuda, Zimbabwe, and Nigeria.[228] But *Soering*'s influence has been felt elsewhere, for example in Canada, where the relevant constitutional provision refers to "cruel and unusual punishment"[229] and is derived not from the European Convention on Human Rights but from the Eighth Amendment to the United States Constitution and from section 10 of the Bill of Rights of 1689.

The second major regional system is that of the Organization of American States. It has the distinction of relying on two instruments, the American Declaration of the Rights and Duties of Man[230] and the American Convention on Human Rights.[231] The Declaration, adopted in May 1948, was originally intended to fulfill a role comparable to that of the Universal Declaration of Human Rights. Somewhat later, the Organization of American States decided to follow the example of the Council of Europe and the United Nations and to prepare a full-blown human rights treaty, the American Convention; this was adopted in 1969 and has been in force since 1978. Emulating the European model, the Convention creates the Inter-American Court of Human Rights and empowers it to adjudicate individual petitions, subject to recognition by the states parties concerned of its jurisdiction in such matters.[232] The Inter-American Commission on Human Rights, which existed before the adoption of the American Convention, operates as a kind of court of first instance, a mechanism roughly analogous to the original Strasbourg procedure. Members of the Organization of American States that have not ratified the American Convention may still be challenged before the Inter-American Commission on Human Rights for violations of the 1948 American Declaration.[233]

The American Declaration of the Rights and Duties of Man contains, in its due process provision, a prohibition of cruel treatment and torture: "Every person accused of an offense has the right to be given an impartial and public hearing, and to be tried by courts previously established in accordance with pre-existing laws, and not to receive cruel, infamous or unusual punishment."[234] However, death penalty litigation under the Declaration has relied on Article I, which guarantees the right to life.[235] The American Convention on Human Rights affirms the guarantee against cruel treatment and torture in its fifth article:

Article 5. RIGHT TO HUMANE TREATMENT.
1. Every person has the right to have his physical, mental, and moral integrity respected.
2. No one shall be subjected to torture or to cruel, inhuman, or

degrading punishment or treatment. All persons deprived of their liberty shall be treated with respect for the inherent dignity of the human person.

3. Punishment shall not be extended to any person other than the criminal.

The first sentence of paragraph 2 is virtually identical to the provisions in the Universal Declaration of Human Rights and the International Covenant on Civil and Political Rights, except that the terms "treatment" and "punishment" are reversed, for no apparent reason.

Although there has been no shortage of torture cases considered by the Inter-American Commission, its caselaw and that of the Court is relatively less sophisticated than that of the European Convention organs. The Inter-American Court of Human Rights has stated that "prolonged isolation and deprivation of communication are in themselves cruel and inhuman treatment, harmful to the psychological and moral integrity of the person and a violation of the right of any detainee to respect for his inherent dignity as a human being. Such treatment, therefore, violates Article 5 of the Convention . . ."[236] The Inter-American Commission has interpreted the provision in an application dealing with prolonged detention on death row in Jamaica.

> Pratt and Morgan suffered a denial of justice during the period 1980–1984 violative of Article 5(2) of the American Convention on Human Rights. The Commission found that the fact that the Jamaican Court of Appeal issued its decision on December 5 1980 but did not issue the reasons for that decision until four years later, September 24, 1984, was tantamount to cruel, inhuman, and degrading treatment because during that four year delay the petitioners could not appeal to the Privy Council and had to suffer four years on death row awaiting execution. The Inter-American Commission on Human Rights, pursuant to its cable of July 7 1987 requests that the execution of Messrs. Pratt and Morgan be commuted for humanitarian reasons.[237]

The commission's decision constitutes the first reported determination by a judicial or quasi-judicial body in any human rights system to the effect that prolonged detention on death row may amount to cruel treatment and torture.

The third regional human rights instrument is the African Charter of Human and Peoples' Rights, adopted by the Organization of African Unity in 1981 and in force since 1986.[238] The Charter establishes a commission, but no court, although discussions are currently under way with a view to one's creation. The organs of the African system are the least developed of the three regional human rights mechanisms. The African Commission considers reports of states parties, which are of some help in interpretation. Little has been known about its petition procedure, and only recently have the Commission's reports begun to be rendered public. Nigeria has been condemned at least twice by the African Commission on Human and Peoples' Rights for violations of the African Charter on Human and Peoples' Rights, in cases initiated by the Constitutional Rights Project on behalf of death row inmates attacking the fairness of their convictions.[239]

Article 5 of the African Charter states:

> Every individual shall have the right to the respect of the dignity inherent in a human being and to the recognition of his legal status. All forms of exploitation and degradation of man particularly slavery, slave trade, torture, cruel, inhuman or degrading punishment and treatment shall be prohibited.

Although the African Charter makes no mention of the death penalty in its right-to-life provision (unlike the comparable instruments of the universal, European, and American systems), scholars have considered that its unqualified recognition of the right to life does not mean that the death penalty, whose use is still widespread in Africa, is not prohibited, providing it is imposed in accordance with the law.[240] However, the African Charter provides explicitly, in article 60, that it is to be construed with reference to the Universal Declaration of Human Rights. Moreover, like all other human rights treaties, it should be interpreted in a dynamic fashion. Litigants have now begun to argue that the "death row phenomenon" is incompatible with the current state of African human rights law and more specifically with the African Charter of Human and Peoples' Rights;[241] this position is undoubtedly strengthened by developments like the judicial abolition of the death penalty in the Republic of South Africa.[242]

INTERNATIONAL HUMANITARIAN LAW

With its increased focus on the protection of civilians as well as its enhanced application to civil strife, international humanitarian law has become a close relative of human rights law. As the law applicable to armed conflicts, it includes a body of norms whose mission is to protect the victims of war—principally civilians and prisoners of war—from ill treatment. The humanitarian law treaties contain a number of provisions concerning application of the death penalty. In particular, there are rules forbidding execution of pregnant women, young mothers, and individuals for crimes committed while under the age of eighteen.[243] International humanitarian law also considers that in the case of sentence of death upon a civilian or a prisoner of war, there shall be a moratorium of six months before the sentence is carried out.[244] The purpose of these provisions is to allow time for the protecting power to intervene on behalf of the condemned person. There is also, implicitly, the hope that the conflict will end and that a subsequent search for reconciliation will bring amnesty or commutation. But this moratorium is of interest because it shows that some modest delay in execution has, in certain contexts, been deemed acceptable by international law.

Universal recognition of the norm prohibiting cruel treatment and torture is consigned in common article 3 to the four Geneva Conventions of 1949.[245] These minimum standards apply, according to the Conventions, in armed conflicts not of an international character. The Geneva Conventions of 1949 have been ratified by virtually every state in the world, and common article 3 has been declared by the International Court of Justice to express principles of customary international law.[246] If the norms of common article 3 are recognized in the extreme conditions of noninternational armed conflict to constitute the lowest common denominator of humane conduct, then *a fortiori* they most surely obtain during international armed conflict and in time of peace. There is, however, little interpretative material, such as caselaw or scholarly writings, permitting insight into the nuances of the interpretation to be given to common article 3.

SPECIALIZED TREATIES

The prohibition of cruel treatment and torture is also ensured by certain specialized instruments, of which the most important is the United Nations Convention Against Torture and Other Cruel, Inhuman and Degrading Treatment or Punishment.[247] Adopted by the General Assembly in 1984, it was preceded by the Declaration on the Protection of All Persons from Being Subjected to Torture and Other Cruel, Inhuman or Degrading Treatment or Punishment,[248] adopted by the same body in 1976. As of December 31, 1994, the Convention had been ratified by eighty-six states.[249] Like a number of other international human rights treaties, this instrument creates a committee charged with overseeing its implementation. An expert body composed of ten members, the Committee Against Torture's principal activity has been the consideration of periodic reports, filed by states parties pursuant to article 19 of the Convention. The treaty also provides for an individual petition mechanism, but this requires an optional declaration by states parties and, in practice, it has been little used by international litigants to date.

A literal reading of the Convention might suggest that the death penalty does not fall within its scope—article 1, which defines torture, excludes "pain or suffering arising only from, inherent in or incidental to lawful sanctions." Nevertheless, pursuant to its article 16, "Each State Party shall undertake to prevent in any territory under its jurisdiction other acts of cruel, inhuman or degrading treatment or punishment which do not amount to torture as defined in article 1, when such acts are committed by or at the instigation of or with the consent or acquiescence of a public official or other person acting in an official capacity." Many of the states parties' periodic reports to the Committee Against Torture make reference to norms concerning application of the death penalty,[250] extradition to other states for capital crimes,[251] or to the fact that capital punishment has been or is being abolished.[252] In many cases, comments on the subject are provoked by questions from members of the committee, demonstrating that the committee considers the death penalty to fall clearly within its jurisdiction.[253] Confirmation can also be found in the reservation that was formulated by the United States at the time it ratified the Convention, dealing with the death row phenomenon and intended to avoid an interpretation similar to that of the European Court of Human Rights in the *Soering* case.[254] Moreover, the United States also produced an "understanding," which it said would apply to its obligations under the Convention: "The United States understands that international law does not prohibit the death penalty, and does not consider this Convention to restrict or prohibit the United States from applying the death penalty consistent with the Fifth, Eighth and/or Fourteenth Amendments to the Constitution of the United States, including any constitutional period of confinement prior to the imposition of the death penalty."[255] However, in none of these materials is there any useful indication of whether the committee or the states parties consider the death penalty to be subsumed within article 16, article 1, or both.

The Convention Against Torture and Other Cruel, Inhuman and Degrading Treatment or Punishment expands upon the general principles set out in article 5 of the Universal Declaration of Human Rights and in article 7 of the International Covenant on Civil and Political Rights. Of particular interest is its prohibition of *refoulement* (forced repatriation) where an individual is threatened with torture.[256] Although there is already a sizeable body of human rights jurisprudence concerned with the issue of extradition to countries where the death penalty is still applied,[257] the Committee Against Torture has yet to address the question.[258]

Also of interest are the Standard Minimum Rules for the Treatment of Prisoners, adopted by the Economic and Social Council in 1957 and revised by the council in 1977.[259] Although they make no special provision for individuals condemned to death or for the imposition of the death penalty, they do set out a number of basic norms that must be respected on death row.[260] The Standard Minimum Rules deal with a number of special categories of prisoner, but they make no provision or even mention of those condemned to death. Because consideration of death row might have been viewed as implicitly legitimizing capital punishment, this may be seen as an early manifestation of the commitment within United Nations bodies to abolition of the death penalty. Certain of the rules have a particular resonance to the often appalling conditions of prisoners sentenced to death:

> Discipline shall be no more restrictive than what is necessary to ensure custody and order.
> Prisoners are to be allowed regular contact with family and friends, by both correspondence and personal visits.
> The prison system must not aggravate unnecessarily the suffering inherent in a prisoner's loss of self-determination and liberty.

It is clear that at least one of the norms in the Standard Minimum Rules is simply inapplicable to those on death row:

> Treatment of prisoners under sentence shall be directed to achieve the capacity for law-abiding and self-supporting lives, utilizing professional services whenever possible.

Specialized conventions dealing with cruel treatment and torture also exist on a regional level. These are the European Convention for the Prevention and Suppression of Torture and Inhuman or Degrading Treatment or Punishment[261] and the Inter-American Convention to Prevent and Punish Torture.[262] Because the death penalty has been abolished in all of the states parties to these two instruments, it seems improbable that questions related to imposition of capital punishment will arise.

ELEMENTS OF THE NORM

Although I have chosen to refer, in a general sense, to the norm prohibiting "cruel treatment and torture," domestic constitutions and international legal instruments use a somewhat larger spectrum of terms, notably "inhuman," "degrading," and "unusual." The attempt to simplify terminology by using a single phrase is not meant to obscure semantic distinctions in the norms, although it certainly reflects the fact that by and large courts do not attempt to draw too fine a line between the various categories. Nor should they, in my view. The willingness of various domestic and international courts to use comparative caselaw in this area indicates that they, too, attach little significance to subtle textual distinctions. In at least one case, that of the Indian Constitution, there is no prohibition whatsoever of either torture or cruel punishment, but courts have perceived such a norm within the context of due process provisions.[263]

The first significant distinction to be made is between torture and treatment or punishment. Many domestic constitutional instruments—including the English Bill of Rights, the United States Constitution, the French Déclaration des droits de l'homme et du citoyen, and the Canadian Charter of Rights and Freedoms—make no mention whatsoever of torture. Although torture is undoubtedly prohibited by these instruments, it seems to be subsumed within the notion of cruel treatment or punishment. The description of the norm prohibiting cruel punishment became somewhat more elaborate with the Universal Declaration of Human Rights in 1948. It adds the term "torture" to the prohibition, as well as using the word "treatment."[264] Since adoption of the Universal Declaration and the various instruments that it has inspired, it is clear that the term "torture" has taken on a meaning which is autonomous from that of punishment or treatment. This first appeared in the early caselaw of the European Commission on Human Rights;[265] it is readily apparent from the distinction that is made between "torture" and "cruel, inhuman, and degrading treatment or punishment" in the 1984 United Nations Convention on the subject:[266]

> 1. For the purposes of this Convention, the term "torture" means any act by which severe pain or suffering, whether physical or mental, is intentionally inflicted on a person for such purposes as obtaining from him or a third person information or a confession, punishing him for an act he or a third person has committed or is suspected of having committed, or intimidating or coercing him or a third person, or for any reason based on discrimination of any kind, when such pain or suffering is inflicted by or at the instigation of or with the consent or acquiescence of a public official or other person acting in an official capacity. It does not include pain or suffering arising only from, inherent in or incidental to lawful sanctions.
>
> 2. This article is without prejudice to any international instrument or national legislation which does or may contain provisions of wider application.[267]

It can be seen that the definition includes punishment, but it excludes "pain or suffering arising only from, inherent in or incidental to lawful sanctions." This rather enormous exception was conceived so as to allow countries to continue imposing methods of corporal punishment in accordance with their domestic law. Such tolerance would, presumably, facilitate ratification of the Convention.[268] However, it is doubtful whether the "lawful sanctions" exception applies to other instruments that prohibit torture.[269] It has been suggested that the term "lawful" must be judged in light not only of domestic law but also of international law.[270] However, as one scholar has noted, this leads to a tautology, because what is lawful under international law must be judged by what is lawful under international law.[271] The Convention Against Torture also refers to "other cruel, inhuman and degrading treatment or punishment." Article 16 of the Convention specifies that states parties must prevent "other acts of cruel, inhuman or degrading treatment or punishment which do not amount to torture as defined in article 1." Unlike torture, "cruel, inhuman and degrading treatment or punishment" is not defined by the Convention Against Torture, but it appears to denote a less severe form of unacceptable treatment. The earlier Declaration was more explicit, setting out that "[t]orture constitutes an aggravated and deliberate form of cruel, inhuman or degrading treatment or punishment."[272] This notion of gradation in degree rather than in substance is supported by the caselaw of the European Commission on Human Rights[273] and the European Court of Human Rights.[274] In the case of *Ireland* v. *United Kingdom*, the European Court stopped short of describing acts committed against prisoners in Northern Ireland's prisons as torture, but it did use the term "inhuman treatment."

Although the distinction between "torture" and "cruel, inhuman and degrading treatment or punishment" is not an easy one, it pales in comparison with efforts to dissect the individual terms "cruel," "inhuman," and "degrading." "Cruel" punishment is prohibited by many international and domestic instruments, although it was not included in the relevant prohibition of the European Convention on Human Rights. In a definition that simply turns us back to the other legs of the norm, Chief Justice Wright of the Supreme Court of California spoke of what he called the "ordinary meaning of cruel": "causing physical pain or mental anguish of an inhumane or torturous nature."[275] A notion of gradation or degree may be present. As one United States court noted, "All punishments might be said to be cruel, but what we examine here is the question of punishment which is too cruel under constitutional standards."[276] In another United States judgment, it is noted that "[c]ruelty does not necessarily involve pain. Indignities can be inflicted even after a person has died."[277] "Inhuman" treatment has been defined by the European Commission on Human Rights as being "at least such treatment as deliberately causes severe suffering, mental or physical."[278] In *Ireland* v. *United Kingdom*, the European Court of Human Rights held that treatment was inhuman if it was premeditated, if it was applied for hours at a time, and if it resulted in intense physical and mental suffering, even if it did not cause actual bodily injury.[279] "Degrading" punishment seems easier to distinguish, since it normally involves an element of humiliation. For the European Commission on Human Rights, punishment is degrading to an individual when it "grossly humiliates him before others or drives him to act against his will or conscience."[280] In the *East African Asians case*, the European Commission described degrading treatment as "conduct of a certain level of severity which lowers the victim in rank, position, reputation or character whether in his eyes or in the eyes of other people."[281] The European Court of Human Rights described degrading treatment as being "such as to arouse in its victims feelings of fear, anguish and inferiority capable of humiliating and debasing them."[282] According to the Human Rights Committee, "For punishment to be degrading, the humiliation or debasement involved must exceed a particular level and must, in any event, entail other elements beyond the mere fact of deprivation of liberty."[283]

The only international law instrument to use the term "unusual" is the American Declaration of the Rights and Duties of Man (adopted in May 1948),[284] although the Philippines tentatively proposed that this word be inserted between "inhuman" and "degrading" in the draft text of article 7 of the International Covenant on Civil and Political Rights.[285] There were objections to the proposal on the grounds that the term was vague and that what might be considered "unusual" in one country might not be so viewed in another.[286] "Unusual" punishment is prohibited by the English Bill of Rights, the United States Constitution, and most of the state constitutions within the United States. Canada opted for the term in enacting its Bill of Rights in 1960[287] and retained it in the 1982 Canadian Charter of Rights and Freedoms,[288] despite a general tendency to follow the terminology of the Universal Declaration of Human Rights and the other major international instruments.[289] Chief Justice Earl Warren, in *Trop* v. *Dulles*, doubted whether "unusual" added anything to the norm prohibiting cruel punishment:

> Whether the word "unusual" has any qualitative meaning different from "cruel" is not clear. On the few occasions this Court has had to consider the meaning of the phrase, precise distinctions between cruelty and unusualness do not seem to have been drawn. . . . If the word "unusual" is to have any meaning apart from the word "cruel," however, the meaning should be the ordinary one, signifying something different from that which is generally done. Denationalization as a punishment certainly meets this test.[290]

When it was first introduced into the language of human rights law, by the English Parliament in 1689, the term "unusual" was apparently meant to prohibit illegal punishments.[291] But in the caselaw of the United States and Canada, there is little or no attempt to give an autonomous meaning to this word.

Often, courts read in an additional term, "dignity," to the prohibition of cruel punishment. There is no reference to the word in the Eighth Amendment of the United States Constitution, but "dignity" appears frequently in judgments dealing with that provision. According to Chief Justice Warren, "The basic concept underlying the Eighth Amendment is nothing less than the dignity of man."[292] For his colleague Justice Brennan: "[F]oremost among the 'moral concepts' recognized in our cases and inherent in the Clause is the primary moral principle that the State, even as it punishes, must treat its citizens in a manner consistent with their intrinsic worth as human beings—a punishment must not be so severe as to be degrading to human dignity. A judicial determination whether the punishment of death comports with human dignity is therefore not only permitted but compelled by the [Eighth Amendment]."[293] Elsewhere in the same judgment, Brennan described "human dignity" as the Eighth Amendment's "fundamental premise."[294] Chief Justice Gubbay of the Zimbabwe Supreme Court has described his country's cruel-punishment provision as enshrining "nothing less than the dignity of man," as embodying "broad and idealistic notions of dignity, humanity and decency."[295]

As with the term "degrading," the cases frequently note that breaches of human dignity are offensive both to the specific victim and to society in general. According to Chief Justice Wright of the California Supreme Court, "The dignity of man, the individual and the society as a whole, is today demeaned by our continued practice of capital punishment."[296] Justice Liacos of the Massachusetts Supreme Judicial Court asks, "What dignity can remain for the government that countenances its use?"[297] These comments echo those of Clarence Darrow:

> We teach people to kill and the State is the one that teaches them. If the State wishes that its citizens respect human life, then the State should stop killing. The greater the sanctity that the State pays to life, the greater the feeling of sanctity the individual has for life.[298]

Similar sentiments have been expressed by Chief Justice Hennessey of the Massachusetts Supreme Judicial Court: "There is an impetus to respond in kind in punishing the person who has been convicted of murder, but the death penalty brutalizes the State which condemns and kills its prisoners."[299]

Some authorities support the view that whether punishment is cruel, inhuman, or degrading depends on the intent of the person who inflicts it. In *Pratt and Morgan* v. *Jamaica*, the Human Rights Committee appeared to adopt such an approach when it condemned Jamaica because prison officials had waited several hours before telling two condemned men of a reprieve. The reprieve itself could hardly be considered cruel; from the prisoners' standpoint it was welcome news. They did not learn until later that delivery of the information had been intentionally delayed.[300] One member of the Human Rights Committee, Nisuke Ando, has stated that the death penalty cannot be said to be imposed in a cruel or inhuman manner if the state has no intention of prolonging suffering.[301] The European Commission on Human Rights, in its early decisions dealing with article 3 of the European Convention, defined inhuman treatment as "such treatment as deliberately causes severe suffering, mental or physical . . ."[302] But, as one scholar has observed, the effect of defining article 3 of the European Convention in terms of intent "was to eliminate from scrutiny some forms of treatment or punishment that clearly merited further consideration so as to better protect the individual's physical integrity."[303] The issue is of some relevance to the death penalty debate, because proponents of legal execution will insist their aim is not to inflict pain but only to bring an end to life.[304]

A similar intent requirement can be found in some judgments of the United States Supreme Court. In *Francis,* the Court held that an unsuccessful electrocution followed by the decision of Louisiana to attempt to execute a man for the second time was not cruel punishment because there was "no purpose to inflict unnecessary pain."[305] In that case, Justice Felix Frankfurter allowed that, hypothetically, "a single, cruelly willful attempt" at execution might offend the Constitution.[306] In a judgment dating to the turn of the century, Oliver Wendell Holmes, then of the Massachusetts Supreme Judicial Court, considered the significance of intent in assessing the inherent cruelty of methods of execution: "[W]hen, as here, the means adopted are chosen with just the contrary intent, and are devised for the purpose of reaching the end proposed as swiftly and painlessly as possible, we are of opinion that they are not forbidden by the constitution."[307] In a 1994 judgment of the Court of Appeals for the Ninth Circuit, where the method of execution (hanging) was challenged, the majority of the Court held that the petitioner was not entitled to an execution free of pain, but only to one free of purposeful cruelty.[308] However, the European Court of Human Rights has recognized that the approach should not be overly subjective. In a corporal punishment case, *Campbell and Cosans* v. *United Kingdom,* the Court ruled that "a threat directed to an exceptionally insensitive person may have no significant effect on him but nevertheless be incontrovertibly degrading; and conversely, an exceptionally sensitive person might be deeply affected by a threat that could be described as degrading only by a distortion of the ordinary and usual meaning of the word."[309]

One argument that is invoked in favor of the intent requirement is that it is the only way to exclude pain or suffering intentionally effected by medical professionals in good faith in order to treat patients. In *Tyrer* v. *United Kingdom*, Judge Fitzmaurice asked whether the army surgeon in the field who amputates a soldier's leg without anesthetic to save his patient's life can be considered to have breached the European Convention on Human Rights because his conduct causes considerable suffering.[310] However, in my view, reference to medical practices is unhelpful. The latter involve "treatment" and not "punishment." The matter should be viewed as being sui generis. In any case, medical treatment necessarily involves a form of implied or express consent, distinguishing it from penal sanctions.

These examples of the subjective component in cruelty are actually rather isolated. Most cases on the subject of cruel punishment make no reference to intent. In perhaps its most celebrated decision dealing with cruel punishment, *Soering* v. *United Kingdom*, the European Court of Human Rights clearly did not apply any intent requirement. It was most certainly not the United Kingdom's intent to subject Soering to the death row phenomenon; Her Majesty's Government had already asked for an assurance that he be spared the death penalty, although the assurance was criticized as being insufficient.[311] To suggest that application of the prohibition of cruel treatment and torture depends on the intent of the executioner would seem to emasculate the provision, whose principal purpose is to protect the rights of individuals, and not primarily to sanction the behavior of state officials. As David Pannick has written, "State action is unconstitutional if its consequence is to inflict unacceptable levels of cruelty, albeit that is not the intention of the organizers of the State action."[312] Perhaps the better view, then, is that treatment or punishment that is not intrinsically cruel may become so if administered with cruel intent, but that treatment or punishment may be cruel even where there is no identifiable cruel intent.

Cultural factors are also extremely important in evaluating whether punishment is cruel, inhuman, or degrading. Notions of cruelty, inhumanity, and degradation, as well as of pain, distress, and humiliation, will depend on a number of personal elements that are socially conditioned. A rather mundane example is provided by the European Court of Human Rights, in *Tyrer* v. *United Kingdom*. The Continental judges were shocked at the practice of "birching," but their English colleague, Judge Fitzmaurice, was not at all outraged. He confessed that his attitude might have been "colored by the fact that I was brought up and educated under a system according to which the corporal punishment of schoolboys (sometimes at the hands of the senior ones—prefects or monitors—sometimes by masters) was regarded as the normal sanction for serious misbehavior, and even sometimes for what was much less serious. . . . Yet I cannot remember that any boy felt degraded or debased."[313] The European

Commission on Human Rights has attempted to determine when ill-treatment of prisoners will reach the threshold of inhumanity, and has said that "the point up to which prisoners and the public may accept physical violence as being neither cruel nor excessive varies between different societies and even between different sections of them."[314] But there must be a limit to the role cultural factors may play. Otherwise, the norm prohibiting cruel treatment and torture ceases to have any international scope. Although a "margin of appreciation" in applying fundamental rights is recognized within the European system, such bodies as the Human Rights Committee and the Committee Against Torture have yet to elaborate a doctrine on just how broadly cultural factors may be invoked within the context of cruel treatment and torture.

Should not economic factors also be taken into account? Conditions of detention in many African countries are notoriously harsh, at least when compared with the situation prevailing in the richer countries of Europe and North America. The gruesome state of African prisons is a consequence of economic conditions. The guarantee against cruel treatment and torture is a civil and political right, which states undertake to ensure immediately to all those subject to their jurisdiction.[315] Unlike the situation applicable to economic and social rights, a state is not entitled to plead that these rights are recognized to the "maximum of its available resources."[316] Yet it seems plainly illogical to hold developing countries to the same standard. The purpose of the International Covenants was surely not to incite states to put conditions on death row ahead of such other social priorities as schooling and medical care.

LIMITATIONS ON THE PROHIBITION OF TORTURE AND CRUEL PUNISHMENT

Limitation clauses appear in many domestic and international human rights instruments.[317] The model for them all is article 29 of the Universal Declaration of Human Rights, which allows that "[i]n the exercise of his rights and freedoms, everyone shall be subject only to such limitations as are determined by law solely for the purpose of securing due recognition and respect for the rights and freedoms of others and of meeting the just requirements of morality, public order and the general welfare in a democratic society."[318] Such a clause means that legislation that is prima facie contrary to the norm is "saved" to the extent it can be justified. The international human rights treaties that were inspired by the Declaration did not follow strictly its approach of a general limitations clause. Instead, specific limitations clauses are provided for such norms as freedom of expression, freedom of religion, and freedom of association.[319] None of the international treaties allows for any form of limitation to the prohibition of cruel treatment and torture. Nevertheless, there are suggestions in the international caselaw that implied limits exist on the prohibition of cruel treatment and torture. A member of the European Commission on Human Rights has asserted that "[w]hat ill-treatment constitutes inhuman treatment or torture will depend upon its character and the circumstances in which it is inflicted: the notion of inhuman treatment or torture is not absolute."[320] The commission has also indicated that where a prisoner resists, ill-treatment that would otherwise not be so may become "justifiable."[321] In *Tyrer* v. *United Kingdom*, Sir Gerald Fitzmaurice stated that "[t]he gloss that has to be placed upon the literal effect of [article 3] relates not only to what *constitutes* or amounts to torture, etc., but to what may in certain circumstances *justify* its infliction such as encompassing the greater good of saving the life of the recipient; or, in certain types of cases, the saving of a great many other lives."[322] But these opinions are relatively isolated within the jurisprudence of the Strasbourg organs.

Several domestic constitutional instruments provide expressly for limitation of rights and freedoms. This is the case of the Canadian and South African Constitutions, both of which use a general limitations clause applicable to all fundamental rights, including the prohibition of cruel treatment and torture. Canadian caselaw gives no insight into the application of the limitations clause to the Canadian Charter's prohibition of cruel and unusual punishment. In the case of South Africa, its Constitutional Court examined whether the death penalty provisions in that country's legislation could be "saved" by application of the limitations clause. The South African Court, using an approach borrowed in large part from the Supreme Court of Canada, considered whether capital punishment fulfilled valid state objectives and whether it was proportionate. Pursuant to the interim constitution, limitations must be justifiable in an open and democratic society based on freedom and equality, and must be both reasonable and necessary. According to President Arthur Chaskalson, "The limitation of constitutional rights for a purpose that is reasonable and necessary in a democratic society involves the weighing up of competing values, and ultimately an assessment based on proportionality."[323] The death penalty could not be saved by the limitations clause, said the court, because it was disproportionate and because it did not impair the right being limited as little as possible.

Several instruments have an implied limitation on the prohibition of cruel treatment and torture, in that in other provisions (normally those dealing with the right to life or to due process of law) they explicitly contemplate the death penalty. This makes it clear that at the time the instrument was adopted its framers did not consider the death penalty to breach the norm prohibiting cruel treatment and torture. In domestic law, the United States Constitution provides a clear example, prohibiting cruel and unusual punishment in the Eighth

Amendment, yet recognizing, in the Fifth Amendment, the existence of capital crimes and declaring that life may not be deprived "without due process of law." The point is perhaps even clearer in treaties like the International Covenant on Civil and Political Rights, where article 7 prohibits torture and cruel, inhuman, and degrading punishment, but where article 6 recognizes the death penalty as a permissible limitation on the right to life.[324] However, constitutions and international human rights treaties are to be interpreted in a dynamic fashion, keeping pace with the progressive development and protection of human rights. More specifically, it is generally recognized that the norm prohibiting cruel treatment and torture changes over time to reflect what U.S. Chief Justice Earl Warren termed "the evolving standards of decency that mark the progress of a maturing society." This raises a difficult question of interpretation. May the court charged with interpreting such instruments conclude that the evolution of human rights law creates a conflict within the instrument itself—that while one provision apparently allows the death penalty, the other provision forbids it?

On numerous occasions, the courts of the United States have insisted that the "cruel and unusual punishment" clause cannot be used to attack capital punishment per se because this would violate the intent of the framers. According to Justice Antonin Scalia in *Callins* v. *Collins,* "The Fifth Amendment provides that '[n]o person shall be held to answer for a capital . . . crime, unless on a presentment or indictment of a Grand Jury, . . . nor be deprived of life . . . without due process of law.' This clearly permits the death penalty to be imposed, and establishes beyond doubt that the death penalty is not one of the 'cruel and unusual punishments' prohibited by the Eighth Amendment."[325] Pronouncements to the same effect can be found in the judgments of the Supreme Court of India, based on a constitution with similar provisions: "Article 21 [of the Indian Constitution] clearly brings out the implication, that the Founding Fathers recognized the right of the State to deprive a person of his life or personal liberty in accordance with fair, just and reasonable procedure established by valid law."[326] Likewise, the Judicial Committee of the Privy Council concluded, in a case dealing with the Jamaican Constitution: "Quite apart from section 17 of the Constitution, the continuing constitutional validity of the death sentence is put beyond all doubt by the provision of section 14(1): 'No person shall intentionally be deprived of his life save in execution of the sentence of a court in respect of a criminal offence of which he has been convicted.' "[327] In the context of the international instruments, the Human Rights Committee has held that the death penalty may not be deemed contrary to article 7 of the Covenant because its existence is accepted in article 6§2.[328] In *Soering* v. *United Kingdom,* the European Court of Human Rights refused to follow a dynamic approach to construction of the European Convention, because the legality of the death penalty had been recognized in article 2§1.[329]

But this rather conservative approach has been challenged by some decisions. In *People* v. *Anderson*, the California Supreme Court did not consider the apparent recognition of the death penalty in the state constitution to be a bar to a finding of its incompatibility with the prohibition of cruel or unusual punishment.

> It has been suggested that we are therefore restrained from considering whether capital punishment is proscribed by article I, section 6, since the death penalty is expressly or impliedly recognized in several other provisions of the California Constitution [such as, "no person shall . . . be deprived of life . . . without due process of law"]. We perceive no possible conflict or repugnance between those provisions and the cruel or unusual punishment clause of article I, section 6, however, for none of the incidental references to the death penalty purport to give its existence constitutional stature. They do no more than recognize its existence at the time of their adoption. . . .[330]
>
> The Constitution expressly prescribes cruel or unusual punishments. It would be mere speculation and conjecture to ascribe to the framers an intent to exempt capital punishment from the compass of that provision solely because at a time when the death penalty was commonly accepted they provided elsewhere in the Constitution for special safeguards in its application.[331]

Judge Jan de Meyer of the European Court of Human Rights took the same position in his individual opinion in *Soering*, although his view was not shared by any of his colleagues.[332] Dennis Davis, quoting the American constitutionalists Tribe and Dorf, makes the point a little differently:

> The fact that another constitutional clause evidently contemplates that death might be inflicted by government without offence to that part of the constitution does not answer the question. Indeed, if the Fifth Amendment did answer it we would be left with another dilemma since it also seemed to sanction the hacking off of people's limbs—by its command that no person shall be "twice put in jeopardy of life or limb." No one would seriously argue today that bodily mutilation employed on occasion as a punishment during colonial times could withstand scrutiny under the Eighth Amendment.[333]

The drafters of domestic and international instruments knew that these would require judicial application of certain values, and that this would necessitate taking into account evolving standards of decency. They therefore must have considered that punishments accepted in 1789 or 1791 or 1950 or 1966 would perhaps disappear at a later date. In the case of the International Covenant on Civil and Political Rights, at any rate, the fact that abolition was contemplated is borne out by two precise references to it within the text of article 6, including the final clause: "Nothing in this article shall be invoked to delay or to prevent the abolition of capital punishment by any State Party to the present Covenant."[334]

ARBITRARINESS AND INEQUALITY

CONSTITUTIONAL AND international norms use a variety of terminology, including the words "cruel," "inhuman," "degrading," and "unusual," to define punishment that is unacceptable. These terms are found in article 5 of the Universal Declaration of Human Rights,[1] article 7 of the International Covenant on Civil and Political Rights,[2] article 3 of the European Convention on Human Rights,[3] article 26 of the American Declaration of the Rights and Duties of Man,[4] article 5§2 of the American Convention on Human Rights,[5] article 5 of the African Charter of Human and Peoples' Rights,[6] and the corresponding provisions of most national constitutions. In practice, the courts often read in two other terms, "arbitrary" and "unequal." It is as if the norm reads: "No one shall be subject to cruel, inhuman, degrading, arbitrary, and unequal punishment." This is because punishment is cruel when it serves no rational or logical purpose. In other words, arbitrary punishment is also cruel punishment. The same applies to punishment that is unequal, because either it is overtly discriminatory or simply so capricious as to be incapable of consistent application. The consequence of this approach is that in interpreting a norm derived from human rights law, courts necessarily concern themselves with criminal law policy. They must consider theories of punishment and the goals of penal legislation in order to define the limits of this fundamental right.

For Justice Byron R. White of the United States Supreme Court, in *Furman* v. *Georgia*, imposition and execution of the death penalty were "obviously cruel in the dictionary sense." But capital punishment was not deemed cruel and unusual in the constitutional sense "because it was thought justified by the social ends it was deemed to serve." Therefore, if the death penalty did not fulfill legitimate and coherent penal objectives, it would be arbitrary, and consequently unconstitutional. In Justice White's view, "[I]ts imposition would then be the pointless and needless extinction of life with only marginal contributions to any discernable social or public purposes."[7] In his analysis of the arbitrariness of the death penalty, Justice White focussed on the sanction's alleged purpose or purposes. He found it difficult to prove that it serves the ends of criminal law more effectively than does life imprisonment, and he said that "the penalty is so infrequently imposed that the threat of execution is too attenuated to be of substantial service to criminal justice."[8] The United States Supreme Court also ruled in *Furman* that the existing death penalty statutes violated the Eighth Amendment to the Constitution because they were applied by juries in an arbitrary, capricious, and discriminatory manner.[9] As Justice Potter Stewart noted, the chance of a convicted murderer being sentenced to death was comparable to the chance of being hit by lightning.[10] Punishment that could be no more precise than lightning was "arbitrary and unequal," and therefore "cruel and unusual." A colleague, Justice William J. Brennan, said the death penalty "smacks of little more than a lottery system."[11]

The courts and legislatures of the United States have sought to eliminate the arbitrariness and inequality of capital punishment by erecting a web of judicial safeguards. Complex, time-consuming, and enormously costly procedural structures have been created with a view to answering the Eighth Amendment complaints of arbitrariness and inequality. But in so doing, some new problems have been created, among them the "death row phenomenon," which I address elsewhere in this work.[12] Frustrated after two decades of endeavoring to eliminate arbitrariness and inequality from the application of the death penalty, Justice Harry Blackmun of the United States Supreme Court, on the eve of his retirement in 1994, stated: "[N]o longer will I tinker with the machinery of death."[13] He went on to say that

> although most of the public seems to desire, and the Constitution appears to permit, the penalty of death, it surely is beyond dispute that if the death penalty cannot be administered consistently and rationally, it may not be administered at all. . . .[14]
>
> . . . [I]t soon became apparent [after the judgment in *Furman* v. *Georgia*] that discretion could not be eliminated from capital sentencing without threatening the fundamental fairness due a defendant when life is at stake. Just as contemporary society was no longer tolerant of the random or discriminatory infliction of the penalty of death . . . evolving standards of decency required due consideration of the uniqueness of each individual defendant when imposing society's ultimate penalty. . . . [T]he consistency and rationality promised in *Furman* are inversely related to the fairness owed the individual when considering a sentence of death. A step toward consistency is a step away from fairness.[15]

Justice Blackmun was echoing his colleague Justice Thurgood Marshall, who had said more than a decade earlier that "the effort to eliminate arbitrariness in the infliction of that ultimate sanction is so plainly doomed to failure that it—and the death penalty—must be abandoned altogether."[16]

The American focus on arbitrariness and inequality as an approach to the norm prohibiting cruel treatment and torture has found echoes in the caselaw of other national tribunals called upon to assess the legality of the death penalty. The South Africa Constitutional Court, in its June 1995 judgment declaring the death penalty a violation of the interim constitution's norm prohibiting cruel, inhuman, and degrading treatment or punishment, largely adopted the American focus on arbitrariness and inequality. According to Justice Laurence Ackerman,

> Where the arbitrary and unequal infliction of punishment occurs at the level of a punishment so unique as the death penalty, it strikes me as being cruel and inhuman. For one person to receive the death sentence, where a similarly placed person does not, is, in my assessment of values, cruel to the person receiving it. To allow chance, in this way, to determine the life or death of a person, is to reduce the person to a cypher in a sophisticated judicial lottery. This is to treat the sentenced person as inhuman.[17]

LEGISLATIVE PURPOSE OF PUNISHMENT

Criminal law undoubtedly has a declaratory quality, in that it is important in and of itself that a tribunal affirm the criminal liability of the accused and denounce his or her behavior. If this approach is given priority, then the actual punishment of the offender becomes something of a secondary matter. But while most modern theories of criminal law require punishment of the offender, the goal of such an act is not always so clear. Punishment is said to serve four principal purposes: deterrence, retribution, rehabilitation, and protection of society. Like all other punishments, the death penalty must be justifiable in light of these objectives of criminal law policy. If it fails to meet one or more of these purposes, then the punishment is purely arbitrary and therefore offensive to the norm prohibiting cruel punishment.

Two of the four reasons for punishment, rehabilitation and protection, are relatively easy matters. Clearly, the death penalty does not contemplate rehabilitation of the prisoner.[18] This is one of its great and inherent defects. In the South African Constitutional Court case on the death penalty, three judges—Tole Madala, Ismael Mahomed, and Yvonne Mokgoro—stressed the role of rehabilitation in punishment and the fact that this element is effectively eliminated by a death sentence.[19] Justice Madala questioned whether the rejection of rehabilitation as a possibility could accord with the concept of *ubuntu*, an African notion that regroups values of dignity and community solidarity, and that is expressly recognized in the interim constitution.[20] In India, where appellate courts have the right to review and reconsider death sentences, they have frequently asked whether an accused could be rehabilitated.[21] An example is *Babugowda* v. *Karnataka*, where the court commuted the death sentence to life imprisonment because it could not assume the accused to be irredeemable.[22] In China, an extraordinary procedure condemns individuals to death but then allows a grace period of a few years for their rehabilitation. If they succeed, then the sentence is commuted. The details of this approach are very sketchy, and it has been denounced as constituting cruel, inhuman, and degrading treatment or punishment by members of the United Nations Committee Against Torture.[23]

Protection of the public as a goal of sentencing means simply that the offender is removed from civil society and physically restrained from pursuing his or her antisocial activities. Respect of the right to life of the ordinary citizen requires that dangerous offenders be prevented from committing more crimes. However, this requires a balancing of the interests of the innocent citizen and the offender. Sentences are set following trial; once they have been purged, society does not normally allow prisoners to be detained, even if there is undisputed evidence of dangerousness. To do so would violate another fundamental norm, that which protects the individual against double jeopardy: *non bis in idem.*[24] Clearly, the death penalty offers the certainty of protection for the public, because by physically eliminating the delinquent it removes any chance of recidivism.[25] But this is a poor argument for capital punishment. It may just as readily, and absurdly, be invoked to justify executing petty criminals or, for that matter, those persons who have not even committed breaches of the law but who are determined, perhaps because of mental instability, to represent a threat to others. Certainly detention of one form or another, up to and including life imprisonment, is an equally effective answer to this concern.

To the extent that any form of punishment, whether it be a fine, detention, or some other type of sanction, has a deterrent effect, it must be conceded that the death penalty will also operate to deter. The only real issue in capital punishment is whether the death penalty has a significantly distinct effect, as opposed to other forms of punishment like life imprisonment. Given the generally recognized choices, this boils down to a comparison between capital punishment and life imprisonment. Simply stated, the question is whether there are fewer murders in jurisdictions that do not execute. The general public may tend to believe that the death penalty operates as such a distinct deterrent. Such intuitive conclusions can be misleading, however, when they are made by decent, law-abiding citizens, who are deterred from committing serious crime by their own moral values rather than any threat of punishment, whatever be its form. A study prepared by the criminologist Norval Morris for the United Nations, and cited by Justice Thurgood Marshall of the United States Supreme Court in both *Furman* v. *Georgia* and *Gregg* v. *Georgia,* states: "It is generally agreed between the retentionists and abolitionists, whatever their opinions about the validity of comparative studies of deterrence, that the data which now exist show no correlation between the existence of capital punishment and lower rates of capital crime."[26] A recent literature review of all post-1972 empirical studies dealing with the death penalty found that no criminologist in the United States has claimed to present data demonstrating a long-term deterrent effect of the death penalty that is greater than that exerted by lengthy imprisonment.[27] In *Gregg*, an amicus curiae brief relied heavily on a study by Isaac Ehrlich purporting to show that each additional execution in the United States might have saved eight lives.[28] In his dissenting reasons, Justice Marshall noted that the Ehrlich study had been severely criticized[29] and that it was "of little, if any, assistance in assessing the deterrent impact of the death penalty."[30] In *Furman*, the justice had referred to the massive amount of statistical evidence before the Court on the subject of deterrence, observing that it was not "convincing beyond all doubt, but, it is persuasive."[31] Justice Marshall concluded that the death penalty was "no more effective a deterrent than life imprisonment."[32] A majority of the justices of the Supreme Judicial Court of Massachusetts also concluded that "serious studies of the entire subject, including the report of two Massachusetts legislative commissions, disclosed that the deterrence basis, like the others that might be asserted, had not been established by satisfactory empirical proof or by acceptable *a priori* reasoning."[33]

But recognition of a deterrent effect of the death penalty can be found in the reasons of some United States Supreme Court justices. According to Justice Potter Stewart in *Gregg*, statistical attempts to evaluate whether the death penalty is an effective deterrent have resulted in "inconclusive" results.[34] "Although some of the studies suggest that the death penalty may not function as a significantly greater deterrent than lesser penalties, there is no convincing empirical evidence either supporting or refuting this view," he said. Justice Stewart suggested that it was fair to assume there were murderers who act out of passion, and that the threat of death was for them no deterrent. He went on to say, however, that for many others

> the death penalty undoubtedly is a significant deterrent. There are carefully contemplated murders, such as murder for hire, where the possible penalty of death may well enter into the cold calculus that

precedes the decision to act. And there are some categories of murder, such as murder by a life prisoner, where other sanctions may not be adequate.[35]

Justice Stewart added that deterrence was "a complex factual issue," and he considered that this was a matter better left to legislatures, which can evaluate statistical studies in light of local conditions. In his view, "many of the post-*Furman* statutes reflect just such a responsible effort to define those crimes and those criminals for which capital punishment is most probably an effective deterrent."[36] The Supreme Court of India has also indicated, in some judgments from the 1980s, that it considers the death penalty to operate as a useful and effective deterrent.[37]

Often judges have recognized that if indeed the death penalty has any deterrent effect, this is neutralized if the sanction is only imposed in rare cases, and after lengthy delays. "[C]ommon sense and experience tell us that seldom-enforced laws become ineffective measures for controlling human conduct and that the death penalty, unless imposed with sufficient frequency, will make little contribution to deterring those crimes for which it may be exacted," said Justice White in *Furman.*[38] In *People* v. *Anderson*, the State conceded, and the Court accepted, that any deterrent effect of capital punishment could only be convincingly demonstrated if the punishment were swiftly and certainly exacted. Chief Justice Wright, speaking for the Court, noted that application of the death penalty was neither swift nor certain.[39] Chief Justice William H. Rehnquist of the United States Supreme Court, a believer in the death penalty's alleged deterrent effect, has also acknowledged (as an associate justice) that such an effect is lessened by significant delay in imposition.[40] And in *Furman*, Justice Brennan observed that the proponents of the deterrence argument necessarily admit that its validity depends upon the existence of a system in which the punishment of death is invariably and swiftly imposed. The real situation, he said, was quite different. "A rational person contemplating a murder or rape is confronted not with the certainty of a speedy death, but with the slightest possibility that he will be executed in the distant future." Justice Brennan added:

> The risk of death is remote and improbable; in contrast, the risk of long-term imprisonment is near and great. In short, whatever the speculative validity of the assumption that the threat of death is a superior deterrent, there is no reason to believe that as currently administered the punishment of death is necessary to deter the commission of capital crimes. Whatever might be the case were all or substantially all eligible criminals quickly put to death, unverifiable possibilities are an

insufficient basis upon which to conclude that the threat of death today has any greater deterrent efficacy than the threat of imprisonment.[41]

In South Africa, the Constitutional Court examined the issue of deterrence within the context of the interim constitution's limitations clause, which is based on models found in the Canadian and German[42] constitutional instruments.[43] The constitution appears to authorize exceptions to the prohibition of cruel, inhuman, and degrading punishment, providing this is the result of legislation that is reasonable, necessary, and justifiable in an open and democratic society based on freedom and equality. Although the burden of establishing a breach of the right falls to the appellant, once this has been met it is for the State to demonstrate the legitimacy of the limitation.[44] The State defended the merits of the deterrent effect of capital punishment in this context.[45]

The deterrence argument had found some support in a judgment of the Tanzanian Court of Appeal, rendered only two weeks prior to the hearing of the South African Constitutional Court.[46] The Tanzanian Court had no evidence to suggest that the death penalty was more effective than a lengthy term of imprisonment in determining whether capital punishment was a justifiable limit. However, the Tanzanian Court of Appeal considered that this was a matter for society, not the courts, to determine and that society generally favored the death penalty.[47] In the South African case, the State also focussed on an astronomic rise in the nation's crime rate since the imposition of a moratorium on executions in February 1990.[48] However, President Arthur Chaskalson noted that the crime wave had begun before the moratorium was announced. Furthermore, he explained that the moratorium could have ended at any time, and murderers had therefore no assurance whatsoever that they would not be subject to the death penalty.[49] Justice John Didcott was even more affirmative on this point, arguing that the statistics tendered in evidence actually demonstrate that the moratorium had no effect at all on the murder rate.[50]

The crime wave in modern-day South Africa could be explained by a number of factors, noted President Chaskalson, including political violence, homelessness, unemployment, poverty, and the frustration consequent upon such conditions.[51] Citing evidence before the Court showing that the bulk of violent crime was never solved, President Chaskalson stated that the most effective deterrent is the knowledge that the offender will probably be caught, convicted, and punished:[52]

> We would be deluding ourselves if we were to believe that the execution of the few persons sentenced to death during this period, and of a comparatively few other people each year from now onwards will provide the solution to the unacceptably high rate of crime. There will

always be unstable, desperate, and pathological people for whom the risk of arrest and imprisonment provides no deterrent, but there is nothing to show that a decision to carry out the death sentence would have any impact on the behavior of such people, or that there will be more of them if imprisonment is the only sanction. No information was placed before us by the Attorney General in regard to the rising crime rate other than the bare statistics, and they alone prove nothing, other than that we are living in a violent society in which most crime goes unpunished—something that we all know.[53]

Concluding his remarks on the question of deterrence, President Chaskalson noted that the attorney general had admitted that it was impossible to prove convincingly that the death penalty was a deterrent, and that there was inevitably an element of speculation in such a conclusion. "It is, he said, a proposition that is not capable of proof, because one never knows about those who have been deterred; we know only about those who have not been deterred, and who have committed terrible crimes."[54] As Justice Kriegler stated in his concurring reasons, "[n]o empirical study, no statistical exercise and no theoretical analysis has been able to demonstrate that capital punishment has any deterrent force greater than that of a really heavy sentence of imprisonment."[55] Therefore, "[i]t simply cannot be reasonable to sanction judicial killing without knowing whether it has any marginal deterrent value."[56]

The second major argument invoked in favor of the death penalty is its retributive value. In the case of certain crimes, notably intentional homicide, it is said that society cries out for an appropriate sanction. Although, as I have demonstrated earlier in this book, the *lex talionis* ("an eye for an eye, a tooth for a tooth") has its roots in a search for proportionality in criminal sentencing, the maxim is now usually invoked to legitimize retributive justice. In some legal systems, notably those inspired by Islamic law, offenders may be executed using the same methods that they employed as killers. Criminal justice that is based on retribution can be clearly distinguished from utilitarian approaches, in that it is not essentially concerned with improving society or modifying social behavior. It is directed towards the past and not the future, imposing punishment simply because the delinquent deserves it.

Vengeance, or retribution, has been acknowledged by the United States Supreme Court as a permissible purpose of punishment under the Eighth Amendment, although not as the dominant objective of the criminal law.[57] The case for retribution and its role in capital sentencing was set out by the eminent English jurist Lord Denning in 1949 in testimony before the United Kingdom's Royal Commission on Capital Punishment:

Punishment is the way in which society expresses its denunciation of wrong doing: and in order to maintain respect for law, it is essential that the punishment inflicted for grave crimes should adequately reflect the revulsion felt by the great majority of citizens for them. It is a mistake to consider the objects of punishment as being deterrent or reformative or preventive and nothing else. . . . The truth is that some crimes are so outrageous that society insists on adequate punishment, because the wrong-doer deserves it, irrespective of whether it is a deterrent or not.[58]

But few judges have been prepared to defend the death penalty as a valid exercise of punishment's retributive function. Rather, they have tended to couch the matter in utilitarian arguments, explaining that the failure to provide just punishment may result in social unrest and, in extreme cases, in vigilante action. The desire for retribution is thus treated as an inevitable or at least normal human urge, one that society must satisfy lest it run the risk that individuals will seek "justice" themselves. In a 1994 judgment, the Supreme Court of Trinidad and Tobago evoked the specter of vigilantism, which it said might be a consequence of the Judicial Committee of the Privy Council's decision in *Pratt et al.*[59] A year earlier, the Privy Council had held that inordinate delay in execution was grounds for commutation of sentence, thereby sparing more than a hundred death row prisoners from Caribbean hangmen. According to Justice Hamel-Smith of the Supreme Court of Trinidad and Tobago,

[w]hen law-abiding citizens reach the point where they perceive that the trials of perpetrators of the most vicious and inhuman crimes not only take precedence over their cries for justice but that those perpetrators no longer face their just deserts simply because by their excessive criminal behavior the system of justice affordable in a particular country can no longer keep abreast of prescribed or even self-prescribed deadlines then, amidst the platitudes of the purists and those who perceive capital punishment to be barbaric, the law of the jungle will once again prevail.[60]

Chief Justice Rehnquist of the United States Supreme Court also invoked the threat of vigilante justice in ruling on a death penalty case, suggesting that the potential for mob action is "still with us."[61] Justice Stewart of the United States Supreme Court stated in *Furman* that "[w]hen people begin to believe that organized society is unwilling or unable to impose upon criminal offenders the punishment they 'deserve' then there are sown the seeds of anarchy—of self-help, vigilante justice, and lynch law."[62] He returned to the point in *Gregg*, describing capital punishment as an expression of society's moral outrage, and said that although the retributive function of the death penalty might be unappealing to some, it was "essential in an ordered society that asks its citizens to rely on legal processes rather than self-help to vindicate their wrongs."[63]

Justice William J. Brennan challenged the self-help argument that had been advanced by his brethren, explaining that it was without factual basis. "There is no evidence whatever that utilization of imprisonment rather than death encourages private blood feuds and other disorders,"[64] he said. Justice Thurgood Marshall described the claim as being "wholly inadequate" to justify capital punishment;[65] in his view, the arguments were not retributive in the true sense, but rather utilitarian. The death penalty was portrayed as being valuable to society, observed Justice Marshall, because it had beneficial results—namely, by discouraging self-help.[66] On the merits of the retribution argument, Justice Marshall took a radically opposite position to that of Justices Rehnquist and Stewart, as well as to that of Lord Denning:

> [T]he implication of the statements appears to me to be . . . that society's judgment that the murderer "deserves" death must be respected not simply because the preservation of order requires it, but because it is appropriate that society make the judgment and carry it out. . . . The mere fact that the community demands the murderer's life in return for the evil he has done cannot sustain the death penalty. . . . Under these standards, the taking of life "because the wrongdoer deserves it" surely must fall, for such a punishment has as its very basis the total denial of the wrongdoer's dignity and worth.[67]

Justice Marshall considered that punishment based on retribution was forbidden by the Eighth Amendment.[68] Other judges in other courts have reached the same conclusion. Justice Krishna Iyer of the Supreme Court of India has stated that "[t]he retributive theory has had its day and is no longer valid."[69] In Zimbabwe, Chief Justice Gubbay has affirmed that "retribution has no place in the scheme of civilized jurisprudence."[70] According to Chief Justice Wright of the California Supreme Court, "It is incompatible with the dignity of an enlightened society to attempt to justify the taking of life for purposes of vengeance."[71]

In the South African Constitutional Court, retribution was also rejected, but the matter was treated with slightly more circumspection. President Chaskalson, who wrote the main judgment in the case, conceded that retribution was a valid objective of criminal policy, though one of less importance than deterrence.[72] Punishment must "fit the crime," but there is no reason that it should be equivalent to the crime, he noted. Life imprisonment is entirely adequate in expressing society's moral outrage at the crime of murder, no matter how heinous.[73]

> The state does not put out the eyes of a person who has blinded another in a vicious assault, nor does it punish a rapist, by castrating him and submitting him to the utmost humiliation in gaol. The state does not need to engage in the cold and calculated killing of murderers in order to express moral outrage at their conduct. A very long prison sentence is also a way of expressing outrage and visiting retribution upon the criminal.[74]

President Chaskalson also couched his argument in the political context of post-apartheid South Africa. The country was committed to reconstruction and reconciliation, and this was not the time for either the state or the courts to be encouraging such sentiments as vengeance.[75]

In the same case, Acting Justice Kentridge stated that when the death penalty is imposed for murder, the punishment does not fit the crime, but repeats it.[76] "We are not to stoop to the level of the criminal," said Justice Pius Langa.[77] Justice John Didcott maintained that "retribution smacks too much of vengeance to be accepted, either on its own or in combination with other aims, as a worthy purpose of punishment in the enlightened society to which we South Africans have now committed ourselves, and that the expression of moral outrage which is its further and more defensible object can be communicated effectively by severe sentences of imprisonment."[78]

As with arguments based on deterrence, retribution grows cold as a justification for the death penalty when it is delayed. According to Chief Justice Rehnquist of the United States Supreme Court, "There can be little doubt that delay in the enforcement of capital punishment frustrates the purpose of retribution."[79]

PROCEDURAL ARBITRARINESS

In 1972, in *Furman* v. *Georgia*,[80] the United States Supreme Court sought to eliminate arbitrariness in imposition of the death penalty by declaring that statutes that did not fetter the court's discretion by providing certain guidelines and criteria were contrary to the Constitution's Eighth Amendment. Legislatures quickly responded by defining a variety of mitigating and aggravating factors, and this new approach was deemed acceptable four years later by the majority in *Gregg* v. *Georgia*.[81] But there is perhaps an impossibly fine line to be drawn. If discretion is eliminated or reduced by the erection of a rigorous framework for imposition of the death penalty, this may deprive the sentencer of the possibility of individualizing the sanction and thus commit the same sin of arbitrariness.

The United States Supreme Court does not consider individualized sentencing to be a constitutional requirement in all cases of criminal sanctions, although it has admitted that there is a long tradition to this effect.[82] In *Roberts (Stanislaus)* v. *Louisiana,* Justice John Paul Stevens spoke of "our society's rejection of the belief that 'every offense in a linked legal category calls for an identical punishment without regard to the past life and habits of the particular offender.' "[83] However, in capital cases, what is a recognized principle becomes a constitutional precept. "Given that the imposition of death by public authority is so profoundly different from all other penalties," wrote Chief Justice Warren Burger, "we cannot avoid the conclusion that an individualized decision is essential in capital cases."[84] This is because, he said, there are no corrective or modifying mechanisms once the sentence has been executed. "When the choice is between life and death, that risk is unacceptable and incompatible with the commands of the Eighth and Fourteenth Amendments."[85] In *Callins* v. *Collins,* Justice Blackmun described "individualized sentencing" as an "essential component of fundamental fairness."[86]

The first corollary of these principles is the exclusion of mandatory death penalties. These sanctions are increasingly rare in most legal systems. Because of their harshness, they almost inevitably incite investigators, prosecutors, judges, and juries to perhaps excessive generosity, and this runs contrary to sound principles of penal policy. In the United Kingdom, for example, mandatory death sentencing in previous centuries led to what many consider an exaggerated emphasis on due process safeguards. Judges and juries invoked technical evidentiary and procedural flaws as a way of mitigating the consequences of guilty verdicts. The Supreme Court of the United States has said that the Eighth and Fourteenth Amendments require "in all but the rarest kind of capital case" that there be no mandatory death sentence. Nevertheless, the Court has as yet expressed "no opinion as to whether the need to deter certain kinds of homicide would justify a mandatory death sentence as, for example, when a prisoner—or escapee—under a life sentence is found guilty of murder."[87]

But the requirement of individualized sentencing inevitably leads to a contradiction, because "[t]he power to be lenient is the power to discriminate."[88] As Justice Blackmun wrote in *Callins* v. *Collins,* the consistency that *Furman* promised and the individuality of sentencing required by a subsequent judgment, *Lockett* v. *Ohio,* "are not only inversely related, but irreconcilable in the context of capital punishment." He continued:

Any statute or procedure that could effectively eliminate arbitrariness from the administration of death would also restrict the sentencer's discretion to such an extent that the sentencer would be unable to give full consideration to the unique characteristics of each defendant and the circumstances of the offense. . . . All efforts to strike an appropriate balance between these conflicting constitutional commands are futile because there is a heightened need for both in the administration of death.[89]

After twenty years of a search for procedural solutions to the arbitrariness of the death penalty, Justice Harry Blackmun, who had upheld capital punishment in the past (dissenting in *Furman* and joining the majority in *Gregg*), confessed that he could no longer "tinker with the machinery of death." The endeavor was a failure; it was not possible to eliminate arbitrariness from imposition of the death penalty, and consequently any capital punishment statutes breached the guarantee against cruel punishment found in the Eighth Amendment.[90] Justice Blackmun said the Court had already virtually conceded that fairness and rationality could not be achieved in the administration of the death penalty, in *McCleskey* v. *Kemp*.[91] In that ruling, the United States Supreme Court had dismissed a challenge based on racial discrimination in imposition of the death penalty, not because the case had not been proven but because eliminating racism from the U.S. judicial system seemed too daunting. *McCleskey* showed that "murder defendants in Georgia with white victims are more than four times as likely to receive the death sentence as are defendants with black victims."[92] The Supreme Court in effect threw up its hands, conceding the impossibility of a death penalty system that was free of racism. Justice Lewis F. Powell Jr., who cast the decisive vote in *McCleskey*, later expressed his regrets about the result. He confessed, several years after his retirement, "I have come to think that capital punishment should be abolished."[93] In another death penalty challenge where the issue of racial bias was raised, Chief Justice Hennessey of the Massachusetts Supreme Judicial Court stated:

We reject any suggestion that racial discrimination is confined to the South or to any other geographical area. The experience of Ohio under a post-*Furman* statute through 1977 shows that, of 173 black persons who killed white persons, thirty-seven of them (21.4%) were sentenced to death. Of forty-seven whites who killed blacks, *none* were sentenced to death. Moreover, the existence of racial prejudice in some persons in the Commonwealth of Massachusetts is a fact of which we take notice.[94]

The arbitrariness that is inherent in discretionary sentencing is only aggravated by the factor of race, Justice Blackmun insisted in *Callins* v. *Collins*.[95] Courts in other countries have found the same defects. "Historically speaking, capital sentencing perhaps has a class bias and color bar even as criminal law barks at both but bites the proletariat to defend the proprietariat,"[96] said Justice Krishna Iyer of the Indian Supreme Court. President Arthur Chaskalson of the South African Supreme Court wrote:

> It cannot be gainsaid that poverty, race and chance play roles in the outcome of capital cases and in the final decision as to who should live and who should die. It is sometimes said that this is understood by the judges, and as far as possible, taken into account by them. But in itself this is no answer to the complaint of arbitrariness; on the contrary, it may introduce an additional factor of arbitrariness that would also have to be taken into account. Some, but not all, accused persons may be acquitted because such allowances are made, and others who are convicted, but not all, may for the same reason escape the death sentence.[97]

And Justice Blackmun observed on the eve of his retirement in 1994:

> [D]espite the efforts of the States and courts to devise legal formulas and procedural rules to meet this daunting challenge, the death penalty remains fraught with arbitrariness, discrimination, caprice and mistake. . . . [T]he problems that were pursued down one hole with procedural rules and verbal formulas have come to the surface somewhere else, just as virulent and pernicious as they were in their original form."[98]

Arbitrariness is also said to enter into the imposition of capital punishment by virtue of the quality of defense counsel. A majority of capital defendants are indigent, and they are normally represented by state-appointed counsel, since the professional fees paid are insufficient to attract experienced lawyers. At best, the accused is defended by an eager, well-meaning, but inexperienced advocate. At worst, counsel are lazy or incompetent or both.[99] President Chaskalson of the South African Constitutional Court described a situation that, with minor adjustments, would appear to exist in many countries:

> Most accused facing a possible death sentence are unable to afford legal assistance, and are defended under the *pro deo* system. The defending counsel is more often than not young and inexperienced, frequently of a different race to his or her client, and if this is the case,

usually has to consult through an interpreter. *Pro deo* counsel are paid only a nominal fee for the defence, and generally lack the financial resources and the infrastructural support to undertake the necessary investigations and research, to employ expert witnesses to give advice, including advice on matters relevant to sentence, to assemble witnesses, to bargain with the prosecution, and generally to conduct an effective defence. Accused persons who have the money to do so, are able to retain experienced attorneys and counsel, who are paid to undertake the necessary investigations and research, and as a result they are less likely to be sentenced to death than persons similarly placed who are unable to pay for such services. (I do not want to be understood as being critical of the *pro deo* counsel who perform an invaluable service, often under extremely difficult conditions, and to whom the courts are much indebted. But the unpalatable truth is that most capital cases involve poor people who cannot afford and do not receive as good a defence as those who have means. In this process, the poor and the ignorant have proven to be the most vulnerable, and are the persons most likely to be sentenced to death.)[100]

Moreover, in many countries in the developing world, capital defendants are often not represented at all, there being no system of legal aid whatsoever. International human rights norms require that an accused "have legal assistance assigned to him, in any case where the interests of justice so require, and without payment by him in any such case if he does not have sufficient means to pay for it."[101] According to the United Nations Human Rights Committee, this is one of the rules that must be respected if a state is to impose the death penalty and not run afoul of article 6 of the International Covenant on Civil and Political Rights.[102] In *Reid* v. *Jamaica*, the Human Rights Committee said that "it is axiomatic that legal assistance must be made available to a convicted prisoner under sentence of death."[103] According to the committee, "[I]n cases involving capital punishment, in particular, legal aid should enable counsel to prepare his client's defence in circumstances that can ensure justice. This does include provision for adequate remuneration for legal aid."[104] But, according to one member of the committee, the duty of the state to provide legal counsel did not go beyond the responsibility to act in good faith in assigning counsel. The state should not be held responsible for errors in judgment by the attorneys, because this would amount to holding a court-appointed lawyer to a higher standard of accountability than a privately retained one.[105]

In many poor states, this principle, although presented as being a civil and political right, is in reality an economic and social right requiring resources that are simply unavailable in the existing economy. Here again, then, there is an impasse. States sometimes argue that they are unable to abolish the death penalty because of their level of development, but it is this very level of development that makes it impossible to impose the death penalty without breaching fundamental human rights norms. But the question of poorly remunerated and generally inadequate counsel arises even in the most developed countries, including the United States.[106] Ironically, by the time a cause célèbre makes its way to the Supreme Court or, in the case of states in the Commonwealth Caribbean, to the Judicial Committee of the Privy Council, first-class legal minds are generally at work on the matter. But at this point, it is often too late to correct deficiencies related to the production of evidence or tactical decisions at trial.

In its views in *Reid* v. *Jamaica*, the Human Rights Committee also took the occasion to comment on the legal aid system in Jamaica:

> On the basis of the information before it, the Committee considers that this system, in its current form, does not appear to operate in ways that would enable legal representatives working on legal aid assignments to discharge themselves of their duties and responsibilities as effectively as the interests of justice would warrant. The Committee considers that in cases involving capital punishment, in particular, legal aid should enable counsel to prepare his client's defence in circumstances that can ensure justice. This does include provision for adequate remuneration for legal aid. While the Committee concedes that the State party's authorities are in principle competent to spell out the details of the Poor Prisoner's Defence Act, and while it welcomes recent improvements in the terms under which legal aid is made available, it urges the State party to review its legal aid system.[107]

In *Pinto* v. *Trinidad and Tobago*, the complainant had a court-appointed counsel at trial but did not want the same attorney to act for him on appeal. That attorney nevertheless inscribed the case and prepared the appeal without any consultation with Pinto. The Human Rights Committee said that "the State party should have accepted the author's arrangements for another attorney to represent him for purposes of the appeal, even if this would have entailed an adjournment of the proceedings."[108] The committee concluded that there had been a violation of article 14§3(d) of the International Covenant on Civil and Political Rights,[109] which in turn resulted in a breach of article 6, and that Pinto was entitled to a remedy entailing his release.[110]

The Human Rights Committee has frequently had occasion to comment on the inadequacies of court-appointed counsel. In *Reid* v. *Jamaica*, the prisoner was able to communicate with his legal aid attorney for the first time on the day of the trial. His lawyer asked for a postponement in order to prepare the case, but the judge refused.[111] The committee said this was a violation of article 14§3(b) of the Covenant, which enshrines the right "[t]o have adequate time and facilities for the preparation of [one's] defence and to communicate with counsel of [one's] own choosing."[112] In another case, the trial court had assigned the petitioner two attorneys who met briefly with him prior to the preliminary hearing and for about thirty minutes one month before the trial.[113] On appeal, a court-appointed attorney did not consult with him, despite several letters requesting an interview.[114] The committee, "[b]earing in mind particularly that this is a capital punishment case and that the author was unable to review the statements of the prosecution's witnesses with counsel," went on to conclude "that the time for consultation was insufficient to ensure adequate preparation of the defence, in respect of both trial and appeal," and that consequently there was a breach of the Covenant.[115] In *Thomas* v. *Jamaica*, the accused met his court-appointed lawyer for the first and only time on the day of the trial. The trial continued the same day and, according to Thomas, his attorney did not present all of the facts to the judge and jury. But because of the absence of evidence of a request for postponement, Thomas's international petition was dismissed.[116] Where counsel is privately retained, on the other hand, the Human Rights Committee has considered that any shortcomings in the defense lie with the attorney and that as a result any breach of a right guaranteed by the Covenant cannot be imputed to the state party.[117]

Another significant safeguard against arbitrariness is statutory provision for automatic appeal.[118] The International Covenant on Civil and Political Rights provides for a right of appeal, at the discretion of the convicted person.[119] According to Justice Potter Stewart of the United States Supreme Court, speaking of a mechanism of mandatory review in death penalty cases, "The provision for appellate review in the Georgia capital-sentencing system serves as a check against the random or arbitrary imposition of the death penalty."[120] But, contrary to public impressions, appellate review is often inadequate to correct errors at trial. It is not, after all, a new trial by any sense of the imagination. New evidence is admitted in only the most exceptional of cases, and findings of fact by the court of first instance, particularly those involving credibility, are rarely adjusted. In *Lockett* v. *Ohio*, Justice Thurgood Marshall noted: "That an Ohio trial court could impose the death penalty on petitioner under these facts, and that the Ohio Supreme Court on review could sustain it, cast[s] strong doubt on the plurality's premise [in *Gregg*] that appellate review in state systems is sufficient to avoid the wrongful and unfair imposition of this irrevocable penalty."[121]

The common-law system that obtains in most of the English-speaking world and in the Commonwealth countries is distinct from other systems of criminal law in that it accords a great deal of discretion to the prosecution. The prosecutor may decide whether to proceed with charges based on his or her assessment of the quality of the evidence, as well as other factors, which are often related to bargains struck with the accused. In exchange for favorable testimony against accomplices, or simply in order to avoid trial with a guilty plea, the prosecution may agree to proceed on lesser infractions or, in capital cases, undertake not to seek the death penalty. Courts have noted that such "prosecutorial discretion has resulted in the arbitrary imposition of the death penalty."[122] As Justice Brennan of the United States Supreme Court has observed, the selection process for imposition of the death penalty begins in the prosecutor's office. "Just like the jury, then, where death is the consequence, the prosecutor's discretion must be suitably directed and limited so as to minimize the risk of wholly arbitrary and capricious action," wrote Justice Brennan.[123]

Plea bargaining is one of the most troublesome aspects of prosecutorial discretion in capital cases. Essentially, in return for a guilty plea the accused is saved from the gallows and sentenced to some lesser punishment, normally life imprisonment. Plea bargaining is well accepted within the system and has many advantages for the state, notably the certainty of obtaining convictions and the substantial economies effected by avoiding trials.[124] But like most other "normal" procedures in criminal matters, plea bargaining takes on a special and highly questionable dimension when the death penalty is involved.[125] In effect, the accused is threatened with the most severe form of physical harm, the death penalty; he or she is then promised that this will not be inflicted, but in return for a confession, which takes the form of a guilty plea. Sometimes the choice is actually provided by statute, where a plea of guilt entitles the convicted person to life imprisonment instead of the death penalty. The constitutionality of such provisions has been upheld by the United States Supreme Court.[126] But the Court cautioned that "[i]f the provision had no other purpose or effect than to chill the assertion of constitutional rights by penalizing those who choose to exercise them, then it would be patently unconstitutional."[127]

An early example of plea bargains in death penalty cases goes back to the time of the English Bill of Rights of 1689.[128] During the Bloody Assizes of 1685 after the Monmouth Rebellion, Justice Jeffreys of the King's Bench was appointed to try the rebels. The chief prosecutor, Sir Henry Pollfexen, proposed a plea bargain—any person who pleaded guilty would be spared the death penalty. At the time, execution of this sentence involved being drawn on a cart to the gallows and hanged by the neck; the prisoner was cut down while still alive, then disembowelled; his bowels were burnt before his eyes; and then he was beheaded and quartered.[129] Pollfexen managed to find more than five hundred individuals who were prepared to plead guilty and go to prison for life. (Those who refused to plead guilty and were then convicted were executed in the traditional manner.) The bargain was respected, at least until the work of the chief prosecutor's commission was completed. Justice Jeffreys then undid the deal, signing death warrants for almost two hundred individuals who had accepted the plea bargain![130]

A more contemporary example of the consequences of plea bargaining can be seen in *State* v. *McMurtrey*.[131] The prosecutor offered a sentence of life imprisonment in return for a guilty plea, but the defendant exercised his right to trial by jury, was found guilty, and was sentenced to death. He argued that this violated the Eighth and Fourteenth Amendments to the Constitution. The appeal court, however, refused to reverse the death sentence. The Supreme Court of the United States has held that a defendant who pleads guilty extends a substantial benefit to the state and is therefore entitled to a less harsh sentence in return.[132] But if the plea bargain is refused, then the state may prosecute to the maximum extent of the law.[133]

In an international case, petitioner Keith Cox alleged in a communication presented to the United Nations Human Rights Committee that he would be subjected to torture or to cruel, inhuman, and degrading treatment or punishment, in violation of article 7 of the International Covenant on Civil and Political Rights,[134] as a result of plea-bargaining mechanisms in effect in the State of Pennsylvania. Two alleged accomplices of Cox had earlier negotiated guilty pleas in return for life sentences. In seeking his extradition from Canada, Pennsylvania refused to renounce use of the death penalty in his case. In its written pleadings to the Human Rights Committee, Canada actually justified Pennsylvania's behavior by explaining that plea bargaining was a technique used by prosecutors in the state in order to obtain guilty pleas. The committee was unimpressed with Cox's argument and said, in its typically laconic fashion: "The Committee notes that the author claims that the plea bargaining procedures, by which capital punishment could be avoided if he were to plead guilty, further violates his rights under the Covenant. The Committee finds this not to be so in the context of the criminal justice system in Pennsylvania."[135]

Finally, there is a criterion of proportionality. Punishment that is disproportionate to the crime constitutes arbitrary punishment and is, accordingly, cruel. Justice Harry Blackmun of the United States Supreme Court referred, in *Lockett* v. *Ohio*, to "the limits of the Eighth Amendment proscription, incorporated in the Fourteenth Amendment, against gross disproportionality."[136] The International Covenant on Civil and Political Rights provides that capital punishment may only be imposed for "the most serious crimes."[137] This provision of the Covenant was frequently criticized during the document's drafting, and some state representatives argued for a specific enumeration of serious crimes.[138] The term "most serious crimes" has since been attacked for allowing too much divergence in state practice and for being ineffectual as a check on the inclination of some regimes to resort to capital punishment.[139] Similar provisions appear in the American Convention on Human Rights,[140] the Arab Charter of Human Rights,[141] and in the "Safeguards Guaranteeing the Rights of Those Facing the Death Penalty."[142] The fourth Geneva Convention lists crimes for which the death penalty may be imposed upon civilians in occupied territories: espionage, serious crimes of sabotage of military installations, and intentional murder.[143]

Reports from states parties to the Human Rights Committee indicate that in addition to such undisputably serious crimes as premeditated murder and treason, the death penalty has been also applied in some states for economic crimes,[144] trafficking in currency,[145] banditry,[146] political crimes,[147] adultery,[148] use of narcotic drugs,[149] trafficking in narcotic drugs,[150] homosexuality,[151] offenses against sexual morality,[152] rape,[153] espionage,[154] armed robbery,[155] misuse of public funds,[156] and involuntary crimes.[157] The Human Rights Committee's General Comment 6(16) states that the expression "most serious crimes" must be "read restrictively," because death is a "quite exceptional measure."[158] During consideration of the periodic reports of states parties under article 40 of the Covenant, members of the committee have indicated the restrictive interpretation to be given to the term "serious crimes." Often, they have focussed solely on the length of the list of capital offenses. For example, during presentation of a report from Jordan, a committee member said that eleven capital crimes was "a high number."[159] In response to criticism from members of the committee that the number of capital crimes was too large, the representative of Tunisia, during presentation of its third periodic report, agreed that the list was long and that "it should be shortened as a first step."[160] Some reports have indicated that the list of capital crimes is in the process of being abbreviated. Algeria, in its initial report, said that the reduction of capital crimes is under consideration by a commission responsible for revising the nation's penal code and that opinion favors abolition of the death penalty for economic offenses.[161] The Supreme Court of India has concluded that the country's legislation is in accordance with article 6§2 of the Covenant, because the death penalty only applies in the case of seven offenses that are characterized as heinous crimes.[162]

The Human Rights Committee has singled out a number of individual offenses and suggested that they do not meet the standard of article 6§2 of the Covenant. This is notably the case with respect to political crimes.[163] Attempts during drafting of the Covenant to prohibit the death penalty in the case of such crimes were unsuccessful,[164] although provisions to this effect appear in the American Convention on Human Rights[165] and the Arab Charter of Human Rights.[166] But the argument can be sustained that political crimes are not "the most serious crimes" within the meaning of the Covenant and that consequently the death penalty is forbidden for these crimes, even in the absence of a specific provision.[167] The Human Rights Committee has frequently criticized states parties that impose the death penalty for political offences,[168] conspiracy between civil servants and soldiers,[169] misappropriation of state or public property,[170] treason,[171] espionage,[172] and refusal to divulge previous political activities.[173] During presentation of Democratic Yemen's initial report, members of the Human Rights Committee objected to "vaguely defined crimes" subject to the death penalty, including offenses against "peace, humanity or human rights" or war crimes "motivated by hostility towards the Republic."[174] During presentation of Viet Nam's initial report, members of the committee observed that "political crimes" should not be capital crimes.[175] At the time of the drafting of its General Comment on article 6, one of the members of the Human Rights Committee, Hanga, sought a last-minute amendment stating that capital punishment should not be imposed for political offenses, only to be told that it was too late in the drafting process to make any changes to the text.[176]

The Human Rights Committee has also objected to imposition of the death penalty for offenses against property, among them misuse of public funds,[177] crimes against the economy,[178] theft,[179] and misappropriation of state or public property.[180] When Mauritius imposed the death penalty for drug traffickers, members of the committee said that "to extend the death penalty to all cases of drug trafficking, including those involving the sale and consumption of unprocessed coca leaves, was an excessive measure,"[181] implying evidently that in some cases the death penalty would be acceptable in cases of drug trafficking.[182]

The Committee Against Torture has also shown some interest in the scope of crimes subject to the death penalty. This indicates the view of the committee, and of the states parties, that the death penalty is indeed subsumed within the prohibition of torture and cruel, inhuman, and degrading treatment or punishment. In consideration of the Libyan report to the Committee Against Torture, one of the members, Bent Sorensen, expressed pleasure that application of the death penalty will be limited to a smaller number of offenses, but said he was somewhat astonished that it is applicable in the case of economic crimes.[183] Belarus, during presentation of its report to the Committee Against Torture, answered a question about crimes to which the death penalty is applicable, noting that the number is being reduced to four—aggravated homicide, high treason, genocide, and terrorism.[184]

The secretary-general of the United Nations, in his 1990 quinquennial report on capital punishment to the Economic and Social Council, based on replies from forty-one member states to a questionnaire, noted that not all of the offenses appeared to comply with the standards of the Covenant: "For example, offences aimed at the domination of a social class or at overthrowing the basic economic and social orders (as reported by Turkey), and theft in aggravated circumstances, sexual intercourse with a female relative under fifteen or arousing of religious and sectarian feelings and propagation of Zionist ideas (as reported by Cuba), may not stand the test of a 'most serious crime' in the sense of article 6 of the Covenant."[185]

Few jurists would challenge the suggestion that imposing the death penalty for murder is "proportionate."[186] However, courts in the United States have ruled that punishment of death for some other crimes violates the principle of proportionality. In *Coker* v. *Georgia*, the United States Supreme Court held that capital punishment for rape was contrary to the Eighth Amendment.[187] The death penalty for felony murder, by which participants in a criminal act where murder is committed may be held liable for first-degree murder, even if they had no intention to commit such a crime, has been found by the Supreme Court to be unconstitutional. "The imposition of the death penalty for this crime totally violates the principle of proportionality embodied in the Eighth Amendment's prohibition," said Justice Thurgood Marshall.[188] Justice Byron White also concluded, in *Lockett,* that it was indeed disproportionate to impose the death penalty, because no intent to commit murder had been proven.[189] However, Chief Justice Warren Burger, writing for the majority, found it unnecessary to base his conclusions on the issue of proportionality.[190]

PUBLIC OPINION

DURING DEBATES on the death penalty, it is usually argued by retentionists, and frequently conceded by abolitionists, that public opinion favors its use.[1] This claim is often made even in countries where capital punishment has long been abolished. The apparent enthusiasm for the death penalty is said to increase, or at least to become more visible, when crime rates are high or following news of a particularly atrocious crime. During debates on an international level, where states are called upon to accept new norms concerning limitation and abolition of capital punishment, they frequently invoke public opinion in order to account for their reticence. Even were the government willing to take such a step, they say, public opinion would simply not stand for abolition. This was the position taken by the United States when presenting its initial report to the Human Rights Committee pursuant to article 40 of the International Covenant on Civil and Political Rights.[2] According to this report, "The majority of citizens through their freely elected officials have chosen to retain the death penalty for the most serious crimes, a policy which appears to represent the majority sentiment of the country."[3] In November 1994, when Rwanda opposed the Security Council resolution creating the International Tribunal for Rwanda,[4] it argued that the draft statute was unacceptable to its population because it excluded the death penalty.[5] The United Kingdom has frequently declined to ratify international treaties affirming abolition of the death penalty, including Protocol No. 6 to the Convention for the Protection of Human Rights and Fundamental Freedoms Concerning the Abolition of the Death Penalty.[6] In the view of several governments, this is a matter to be left to the conscience of individual members of Parliament in a free vote, a position not adopted when other fundamental human rights norms are concerned.[7]

Human rights instruments, whether they be international treaties or domestic constitutions, are, first and foremost, aimed at protection of the individual from the state. Although encompassing a significant collective rights dimension, they begin from the premise that the state itself, even where it expresses the legitimate democratic aspirations of the general public, may attempt to oppress the individual for any number of reasons. Consequently, unpopular speech and belief need to be sheltered from majorities that would suppress them, ethnic minorities must be guaranteed the right to survive and to resist assimilation, and accused criminals require protection from unfair prosecution and biased judges. If public opinion were to be canvassed each time individual rights were in jeopardy, there can be little doubt that human rights guarantees would frequently come out the loser. Yet it would contradict the raison d'être of human rights law to make its efficacy contingent on public opinion, one of the very forces it is aimed at counteracting or neutralizing.

Some norms effectively insulate the individual from the vagaries of public opinion. When international law forbids ex post facto prosecution of criminal offenses—proclaiming that no one shall be held guilty on account of any act or omission that did not constitute a crime under national or international law when it was committed—neither legislature nor court may tamper with this principle without expressly violating the state's treaty obligations.[8] The right of the accused to be present at trial, and to cross-examine prosecution witnesses, is similarly protected;[9] although this right is subject to derogation in time of war or national crisis, the state must justify such an exceptional step by objective criteria subject to independent judicial assessment.[10]

However, the guarantee against cruel punishment and torture, fundamental as it may be in the overall human rights scheme, is peculiarly vulnerable to the vagaries of public opinion. The terms "cruel," "inhuman," and "degrading" are enigmatic, resisting judicial interpretation that does not take public opinion into account—they are subjective concepts. What is deemed cruel, inhuman, or degrading by one society, one culture, one religion, even one age group, will often be viewed differently by others. Furthermore, within a particular society such concepts will inevitably change over time. The same may be said of the notion of "punishment." In a judgment issued at the beginning of the century, the majority of the United States Supreme Court held that the prohibition against cruel and unusual punishment "may acquire meaning as public opinion becomes enlightened by a humane justice."[11] Criminal sanctions must be established with reference to public attitudes because effective punishment aims, inter alia, at deterrence and retribution. These goals cannot be attained unless forms of punishment inspire abhorrence and loathing among common citizens. Criminal sentences vary enormously from jurisdiction to jurisdiction, even among societies that are fundamentally similar in many respects. Public opinion must inevitably contribute to an assessment of the line of demarcation between punishment that is effective but not offensive to the fundamental human right to be free of cruelty and punishment that crosses the threshold.

   This feature of the norm has frequently been acknowledged by the judiciary. Chief Justice Earl Warren of the United States Supreme Court said that cruel punishment should be assessed in light of "the evolving standards of decency that mark the progress of a maturing society."[12] The phrase has been invoked on scores of occasions, not only by courts in the United States but throughout the world.[13] The notion of "evolving standards of decency" has frequently been cited before the courts of the United States when the method of execution has been under consideration.[14] In a recent Connecticut case, a judge noted that before the American Revolution burglars had their foreheads branded and an ear cut off, a sanction that would surely no longer pass the test of contemporary standards of decency.[15]

   According to Acting Justice Sydney Kentridge of the South African Constitutional Court, "The accepted mores of one's own society must have some relevance to the assessment whether a punishment is impermissibly cruel and inhuman."[16] However, in construing the prohibition, courts may attach different degrees of weight to the various sources of public opinion. In some cases, they have relied simply on their own intuitive notion of cruelty. This was the approach of the Judicial Committee of the Privy Council in its 1993 judgment on the death row phenomenon. Lord Griffiths, speaking for six of his colleagues, noted an "instinctive revulsion" against executing an individual who had been subject to lengthy detention. "What gives rise to this instinctive revulsion? The answer can only be our humanity; we regard it as an inhuman act to keep a man facing the agony of execution over a long extended period of time."[17] Other courts have attempted to be more scientific, or at least to appear so. Some have gone so far as to invoke public opinion polls,[18] although these are notoriously unreliable and have been shown to be a poor measurement.[19] Often, the behavior of juries is also cited as an indicator of general public sentiment.[20] On at least one occasion, a court has referred to the multitude of religious, social, and other groups filing amicus curiae briefs in support of abolition as evidence of the public's position.[21]

   In the United States, judges have developed an analysis that attaches great significance to legislative activity as a measure of public opinion. Following the Supreme Court ruling in *Furman* v. *Georgia*,[22] which halted the operation of all existing death penalty legislation, many state legislatures responded with new statutes aimed at overcoming the strictures in the plurality's reasons. In a sense, they were provoked by the two unequivocally abolitionist justices, Brennan and Marshall, who had argued that the death penalty violated the Eighth Amendment because it was out of step with contemporary values. This was perceived as a challenge to the "community," and it responded with a vengeance.[23] When the issue was revisited four years later, in *Gregg* v. *Georgia*,[24] the

plurality shifted, creating a new majority. But this was not only because the
new legislation answered the concerns of the wavering justices. The three who
had joined Justices Brennan and Marshall in *Furman* to make up the majority
felt that the legislative activity itself was relevant evidence of public opinion,
and that this was germane to judicial interpretation of the scope of what was
"cruel and unusual."[25] This is a paradox. The legislatures interpret the Constitution; yet the Constitution was aimed precisely at protecting the citizen from
the legislatures. The problem had been anticipated by Justice William J. Brennan in *Furman* v. *Georgia:* "If the judicial conclusion that a punishment is 'cruel
and unusual' 'depend[ed] upon virtually unanimous condemnation of the penalty at issue,' then '[l]ike no other constitutional provision, [the clause's] only
function would be to legitimize advances already made by the other depart-
ments and opinions already the conventional wisdom.' We know that the
Framers did not envision 'so narrow a role for this basic guaranty of human
rights.' "[26]

Some courts, while not totally rejecting the role of public opinion in the
determination of what constitutes cruel punishment and torture, have assigned
it a very subordinate position. The South African Constitutional Court, in assessing whether the death penalty violated that country's interim constitution,
rejected arguments that reliance should be placed on South African public
opinion.[27] President Chaskalson, in reasons that were endorsed by his ten colleagues, said that for the sake of argument he was prepared to admit "that the
majority of South Africans agree that the death sentence should be imposed in
extreme cases of murder."[28] Nevertheless, "The question before us . . . is not
what the majority of South Africans believe a proper sentence for murder
should be. It is whether the Constitution allows the sentence."[29] President
Chaskalson echoed the words of Justice Lewis F. Powell in *Furman,* who said
that public opinion, while not totally irrelevant, lay "at the periphery—not the
core—of the judicial process in constitutional cases. The assessment of popular
opinion is essentially a legislative, and not a judicial, function."[30] Chief Justice
Wright of the California Supreme Court described public acceptance of capital
punishment as "a relevant but not controlling factor" in the judicial debate.[31]

There is, perhaps, a confusion between human rights considerations and
criminal law considerations that it is important to clarify. Advocates of the
death penalty may attempt to defend its use in order to avoid threats of "mob
violence." This was the argument invoked by the Tanzanian government in
answering a 1994 challenge to the death penalty. The State insisted that it was
dangerous to let criminal law policy "jump too far ahead of the population"
because this would result in alienation of the public and its loss of confidence
in the system. "There is abundant evidence that members of the Tanzanian

public often resort to *mob justice* in a situation in which they feel that the criminal justice system, and/or its agencies, lack the competence or the will to protect them against crimes," claimed the State. "Therefore no civilized community should provoke such a situation in the name of a so-called 'progressive' penal policy."[32] But even if this view is to be accorded validity, it is still grounded in the theory of criminal law. The idea that prompt and harsh punishment is important to the maintenance of public confidence in a system of criminal justice seems out of place when the standpoint of human rights is adopted. Human rights tribunals have been alive to the rather delicate nexus between public opinion and human rights. Justice Brian Walsh of the European Court of Human Rights, in a case dealing not with punishment but with the legality of homosexual activity, warned that "[i]f the law is out of touch with the moral consensus of the community, whether by being either too far below it or too far above it, the law is brought into contempt."[33]

ROLE OF THE LEGISLATURE

Constitutional courts will normally exercise a degree of deference for the legislature. There is a presumption that the legislation is valid and, at the very least, the petitioner who alleges that punishment is cruel or torturous has the burden of proof or persuasion to demonstrate a constitutional violation. Justice Potter Stewart of the United States Supreme Court stated, in *Gregg* v. *Georgia:*

> We may not require the legislature to select the least severe penalty possible so long as the penalty selected is not cruelly inhumane or disproportionate to the crime involved. And a heavy burden rests on those who would attack the judgment of the representatives of the people. This is true in part because the constitutional test is intertwined with an assessment of contemporary standards and the legislative judgment weighs heavily in ascertaining such standards.[34]

In an international context, a corollary of this is the "margin of appreciation" doctrine, developed by the European Court of Human Rights.[35] The rationale for such approaches is a desire to temper the scope of judicial lawmaking. If constitutional courts attempt to second-guess every legislative decision, then they usurp the role of the legislator. Justice Felix Frankfurter of the United States Supreme Court explained the importance of such deference:

> Courts aren't representative bodies. They are not designed to be a good reflex of a democratic society. History teaches that the independence of the judiciary is jeopardized when the courts become em-

broiled in the passions of the day and assume primary responsibility in choosing between competing political, economic and social pressures.[36]

For Chief Justice Warren Burger, "[I]n a democratic society legislatures, not courts, are constituted to respond to the will and consequently the moral values of the people."[37] Deference to the legislature may be particularly strong in cases dealing with criminal sanctions, because "these are peculiarly questions of legislative policy."[38] Courts in India have also looked to legislative behavior in assessing whether punishments are constitutionally suspect. In *Bachan Singh* v. *State of Punjab*, the Indian Supreme Court ruled that the death penalty does not violate "the letter or the ethos" of the constitution, relying amongst other points on the fact that "contemporary public opinion channelized through the people's representatives in Parliament" continues to favor it.[39]

The legislative behavior argument, at least within the United States, has been rather decisive. Since *Gregg* v. *Georgia* in 1976, with rare exceptions the legislatures have been relatively intransigent on the question, and the only real movement has been a slow but discernible expansion of the number of states prepared to impose the death penalty. In 1995, Governor George Pataki of New York signed into force a death penalty statute that his predecessor, Mario Cuomo, had vetoed for more than a decade.[40] The death penalty came back into force in New York State on September 1, 1995. The previous year, Congress expanded the scope of the federal death penalty.[41]

In the case of interpretation of the norm prohibiting cruel treatment and torture, legislative action may provide guidance that is helpful in determining the subjective component of the terms "cruel," "inhuman," and "degrading." The legislature may be considered by the courts to be a particularly reliable guide to public opinion. Legislation can be analyzed and assessed with relative precision, something that can less readily be said of such other indicators of public opinion as polls, newspaper editorials, and the behavior of juries. However, the use of legislation for this purpose is, at least theoretically, quite different from the principle of judicial deference. For example, judges in the United States will frequently invoke legislative patterns in other states as evidence that legislation in their own state is out of step with "evolving standards of decency." Clearly, they have no obligation to defer to legislatures from other jurisdicions. Yet the seminal United States Supreme Court decisions on the death penalty, *Furman* v. *Georgia*[42] and *Gregg* v. *Georgia*,[43] show that this distinction between legislative deference and use of legislation in order to determine "evolving standards" is not all that clear.

The classic explanation for the use of legislative materials in evaluating public opinion is that of Justice Potter Stewart of the United States Supreme

Court. In *Gregg*, Justice Stewart noted that since the *Furman* decision of 1972 thirty-five state legislatures had adopted death penalty legislation in an attempt to respond to the ruling's strictures about the inherent arbitrariness of existing death penalty statutes. In his view, this was "[t]he most marked indication" that a large proportion of American society continued to support the death penalty. "[A]ll of the post-*Furman* statutes make clear that capital punishment itself has not been rejected by the elected representatives of the people," Justice Stewart said.[44] Nevertheless, he cautioned that "legislative judgments alone cannot be determinative of Eighth Amendment standards since that Amendment was intended to safeguard individuals from the abuse of legislative power."[45]

Justice Harry Blackmun had made similar comments in his dissent in *Furman*. While admitting his personal satisfaction with the majority decision that declared existing death penalty legislation to be contrary to the Eighth Amendment, Justice Blackmun cautioned that "we should not allow our personal preferences as to the wisdom of legislative and congressional action, or our distaste for such action, to guide our judicial decision in cases such as these."[46] He cited federal death penalty statutes to show that "these elected representatives of the people—far more conscious of the temper of the times, of the maturing of society, and of the contemporary demands for man's dignity, than are we who sit cloistered on this Court—took it as settled that the death penalty then, as it always has been, was not in itself unconstitutional."[47] Members of the Supreme Court continue to echo these pronouncements. According to Justice Antonin Scalia, in *Stanford* v. *Kentucky*, " '[F]irst' among the 'objective indicia that reflect the public attitude toward a given sanction' are statutes passed by society's elected representatives."[48] For Justice Sandra Day O'Connor, in *Penry* v. *Lynaugh*, "The clearest and most reliable evidence of contemporary values is the legislation enacted by the country's legislatures."[49] One enthusiastic United States judge has noted that "[w]hen, in the course of a decade, thirty-seven States call for the death penalty, the probability that the legislature of each State accurately reflects its community's standards approaches certainty."[50]

Answering the legislative opinion argument in *Gregg*, dissenting Justice Thurgood Marshall responded that the enactment of new death penalty statutes should not be regarded as "conclusive." He insisted that only well-informed public opinion could contribute to the constitutional debate, and he cited recent studies demonstrating how little Americans knew about the matter.[51] According to Justice Marshall:

> I would be less than candid if I did not acknowledge that the [enactment of new statutes imposing the death sentence has] a significant

bearing on a realistic assessment of the moral acceptability of the death penalty to the American people. But if the constitutionality of the death penalty turns, as I have urged, on the opinion of an *informed* citizenry, then even the enactment of new death statutes cannot be viewed as conclusive.[52]

Justice Marshall added that if one were to assume the new statutes to be evidence of informed public opinion, an "excessive penalty is invalid under the Cruel and Unusual Punishments Clause even though popular sentiment may favor it."[53] Similar views appear in other judgments. According to Chief Justice Wright of the California Supreme Court, for example:

> Respondent . . . urges that we must accept as controlling indicia of contemporary civilized standards of decency both legislative acts creating new capital crimes and legislative acquiescence in the continuation of capital punishment. Although we accord great deference to the judgment of the Legislature in this respect, we would abdicate our responsibility to examine independently the question were our inquiry to begin and end with the fact that statutory provisions authorizing imposition of the death penalty have been recently enacted or continue to exist.[54]

Canada's Supreme Court looked at legislative behavior during "free votes" on the death penalty in the federal Parliament. During these votes, elected members are not bound by party discipline and may, in such cases, be deemed to reflect more accurately the views of their constituents. According to Justice John Sopinka:

> In 1976, in a free vote, a majority of the members of the House of Commons voted to abolish capital punishment for all offences under the Criminal Code. Its reinstitution was rejected in another free vote in 1987. These votes reflect the view of the majority of the elected members of parliament that the death penalty is incompatible with respect for human dignity and the value of human life. Thus public policy in Canada, reaffirmed as recently as four years ago, stands clearly opposed to the death penalty.[55]

In the same judgment, Justice Peter D. Cory remarked that "[t]hese votes are a clear indication that capital punishment is considered to be contrary to basic Canadian values."[56] But Justice Beverley McLachlin saw the Parliamentary debates in another light. She noted that continued discussion of the matter by the legislature was evidence of important retentionist sentiment. As for the free vote in 1987 calling for revival of the death penalty, even though it was defeated Justice McLachlin considered that "the vote—148 to 127—fell far short of reflecting a broad consensus even among Parliamentarians."[57]

Before United States courts, legislative behavior has been invoked successfully in order to limit some of the more excessive aspects of the death penalty. Arguments of this nature have been presented in cases dealing with the specific crimes for which capital punishment may be imposed, as well as the juvenile death penalty and the method of execution. Within the United States, legislation provides for the death penalty in cases of murder and, under new federal legislation, large-scale drug trafficking.[58] (Since the *Gregg* decision of 1976, in practice it has only been imposed in cases of murder.) In *Coker* v. *Georgia*, the Supreme Court struck down Georgia's death penalty for rape of an adult woman, principally because it was the only state to impose the death penalty for rape of an adult, and one of only three to impose it for rape in any case.[59] In *Enmund* v. *Florida*, the Court considered whether the death penalty could be imposed in cases of "felony murder"—where there is no evidence that the accused attempted to commit murder, but where he or she participated with others in a crime like robbery where a murder was committed. "[O]nly about a third of American jurisdictions would ever permit a defendant who somehow participated in a robbery where a murder occurred to be sentenced to die,"[60] said the Supreme Court, adding that only eight states authorized the death penalty solely for felony murder.[61] Thus, legislative behavior in states other than those having the impugned statutes was viewed by the Supreme Court as a convincing argument for assessing the scope of the Eighth Amendment.

The United States is one of the few jurisdictions in the world in which the execution of individuals for crimes committed while under the age of eighteen is permitted. Imposition of the death penalty in such circumstances is prohibited by several international legal instruments.[62] But even in those jurisdictions within the United States where such executions are legal, there is an enormous variation in the governing legislation as to the age at which capital punishment is definitively forbidden. In *Thompson* v. *Oklahoma*, the plurality looked to the eighteen states that had adopted a minimum age requirement for the death penalty; all of them required the defendant to be at least sixteen years old at the time of the offense.[63] Therefore, Justice O'Connor considered that applying the death penalty to fifteen-year-olds would violate the Eighth Amendment because "almost two-thirds of the state legislatures have definitely concluded that no fifteen-year-old should be exposed to the threat of execution."[64] Similarly, when the United States Supreme Court affirmed in 1986 that execution of the insane would be contrary to the Eighth Amendment,[65] it observed, in this respect, that "no State in the Union permits the execution of the insane."[66]

Finally, courts have frequently looked at legislative behavior in assessing when methods of punishment reach the point where they are no longer "acceptable." This argument has been invoked in the United States in challenges to execution by hanging,[67] by electrocution,[68] and by asphyxiation in the gas chamber.[69] As Justice Stephen Reinhardt of the Court of Appeals for the Ninth Circuit stated, "[O]nce a punishment has been rejected as unacceptable by a sufficiently large number of state legislatures, we can no longer say that it is consistent with our society's standards of decency, regardless of what our view would be in the absence of such clear legislative action."[70] But in that same case, the majority considered that "[t]he number of states using hanging is evidence of public perception, but sheds no light on the actual pain that may or may not attend the practice. We cannot conclude that judicial hanging is incompatible with evolving standards of decency simply because few states continue the practice."[71]

TRENDS IN INTERNATIONAL AND COMPARATIVE LAW TOWARDS ABOLITION

That international law evidences a trend favorable to abolition of the death penalty would seem to be beyond dispute. Four international instruments now prohibit imposition of the death penalty.[72] They have been ratified by approximately fifty states, which are now bound at international law not to pronounce or impose the death penalty.[73] The ad hoc tribunals set up by the Security Council to judge war crimes and crimes against humanity committed in the former Yugoslavia and in Rwanda formally exclude the possibility of capital punishment.[74] The International Law Commission's draft statute for a permanent international criminal court—a body that will likely have jurisdiction over serious violations of humanitarian law, crimes against humanity (including genocide), and certain narcotics-related and terrorist crimes—also excludes the death penalty.[75] Discussions within United Nations bodies concerning the fact that these international penal statutes exclude the death penalty indicate that the matter is uncontroversial. This trend ought to be an important argument before domestic courts in any "evolving standards of decency" argument.

Regrettably, United States courts have yet to show much interest in developments in international law. Note, however, that the Supreme Court, in one of the leading cases on the Eighth Amendment not dealing with capital punishment, considered comparative law sources and observed that the punishment—deprival of citizenship for the crime of desertion—was not authorized in other countries.[76] In a death penalty case, Chief Justice Wright of the Supreme Court of California wrote that "the repudiation of the death penalty in this country is reflected in a world-wide trend towards abolition."[77] In some jurisdictions, this international trend has been given more serious consideration. Justice Peter D. Cory, of the Supreme Court of Canada, in *Kindler* v. *Canada*, cited it,[78] referring explicitly to the abolitionist international instruments.

Other judges, however, have countered the arguments for abolition, pointing out that the death penalty is still used in many countries. In *Bachan Singh* v. *State of Punjab*, Justice Sarkaria of the Indian Supreme Court upheld the legality of the death penalty, noting that "a very large segment of people, the world over, including sociologists, legislators, jurists, judges and administrators still firmly believe in the worth and necessity of capital punishment for the protection of society."[79] Acting Justice Sydney Kentridge stated in the South African Constitutional Court decision that "one cannot say that the death penalty is as yet contrary to international law."[80] Justice Gerald La Forest of the Supreme Court of Canada affirmed that "despite these trends, [there is] no international norm."[81] This is not really accurate though; as noted above, a widely accepted international norm prohibits the death penalty. It is not yet, however, a universal norm. Justice La Forest also admitted "a growing and, in my view, welcome trend among Western nations over the past fifty years to abolish the death penalty[;] but some have gone against this trend, notably the United States, a fact of especial concern having regard to its size and proximity to this country."[82] He too alluded to the international instruments, but claimed that all fall short of actually prohibiting use of the death penalty: "This contrasts with the overwhelming universal condemnation that has been directed at practices such as genocide, slavery and torture." His comment that all fall short of prohibiting the death penalty is puzzling, because this is most certainly the vocation of the three above-mentioned protocols.[83]

EXECUTIVE ACTION

One of the features of modern death penalty practice is that despite legislation permitting capital punishment and courts prepared to impose it, the executive, which often has the final say in an execution, refuses to authorize the deed itself. The growing list of abolitionist countries includes a large number of nations in which capital punishment exists in law but is no longer carried out. Amnesty, pardon, and commutation of death sentences are contemplated by article 6§4 of the International Covenant on Civil and Political Rights: "Anyone sentenced to death shall have the right to seek pardon or commutation of the sentence. Amnesty, pardon or commutation of the sentence of death may be granted in all cases."[84] The executive will often exercise this function on a case-by-case basis. Sometimes, a collective commutation will be offered to mark some significant political anniversary. In recent times, general moratoria on the death penalty have been imposed, frequently because a country has undertaken a formal debate on whether to abolish capital punishment. Courts have looked at these developments as evidence of public opinion and societal values. As the California Supreme Court noted in 1972, "Although death penalty statutes do remain on the books of many jurisdictions, and public opinion polls show opinion to be divided as to capital punishment as an abstract proposition, the infrequency of its actual application suggests that among those persons called upon to actually impose or carry out the death penalty it is being repudiated with ever increasing frequency."[85] Chief Justice Wright pointed to the steady decrease in executions in the United States, which hit a peak of 199 in 1935 and steadily plummeted to 2 in 1967. "[I]n spite of a growing population and notwithstanding the statutory sanction of the death penalty," he said, this fact "persuasively demonstrates that capital punishment is unacceptable to society today."[86] Similar statistics were examined in a Massachusetts judgment. Noting that executive action had resulted in commuting sentences in Massachusetts since 1948 (forty-three cases), Chief Justice Edward F. Hennessey of the Supreme Judicial Court observed that "[t]he complete absence of executions in the Commonwealth through these many years indicates that in the opinion of those several Governors and others who bore the responsibility for administering the death penalty provisions and who had the most immediate appreciation of the death penalty, it was unacceptable."[87]

Courts have juxtaposed to this executive reluctance to execute the apparent enthusiasm for capital punishment revealed by public opinion polls. The refusal of the executive to comply with public enthusiasm for executions may be viewed as elitist. For example, in the 1994 elections a prominent politician, Governor Mario Cuomo of New York, paid with his career for systematic and uncompromising vetoes each time the state legislature passed a capital punishment statute. Yet politicians are elected to lead, not to follow, and they often take unpopular decisions that are respected by voters as being for the greater good. If elected officials determined fiscal policy based on the impulsive opinions of their electorate, the state would quickly go bankrupt. In one recent judgment, Associate Justice Berdon of the Connecticut Supreme Court considered that the real practice of those responsible for carrying out the death penalty was a far more useful guide to public opinion than such indicators as opinion polls. "[P]ublic opinion must be gleaned from a society's actual record in carrying out the death penalty,"[88] he said. According to Chief Justice Hennessey of the Massachusetts Supreme Judicial Court, "What our society does in actuality is a much more compelling indicator of the acceptability of the death penalty than the responses citizens may give upon questioning."[89]

Officially proclaimed moratoria have prevented executions for significant periods of time in such states as Jamaica, Trinidad and Tobago, Zimbabwe, and South Africa. Although they do not necessarily lead to abolition, these mandated pauses do indicate a reluctance by officials to proceed with executions and suggest a degree of hesitation in the general public.[90] Acting Justice Sydney Kentridge, in his individual reasons for judgment in the South African Constitutional Court case, opined that the proclamation of a moratorium by President F. W. De Klerk in 1990 might support contentions that South African public opinion was at least ambivalent on the subject of capital punishment.[91]

ROLE OF JURIES AND JUDGES IN SENTENCING

Although determination of criminal sentences is normally left to judges in most jurisdictions, within the United States, at least, the death penalty is usually imposed by a jury.[92] American state judges are often elected, making them particularly vulnerable to political pressures and therefore unsuited for such life-and-death decisions.[93] According to the United States Supreme Court, "[O]ne of the most important functions any jury can perform in making . . . a selection [between life imprisonment and death for a defendant convicted in a capital case] is to maintain a link between contemporary community values and the penal system—a link without which the determination of punishment could hardly reflect 'the evolving standards of decency that mark the progress of a maturing society.' "[94] The role of juries in determining these "evolving standards" was considered by Chief Justice Wright of the Supreme Court of California in *People* v. *Anderson:* "Jury sentencing has been considered desirable in capital cases," he wrote, going on to quote the U.S. Supreme Court.[95] For this reason, jury involvement in capital sentencing is a source of arguments that help to fix the position of public opinion with respect to the death penalty. This was also recognized by the majority of the Supreme Court in *Gregg* v. *Georgia,* which considered the jury to be "a significant and reliable objective index of contemporary values because it is so directly involved."[96]

In the twentieth century, the principle of jury discretion was adopted by legislators in the United States as a replacement for mandatory death penalties. Indeed, the resistance of juries to the imposition of mandatory death sentences has been manifested for centuries. In *Kindler* v. *Canada,* Justice Peter D. Cory considered this to be evidence of a historic revulsion to capital punishment. He observed that records going back as far as the fourteenth century indicate an unwillingness of juries to convict for felonies, in order to avoid the possibility that capital punishment would be imposed.[97] By the seventeenth century, juries were using their power to convict for lesser but included offenses in order to avoid the death penalty. As Justice Cory noted, in the eighteenth century, despite a dramatic increase in the number of capital crimes, the frequency of convictions and the harshness of sentences decreased.[98] "Quite simply," he remarked, "juries tended to refuse to convict or, if they did convict, refused to find the accused guilty of a capital offence."[99] The justice went on to say:

> This marked resistance to the death penalty speaks volumes for the basic decency and compassion of jurors. It is reflected in their decisions over the centuries and constitutes a long and lasting record of social values that is worthy of consideration. The compassionate views of the jurors are echoed in over 300 years of writings by reformers.[100]

But in *Gregg* v. *Georgia*, Justice Stewart was not prepared to concede that the reluctance of juries to impose the death penalty was evidence of public disapproval of capital punishment. "Rather, the reluctance of juries in many cases to impose the sentence may well reflect the human feeling that this most irrevocable of sanctions should be reserved for a small number of extreme cases," he said.[101] For Chief Justice Burger in *Furman* v. *Georgia*, "[T]he very infrequency of death penalties imposed by jurors attests to their cautious and discriminating reservation of that penalty for the most extreme cases."[102]

PUBLIC OPINION POLLS

Periodically, soundings of public opinion (of varying degrees of scientific rigor) are conducted in different countries, including many where the death penalty has been abolished. These polls are often undertaken following a particularly atrocious crime; they are said to show that even in the most enlightened societies the majority of the public supports the use of capital punishment. The surveys themselves are rarely cited in legal literature or caselaw, but usually there is in effect a rather ready concession by abolitionists, based essentially on intuition, that they will confirm the existence of widespread support for capital punishment.[103]

Such polls have been subjected to many critiques. It is frequently argued that public opinion is poorly informed about the detailed issues involved and the contributions of scientific research on the death penalty. The more the respondent knows about capital punishment, the less likely he or she is to support its retention. The problem of information was articulated by Justice Mwalusanya, of the High Court of Tanzania:

> The government must assume responsibility for ensuring that their citizens are placed in a position whereunder they are able to base their

views about the death penalty *on a rational and properly informed assess-ment.* It is clear that many people base their support for the penalty on an erroneous belief that capital punishment is the most effective deter-rent punishment, and so the government has a duty to put the true facts before them instead of holding out to the public that the death penalty is an instant solution to violent crime.[104]

Likewise, in the view of Justice Thurgood Marshall, of the United States Su-preme Court, "the American people, fully informed as to the purposes of the death penalty and its liabilities, would in my view reject it as morally unaccept-able."[105]

Perhaps the most significant criticism of public opinion polling concerns the wording of the questions asked. When alternative punishments are pro-posed, such as life imprisonment without possibility of parole, the majorities tend to evaporate.[106] Polls that take this approach, it may be argued, show the opposite—namely, that public opinion is actually uncomfortable with capital punishment. Some judges have been attuned to this degree of ambiguity in poll results, refusing to see the findings as confirmation of public support for the death penalty. Justice Robert I. Berdon, of the Connecticut Supreme Court, wrote:

> Even public opinion polls demonstrate public reluctance and concern over the imposition of the death penalty. While a majority of the pub-lic may support the death penalty in the abstract, public support for the penalty drops to below 50 percent when alternative sentences are considered. Given the choice, more people would support life impris-onment without parole plus restitution to the victim's family over the death penalty. In addition, many people have significant doubts about various aspects of the death penalty. Fifty-eight percent of those sur-veyed in an April, 1993 poll were concerned about the danger of exe-cuting innocent people. Forty-eight percent were concerned about racism in the application of the penalty, and another 42 percent had doubts about the ability of the death penalty to deter crime.[107]

He considered that polls supported the conclusion that if alternative sentences were offered the public would significantly change its answer to questions on the death penalty.[108] Justice Harry A. Blackmun of the United States Supreme Court also felt that canvasses of public opinion were in no way decisive indica-tors of support for capital punishment: "More than 75 percent of those sur-veyed indicated that if they were called upon to make a capital-sentencing decision as jurors, the amount of time the convicted murderer actually would have to spend in prison would be an 'extremely important' or a 'very important' factor in choosing between life and death."[109] Chief Justice Wright of the California Supreme Court also referred to such surveys, concluding that "public opinion polls show opinion to be divided as to capital punishment as an abstract proposition."[110] Associate Justice Berdon of the Connecticut Supreme Court considered that public sentiment "cannot appropriately be measured by abstract polls that elicit generalized, emotional responses from participants."[111]

Despite these limitations on their conclusiveness, some courts have felt such surveys to be useful evidence of public support for capital punishment. In *Gregg* v. *Georgia*, reference was made to public opinion polls favoring the death penalty.[112] In *Kindler* v. *Canada*, Justice Beverly McLachlin of the Supreme Court of Canada stated that such polls continued to show considerable support among Canadians for the return of the death penalty for certain offenses.[113] Justice La Forest, who drafted the reasons for the majority in that case, cautioned against determining acceptability of the death penalty "in terms of statistical measurements of approval or disapproval by the public at large," but added that "it is fair to say that they afford some insight into the public values of the community."[114]

CONCLUSION

The norm prohibiting cruel treatment and punishment is unique, as I have explained elsewhere in this work, because its interpretation is so closely related to public attitudes. This is a troubling situation, in that constitutional or international norms have been created to protect individuals *from* public opinion. Assuming that the democratically elected representatives of the population do in fact carry out the people's wishes, implicit in the notion of supralegislative norms is the idea that at times democracy will oppress individuals or minority groups. But as Justice Brennan put it so eloquently in *Furman*,

> The right to be free of cruel and unusual punishments, like the other guarantees of the Bill of Rights, "may not be submitted to vote; [it] depend[s] on the outcome of no elections." "The very purpose of a Bill of Rights was to withdraw certain subjects from the vicissitudes of political controversy, to place them beyond the reach of majorities and officials and to establish them as legal principles to be applied by the courts." *Board of Education* v. *Barnette*, [319 U.S. 624, 638, 63 S.Ct. 1178, 1185, 87 L.Ed. 1628] (1943).[115]

If public opinion is removed from the equation, however, on what are judges to rely? Justice Antonin Scalia of the United States Supreme Court has warned that "the risk of assessing evolving standards is that it is all too easy to believe that evolution has culminated in one's own views."[116]

Reliance on legislative behavior seems to be peculiarly American. This is perhaps because of the particularities of the U.S. federal system, which creates more than fifty distinct criminal law jurisdictions and therefore facilitates a form of internal comparative law. Other jurisdictions have tended to consider public opinion more abstractly or, in the case of the Human Rights Committee, to ignore it altogether. No matter what is said, it is a rare judge indeed who is immune to the influence of public sentiment, even where tenure of office is assured. Judges will say they are concerned with the image of the court, and be careful not to let its findings come unhinged from societal attitudes as a whole. On an international level, the problem takes on different dimensions. Such tribunals as the European Court of Human Rights and the Human Rights Committee realize that if they become too isolated from "public opinion" this may result in denunciations of the relevant treaty or inhibit ratifications.

Perhaps it is wrong to give public opinion too much importance in judicial consideration of the norm prohibiting cruel punishment and torture. Courts, as well as legislatures, should be more aggressive in their role as molders of public opinion. In this respect, the Judicial Committee of the Privy Council set an interesting example when it affirmed that its members were shocked at the notion of prolonged detention prior to execution.[117] They cited no polls, no legislative trends. Their judgment will make public opinion, even if it does not follow it.

THE DEATH ROW

PHENOMENON

D EATH ROW is the cell or block of cells in which inmates condemned to death are held while awaiting execution.[1] There may be within this death row one or more "death cells," special units in which the condemned person is kept for a period of hours or a few days immediately prior to imposition of the sentence. Death row inmates are normally segregated from other convicts serving fixed terms of imprisonment. The reasons for this are somewhat obscure. There may be a suggestion that the individual is already a "dead man"[2] and thus no longer belongs with the living. Another explanation may be the security of other prisoners and prison guards, for whom exposure to a desperate individual with literally nothing to lose may be dangerous. Yet those sentenced to life terms are commonly mixed with the general inmate population, and so this argument seems flawed.

Death row is often characterized by particularly harsh prison conditions: cells without amenities, little or no time outdoors for recreation, an absence of activities related to work or education (after all, rehabilitation has been excluded), contemptuous prison personnel, rare opportunities for visits from family and friends or other forms of communication. Prison systems are normally structured according to a gradation of conditions, a form of behavioral modification by which an inmate progresses from "maximum security" to "minimum security" during the sentence in return for compliance with regulations and orders and participation in prison labor. Yet the death row prisoner is invariably kept at the most extreme end of the spectrum, no matter how positive his or her behavior or how long the wait. "Death row is a prison within a prison, physically and socially isolated from the prison community and the outside world," notes Robert Johnson. "Condemned prisoners live twenty-three and one-half hours alone in their cells . . ."[3]

The length of detention on death row is one of its more egregious and contested features. As Albert Camus wrote, a man is destroyed by the wait for death long before he really dies. Two deaths are inflicted, of which the first is worse than the second, even though he may only have killed once.[4] The California Supreme Court described detention on death row as being "often so de-grading and brutalizing to the human spirit as to constitute psychological torture."[5] The Supreme Judicial Court of Massachusetts referred to the prisoner's "extreme anguish in anticipation of the extinction of his existence."[6] For Justice John Paul Stevens of the U.S. Supreme Court, a death sentence involves punishment in two stages:

> Imprisonment follows immediately after conviction; but the execution normally does not take place until after the conclusion of post-trial proceedings in the trial court, direct and collateral review in the state judicial system, collateral review in the federal judicial system, and clemency review by the executive department of the State. However critical one may be of these protracted post-trial procedures, it seems inevitable that there must be a significant period of incarceration on death row during the interval between sentencing and execution. If the death sentence is ultimately set aside or its execution delayed for a prolonged period, the imprisonment during that period is nevertheless a significant form of punishment. Indeed, the deterrent value of incarceration during that period of uncertainty may well be comparable to the consequences of the ultimate step itself.[7]

The scope of the problem may be a recent development,[8] although the cruelty involved in prolonging capital punishment has long been recognized. As Lords Scarman and Brightman of the Judicial Committee of the Privy Council noted in *Riley* v. *Attorney-General of Jamaica,* "It is no exaggeration, therefore, to say that the jurisprudence of the civilized world, much of which is derived from common law principles and the prohibition against cruel and unusual punishments in the English Bill of Rights, has recognized and acknowledged that prolonged delay in executing a sentence of death can make the punishment when it comes inhuman and degrading."[9]

Many decades ago, execution normally followed sentencing within weeks or months. The progressive limitations on the death penalty that are compelled by human rights law, coupled with the growth of abolitionist sentiment, have been responsible for much of this prolonged delay. Prisoners launch what seem to be unending challenges to conviction and sentence, directed to domestic courts responsible for appeal, judicial review, and constitutional litigation. When these fail, there are requests for pardon or commutation. Death sentences are also attacked before international human rights bodies, like the United Nations Human Rights Committee or the Inter-American Commission on Human Rights. Delay in execution is also the unintended by-product of moratoria, which are normally respected in order to permit politicians and jurists to debate whether to abolish the death penalty.

Ironically, then, prolonged detention on death row, which may itself constitute a violation of an individual's human rights, is the consequence of efforts to limit and eventually abolish the death penalty that can be directly attributed to the influence of contemporary human rights law. This creates a dilemma for a state that hopes to retain the death penalty. If it is to provide the full range of procedural guarantees that are prescribed by international and domestic law, then it may be simply impossible to complete the process within an acceptably short period. The Royal Commission on Capital Punishment of the United Kingdom, considering the question in the early 1950s when normal stays on death row amounted only to weeks and not years, was already well aware of the conflicting imperatives:

> We have examined the possibility of reducing the length of time between sentence of death and execution . . . in order to shorten the period of strain on the prisoner and those about him. It seems, however, that to do this would be to run the risk of handicapping the prisoner and his advisers in arranging for an appeal and bringing forward information that might justify a reprieve. It is also necessary for the Secretary of State to have enough time to make such enquiries as may be necessary before deciding whether the sentence should be carried out. In 1950, when there were 19 executions in England and Wales, the average period was about five weeks; in the twelve cases in which there was an appeal the average was slightly over six weeks, and in seven where there was not, it was just under three. In general, the interval between sentence and execution is shorter here than in most Commonwealth countries and much shorter than is usual in the United States.[10]

As the author David Pannick has argued, "A legalistic society will be unable to impose the death penalty without an unconstitutionally cruel delay, and hence it will be unable lawfully to impose the death penalty at all."[11]

Although delay is usually welcomed by the condemned individual, there are some who refuse all remedies against their sentence and plead to be executed promptly. Perhaps they feel a desire to atone for their crimes, but they may also be simply expressing pre-existent suicidal tendencies or a horror of any prolongation of the agony on death row. This agony haunts those sentenced to death, who are condemned not only to lose their lives but also to contemplate their fate. There is more involved than the fear of "meeting one's maker"; often the prisoner is troubled by the horror of so-called botched executions, which make extinction of life a moment of excruciating and terrifying pain. As Justice William J. Brennan of the United States Supreme Court said in *Furman* v. *Georgia,* "[T]he prospect of pending execution exacts a frightful toll during the inevitable long wait between the imposition of sentence and the actual infliction of death."[12] Years earlier, Justice Felix Frankfurter of the Supreme Court admitted that "the onset of insanity while awaiting execution of a death sentence is not a rare phenomenon."[13]

While serving a term in an English jail, Oscar Wilde had a brush with death row. One of his fellow inmates was a trooper of the Royal Horse Guards, condemned for murdering his lover, and sentenced to die within six weeks. Wilde's poem *The Ballad of Reading Gaol* attempts to convey the mental suffering of the condemned man, forced to brood upon "[h]is anguish night and day."[14] Death row is, indeed, the stuff of poets, because so much of the suffering that is involved belongs to the spirit rather than the body. This is not torture that can be easily proven with photographs, X rays, and medical reports, although psychiatrists and psychologists have attempted to study the matter.[15] The Indian Judge Krishna Iyer put the matter more bluntly in the case of Rajendra Prasad, who had lived with the agony of impending hanging for six years: "He must, by now, be more a vegetable than a person and hanging a vegetable is not death penalty."[16] Virtually all of the courts that have examined the matter concur that there is some inherent suffering in awaiting the hangman, although, as I shall point out, some judges have taken the view that the struggle to stay alive through the exercise of various appellate remedies is in some sense an antidote. The latter position was expressed by Lord Diplock, in *Abbott* v. *A.-G. of Trinidad and Tobago,* who said, "[W]here there's life, there's hope."[17] Others see in this battle against execution only an aggravation of the suffering, citing the "ineradicable human desire" to stay alive that makes prolongation of execution cruel, inhuman, and degrading.[18]

Within death row itself, there is usually a special regime applicable to the hours or days immediately preceding execution. Faced with imminent death, the prisoner is usually kept in total isolation and under constant surveillance. He or she may be entitled to special dining privileges, the famous "last meal." Sometimes the prisoner is subject to a set of strictures that is even more rigorous than the death row routine. In the British prison in Cyprus, where political prisoners were held awaiting execution, they were deprived of all meals during their twenty-four-hour wait in the so-called death cell. To this day,[19] the wire mesh of the cell doors evidences small holes, large enough for a cigarette to poke through; smoking was the only "luxury" to which the condemned prisoners were entitled. In South Africa under apartheid, a week prior to execution death row prisoners were moved to cells known as the "pot," so called because prisoners were to "stew before they die."[20] The night before the execution, the South African prisoner would be given a last meal of chicken, deboned so as to foil any suicide attempts. In a recent Jamaican case, the Human Rights Committee described how a prisoner was placed in the death cell adjacent to the gallows for five days, subject to round-the-clock surveillance. During this period, he was weighed in order to calculate the length of the rope that would be required for an efficient and successful "drop." He was, moreover, taunted by the executioner about the impending execution date, and could hear the gallows being tested. For the committee, these were among the factors in the prisoner's case justifying the conclusion that he had been subject to torture or cruel, inhuman, and degrading treatment or punishment.[21]

Another feature of death row that may be the source of additional suffering for prisoners is the periodic fixing of execution dates, followed by reprieves. Many of those condemned to die go through this process several times. When the death sentence is finally carried out, it follows "one or more agonizing stays of execution."[22] Justice Liacos, of the Massachusetts Supreme Judicial Court, noted how "[l]engthy delays, especially if punctuated by a series of last minute reprieves, intensify the prisoner's suffering."[23] Naturally, the reprieve is greeted with relief and satisfaction, but the process of preparing for execution is nonetheless tormenting. The Judicial Committee of the Privy Council, in its 1993 decision in *Pratt et al.* v. *Attorney General for Jamaica et al.*, referred to the repeated fixing of execution dates as an aggravating factor contributing to the inhuman and degrading treatment that the two petitioners suffered during their fourteen-year stay on Jamaica's death row.[24] Perhaps the most extreme example of this is the finding, by the United Nations Human Rights Committee, that a delay of several hours in informing Pratt and Morgan of one of these stays of execution constituted cruel, inhuman, and degrading treatment.[25] There is a suggestion that an element in the committee's consideration was the fact that the delay by the Jamaican prison authorities was intentional and apparently malicious,[26] although this suggestion has been challenged by the country's government.[27]

In a November 1995 judgment, *Guerra* v. *Baptiste*, the Judicial Committee of the Privy Council concluded that condemned prisoners must also receive sufficient notice of execution. The warrant of execution in Guerra's case had been read to him only seventeen hours prior to the time fixed for execution. Writing for the council, Lord Goff of Chieveley stated that "justice and humanity require that a man under sentence of death should be given reasonable notice of the time of his execution. Such notice is required to enable a man to arrange his affairs, to be visited by members of his intimate family before he dies, and to receive spiritual advice and comfort to enable him to compose himself, as best he can, to face his ultimate ordeal."[28] Adequate notice is also important because it provides the prisoner with time to take legal proceedings with a view to challenging the execution. In support of the conclusions, Lord Goff noted that the principle had been long recognized in England in times when capital punishment was still in effect, and that it was a settled practice in Trinidad and Tobago for a condemned individual to be advised of the time and date of his execution by the reading of a death warrant to him on a Thursday for execution on the following Tuesday. Their Lordships concluded that Trinidad's constitutional norm prohibiting cruel and unusual punishment had been violated, as had the guarantee of due process.

But not all tribunals have viewed death row in the same manner. A judge of the United States District Court has stated:

> The process of which petitioner complains serves the important state interest of keeping the post conviction process moving forward at the same time it preserves petitioner's due process rights. The extensive and repeated review of petitioner's death sentence was sought by petitioner and is afforded by the Eighth and Fourteenth Amendments and by federal law. To accept petitioner's argument would create an irreconcilable conflict between constitutional guarantees and would be a mockery of justice.[29]

In some cases, the courts have attempted to document the mental suffering of the condemned man. Chief Justice Gubbay of the Zimbabwe Supreme Court, in *Catholic Commission for Justice and Peace in Zimbabwe* v. *Attorney-General*, quoted extensively from an affidavit of Admire Mthombeni, who had been sentenced to death in a politically related murder and then pardoned some years later. Mthombeni's evidence was not disputed by the State. Mthombeni said:

> Because you spend so much time in your cell alone you endlessly brood over your fate and it becomes very difficult, and for some people impossible, to cope with it all.
>
> The treatment meted out to you by the warders is very harsh. They are continuously hassling you and chasing you up.
>
> If you make any complaint about anything to do with the condition you run the risk of receiving a beating. One of the warders blows a whistle. Other warders come running and without further ado they start beating you with their baton sticks. The warders are also continuously reminding you of the hanging which awaits you. They continually taunt and torment you about it. For instance, they would ask you

why you are bothering to read when you are going to hang. They also say that you are not fat enough to hang.

The gallows themselves are situated within the condemned section itself. Whilst I was there, people were hanged in 1987 and 1988. Although apparently five people can be hanged at the same time the hanging used to take place in stages. This meant that for the rest of us the agony was prolonged.

In 1987 a total of 11 people were hanged. However, the process went on for about two weeks. Two people were hanged one day. The next day nobody was hanged. The following day another two people were hanged and so it went.

During this period, the warders rattled our doors at 4:00 AM which is the time they remove people from their cells for hanging. The effect was of course that I woke up suddenly terrified that I was about to be hanged. This was just another way in which they tormented us.

When a person was to be taken out for hanging the warders came into his cell in a group. They leg ironed him and handcuffed him. Often, the person to be hanged resisted and the warders then used electric prodders to subdue him. I saw this through the peep-hole in my cell. The warders also told us that they did this.

We heard the sounds of wailing and screaming of those about to be hanged from the time they are removed from their cells at 4:00 AM up to the time they were hanged at about 9:00 AM.

We also heard the sounds of the gallows themselves . . .

The warders often told us detailed and lurid stories about the hangings themselves which they had witnessed. The aim of this was to torture us.

For instance, after one lot of hangings, they told us that the machine did not work properly. As a result, one of those to be hanged called Chitongo did not die. Instead, he somehow managed to get hold of the hangman and would not let go. We were told that the warders eventually had to get a hammer and then they hammered him to death.

On another occasion one of the warders showed one condemned man called Vundla a newspaper showing that he was about to be executed. We were not allowed access to any newspapers. The warder therefore deliberately showed this condemned person the newspaper to torture him.

As a result, Vundla managed to climb up to the window at the top of his small cell and from there he dived on to the floor and killed himself.

Many people could not cope with all this and became mentally disturbed. The warders treated these kind of people even worse than us. For instance, if a mentally disturbed prisoner soiled his cell the warders refused for days to have it cleaned up.[30]

A brief by another death row inmate, Henry Arsenault,[31] was quoted by Justice Liacos of the Massachusetts Supreme Judicial Court in a 1980 judgment:

For over two years, Henry Arsenault "lived on death row feeling as if the Court's sentence were slowly being carried out." Arsenault could not stop thinking about death. Despite several stays, he never believed he could escape execution. "There was a day to day choking, tremulous fear that quickly became suffocating." If he slept at all, fear of death snapped him awake sweating. His throat was clenched so tight he often could not eat. His belly cramped, and he could not move his bowels. He urinated uncontrollably. He could not keep still. And all the while a guard watched him, so he would not commit suicide. The guard was there when he had his nightmares and there when he wet his pants. Arsenault retained neither privacy nor dignity. Apart from the guards he was alone much of the time as the day of his execution neared.

And on the day of the execution, after three sleepless weeks and five days' inability to eat, after a night's pacing the cell, he heard the warden explain the policy of the Commonwealth—no visitors [only members of the prisoner's immediate family were allowed to visit before the execution; Arsenault had no immediate family], no special last meal, and no medication. Arsenault asked the warden to let him walk to the execution on his own. The time came. He walked to the death chamber and turned toward the chair. Stopping him, the warden explained that the execution would not be for over an hour. Arsenault sat on the other side of the room as the witnesses filed in behind a one-way mirror. When the executioner tested the chair, the lights dimmed. Arsenault heard other prisoners scream. After the chaplain gave him last rites, Arsenault heard the door slam shut and the noise echoing, the clock ticking. He wet his pants. Less than half an hour before the execution, the Lieutenant Governor commuted his sentence. Arsenault's legs would not hold him up. Guards carried him back to his cell. He was trembling uncontrollably. A doctor sedated him. And he was moved off death row.[32]

For Justice Liacos, "The raw terror and unabating stress that Henry Arsenault experienced was torture; torture in the guise of civilized business in an advanced and humane polity. This torture was not unique, but merely one degrading instance in a legacy of degradation."[33]

That the threat of death constitutes punishment in itself is perhaps no more vividly demonstrated than in the fact that some condemned individuals renounce all appeals in order to avoid this additional suffering.[34] When Gary Gilmore waived his rights of appeal and literally challenged the authorities in Utah to execute him, Chief Justice Warren Burger spoke of a petition filed by Gilmore's mother in order to block the execution as being "unique in the annals of the Court." (Faced with her son's refusal to act, Gilmore's mother had instituted proceedings on his behalf and contrary to his instructions in the hope of blocking execution.) Actually, Gilmore, who stated that he did not "care to languish in prison for another day,"[35] represents only one of many of those involved in "death wish" cases.[36] In *Townsend* v. *Twomey*, a psychiatric evaluation revealed that the offender "had been subject to the agony of doubt for such a long period of time in prison that he would welcome any conclusion to the daily threat of death, including the death penalty itself, in order to overcome the agony which he experienced."[37] Doris Ann Foster, confined to the Maryland Correctional Institution for Women, claimed that waiting on death row "is ruining my body and eventually would ruin my mind. . . . I have no desire to continue on in such an inhumane existence."[38] Robert Lee Massie sought execution, saying: "Would [Christ] condemn me to a four-by-ten cell year after year, giving me dates of execution, and bringing me from the brink of death each time the sentence was about to be executed? Would He subject me to this kind of mental torment?"[39] Dennis Stanworth sought execution because "it would save me many months of useless existence here on Death Row."[40] In another case, the United States District Court recognized that "the deplorable conditions on death row undoubtedly have had some effect on Smith," who chose not to challenge his death sentence."[41]

Professor Hugo Adam Bedau has argued that this acquiescence in capital punishment constitutes "prima facie evidence of mental disturbance."[42] But it would be wrong to think the prisoner is merely choosing between life and death, because life on death row is a "living death." The United States District Court for Alabama, in an application by the mother of John Louis Evans III attempting to block her son's execution after he had refused to exercise his appellate remedies, observed that "John Evans has confronted his option of life imprisonment or death by execution and has elected to place his bets on a new existence in some world beyond this. The Court finds no evidence of irrationality in this; indeed, in view of the allegations in the case of *Jacobs* v. *Locke*, the [case concerning] death row conditions of confinement case presently pending in this Court, it may well be that John Evans has made the more rational choice."[43] Rational or not, Evans's choice is certainly not an uncommon one.

These matters are sometimes collectively referred to as the "death row phenomenon." The phenomenon appears to have been recognized for many decades, in that executive clemency was often considered when, for whatever reason, sentence of death was not imposed promptly. There was no right to commutation as such, but in a benign gesture of humanitarian sentiment the head of state implicitly admitted that prolonged detention following pronouncement of a sentence of death was simply unacceptable. There are rare indications in the cases that there was some inherent common-law power vested in the courts to stay executions in such circumstances,[44] although there is an absence of real authority on the point in cases where this power was actually exercised. More recently, the death row phenomenon has received judicial recognition. Applying domestic or international norms prohibiting cruel punishment and torture, some tribunals have held that when execution is not carried out with reasonable promptness, then there is a breach of the condemned person's human rights. The remedy for such violation, it is generally held, is commutation of the sentence to one of life imprisonment.

This chapter deals with the death row phenomenon in a general sense. Domestic and international courts have now tackled the matter in a number of cases, many of which make widespread use of comparative and international law. Although general themes emerge, the authorities are far from consistent. Surprisingly, the United States Supreme Court, with its extremely abundant caselaw on virtually all aspects of the death penalty, has yet to pronounce itself on this matter.[45] After a general discussion of the caselaw, I shall consider specific aspects of the problem that continue to vex jurists, such as the length of delay that is acceptable, whether delay must not only be imputable to the authorities but also go beyond what is "normal" under existing procedures, mitigating and aggravating factors, and the acceptability of the conditions of confinement themselves.

HISTORICAL BACKGROUND

One of the first reported cases dealing with the death row phenomenon is that of Caryl Chessman, sentenced to die in the California gas chamber in 1948. As a result of a series of judicial challenges, in 1959 he still had not been executed.[46] Chessman filed a new petition, arguing that the eleven years he had spent on death row constituted mental suffering incompatible with the Eighth Amendment to the United States Constitution. The California Court of Appeal con ceded that Chessman's time in prison was an unusual occurrence, and that mental suffering was inevitably to be expected from such detention.[47] It concluded, however, that the California courts had proceeded with diligence, in good faith, and without unreasonable delay, and that as there has been no violation of due process there was therefore no issue of cruel and unusual punishment caused by the delay. Several years later, in another death row case, the California Supreme Court would note: "[In *Chessman*, w]e recognized that mental suffering undoubtedly attended his detention, indicated that there had not been unreasonable delay by California in the proceedings, and concluded that unconstitutionally cruel or unusual punishment had not been imposed."[48]

In a subsequent appeal, this time through the federal courts, Chessman's arguments impressed the district court judge hearing the application. While agreeing that the judicial remedy must fail, the Court conceded that "extrajudicially speaking, the appeal of the petitioner in this regard is impressive."[49] This obiter dictum, motivated purely by humanitarian concerns, earned the district court judge a reproach from the Ninth Circuit Court of Appeals. It said that the district court judge "turned sideways and suggested that the governor of California and the California Supreme Court should consider this long incarceration as a ground for commutation of sentence."[50] In the opinion of the Ninth Circuit Court of Appeals:

> It may show a basic weakness in our government system that a case like this takes so long, but I do not see how we can offer life (under a death sentence) as a prize for one who can stall the processes for a given number of years, especially when in the end it appears the prisoner never really had any good points. If we did offer such a prize, what year would we use as a cutoff date? I would think that the number of years would have to be objective and arbitrary. But counsel for petitioner suggest that we take a subjective approach on this man's case. We are told of his agonies on death row. True, it would be hell for most people. But here is no ordinary man. In his appearance in court one sees an arrogant, truculent man, the same qualities that Regina and Mary [Chessman's victims] met, spewing vitriol on one person after another. We see an exhibitionist who never before had such opportunities for exhibition. . . . And, I think he has heckled his keepers long enough.[51]

Chessman's case received much international attention, but both the courts and governor of California remained steadfast in their determination to execute, and he was eventually gassed in 1960. There has been speculation that had there been any further delay, even for a matter of weeks, "Chessman's life would almost certainly have been saved, if not on the merits then at least due to a change in personnel of the California Supreme Court."[52]

Another instance of early recognition of the death row phenomenon in the United States is found in a 1971 case before the Alabama Court of Criminal Appeals. Alabama's statue provided that execution must take place in the Kilby Prison, which had been closed and demolished. Brown could not be executed until the legislature had reconvened and designated another place for execution. This had the effect of leaving "a molecular Sword of Damocles suspended to fall *if and whenever*" the legislature amended the statute. The Court refused to conclude that Alabama would designate a new location for execution, and speculated as to whether such a step might constitute a breach of the rules against ex post facto laws and cruel and unusual punishment.[53] In any case, said the Court, "[T]he State of Alabama has (or has not) delayed too long in bringing him to the electric chair. This uncertainty constitutes psychological cruelty. Moreover, it is unusual."[54]

At about the same time, the Supreme Court of California struck down the death penalty, in part because of the death row phenomenon. According to Chief Justice Wright, "The cruelty of capital punishment lies not only in the execution itself and the pain incident thereto, but also in the dehumanizing effects of the lengthy imprisonment prior to execution during which the judicial and administrative procedures essential to due process of law are carried out."[55] Although it had admitted delays were lengthy, the State argued that they were acceptable because they resulted from the assertion of a prisoner's rights. The Court rejected this submission: "An appellant's insistence on receiving the benefits of appellate review of the judgment condemning him to death does not render the lengthy period of impending execution any less torturous or exempt such cruelty from constitutional proscription."[56]

In another early case, *Townsend* v. *Twomey*, the United States District Court acknowledged that a prolonged stay on death row appeared to be unconstitutional. However, it fell back on the dicta of the United States Supreme Court in *Trop* v. *Dulles* that recognized the constitutionality of the death penalty despite the Eighth Amendment, or rather as an exception to it.[57] Yet the issue of the death row phenomenon is quite distinct from that of capital punishment, as such.

The Appellate Division of the High Court of Rhodesia also considered the death row phenomenon in a case heard during the late 1960s. Delay in execution was invoked as an alleged breach of that country's 1961 Constitution, whose cruel treatment and torture provision was modelled on that of article 3 of the European Convention on Human Rights.[58] Although dismissing the application, Chief Justice Beadle recognized that prolonged delay in execution might constitute "inhuman treatment," although he said it could not be deemed "inhuman punishment." The result of this conclusion was of significance with respect to the proposed remedy, for Chief Justice Beadle argued that where "treatment" is inhuman, then the Court must order that such treatment be stopped. And in the case of a prisoner awaiting the gallows, the way to stop the breach would be to accelerate the execution. He wrote: "If during the course of his punishment, a prisoner is subjected to inhuman 'treatment,' he can move the Court for relief and the Court will see that the 'treatment' is stopped, but that does not affect the original 'punishment' which cannot, itself, become tainted with the inhumanity of the 'treatment.' "[59] The chief justice admitted that the condemned inmate was unlikely to be very pleased with his proposed remedy, and that it was "something which no person sentenced to death is ever likely to [request]. Even if, therefore, in certain circumstances, delay may be considered as inhuman treatment, the remedy given an accused who is under sentence of death under s. 60(1) [of the 1961 Rhodesian Constitution] is not one which is likely to be of much value to him, as it gives him no more than the right to ask for the delay to cease."[60]

The Judicial Committee of the Privy Council, still the highest court of appeal for many Commonwealth countries (of which the largest involved is now perhaps New Zealand),[61] examined the death row phenomenon in a series of cases originating in independent Caribbean states. In the first of these, *de Freitas* v. *Benny*, the prisoner had been sentenced to death by the courts of Trinidad and Tobago in August 1972; his constitutional appeal was presented to the Privy Council in May 1975. De Freitas relied on evidence that prior to independence in 1962 the normal period spent in cells before execution was five months. This was, he said, an "unwritten rule of law." Consequently, detention lasting longer than five months was unconstitutional, being a breach of section 2(b) of Trinidad's Constitution, which prohibits the imposition of cruel and unusual treatment or punishment, as well as being contrary to common law.[62] The Privy Council summarily dismissed the application, not even calling upon respondents for argument. It was suggested in *de Freitas* that there is evidence that before independence, the normal period spent in cells prior to execution was five months; that this waiting period has become much longer since independence; and that it has given rise to a new "unwritten rule of law" that is unconstitutional.[63] The Law Lords confessed that they had "difficulty in formulating" the argument based on delay.[64]

Four years later the issue returned to the Privy Council in another Trinidadian case. Appellant Abbott's execution was delayed extensively because of his applications for various forms of review. The Privy Council acknowledged "[t]hat so long a total period should have been allowed to elapse between the passing of a death sentence and its being carried out is . . . greatly to be deplored."[65] Such inordinate delay brings the administration of criminal justice into disrepute among law-abiding citizens, it said.[66] However, "[T]heir Lordships doubt whether it is realistic to suggest that from the point of view of the condemned man himself he would wish to expedite the final decision as to whether he was to die or not if he thought that there was a serious risk that the decision would be unfavorable."[67] Consequently, said Lord Diplock, delay caused by the prisoner's use of different forms of judicial review could never be invoked as evidence of inhumanity. This eliminated from the calculation a full three years of appeals and two years of pardon applications, leaving only a matter of eight months between the filing of Abbott's application for pardon and its dismissal by the president. A delay of eight months, concluded Lord Diplock, could hardly be considered to be offensive to the offender's fundamental human rights.[68]

The Privy Council examined the issue of the death row phenomenon once again in the early 1980s, in *Riley* v. *Attorney-General of Jamaica.*[69] This case applied section 17 of the Jamaican Constitution, for which the model was article 3 of the European Convention on Human Rights.[70] Like much landmark caselaw, *Riley* is now known more for the powerful dissent of Lords Scarman and Brightman than for the majority view, which dismissed the application on what amounts to little more than a technicality in the Jamaican Constitution. Writing for the majority, Lord Bridge of Harwich relied on section 17§2 of that document, which preserved all punishments that were lawful in Jamaica prior to independence from scrutiny under section 17§1, the "inhuman and degrading punishment" provision.[71] He cited burning at the stake as an example of a punishment that would not be saved by section 17§2, because it clearly was beyond the pale of English law in 1960, when Jamaica was decolonized. For this reason, the majority concluded that "the legality of a delayed execution by hanging of a sentence of death lawfully imposed . . . could never have been questioned before independence."[72]

The two dissenting judges ably dismissed the argument based on section 17§2. Lords Scarman and Brightman noted that "what is challenged is not the judicial sentence authorized by pre-existing law, but the exercise by the executive of a power conferred on it by the constitution itself."[73] While conceding "that a period of anguish and suffering is an inevitable consequence of sentence of death,"[74] they insisted that "a prolongation of it beyond the time necessary for appeal and consideration of reprieve is not."[75] Replying, implicitly, to Lord Diplock in *Abbott* (who said, "[W]here there's life, there's hope"),[76] they declared: "And it is no answer to say that the man will struggle to stay alive. In truth, it is this ineradicable human desire which makes prolongation inhuman and degrading."⁷⁷ Then the minority proceeded to elaborate upon the applicable principles in the case of delayed execution. According to Lords Scarman and Brightman:

> Prolonged delay when it arises from factors outside the control of the condemned man can render a decision to carry out the sentence of death an inhuman and degrading punishment. It is, of course, for the applicant for constitutional protection to show that the delay was inordinate, arose from no act of his, and was likely to cause such acute suffering that the infliction of the death penalty would be in the circumstances which had arisen inhuman or degrading.⁷⁸

The majority view in *Riley* stood for slightly more than a decade. Binding on jurisdictions that still recognized Privy Council appeals, it was also a persuasive precedent throughout the common-law world.

A few years after *Riley*, the High Court of Trinidad and Tobago was faced with a new attack on the death row phenomenon. Thomas and Paul were sentenced to death for murder in 1975. Their appeals were dismissed some eighteen months later, and their ultimate application to the Privy Council was rejected in 1981. Constitutional motions impugning the death penalty were not heard until 1984, more than nine years after imposition of the death sentence. Judge Collymore of the High Court of Trinidad and Tobago highlighted a conflict in the dicta of the Privy Council.⁷⁹ He noted that in *Riley* Lord Bridge of Harwich had held that "[w]hatever the reason for, or length of, delay in executing a sentence of death lawfully imposed, the delay can afford no ground for holding the execution to be a contravention of section 17(1)," whereas in *Abbott* Lord Diplock had said that "it is possible to imagine cases in which the time allowed by the authorities to elapse between the pronouncement of a death sentence and notification to the condemned man that it was to be carried out was so prolonged as to arouse in him a reasonable belief that his death sentence must have been commuted to a sentence of life imprisonment."⁸⁰ Judge Collymore attributed the dissent in *Abbott* to the context of the case, namely, a national debate on the death penalty that "would, without a doubt, have raised the hopes of all the prisoners awaiting execution that the possibility existed of the commutation of their sentences."⁸¹

Troubled by *Riley*, and unconstrained by the technical peculiarities of the Jamaican Constitution, Judge Collymore fell back on *Abbott*. According to his reading of that case, "[A]ny protracted and unreasonable incarceration for which a condemned person is not responsible might conceivably give cause for redress, and . . . such a case would involve delay measured in years rather than in months."⁸² In other words, delayed execution could give rise to a remedy, providing it passed a threshold of years and on the further condition that the delay was imputable to the State, and not to the offender.[83] In the matter of Thomas and Paul, Judge Collymore appeared to consider that the delay of four and a half years was constitutionally suspect, but he also concluded that this was not Trinidad's responsibility. On the issue of what he called "appellate delay," that is, delay subsequent to pronouncement of the death sentence, Judge Collymore cited a 1977 judgment of Chief Justice Hyatali of the High Court of Trinidad and Tobago: "My decision in so holding, however, must not be construed or taken as meaning that delay which is manifestly protracted and unreasonable in bringing to trial an accused charged on a non-bailable offence and in disposing his appeals against his conviction to the higher courts of the land, gives him no cause for complaint and no right to claim redress for the period of any protracted and unreasonable incarceration for which he is not responsible."[84]

In a 1992 judgment, the Court of Appeal of the Eastern Caribbean States, on a matter originating in St. Kitts and Nevis, declined an invitation to follow the minority opinion in *Riley*, and considered itself bound by the views of the majority.[85] But like Judge Collymore in *Thomas and Paul*, Justice Matthew relied on *Abbott*, suggesting that he considered excessive delay in execution to be susceptible of giving rise to a constitutional violation. However, as the delay in the case at bar was only one of six to seven months, he too agreed with dismissing the petition.[86] In a 1992 Bahamian case, the Supreme Court similarly refused a suggestion that it adopt the reasoning of Lords Scarman and Brightman in *Riley*, noting that the majority opinion "exploded precisely the very constitutional argument that counsel sought to have me uphold."[87] In that case, the delay was one of two and a half years.

In 1993, the Privy Council reversed its precedents in *Riley* and *Abbott*. It did so, however, under the impulsion of developments on an international level, which it is necessary to examine first. There are three major international petition mechanisms in the area of human rights. Individuals may "appeal" final judgments of domestic courts to the Human Rights Committee pursuant to the International Covenant on Civil and Political Rights and its Optional Protocol,[88] to the European Commission and Court of Human Rights pursuant to the European Convention on Human Rights,[89] and to the Inter-American Commission and Court of Human Rights pursuant to the American Declaration of the Rights and Duties of Man[90] and the American Convention on Human Rights.[91] By the end of the 1980s, all three of these systems had been confronted with cases raising the issue of the death row phenomenon.

The first to face this difficult issue was the Inter-American Commission on Human Rights, in the case of *Pratt* v. *Jamaica*.[92] Earl Pratt had been convicted

in January 1979 of a homicide that took place on October 6, 1977. His appeal
was dismissed in December 1980, but no reasons were given by the Court of
Appeal until September 24, 1984, effectively blocking further recourse to the
Privy Council. Pratt's petition charged that delays in obtaining the Jamaican
Court of Appeal judgment, which he said was a preliminary to any subsequent
application before the Judicial Committee of the Privy Council, violated his
rights under the American Convention on Human Rights. The Inter-American
Commission examined the question from the standpoint of Pratt's due process
rights, rather than as an issue of cruel, inhuman, or degrading treatment. The
commission was sufficiently disturbed by the failure to document the appeal
that on October 14, 1983, it made a special request to the government of Jamaica to this effect. On October 3, 1984, the Inter-American Commission dismissed the petition, noting that "the rules of criminal procedure were observed
and that the plaintiff received a fair trial," that all domestic legal remedies had
been exhausted, and that Pratt had been assisted adequately by legal aid attorneys. Concluding that "the requirements of due process have been fulfilled,"
the commission resolved that there was no evidence of a breach of the Convention, although it urged Jamaica, on humanitarian grounds, to commute the
death sentence and to take legislative steps aimed at abolition.[93]

For obscure reasons, the Inter-American Commission on Human Rights
reopened the case of Pratt, and that of his accomplice Ivan Morgan; on July 9,
1987, it reached the following conclusion:

> Pratt and Morgan suffered a denial of justice during the period 1980–
> 1984 violative of Article 5(2) of the American Convention on Human
> Rights. The Commission found that the fact that the Jamaican Court
> of Appeal issued its decision on December 5, 1980, but did not issue
> the reasons for that decision until four years later, September 24, 1984,
> was tantamount to cruel, inhuman and degrading treatment because
> during that four year delay the petitioners could not appeal to the
> Privy Council and had to suffer four years on death row awaiting
> execution. The Inter-American Commission on Human Rights, pur-
> suant to its cable of July 7, 1987, requests that the execution of Messrs.
> Pratt and Morgan be commuted for humanitarian reasons.[94]

For the commission, then, the fact that the petitioners "had to suffer four years
on death row awaiting execution" was "tantamount to cruel, inhuman and degrading treatment." The views of the commission were issued informally and
have never been published in its annual reports. They came to light only in
1993, when the conclusions were cited in a judgment of the Judicial Committee
of the Privy Council.

Pratt and Morgan also raised the issue before the United Nations Human Rights Committee in a communication filed on January 28, 1986.[95] Following the unfavorable 1984 report of the Inter-American Commission, they had applied for leave to appeal to the Judicial Committee of the Privy Council in London, but that case had yet to be adjudicated.[96] Before the Human Rights Committee, they again alleged unfairness in the trial and inexcusable delay in the proceedings, constituting a breach of articles 6, 7, and 14 of the International Covenant on Civil and Political Rights.[97] The Human Rights Committee took the trouble to note that "although the authors' cases were considered by the Inter-American Commission on Human Rights, they are no longer being examined under another procedure of international investigation or settlement."[98] It is unclear whether the committee was aware that the Inter-American Commission had recognized the "death row phenomenon" and ruled that a four-year wait on death row constituted a breach of the provision in the American Convention on Human Rights prohibiting cruel, inhuman, or degrading treatment.[99]

On April 6, 1989, the Human Rights Committee reached the same conclusion as the Inter-American Commission as to the adequacy of Pratt's legal representation at trial.[100] It also concluded that the delays in the proceedings, and more specifically the time lapse of nearly four years between the decision of the Jamaican Court of Appeal and the issuance of its written reasons, constituted a violation of article 14§3(c) of the Covenant ("the right to be heard within a reasonable time") and that this suggested a breach of article 6 because it was a capital case. Moreover, even though a temporary stay of execution had been granted on February 23, 1988, by the Jamaican authorities, Pratt and Morgan were not notified of this for twenty hours, leaving them in the agony of imminent execution until forty-five minutes before the scheduled hanging. According to the committee, this delay from the time the stay of execution was granted to the time they were removed from their death cell constituted cruel and inhuman treatment within the meaning of article 7.[101] The committee added that such a breach of the Covenant called for commutation of the sentence as a remedy.[102]

By the time the Human Rights Committee reached its decision and issued its views, Pratt and Morgan had been held on Jamaica's death row for nearly ten years. However, the committee concluded that the delay in *Pratt and Morgan's case*, that is, the death row phenomenon, did not constitute cruel, inhuman, and degrading treatment prohibited by article 7 of the Covenant.

The possibility that such a delay as occurred in this case could constitute cruel and inhuman treatment was referred to by the Privy Council. In principle prolonged judicial proceedings do not *per se* constitute cruel, inhuman or degrading treatment even if they can be a source of mental strain for the convicted prisoners. However, the situation could be otherwise in cases involving capital punishment and an assessment of the circumstances of each case would be necessary. In the present case the Committee does not find that the authors have sufficiently substantiated their claim that delay in judicial proceedings constituted for them cruel, inhuman and degrading treatment under article 7.[103]

The committee ought to have been embarrassed by the fact that it took nearly four years to reach its conclusions.[104]

How could the Human Rights Committee find a delay of twenty hours to be offensive, yet a delay of ten years to be acceptable? In its views it noted that "the issue of warrants for execution necessarily causes intense anguish to the individual concerned."[105] What appears to have shocked the committee, however, is not the cruel effect of the execution order but rather the cruel intention of those who stalled for nearly a day before informing Pratt and Morgan of their reprieve. This was cruelty administered with malice and intended only to heighten the suffering of the victim. Implicitly, at any rate, the committee was suggesting that cruelty be viewed from the standpoint of its perpetrator and not of its victim. Pratt and Morgan might well never have learned of the delay in informing them that execution had been postponed. Under such a hypothesis, the two men would presumably have greeted the announcement with enthusiasm, unaware of the cruel behavior of the bearer of good news.

Three months after the views of the Human Rights Committee in the case of Pratt and Morgan were issued, the European Court of Human Rights faced a death row phenomenon argument in a case involving extradition from the United Kingdom to the United States. Jens Soering was charged with murder, in the State of Virginia; when he was apprehended in the United Kingdom, he asked that its government insist upon assurances that he would not be executed if it were to grant extradition. The applicable treaty between London and Washington included a provision, which has become rather customary in such instruments, allowing the requested state to insist upon such an assurance. The United Kingdom did in fact formally ask that the death penalty not be imposed, but Soering considered that the undertaking of the United States was insufficient and decided to pursue the matter in court. However, his motions in habeas corpus before the English courts were unsuccessful.

The European Commission on Human Rights, which handles the first stage of applications under the European Convention on Human Rights,[106] already had an established line of decisions recognizing the application of the

Convention in extradition cases, despite arguments that this gave the treaty an extraterritorial scope.[107] However, it had refused to intervene in an earlier case (involving extradition to California),[108] and the majority felt that it should not depart from this precedent. Nevertheless, by seven votes to four it held there was a violation of article 13 of the Convention (the right to a remedy) because of shortcomings in English law.[109] The case was then submitted to the European Court of Human Rights; in a unanimous judgment issued on July 7, 1989, it granted Jens Soering's application.[110]

Although capital punishment may have been acceptable in 1950, when the European Convention on Human Rights was adopted, views on the issue had evolved to a point where the death penalty could no longer be considered compatible with article 3 of the Convention, which prohibits inhuman and degrading treatment or punishment. For this reason, it was argued, the Court should order the United Kingdom to reject the United States extradition request. This, however, it was not prepared to do. In article 2§1 of the Convention, which enshrines the right to life, the death penalty is recognized as an exception to that right. If it were to comply with such pretensions, the Court would have to give article 3 an aggressively dynamic interpretation and, in effect, disregard article 2§1. The Court considered that this went beyond a mere question of interpretation, and would be tantamount to amending the Convention by judicial means. In this respect, it noted the 1983 adoption of an optional protocol abolishing the death penalty in time of peace[111] as evidence of the intention of the states parties to amend the Convention by subsequent agreement and not to leave this matter to the Court.

However, the Court held that extradition to the United States would violate the Convention because it would expose Soering to the death row phenomenon.[112] Evidence had been led demonstrating that the average stay in Mecklenburg Penitentiary, home to Virginia's death row, was six to eight years. Delay was essentially caused by the time taken for various procedural remedies sought by prisoners. The conditions on death row were shown to be extremely harsh. The Court also identified several mitigating factors in Soering's favor: youth, mental instability, a secondary role in the crime, and Germany's competing request for extradition, which would not expose Soering to capital punishment. Soering was a German citizen, and under that country's law he could be tried even for offenses committed elsewhere.

With the European Court's judgment in *Soering*, the term "death row phenomenon" entered the mainstream of the human rights vocabulary. In the United States, the decision prompted the Senate to insist upon "Soering reservations" to both the Convention Against Torture and Other Cruel, Inhuman and Degrading Treatment or Punishment[113] and the International Covenant on Civil and Political Rights;[114] the reservations were aimed directly at any interpretation of the phrase "cruel, inhuman or degrading treatment or punishment" that might include recognition of the death row phenomenon. The reservation to article 7 of the Covenant declares: "The United States considers itself bound by Article 7 to the extent that 'cruel, inhuman or degrading treatment or punishment' means the cruel and unusual treatment or punishment prohibited by the Fifth, Eighth and/or Fourteenth Amendments to the Constitution of the United States."[115] The United Nations Human Rights Committee has declared this to be an illegal reservation.[116] In the case of the Convention Against Torture, the United States attempted to be even more precise. Not only is there a reservation phrased in terms similar to the text formulated for the Covenant; there is also an "understanding" stating that "international law does not prohibit the death penalty" and that the Convention does not "restrict or prohibit the United States from applying the death penalty consistent with the Fifth, Eighth and/or Fourteenth Amendments to the Constitution of the United States, *including any constitutional period of confinement prior to the imposition of the death penalty.*"[117]

The *Soering* case was soon being cited in other legal systems, where, although it might not have precedential value, it constituted a source of compelling and persuasive authority for recognizing the death row phenomenon. For a few years, however, the European Court appeared to be rather isolated in its position. In September 1991, the Supreme Court of Canada considered *Soering* in two cases involving extradition to the United States.[118] The country's 1976 extradition treaty with the United States provides that the requested state may require assurances that the death penalty will not be imposed before complying with an application to return fugitives.[119] In the matters of Joseph Kindler and Charles Ng, the Canadian minister of justice decided not to seek such assurances. Before escaping custody in the United States, Kindler had been sentenced to death by a Pennsylvania jury. (His appeals had not been fully exhausted at the time of his escape.) Ng had fled California before being charged; he was arrested in Calgary for shoplifting. Both cases involved brutal murders, and neither fugitive could lay claim to significant mitigating factors that might arouse the sympathy of bureaucrats, judges, or jurors.

Both Kindler and Ng argued that the justice minister's refusal to exercise what was a discretionary power, namely, a request for assurances under article 6 of the extradition treaty, breached their fundamental rights under the Canadian Charter of Rights and Freedoms.[120] Their claims pointed specifically to section 12, which protects individuals from "cruel and unusual treatment or punishment," and to section 7, which guarantees that no person shall be deprived of "life, liberty and security of the person . . . except in accordance with the principles of fundamental justice." In a four-to-three decision, the Supreme Court of Canada dismissed the applications. The minority relied on *Soering* in support of its conclusions. The majority, in reasons drafted by Justice G. La Forest, took the view that *Soering* was distinguishable: "Apart from torture, the nature of the offence, the age or mental capacity of the accused (see the Soering case . . .), and other circumstances may constitutionally vitiate an order for surrender. No such considerations are raised in this case, however."[121] Justice La Forest was embarrassed by an earlier judgment he had signed holding that extradition to a country where torture was threatened would constitute a violation of the Charter.[122] Here too, however, a distinction was made between torture and the death penalty. In Canada, therefore, it is illegal to extradite an individual to a state where electric shock treatments may be imposed—unless this is done in the electric chair with an intent to kill.

Soering fared no better before the Human Rights Committee, which had of course already taken a position on the question, in *Pratt and Morgan* v. *Jamaica*,[123] refusing to consider the death row phenomenon as a breach of the prohibition of cruel, inhuman, and degrading punishment. Its views in another Jamaican case raising similar issues, that of Barrett and Sutcliffe, were issued in 1992, more than two years after the European Court's judgment in *Soering*. In addition to beatings the pair had suffered while in detention,[124] it was claimed that their thirteen-year wait on death row constituted cruel, inhuman, and degrading treatment within the meaning of article 7 of the International Covenant. Counsel argued that "the execution of a sentence of death after a long period of time is widely recognized as cruel, inhuman and degrading, on account of the prolonged and extreme anguish caused to the condemned man by the delay."[125] The Human Rights Committee answered:

> [P]rolonged judicial proceedings do not *per se* constitute cruel, inhuman and degrading treatment, even if they may be a source of mental strain and tension for detained persons. This also applies to appeal and review proceedings in cases involving capital punishment, although an assessment of the particular circumstances of each case would be called for. In States whose judicial system provides for a review of criminal convictions and sentences, an element of delay between the lawful imposition of a sentence of death and the exhaustion of available remedies is inherent in the review of the sentence; thus, even prolonged periods of detention under a severe custodial regime on death row cannot generally be considered to constitute cruel, inhuman or degrading treatment if the convicted person is merely availing himself of appellate remedies. A delay of ten years between the judgment of the Court of

Appeal and that of the Judicial Committee of the Privy Council is disturbingly long. However, the evidence before the Committee indicates that the Court of Appeal rapidly produced its written judgment and that the ensuing delay in petitioning the Judicial Committee is largely attributable to the authors.[126]

The views of the majority of the Human Rights Committee in *Barrett and Sutcliffe* were challenged by Christine Chanet, a committee member, in an individual opinion. Chanet refused to accept the blame being placed on the two prisoners for the length of their detention on death row. "The conduct of the person concerned with regard to the exercise of remedies ought to be measured against the stakes involved," she wrote. "Without being at all cynical, I consider that the author cannot be expected to hurry up in making appeals so that he can be executed more rapidly." Chanet said she found support for her views in the decision of the European Court of Human Rights in *Soering* v. *United Kingdom*, which noted that it was "equally part of human nature that the person will cling to life by exploiting those safeguards to the full."[127] She concluded: "A very long period on death row, even if partially due to the failure of the condemned prisoner to exercise a remedy, cannot exonerate the State party from its obligations under article 7 of the *Covenant*."[128]

The issue arose again in 1993, when the Human Rights Committee considered the application of Joseph Kindler, following dismissal of his case by the Supreme Court of Canada.[129] By this time Kindler was back in Pennsylvania, because Minister of Justice Kim Campbell had chosen to defy a request, made by the committee's special rapporteur,[130] to stay the extradition pending consideration of the petition. On July 31, 1992, the committee ruled Kindler's communication partially admissible, with respect to grievances founded on articles 6 and 7 of the Covenant;[131] on July 30, 1993, it concluded on the merits that there was no breach of these norms.[132] Five of the eighteen members wrote individual dissenting opinions, evidence of the increasing difficulty the committee was having with cases concerning capital punishment in general.

With respect to article 7, the Human Rights Committee recalled its earlier jurisprudence, where it held that "prolonged periods of detention under a severe custodial regime on death row cannot generally be considered to constitute cruel, inhuman or degrading treatment if the person is merely availing himself of appellate remedies."[133] It noted that it had paid "careful regard" to the *Soering* decision of the European Court of Human Rights, but stressed the many distinctions between the two cases, particularly the age and mental state of the offenders and the prison conditions in Pennsylvania. Taking a view not unlike that of Justice La Forest of the Supreme Court of Canada, the committee stated that "important facts leading to the judgment of the European Court are distinguishable on material points from the facts in the present case."[134] Kindler's attorney had not led any evidence before the committee on the issue of prison conditions,[135] nor about the specific method of execution in Pennsylvania, which was by then lethal injection.[136] Kindler, who is white, had also raised the possibility that the death penalty was imposed in the United States in a racist manner, but he had failed to substantiate how such bias affected him personally.[137]

Kurt Herndl and Waleed Sadi penned one of the individual opinions that were annexed to the committee's views in the *Kindler* case. Herndl and Sadi said they agreed with the Human Rights Committee's established jurisprudence, whereby "the so-called 'death row phenomenon' does not *per se* constitute cruel, inhuman and degrading treatment, even if prolonged judicial proceedings can be a source of mental strain for the convicted prisoners."[138] The two members added that the prolonged periods of detention were the result of the offender's recourse to appeal remedies.[139] Five members dissented from the committee's views. Bertil Wennergren, in his individual opinion, did not address the issue of the "death row phenomenon." He considered that the Covenant simply did not allow a state, such as Canada, that had already abolished the death penalty to reintroduce it indirectly by cooperating in its implementation by another state.[140] Similar views were expressed by the dissenting members Rajsoomer Lallah, Fausto Pocar, Christine Chanet, and Francisco José Aguilar Urbina. Both Pocar and Aguilar Urbina noted that they agreed with the committee on the subject of article 7, that is, on the relatively conservative approach to the death row phenomenon.[141]

But other courts were soon to take a larger view of *Soering*. In March 1993 Zimbabwe's minister of justice, legal, and parliamentary affairs announced that four individuals who had been on death row for approximately five years were soon to be executed. Within days, a petition lodged on behalf of the condemned men by a local religious organization, the Catholic Commission for Justice and Peace in Zimbabwe, was presented to the country's supreme court. In an eloquent judgment, Chief Justice Gubbay granted the application, relying heavily on the European Court's ruling in *Soering* and on Christine Chanet's dissenting reasons in *Barrett and Sutcliffe*, and expressly disapproving of the views of Justice La Forest of the Supreme Court of Canada in *Kindler*.[142] The legal basis for the application was section 15(1) of the Zimbabwe Constitution, a provision that had been derived from article 3 of the European Convention on Human Rights. Chief Justice Gubbay spoke of the "impressive judicial and academic consensus concerning the death row phenomenon,"[143] referring at a number of points in his judgment to the "demeaning" or "harsh" conditions of deten-tion:[144]

> From the moment he enters the condemned cell, the prisoner is en-meshed in a dehumanizing environment of near hopelessness. He is in a place where the sole object is to preserve his life so that he may be executed. The condemned prisoner is "the living dead."[145]

Unfortunately, the judgment provoked a vigorous riposte from Zimbab-we's legislature, and a constitutional amendment to neutralize its effects was adopted in a matter of months: "Delay in execution of a sentence of death, imposed upon a person in respect of a criminal offence of which he has not been convicted, shall not be held to be a contravention" of the provision prohib-iting cruel, inhuman, and degrading treatment or punishment.[146] But Zimbab-we's Supreme Court has not let the matter lie, and in a judgment subsequent to the constitutional amendment Chief Justice Gubbay held the latter to be inapplicable, at least with respect to persons sentenced to death before the amendment came into force.[147]

In the *Catholic Commission* case the chief justice also analyzed the state of the law in India, where there had been several ostensibly contradictory cases concerning the death row phenomenon during the 1980s. In 1983, a bench of the Indian Supreme Court, in *Vatheeswaran* v. *State of Tamil Nadu*, granted a stay in a case where delay had been only two years.[148] Writing for the Court, Justice Chinnappa Reddy concluded that "the cause of the delay is immaterial when the sentence is death. Be the cause for the delay, the time necessary for appeal and consideration of reprieve or some other cause for which the accused him-self may be responsible, it would not alter the dehumanizing character of the delay."[149] In *Vatheeswaran*, the Court referred to the right to a speedy trial, which is implicit in the right to life and liberty (article 21 of the Constitution), according to the established jurisprudence in India's courts.[150] The implication, at any rate, is that the speedy trial continues until the execution of the sentence, and that this right has been breached. Even though the Indian Constitution does not contain a provision dealing with cruel punishment and torture, this norm has been incorporated into the document by judicial interpretation.[151] "True our Constitution [India] has no 'due process' clause or the VIII Amend-ment," said the Indian Supreme Court in a 1979 judgment. "[B]ut in this branch of law . . . the consequence is the same. For what is punitively outra-geous, scandalizingly unusual or cruel and rehabilitatively counter-productive, is arguably unreasonable and arbitrary."[152]

The threshold of two years' delay was promptly repudiated by three judges of the same court in *Sher Singh*,[153] although the principles elaborated in

Vatheeswaran finding a breach of the Constitution where there was a prolonged wait prior to execution remained unchallenged.[154] Chief Justice Chandrachud disagreed with Justice Chinnappa Reddy about the length of the delay: "[N]o hard and fast rule can be laid down as our learned Brethren have done that 'delay exceeding two years in the execution of a sentence of death should be considered sufficient to entitle the person under sentence of death to invoke Art. 21.' "[155] He said the "two-year rule" was not consistent with the practice of the courts and the usual time that it takes to exhaust appeals; no absolute rule should be laid down, and several other factors should be taken into account. However, on the principles set out in *Vatheeswaran* concerning the death row phenomenon, Chief Justice Chandrachud was in full agreement. He suggested that there is some inherent or common-law basis for a stay of execution pursuant to the death row phenomenon; subsidiarily, he founded it on the due process guarantee of the Constitution:

> A prisoner who has experienced living death for years on end is therefore entitled to invoke the jurisdiction of this Court for examining the question whether, after all the agony and torment he has been subjected to, it is just and fair to allow the sentence of death to be executed. That is the true implication of Art. 21 of the Constitution and to that extent, we express our broad and respectful agreement with our learned Brethren [in *Vatheeswaran*] in their visualization of the meaning of that article. . . . The essence of the matter is that all procedure, no matter what the stage, must be fair, just and reasonable. It is well-established that a prisoner cannot be tortured or subjected to unfair or inhuman treatment. . . . It is a logical extension of the self-same principle that the death sentence, even if justifiably imposed, cannot be executed if supervening events make its execution harsh, unjust or unfair.[156]

Justice Chinnappa Reddy returned to the issue in *Javed Ahmed*, observing that sentence of death had been pending for two years and nine months, although the case was actually decided on other grounds.[157] He did not consider that he had been overruled by *Sher Singh*, because it "may be inappropriate" for one bench to overrule another.[158] Justice Chinnappa Reddy observed that Chief Justice Chandrachud, who drafted the judgment in *Sher Singh*, "while expressing almost complete agreement with most of what had been said in *Vatheeswaran*, dissented from the opinion expressed therein that a delay of two years and more was sufficient to entitle a person under sentence of death to invoke Art. 21 of the Constitution."[159] Justice Chinnappa Reddy also noted that the delay occurred not in the High Court but in the Supreme Court, and that surely, our inability to devise a procedure to deal expeditiously with such matters of life and death can be no justification for silencing what the learned Chief Justice has himself so eloquently described as "the voice of justice and fair play which demands that 'so long as life lasts, so long shall it be the duty and endeavor of this Court to give to the provisions of our Constitution a meaning which will prevent human suffering and degradation.' "[160]

Subsequently, in 1987, a high court judgment followed Justice Chinnappa Reddy's pronouncements in *Vatheeswaran/Javed Ahmed.* Appeal and review having taken three years, the sentence was commuted to life.[161]

Then, in 1989, the Supreme Court of India concluded that "the only delay which could be considered in a writ petition was from the date the judgment of the apex Court was pronounced."[162] In other words, delay began after the exhaustion of all regular appeal avenues, not upon pronouncement of sentence of death at the conclusion of the trial. One scholar has noted that the somewhat more restrained view of the Indian courts on this subject may have been due to the aftershocks of the trials of the assassins of Prime Minister Indira Gandhi.[163] One member of the bench, Justice Shetty, would have allowed the sentencing court to take account of excessive delay in trial,[164] and there is some suggestion that the Indian courts are now endeavoring to temper the harshness of the decision in *Triveniben.*[165]

In November 1993 the Judicial Committee of the Privy Council revisited the issue of the death row phenomenon.[166] The committee sat as a panel of seven, the first time it had done so since the late 1940s. Oral argument lasted three weeks, an extraordinarily long time for any appellate court. The applicants were once again Pratt and Morgan, by then on Jamaica's death row for more than fourteen years. Writing on behalf of the entire bench, Lord Griffiths reversed Lord Diplock in *Abbott,*[167] who had stated that delay imputable to the prisoner could never be grounds for relief. Instead, he expressly adopted the views of the minority in *Riley,*[168] concluding that a prolonged wait for execution, in and of itself, constitutes inhuman treatment. The error of the majority in *Riley,* said the committee, was in construing section 17§2 of the Jamaican Constitution, which specified that punishment that was lawful at the time the country gained independence was deemed consistent with the protection against inhuman treatment or punishment. But, said the Lords, although the death penalty by hanging may well have been lawful and therefore not subject to constitutional attack, a prolonged wait for execution was not, and it could never be sheltered by the provision. The only exceptions would be where execution is delayed because an inmate escapes[169] or employs frivolous appeal procedures in bad faith.[170] On this point, Lord Griffiths said that the majority in *Riley* was wrong to suggest there was no possibility of contesting a long-delayed execution before Jamaican independence. He said the Lords "are satisfied that such an execution could have been stayed as an abuse of process."[171] This remarkable conclusion implies that the death row phenomenon is part of the common law.[172]

"[I]n any case in which execution is to take place more than five years after sentence there will be strong grounds for believing that the delay is such as to constitute 'inhuman or degrading punishment or other treatment,' " concluded the Lords.[173] The reasoning of the Judicial Committee of the Privy Council was eloquent but uncomplicated:

> There is an instinctive revulsion against the prospect of hanging a man after he has been held under sentence of death for many years. What gives rise to this instinctive revulsion? The answer can only be our humanity; we regard it as an inhuman act to keep a man facing the agony of execution over a long extended period of time.[174]

Unfortunately, however, the committee provides no real guidance to the interpretation of the norm. It fails to indicate whether the death row phenomenon constitutes "torture," or whether it is "inhuman" or "degrading."[175]

In fixing an outer limit of five years, the Judicial Committee assessed the time necessary for appeal, petition to the committee, and communication to international human rights organs like the Human Rights Committee and the Inter-American Commission on Human Rights. With respect to such international bodies the committee, although admitting that their conclusions were nonbinding, nonetheless noted that "the wisdom of their deliberations" will be of "benefit" to domestic courts and governments.[176] In a case subsequent to *Pratt*, the Judicial Committee of the Privy Council has reiterated the importance of proceedings before such international bodies: "Their Lordships consider that it would be wrong in principle to exclude altogether any time taken to pursue such petitions. The acceptance of international conventions on human rights has been an important development since the Second World War and where a right of individual petition has been granted, the time taken to process it cannot possibly be excluded from the overall computation of time between sentence and intended execution."[177]

Referring to the European Court's 1989 judgment in *Soering*, the Lords observed that it stands for the unacceptability of prolonged delay on death row, making no mention of the mitigating factors in Soering's case upon which the Human Rights Committee and the Supreme Court of Canada had focussed.[178] The Lords are clear in their conclusion that delay occasioned by legitimate resort of a prisoner to appellate procedures, including international remedies, should in no way be imputed to the accused, and they expressly disagree with judgments of the United States and Canadian courts that hold the contrary.[179]

The Judicial Committee of the Privy Council's finding in *Pratt* has thus strengthened the impact of the European Court's judgment in *Soering*. Not only does it provide a new authority supportive of *Soering*, it helps to clarify the issue of "mitigating factors" which had suggested that *Soering* might be only an isolated decision based on a rather special set of facts. *Pratt and Morgan* may prove to be particularly compelling in courts of common-law tradition, steeped as they are in respect for the findings of "their Lordships" even where Privy Council appeals no longer obtain.[180] The 1990s have seen at least three examples of this. In September 1994, the Supreme Court of Nigeria examined an application alleging excessive delay on death row. Although the Court dismissed the petition for procedural reasons, one of its members had clearly been influenced by the judgment of the Privy Council. According to Justice Ogwuegbu: "Since capital punishment is part of our law, persons charged with capital offences and indeed all criminal cases are entitled to trial and appeal without delay. The Executive and judicial authorities must accept the responsibility of ensuring that execution follows as swiftly as practicable after sentence, allowing reasonable time for appeal and consideration of reprieve."[181] Although the case before it did not directly concern the death row phenomenon, the Constitutional Court of South Africa, in its June 1995 judgment, also considered the significance of the Privy Council's decision in *Pratt and Morgan*. Acting Justice Sydney Kentridge said that "[t]he 'death row' phenomenon as a factor in the cruelty of capital punishment has been eloquently described by Lord Griffiths in *Pratt* . . . [as a case] of inordinately extended delay in the carrying out of the death sentence; but the mental agony of the criminal, in its alternation of fear, hope and despair must be present even when the time between sentence and execution is measured in months or weeks rather than years."[182] Even the rather conservative United States Supreme Court does not seem to be entirely unmoved by the Privy Council decision. In March 1995, it considered the admissibility of an application for judicial review in a case where a prisoner had waited seventeen years on death row. In staying Clarence Lackey's execution and sending the case back to the district court for habeas corpus proceedings, Justice John Paul Stevens called the question "novel" but "not without foundation." He described the claim that this violated the Eighth Amendment to the Constitution as "arguable," because execution after prolonged detention might no longer satisfy the grounds justifying use of the death penalty that had been recognized by the Court in *Gregg* v. *Georgia*,[183] namely, deterrence and retribution. "Such a delay, if it ever occurred, certainly would have been rare in 1789, and thus the practice of the Framers would not justify a denial of petitioner's claim," said Justice Stevens. "Moreover, after such an extended time, the acceptable state interest in retribution has arguably been satisfied by the severe punishment already inflicted." Citing *Pratt,* Justice Stevens also observed that "the highest courts in other countries have found arguments such as petitioner's to be persuasive."[184]

In his memorandum in *Lackey,* Justice Stevens referred to a century-old precedent of the United States Supreme Court. In *Medley,*[185] the Court held that a solitary-confinement regime that came into force after conviction constituted an additional punishment and was thus ex post facto legislation. According to the *Medley* decision of 1890, uncertainty as to time of execution creates such mental anxiety that it amounts to a great increase in punishment: "[W]hen a prisoner sentenced by a court to death is confined in a penitentiary awaiting the execution of the sentence, one of the most horrible feelings to which he can be subjected during that time is the uncertainty during the whole of it . . . as to the precise time when his execution shall take place."[186] According to Justice Stevens: "If the Court accurately described the effect of uncertainty in *Medley,* which involved a period of four weeks, see *ibid.,* that description should apply with even greater force in the case of delays that last for many years. Finally, the additional deterrent effect from an actual execution now, on the one hand, as compared to seventeen years on death row followed by the prisoner's continued incarceration for life, on the other, seems minimal."[187] Justice Stevens's reasons were endorsed by Justice Stephen Breyer, and subsequently appear to have obtained the approval of the entire Court, which entered a stay of Clarence Lackey's execution pending consideration by the district court of his petition for a writ of habeas corpus.[188]

Since Justice Stevens's memorandum, *Lackey* appears to have foundered in the lower courts, and it seems unlikely that the Supreme Court will address the merits of the death row phenomenon in that case. Indeed, the initial reaction to *Lackey* by the courts of appeal has been far from enthusiastic. Although the Court of Appeals for the Tenth Circuit took note of the case, it dismissed an application based on a fifteen-year wait on death row, noting that Justice Stevens's views "do not constitute an endorsement of the legal theory, which has never commanded an affirmative statement by any justice, let alone a majority of the Court."[189] The Ninth Circuit Court of Appeals dismissed another such claim: "[W]e read the Supreme Court's laconic stay in *Lackey* as an indication that the justices wish to see the matter explored in cases where it is properly raised, not as a ruling that stays must be entered in all cases raising *Lackey* claims in disregard of all other equitable considerations. . . . Without more explicit guidance, we cannot conclude that the Supreme Court intends to halt virtually all executions in this country for the many months, perhaps years, it will take for the issue to be fully explored and resolved."[190] In the same case Justice Norris, in dissent, referred to *Lackey* and to the precedents in international and comparative law, concluding that "it is simply beyond dispute that McKenzie's Eighth Amendment claim is substantial, important, and deserving of careful and thoughtful adjudication."[191] However, the delays in the United States system are extraordinarily long, and getting longer. Clarence Lackey's seventeen-year wait is not exceptional but typical. It is only a matter of time before the United States Supreme Court must wrestle with the reasoning of *Pratt and Morgan*, *Soering*, and *Catholic Commission*.

The Human Rights Committee, which had differed quite markedly with the European Court of Human Rights, also appears to be softening its position since the Privy Council decision in *Pratt*. In December 1994, in *Cox* v. *Canada*, the committee declared that the "state party must ensure that the possibilities for appeal are made available to the condemned prisoner within a reasonable time."[192] The individual concurring opinion of committee members Kurt Herndl and Waleed Sadi suggests the impact of *Pratt and Morgan:*

> We further believe that imposing rigid time limits for the conclusion of all appeals and requests for clemency is dangerous and may actually work against the person on death row by accelerating the execution of the sentence of death. It is generally in the interest of the petitioner to remain alive for as long as possible. Indeed, while avenues of appeal remain open, there is hope, and most petitioners will avail themselves of these possibilities, even if doing so entails continued uncertainty. This is a dilemma inherent in the administration of justice within all those societies that have not yet abolished capital punishment.[193]

Another member, Bertil Wennergren, also appeared to be influenced by the Privy Council judgment in *Pratt and Morgan:*

> The Committee has been informed that no individual has been executed in Pennsylvania for over twenty years. According to information available to the Committee, condemned prisoners are held segregated from other prisoners. While they may enjoy some particular facilities, such as bigger cells, access to radio and television sets of their own, they are nonetheless confined to death row awaiting execution for years. And this *not* because they avail themselves of all types of judicial appellate remedies, but because the State party does not consider it appropriate, for the time being, to proceed with the execution. If the State party considers it necessary, for policy reasons, to have resort to

the death penalty as such but not necessary and not even opportune to carry out capital sentences, a condemned person's confinement to death row should, in my opinion, last for as short a period as possible, with commutation of the death sentence to life imprisonment taking place as early as possible. A stay for a prolonged and indefinite period of time on death row, in conditions of particular isolation and under the threat of execution which might by unforeseeable changes in policy become real, is not, in my opinion, compatible with the requirements of article 7, because of the unreasonable mental stress that this implies.[194]

Tamar Bam also cited the psychological harm done to the offender on death row. He referred to "an ever increasing fear which gradually fills the mind of the sentenced individual, and which, by the very nature of the situation, amounts—depending on the length of time spent on death row—to cruel, inhuman and degrading treatment, in spite of every measure taken to improve the physical conditions of the confinement."[195]

That there is an evolution in the Human Rights Committee's thinking became more apparent in a Jamaican decision, issued in the summer of 1995. The committee concluded in *Francis* v. *Jamaica*, that a thirteen-year delay by the Court of Appeal in issuing a written judgment was, of course, attributable to the state party. "Whereas the psychological tension created by prolonged detention on death row may affect persons in different degrees, the evidence before the Committee in this case, including the author's confused and incoherent correspondence with the Committee, indicates that his mental health seriously deteriorated during incarceration on death row," the body observed. It found that there had been a violation of article 7 in this case, taking special note of Francis's description of prison conditions, of abusive treatment by prison guards, and the ridicule and strain involved in a five-day stay in the death cell in 1988.[196]

More so than perhaps any other issue, the death row phenomenon has generated a tremendous synergy among international and domestic courts. Although *stare decisis* is of course inapplicable, it is evident that these courts accord great credit to each other's opinions.

HOW LONG IS TOO LONG?

In *Pratt and Morgan*, the Judicial Committee of the Privy Council suggested that five years on death row was excessive, although it stopped slightly short of imposing this as an immutable rule. According to Lord Griffiths, "[I]n any case in which execution is to take place more than five years after sentence there will be strong grounds for believing that the delay is such as to constitute 'inhuman or degrading punishment or other treatment.' "[197] Pratt and Morgan had been held on death row for fourteen years; the Court noted that twenty-three prisoners had been awaiting execution in Jamaica for at least ten years, and another eighty-two had been under sentence of death for at least five years.[198] In *Riley*, the five applicants had been waiting for between six and seven years when their case was heard by the Privy Council; for the dissenters, this was too long.[199] Some judges of the Supreme Court of India have taken a more rigorous view, holding delay of even two years to be unacceptable;[200] in other cases, they set the limit at two and a half years[201] and at three and a half years.[202] But two years was felt to be too extreme by some of their colleagues who, while not challenging the fact that in some cases two years might be offensive, resisted adopting a "hard and fast rule."[203] The cases before the Zimbabwe Supreme Court, when it granted petitions based on delay in execution, were between fifty-four and seventy-two months.[204] For the European Court of Human Rights, the delay that threatened Jens Soering would be, on average, between six and eight years.[205]

In *de Freitas* v. *Benny*, the applicant argued that, because before Trinidad's independence the time between sentence and execution averaged five months, an execution that involved a lengthier delay was open to attack as cruel and unusual punishment. Commenting upon the case, Lord Griffiths in *Pratt* noted that "the argument and the extent of the delay are so different from the present appeal that their Lordships are unable to gain any assistance from this decision."[206] In *de Freitas*, the delay was considerably longer than five months, in fact approaching three years. Yet even petitioner de Freitas did not attempt to argue that most of this delay was relevant, as he did not question the pretension that delay caused by his own appeals was irrelevant. This is, according to the Privy Council in *Pratt*, not the case. Lord Griffiths's discussion of *de Freitas* is rather careful, and it does not lead to the conclusion that prima facie a delay of months rather than years, and certainly a delay of less than five years, is not subject to judicial scrutiny. The remarks of Acting Justice Kentridge, in the 1995 South African case, are germane in this context. He said that even delay measured "in months or weeks rather than years"[207] could be unacceptable. And Justice Liacos, of the Massachusetts Supreme Judicial Court, said: "My argument that the ordeal imposed on the condemned is cruel and unusual punishment does not depend on the existence of lengthy delays between sentence and execution. Two months—or for that matter one day—of torture offends the constitution."[208]

Following the Privy Council's decision in *Pratt and Morgan*, death sentences were commuted in Jamaica and in Trinidad and Tobago, complying with the five-year rule. In a 1994 case falling only months short of five years, a Trinidadian petitioner challenged the executive's decision to proceed with his execution. The Supreme Court of Trinidad and Tobago indicated that public opinion was dissatisfied with the Privy Council's decision, and went on to state:

> When the highest court of the land imposes a time limit on due process and as a result some fifty three murderers have their sentences commuted to life imprisonment those very citizens have every right to expect that where there has been compliance with the time limit imposed contrary to their wishes . . . , they now expect that the condemned man will be executed as swiftly as possible. To become embroiled in semantics, whether four years and five months is the equivalent to five years or that the time is so close that it satisfies the limitation, is to *play* with the enforcement of the law. In this court's view the period in question cannot be considered unreasonable or inordinate and certainly not enough to be considered a breach of the right in question.[209]

In a post-*Pratt* case originating from the Bahamas Court of Appeal, the Privy Council refused to lower the five-year limit. The applicant had spent four and a half years on death row, and the council described his attempts to invoke *Pratt* in order to obtain a stay of execution as being "hopeless."[210]

However, in a November 1995 judgment, *Guerra* v. *Baptiste*, the Judicial Committee of the Privy Council refined the conclusions it had reached in *Pratt and Morgan* with respect to length of delay, and considerably enlarged their scope. Guerra's delay amounted to four years and ten months. Lord Goff of Chieveley noted that in the council's view, "no fixed time is specified for the period within which execution would take place after conviction and sentence. On the contrary, the period is to be ascertained by reference to the requirement that execution should follow as swiftly as practicable after sentence, allowing a reasonable time for appeal and consideration of reprieve."[211] Lord Goff added that:

> If capital punishment is to be carried out it must be carried out "with all possible expedition." It is in this sense that a "reasonable time" for appeal is to be understood. In the assessment of such reasonable time, great importance must be attached to ensuring that, consonant with the tradition of the common law and the recognition of the inhumanity involved in prolonging the period awaiting execution in a condemned cell on death row, such delay will not occur and any delay which does occur will be curtailed."[212]

His Lordship proceeded to examine the actual period of delay and compare it with what he called "realistic targets." In Guerra's case, the period of four years and ten months that had elapsed between sentencing and exhaustion of domestic remedies should have taken only two years. Lord Goff also objected to the four-year period between sentencing and appeal judgment, which should have taken twelve months. His conclusion was that "there has been a substantial and unjustifiable period of delay in the disposal of the appellant's appeal, a period which in all probability exceeds three years."[213] In conclusion, Guerra had suffered cruel and unusual punishment, contrary to the constitution of Trinidad and Tobago.

But what are the factors that assist in determining the length of acceptable delay and the threshold where it crosses into the realm of illegality? Most of the reported judgments are silent on this point. In *Soering*, for example, the European Court of Human Rights made no effort whatsoever to determine the length of acceptable delay, or to suggest the factors that may assist in making such a determination.[214] The few examples where this exercise has been undertaken attempt to estimate the length of delays that are "normal," given the historical functioning of the system.

Lord Griffiths, in *Pratt and Morgan*, described English practice with respect to delays of execution. An English statute of the eighteenth century specified "that all persons convicted of murder should be executed on the next day but one after sentence, unless convicted on Friday in which case they were to be executed on Monday and kept in solitary confinement upon bread and water until executed."[215] Somewhat later, the practice was for the sheriff to fix a date of execution in the fourth week after the death sentence was passed.[216] In Scotland, the date of execution was set by the court and varied from fifteen to twenty-seven days after sentencing, depending on the location. An appeal in such cases was heard within three weeks of the verdict; if the appeal was dismissed, an execution date was set within fourteen to eighteen days, so as to provide for time to examine the possibility of commutation.[217] According to the United Kingdom's Royal Commission on Capital Punishment, the average delay between imposition of sentence and execution in 1950 was six weeks if there was an appeal and three weeks if there was not. In *Pratt*, Lord Griffiths related a 1947 case from the Gold Coast, where an individual sentenced to death for murder had been awaiting execution for two years.[218] The case was sufficiently shocking to provoke a debate in Parliament, and the colonial secretary undertook to adopt a rule that would prevent recurrence of such a situation. At the time, Winston Churchill stated that "people ought not to be brought up to execution, or believe that they are to be executed, time after time whether innocent or guilty, however it may be, whatever their crime. That is a wrong thing."[219]

The Privy Council, in *Pratt*, examined the "normal" period of time for the various judicial and extrajudicial remedies, coming to the conclusion that this should not take more than five years. According to Lord Griffiths, once a death sentence is imposed, an appeal should be heard within a period of twelve months. A further appeal to the Jamaican Privy Council ought to take no longer than another twelve months. He remarked: "Their Lordships do not purport to set down any rigid timetable but to indicate what appear to them to be realistic targets which, if achieved, would entail very much shorter delay than has occurred in recent cases and could not be considered to involve inhuman or degrading punishment or other treatment."[220] Any subsequent recourse to the Judicial Committee of the Privy Council would of course be treated with dispatch. Note that Lord Griffiths, in determining that two years should be sufficient for exercise of all domestic remedies, came rather close to the conclusion of Justice Chinnappa Reddy in *Vatheeswaran*,[221] the Indian case that provoked so much controversy because of the heavy onus it put on the state to expedite appellate procedures.

But even upon exhaustion of all domestic remedies, there is still the issue of applications to international bodies like the Human Rights Committee and the Inter-American Commission on Human Rights. Unlike remedies of international tribunals such as the Inter-American Court of Human Rights or the European Court of Human Rights, the views or reports of these bodies are not binding. Jamaica could well have recognized the jurisdiction of the Inter-American Court, but chose not to do so. Yet the Privy Council insists upon the importance of these extrajudicial remedies: "Their Lordships wish to say nothing to discourage Jamaica from continuing its membership of these bodies and from benefiting from the wisdom of their deliberations."[222] Consequently, to the two years it has allowed for domestic appeals, the Privy Council is prepared to admit another eighteen months or so for applications to the Human Rights Committee and the Inter-American Commission. This is surely wishful thinking, because these international bodies, understaffed and underfunded, are hardly known for their celerity. Perhaps the importance that the Privy Council attributes to their functions may help to alleviate such problems.

In *Catholic Commission*, Chief Justice Gubbay of the Supreme Court of Zimbabwe said that "[i]n the making of a value judgment regard is to be had, *inter alia*, to how the periods of delay from sentence to the proposed dates of execution compare with the average delays over those years from 1978 when executions were carried out in this country."[223] He found this to average about seventeen months, and concluded that in the instant case "[m]aking all reason-

able allowance for the time necessary for appeal and the consideration of reprieve, these delays are inordinate." The Indian Supreme Court examined the
procedural requirements of appellate review, including a statutory requirement
that sentence of death be confirmed by the High Court, in concluding "that
delay exceeding two years in the execution of a sentence of death should be
considered sufficient to entitle the person under sentence of death to . . . de-
mand the quashing of the sentence of death."[224]

The purpose of the analysis, according to the courts, is to establish what
length of time is so inordinate as to be "shocking." But what is it that the courts
actually find shocking, the suffering of the prisoner or the dysfunctions of the
judicial system? The "death row phenomenon" argument is often couched in
concerns about the terrible toll on the condemned individual, yet the discussion
of the relevant factors focusses exclusively on systemic issues. For example,
Chief Justice Gubbay, in *Catholic Commission,* says that excessive delays

> create a serious obstacle in the dispensation and administration of jus-
> tice. They shake the confidence of the people in the very system. It is
> my earnest belief that the sensitivities of fairminded Zimbabweans
> would be much disturbed, if not shocked, by the unduly long lapse of
> time during which these four condemned prisoners have suffered the
> agony and torment of the inexorably approaching foreordained death
> while in demeaning conditions of confinement.[225]

In this context, the suggestion by Lord Griffiths in *Pratt* that excessive delay
would have been controlled by the doctrine of abuse of process—even before
the entrenchment of a constitutional guarantee against cruel, inhuman, and
degrading treatment—is instructive.[226] Abuse of process is a common-law doctrine aimed at sanctioning misconduct of the state, and it does not necessarily
concern itself with the existence of a particular prejudice to the individual liti-
gant. Normally, where abuse of process is established, there will be a stay of
proceedings, even in cases where the guilt of the accused is hardly in question.
The purpose is to teach the authorities a lesson, and to protect the integrity of
the courts and the other components of the judicial system.[227]

A useful comparison may be made with the application of another human
rights norm, one that has many analogies with the issue of delay in execution—
the right to be tried "without undue delay."[228] The issue is framed as one of
fairness for the accused. Yet much of the caselaw on the subject, particularly in
comparative jurisprudence, emphasizes the notion of abusive procedure, as if it
were a collective, social right that is in question rather than an individual one.[229]
The jurisprudence on the death row phenomenon appears to reflect the same
considerations. Yet the death row phenomenon is premised on a totally differ-

ent right, one that is unquestionably an individual right and where such collective or social factors really have no place. This is why the prohibition of cruel treatment and torture has been elevated to an entirely different level in the catalog of human rights. Unlike the right to a speedy trial, it is a right not subject to derogation or suspension.

There is, consequently, something fundamentally unsatisfactory in the explanations offered in certain judgments for the calculation of how delay in execution passes from what is acceptable to what is unacceptable. The notion of abusive process should be totally foreign to this debate. The law is caught in a tautology, where the only real way to avoid gratuitous suffering while awaiting execution is to perform it immediately, yet where other rights, notably the right to due process, require that proceedings not be rushed. According to Lord Griffiths: "In the last resort the courts have to accept the responsibility of saying whether the threshold has been passed in any given case and there may be difficult borderline decisions to be made."[230]

CAUSE OF DELAY

Those courts prepared to recognize that delay may constitute cruel punishment and torture, and therefore be subject to judicial control, are far from unanimous as to what delays are relevant. If it is cruel, inhuman, and degrading to prolong the period a person must wait before being executed, then logically the matter ought to reduce itself to a simple calculation. The longer the delay, such reasoning would go, the larger the suffering. Yet a great deal of attention has been devoted to distinguishing between types of delay, depending on their cause. In his memorandum in *Lackey* v. *Texas,* Justice Stevens of the United States Supreme Court identified three sources of delay: a petitioner's legitimate exercise of his right to review; negligence or deliberate action by the state; and a petitioner's abuse of the judicial system by escape or by repetitive, frivolous filings.[231]

There is no suggestion in the caselaw that delay might begin to run from the moment of arrest or charge. Nevertheless, such delay may be very significant, particularly where extradition is involved. For example, in the case of *Ng* v. *Canada* the prisoner was arrested in 1987 but not extradited to the United States until 1991;[232] in 1995, he had yet to stand trial. Similarly, Keith Cox was arrested in Canada early in 1991, but he was not extradited to the United States until the final days of 1994.[233] The argument as to the relevance of delay before sentencing does not even appear to have been advanced by petitioners in death row litigation. Yet it is from this point that the accused person is put in jeopardy of sentence of death, and it is here that the horror of contemplating the sentence would normally begin. Indeed, the reality of the threat of a death sentence is actually exploited by the state, which will use it to incite the accused to accept a plea bargain of life imprisonment or some other reduced sentence.

Moreover, the significance of delay prior to sentence is recognized in another human rights norm, the procedural guarantee that a trial be held without undue delay.[234] Remedies may vary where there is a violation of the right to trial without undue delay, but this will often lead to a stay of proceedings. Of course, it may be argued that the death sentence becomes a certainty only upon conviction and imposition of sentence. Yet the existence of various forms of review, including appeal, judicial review, and application for commutation, demonstrates that even this is not the case. The death sentence is never really a certainty until after it has been carried out, although it would seem fair to say that the probability of death increases once a conviction has been entered and sentence actually passed.

Delay Not Attributable to the Prisoner

Several factors may account for delay that is independent of the will of the condemned person. Legislation can, in some jurisdictions, require that all death sentences be examined on appeal, even if the prisoner has decided not to contest the judgment at first instance.[235] In the case of prisoners of war, delay is actually imposed as an obligation by the third Geneva Convention,[236] article 101 of which establishes a moratorium of six months between imposition of the penalty and its execution.[237] The moratorium exists in order to permit the prisoner's own government to be informed of the sentence, through the Protecting Power. A similar provision exists in the fourth Geneva Convention, specifying a moratorium of six months in the case of sentences imposed on protected civilians during an international armed conflict.[238] There were also unsuccessful attempts to introduce a moratorium on executions into the Additional Protocol to the Geneva Conventions dealing with noninternational armed conflicts. The hope of the International Committee of the Red Cross, in advancing such a proposal, was that moratorium would eventually lead to amnesty.[239]

Delay may also be attributable to executive action in the form of consideration of pardon, amnesty, or commutation. Again, international law imposes requirements in this respect,[240] and in many countries any death sentence will be examined by the head of state or some other official irrespective of whether the prisoner actually applies for such consideration.[241]

In China, execution is apparently suspended for two years following sentence. If a prisoner demonstrates during this period that he or she is "repentant or of exemplary conduct, the sentence might be reduced to fifteen to twenty years."[242] When China described this procedure during presentation of its initial report to the Committee Against Torture, one member, Christine Chanet, said she found the suspended death sentence to be "particularly cruel."[243] Another member of the committee, Dipanda Mouelle, said that the suspended death sentence "amounted to inhuman and degrading treatment."[244] Nevertheless, the suspension of the death sentence in China has deep historical roots based upon humanitarian considerations.[245] It benefitted two members of the so-called Gang of Four, Jiang Qing (the widow of Mao Zedong) and Zhang Chunqiao, who survived the two-year moratorium and had their sentences commuted to life imprisonment. Chinese officials and jurists have cited this built-in delay as evidence that the country's policy is to restrict use of the death penalty.[246]

Many states have suspended capital punishment for a period that often extends over several years in order to examine whether the death penalty should be abolished. During this time, the individuals concerned remain on death row and, frequently, death sentences continue to be imposed by the courts, even though they are not carried out.[247] This was the situation in the *Catholic Commission* case, where a moratorium came to an end and prisoners were threatened with a renewal of executions.[248] They had in no fashion contributed to the delay, which had been imposed by the state in a process that might ultimately be to their benefit (although this did not turn out to be the case). The goodwill of the state could hardly be faulted, because it might well have decided to continue with executions pending consideration of the matter of abolition. For instance, a moratorium at the end of the 1970s while abolition of the death penalty was being debated contributed to death row delay in Jamaica.[249] Lords Scarman and Brightman of the Judicial Committee of the Privy Council considered "[i]f the criterion be the effect of the delay upon those subjected to it, the uncertainty engendered by the debate was an aggravating factor in the cruelty imposed upon them."[250]

During presentation of Poland's initial report to the Committee Against Torture, the government representative noted that there had been a moratorium since 1988 on imposition of the death penalty, and that although nobody had been executed, three persons had been sentenced; it was essential to resolve the matter quickly, if for no other reason than not to leave the three in a state of uncertainty.[251]

Delay can also be caused by third parties who initiate judicial challenges in the name of the condemned person without his or her authorization. There have been several cases in the United States in which a prisoner renounces to all appeals but a well-meaning relative or human rights activist insists upon review.[252]

All of the above cases involve no obvious malice or even negligence on the part of the state or third parties. The purpose of the delay is to spare the life of the accused person, through commutation of sentence or even release by executive, legislative, or judicial means. Can such delay be germane to the issue of cruel treatment?

There are also examples of such "benign" delay in the case of Pratt and Morgan. Upon dismissal of their appeals in December 1980, the governor-general of Jamaica should have submitted the matter to the Jamaican Privy Council to determine whether pardon or commutation should be granted, as provided for in sections 90 and 91 of the Constitution. And as Lord Griffiths observed, such provisions, adopted in a context whereby such matters were heard with great dispatch, "must be construed as imposing a duty on the Governor-General to refer the case to the [Jamaican Privy Council] and the JPC to give their advice as soon as practical."[253] A short delay at this point may have been due to a Senate decision to suspend executions for eighteen months, pending discussion on the question of capital punishment in general.[254] However, by May 1981 executions had resumed and, stated Lord Griffiths, "it is difficult to see why at about that time [the Jamaican Privy Council] should not have considered and advised upon the appellants' case."[255] Nearly ten years later, after an unsuccessful application to the Judicial Committee of the Privy Council, and following two successful applications to international human rights bodies, the authorities again failed to submit the matter to the Jamaican Privy Council, something Lord Griffiths suggested may have been a result of political wavering with respect to the death penalty.[256]

Delay may also be attributable to negligence on the part of the state, as demonstrated by several examples in the caselaw. In the case of Pratt and Morgan, the Privy Council designated a number of points at which delay was due to the state's lack of diligence in advancing the proceedings. In a general sense, the council found itself unable to account for the repeated failure of the Jamaican authorities to submit the matter to the Jamaican Privy Council for determination on the issues of pardon and commutation, a constitutional requirement. A few short periods were accounted for, as mentioned above, but for the bulk of the delay no explanation was provided. In the detailed and somewhat confusing saga of the Pratt and Morgan case during the 1980s that is related by Lord Griffiths, what stands out is that the Jamaican Privy Council should have considered the case in 1981 and did not do so until 1986. Nevertheless, since Pratt and Morgan failed to press their case at the Judicial Committee of the Privy Council until 1986, this factor is actually rather neutral in the entire calculation.

Other examples of negligence by the State are also cited by Lord Griffiths, although their connection with the delay is generally minor or, in the case of the judgment of the Court of Appeal, without significance. The appeal by Pratt and Morgan to the Jamaican Court of Appeal was filed in January 1979, within a few days of sentencing, yet it was not heard until December 1980. "Making every allowance for the pressure of work on the Jamaican courts this does seem a long time to arrange a hearing in a capital case which one would have expected to have been expedited," noted Lord Griffiths.[257] He added that at least part of the delay was because legal aid was not provided for until May 1980; again, no explanation was offered. Upon dismissal of the appeal, Pratt and Morgan wrote to the registrar of the Court of Appeal asking for the relevant papers to be prepared so that the case could be taken to the Judicial Committee of the Privy Council.[258] However, the Jamaican judge responsible for drafting the judgment forgot all about it. "This was a serious oversight by the judge and by those in the office of the Court of Appeal who should have reminded him that reasons had not been provided in accordance with the practice of the Court of Appeal, which is to provide a reserved judgment or reasons within three months of a hearing," Lord Griffiths noted.[259] Pratt and Morgan did not press the matter until three years later, in 1984. "[W]hether this was a deliberate policy adopted by the appellants and their advisers or, as seems more likely, due to the appellants' lack of access to legal advice, cannot be determined with any certainty," wrote Lord Griffiths.[260] Reasons for judgment were then drafted (although Pratt and Morgan did not in fact seek special leave from the Judicial Committee of the Privy Council until 1986), and their application was promptly dismissed.[261] Lord Griffiths pointed out that the delay in drafting the judgment was inexcusable, but it was not the reason that Pratt and Morgan's application to the Privy Council was delayed.[262]

The Inter-American Commission on Human Rights and the Human Rights Committee were both, however, under the impression that Pratt and Morgan's hearing before the Judicial Committee of the Privy Council had been delayed because of the Appeal Court judge's failure to draft reasons for judgment for more than three and a half years. They had probably got this impression from the Privy Council itself, because in its reasons dismissing Pratt and Morgan's application in 1986, Lord Templeton affirmed that this delay had prevented the petitioners from exercising such a remedy.[263] According to the Inter-American Commission on Human Rights,

> Pratt and Morgan suffered a denial of justice during the period 1980–1984 violative of Article 5(2) of the American Convention on Human Rights. The Commission found that the fact that the Jamaican Court of Appeal issued its decision on December 5 1980 but did not issue the reasons for that decision until four years later, September 24, 1984, was tantamount to cruel, inhuman and degrading treatment because during that four year delay the petitioners could not appeal to the

Privy Council and had to suffer four years on death row awaiting execution. The Inter-American Commission on Human Rights, pursuant to its cable of July 7 1987 requests that the execution of Messrs. Pratt and Morgan be commuted for humanitarian reasons.[264]

Interestingly, the Inter-American Commission had earlier considered the same case, and reached the opposite conclusion.[265]

The Human Rights Committee also examined this rather appalling failure of the Court of Appeal to draft its reasons for judgment. It concluded:

> 13.4 The State party has contended that the time span of three years and nine months between the dismissal of the authors' appeal and the delivery of the Court of Appeal's written judgement was attributable to an oversight and that the authors should have asserted their right to receive earlier the written judgement. The Committee considers that the responsibility for the delay of 45 months lies with the judicial authorities of Jamaica. This responsibility is neither dependent on a request for production by the accused in a trial nor is non-fulfillment of this responsibility excused by the absence of a request from the accused. The Committee further observes that the Privy Council itself described the delay as inexcusable. . . .
>
> 13.5 In the absence of a written judgement of the Court of Appeal, the authors were not able to proceed to appeal before the Privy Council, thus entailing a violation of article 14, paragraph 3(c), and article 14, paragraph 5. In reaching this conclusion it matters not that in the event the Privy Council affirmed the conviction of the authors. The Committee notes that in all cases, and especially in capital cases, accused persons are entitled to trial and appeal without undue delay, whatever the outcome of those judicial proceedings turns out to be.[266]

The legal basis of the two decisions of these international bodies is somewhat different. The Inter-American Commission, in its second assessment in the Pratt and Morgan case, considered the norm against cruel, inhuman, and degrading treatment to have been violated. However, the Human Rights Committee, considering an identical fact situation, did not agree. Its views in *Pratt* express what was to become its position in a large number of death row cases, namely, that delay in and of itself does not violate the prohibition of cruel, inhuman, and degrading treatment or punishment. The Human Rights Committee found a violation, but with respect to article 14§3(c) of the International Covenant on Civil and Political Rights,[267] that is, the right to a speedy trial that comprises one element of the due process guarantee.

At the root of this distinction are two fundamentally different views of the problem of delay due to negligence or malice on the part of the authorities. If it is the length of the delay that is the cause of suffering for the prisoner, then the cause of the delay is virtually irrelevant; the prisoner may never even know it. As the Pratt and Morgan case demonstrates, it is frequently difficult to identify the cause of the delay. All that the prisoner knows is that the delay makes him suffer, and that consequently the treatment he receives is cruel, inhuman, and degrading. But if the norm of a speedy trial is being invoked, as in the Human Rights Committee's views in *Pratt and Morgan*, then it is the conduct of the authorities that is offensive. It matters little whether the prisoner actually suffers any real prejudice. The state is being sanctioned for misconduct. Here, human rights law comes rather close to the old common-law doctrine of abuse of process.[268] Indeed, it is hardly surprising that the Judicial Committee of the Privy Council suggests that even prior to the existence of constitutional guarantees, courts had a common-law authority to stay executions that had been delayed for excessive periods.[269]

Delay Attributable to the Prisoner

As the *Pratt and Morgan* case shows so clearly, delay may often be the result of a number of factors. Even where the prisoner is not directly responsible for the delay, such as the failure of the Jamaican judge to draft his reasons for judgment, it will be a rare prisoner who complains about such situations. At the heart of this dilemma is whether the responsibility lies with the prisoner-applicant or with the state-respondent to see that proceedings are conducted without undue delay. The due process guarantees say this is the duty of the state. But the courts, in assessing the significance of the death row phenomenon, have been more equivocal.

Several courts have held that delay attributable to the condemned person's exercise of various remedies to challenge the sentence should be excluded from the calculation, and that only delay imputable to the state's lack of diligence in advancing the case should be counted. Another body of jurisprudence considers that the clock begins to run from the moment sentence is imposed, and that from that point on it is the state's duty to ensure that all useful appeal remedies are exercised promptly. It is usual for courts to consider delay, at any stage of the proceedings and whatever the cause, in fixing sentence. An appellate court would normally also be in a position to adjust sentence by taking into account delay since the pronouncement of sentence. This is because in noncapital cases sentence is inherently a question of time. Not only do the various objectives of sentencing—retribution, deterrence, rehabilitation, protection of the public— tend to grow cold and even irrelevant with the passage of time, but the existence of delay means that the prisoner is in effect already serving time before the sentence is definitively established. The significance of delay, particularly that involved in the regular judicial process of trial and appeal, is not nearly so clear.

The position maintaining that delay caused by appeal should not be counted has been stated quite emphatically by a number of United States courts. As early as 1971, the United States District Court, N. D. Illinois, E.D., stated:

> The Court finds and concludes, however, that petitioner's confinement for more than seventeen years, and his remaining under sentence of death for fifteen years and nine months, has not been caused solely by delays in proceedings by the State of Illinois. Rather, the fact that the death sentence has not been carried out and petitioner is still living is due principally to the skillful, persistent and conscientious efforts on petitioner's behalf by his own counsel to save him from the death penalty and secure his release from confinement.[270]

As a result, a complaint based on delay in execution was dismissed.

A similar position was adopted in the case of *Richmond* v. *Lewis.* Richmond had spent sixteen years on death row. Originally convicted in 1974, his sentence was reimposed in 1980 after the state trial court found no mitigating circumstances sufficient to warrant leniency. The District Court considered that "[t]he delay in the execution was prompted by Richmond's request, through his attorneys, to have his challenges to the sentence of death heard by several courts. The fact that this review has taken a long time does not indicate that the delay is unwarranted."[271] The Court said it was better "to take the time to consider each issue thoroughly rather than quickly dispatching someone to the gas chamber."[272]

On appeal, the Ninth Circuit Court of Appeals considered that "the relevant period of his residency on death row is actually ten years."[273] The Court noted that there was yet no formal decision by the United States Supreme Court[274] or the Ninth Circuit on the point; citing several United States judgments in which delay caused by the prisoner's exercise of various remedies had been disregarded,[275] the Court concluded that "in light of the relative absence of contrary precedents, we believe that the reasoning of these cases is sound."[276] In the view of the Ninth Circuit Court of Appeals,

> [a] defendant must not be penalized for pursuing his constitutional rights, but he also should not be able to benefit from the ultimately unsuccessful pursuit of those rights. It would indeed be a mockery of

justice if the delay incurred during the prosecution of claims that fail on the merits could itself accrue into a substantive claim to the very relief that had been sought and properly denied in the first place. If that were the law, death-row inmates would be able to avoid their sentences simply by delaying proceedings beyond some threshold amount of time, while other death-row inmates—less successful in their attempts to delay—would be forced to face their sentences. Such differential treatment would be far more "arbitrary and unfair" and "cruel and unusual" than the current system of fulfilling sentences when the last in the line of appeals fails on the merits. We thus decline to recognize Richmond's lengthy incarceration on death row during the pendency of his appeals as substantively and independently violative of the Constitution.[277]

An earlier decision of the United States District Court for the District of Utah, later affirmed by the Tenth Circuit, rejected a claim for relief after ten years on death row. The Court said that the petitioner's argument was "a mockery of justice," because delay was more attributable to his own actions than to those of the state, adding that he had sought "extensive and repeated review of [his] death sentence."[278]

Justice Quirico of the Massachusetts Supreme Judicial Court made an eloquent plea for rejecting all such delay in considering the issue of the death row phenomenon:

I find it difficult to understand or appreciate how it is constitutionally cruel or unusual punishment to permit a person who has been sentenced to death to pursue appellate procedures almost *ad infinitum* when, as stated by the Justices taking that position, the procedures always end in a commutation of the death sentence. To the extent that a defendant resorts to those endless appellate procedures, he should not be heard to complain about the prolongation of his period of anxiety and agony over his possible execution. To the extent that the delays are due to the actions of intermeddlers, the court is not without power to deal with them.[279]

In *Kindler* v. *Canada*, Justice La Forest, writing for the majority of the Supreme Court of Canada, adopted a similar position. He expressly endorsed the views of the Court of Appeals (Ninth Circuit) in *Richmond* v. *Lewis*. Referring to practice in death row appeals in the United States, the Canadian jurist noted that "[t]he unwieldy and time-consuming nature of this generous appeal process has come under heavy criticism,"[280] but added that the psychological stress inherent in the death row phenomenon cannot be dismissed lightly, it ultimately pales in comparison to the death penalty. Besides, the fact remains that a defendant is never forced to undergo the full appeal procedure, but the vast majority choose to do so. It would be ironic if delay caused by the appellant's taking advantage of the full and generous avenue of the appeals available to him should be viewed as a violation of fundamental justice.[281]

The views of the Human Rights Committee are to the same effect although, as I have mentioned earlier in this chapter, they appear to be evolving.[282]

It may be necessary to make some distinctions with respect to the type of remedy that is being exercised. In the United States, most of these are not part of the normal appellate process but are forms of judicial review by means of applications for habeas corpus. There is the implication that repeated applications for judicial review are in some way vexatious or abusive. Chief Justice Chandrachud of the Indian Supreme Court, in *Sher Singh*, insisted upon close scrutiny to establish whether procedures were merely taken to buy time:

> But it is, at least, relevant to consider whether the delay in the execution of the death sentence is attributable to the fact that [the appellant] has resorted to a series of untenable proceedings which have the effect of defeating justice. It is not uncommon that a series of review petitions and writ petitions are filed in this Court to challenge judgments and orders which have assumed finality, without any seeming justification. Stay orders are obtained in those proceedings and then, at the end of it all, comes the argument that there has been prolonged delay in implementing the judgment or order. We believe that the Court called upon to vacate a death sentence on the ground of delay caused in executing that sentence must find why the delay was caused and who is responsible for it. If this is not done, the law laid down by this Court will become an object of ridicule by permitting a person to defeat it by resorting to frivolous proceedings in order to delay its implementation. And then, the rule of two years will become a handy tool for defeating justice.[283]

Yet these remedies are normally granted within a constitutional context, rights accruing to condemned persons as part of their due process or procedural guarantees. It would seem extravagant indeed to suggest that the exercise of constitutional rights is vexatious or abusive. And aside from innuendo on this point, it is hard to find examples in the caselaw where the courts have actually contended that a death row petition was vexatious or abusive. In any event, this should hardly be a source of further delay. Mechanisms exist for any such frivolous proceeding to be summarily dismissed, and it ought to be the duty of the state to see that these mechanisms are in fact applied. Note, on this point, that even the proponents of the other view, who hold that petitioner-caused delay should be counted in the calculation, exclude from this any such vexatious or abusive delay. For Lord Griffiths, in *Pratt and Morgan*, "If delay is due entirely to the fault of the accused such as an escape from custody or frivolous and time wasting resort to legal procedures which amount to an abuse of process the accused cannot be allowed to take advantage of that delay for to do so would be to permit the accused to use illegitimate means to escape the punishment inflicted upon him in the interest of protecting society against crime."[284] But in a subsequent judgment the Privy Council cautioned against quibbling over responsibility for specific portions of the delay. Citing the words of Lord Griffiths in *Pratt and Morgan*, their Lordships said this would only be relevant where responsibility was *due entirely* to the prisoner:

> Their Lordships wish to discourage the minute examination of weeks and even months when such delay can be said to have occurred and to be the responsibility of one or other party or of both so that it must be appointed as was suggested here. The right approach is to take the total period of time which has elapsed and then to ask, as indicated in *Pratt and Morgan*, whether the "delay is due entirely to the fault of the accused such as an escape from custody or frivolous and time wasting resort to legal procedures which amount to an abuse of process" (pages 29–30). If they do the defendant cannot take advantage of delay. It is right to recall what was said in *Pratt and Morgan* at page 33: "It is part of the human condition that a condemned man will take every opportunity to save his life through use of the appellate procedure. If the appellant procedures enable the prisoner to prolong the appellate hearings over a period of years, the fault is to be attributed to the appellate system that permits such delay and not to the prisoner who takes advantage of it." That assessment does not depend on considering whether the time which has elapsed "was so prolonged as to arouse in him a reasonable belief that his death sentence must have been commuted to a sentence of life imprisonment," one possible exception referred to by Lord Diplock in *Abbott* v. *Attorney General of Trinidad and Tobago*, [1979] 1 W.L.R. 1342 at page 1348. The test is the wider objective one laid down in *Pratt and Morgan*.[285]

The Supreme Court of India shares the narrower view of the death row phenomenon adopted by U.S. and Canadian courts, but it limits this to the statutory appeal procedure. Justice Oza of the Supreme Court of India, in *Triveniben* v. *State of Gujarat*, expressed the view that the only delay that a court might consider in such constitutional review is that starting "from the date the judgment by the apex Court is pronounced, i.e., when the judicial process has come to an end."[286] The Indian Court of Appeal is empowered to revise a sentence of death, taking into account factors arising since imposition of sentence, including unusual delay.[287] This is not the case in most other legal systems, and the Indian precedent is therefore of rather limited interest.

In a European Court of Human Rights case delay in administering corporal punishment was measured in weeks. Judge Fitzmaurice of the United Kingdom, who dissented in the judgment, said: "Most of this delay was due to the fact that there was an appeal against the sentence which was not finally heard for some five weeks."[288] He went on to observe that "during the period when the appeal was still outstanding, therefore, any mental anguish caused by the delay resulted from Mr Tyrer's own act, and probably would have been more than compensated for by the hope that the appeal would succeed."[289] The majority noted that the relevant legislation provided for birching to be inflicted no later than six months after passing sentence, but said this did not alter the fact that there had been unnecessary delay in imposing it since conviction by the juvenile court. According to the majority of the Court, "Mr Tyrer was subjected to the mental anguish of anticipating the violence he was to have inflicted on him."[290]

The European Court of Human Rights took a similar line of reasoning in the *Soering* case. The delay was hypothetical, because Soering has not yet stood trial. The Court was concerned with "normal" delay in Virginia, consisting of several years, which would be consumed with the exhaustion of the various appeal and judicial review procedures available by statute and pursuant to constitutional due process rights. Delay in such cases was largely of the prisoner's own making,[291] noted the Court, adding that it is "part of human nature that the person will cling to life by exploiting those safeguards to the full."[292] According to the Court, "however well-intentioned and even potentially beneficial is the provision of the complex of post sentence procedures in Virginia, the consequence is that the condemned prisoner has to endure for many years the conditions on death row and the anguish and mounting tension of living in the ever present shadow of death."[293] The European Court held that this delay was relevant, although by citing some factors particular to the applicant, including age and psychological makeup, it left an unfortunate aura of ambiguity surrounding its position.[294]

The clearest statement of the larger view that considers delay in and of itself to be offensive to the norm prohibiting cruel punishment and torture—

even absent any mitigating or aggravating factors, and irrespective of whether the prisoner's use of various judicial remedies to challenge the sentence is responsible for the delay—comes from the Judicial Committee of the Privy Council in *Pratt and Morgan*. But this judgment reversed earlier pronouncements of the Privy Council. In the first of its cases dealing with the death row phenomenon, *de Freitas* v. *Benny*, Lord Diplock excluded the period when appeals were being exercised: "The initiative for securing expedition in all these proceedings lay with the appellant; procrastination on the part of the Crown or the courts is not alleged."[295] In *Abbott*, the second Privy Council case, delay between sentence and dismissal of appeal was again deemed to be irrelevant:[296] "It has to be conceded that the applicant cannot complain about the delay totalling three years subsequent to the rejection of his petition caused by his own action in appealing against his conviction or about the delay totalling two years subsequent to the rejection of his petition caused by his own action in appealing against the sentence on constitutional grounds."[297] This meant that of the six-year lapse between sentence and execution, less than eight months were in dispute.

David Pannick, in his pioneering study of the question, criticized Lord Diplock's views:

> [I]t ignores the degree of mental torture suffered; it deters the defendant from claiming his rights to review by Appellate Courts of the penalty of death; and it penalizes the claiming of the right to appeal by providing that the exercise of that right prevents the defendant from claiming that his treatment has breached his right not to suffer cruel or inhuman punishment. The defendant's reluctance to suffer a long delay before execution, his knowledge that if he appeals against sentence or conviction any delay resulting therefrom will not render his execution unconstitutionally cruel, and his failure accurately to assess his chances of winning an appeal against conviction or sentence, may deter the defendant from appealing, and thereby overturning, a sentence of death unlawfully imposed.[298]

Then, in *Riley*, two members of the Judicial Committee of the Privy Council, Lords Scarman and Brightman, took a more liberal view of the matter. However, even they admitted that "a period of anguish and suffering is an inevitable consequence of sentence of death," adopting the position that "prolongation of it beyond the time necessary for appeal and consideration of reprieve is not."[299] This suggests that even the dissenters in *Riley* would have excluded delay attributable to exercise of judicial remedies.[300]

The views of Lords Scarman and Brightman were soon endorsed by the

Indian Supreme Court, which went a step further by including appellate delay that was ostensibly attributable to the prisoner. In *Vatheeswaran* v. *State of Tamil Nadu,* Justice Chinnappa Reddy said:

> While we entirely agree with Lord Scarman and Lord Brightman about the dehumanizing effect of prolonged delay after the sentence of death, we enter a little caveat, but only that we may go further. We think that the cause of the delay is immaterial when the sentence is death. Be the cause for the delay the time necessary for appeal and consideration of reprieve or some other cause for which the accused himself may be responsible, it would not alter the dehumanizing character of the delay.[301]

Shortly afterwards, another panel of the same court questioned whether a two-year delay for execution, as declared in *Vatheeswaran,* was really appropriate. It noted that the danger in imposing a strict time limit was that it might enable a prisoner to avoid execution by means of a series of frivolous and untenable proceedings. The Court recognized that it was perfectly understandable for offenders to use all available remedies to challenge their sentences, and suggested that time consumed in such legitimate exercise of rights would not be subtracted from any calculation of excessive delay. It merely cautioned that "it is, at least, relevant to consider whether the delay in the execution of the death sentence is attributable to the fact that [the prisoner] has resorted to a series of untenable proceedings which have the effect of defeating the ends of justice."[302]

Some United States courts, although they most certainly constitute a minority, have also held the view that the cause of delay is irrelevant. As Chief Justice Hennessey, of the Massachusetts Supreme Judicial Court, observed, "The fact that the delay may be due to the defendant's insistence on exercising his appellate rights does not mitigate the severity of the impact on the condemned individual, and the right to pursue due process of law must not be set off against the right to be free from inhuman treatment."[303]

In May 1993, the Supreme Court of Zimbabwe took the position that the cause of delay was irrelevant to the issue of whether there was a breach of the prohibition against cruel punishment and torture. Chief Justice Gubbay expressly endorsed David Pannick's criticism of the Privy Council's position, cited above—"This criticism is impressive in its logic and I adopt it."[304] He concluded: "Accordingly, I am entirely satisfied that in the determination of whether there has been a breach of s. 15(1) of the Constitution, the period the prisoner has spent in the condemned cell must be taken to start with the imposition of sentence of death. After all, it is from that date that he begins to suffer what is termed the 'death row phenomenon.' "[305] The Supreme Court of

Zimbabwe expressly criticized the views of the United States Court of Appeals (Ninth Circuit) in *Richmond*[306] and the Supreme Court of Canada in *Kindler*,[307] while endorsing the position of the European Court of Human Rights in *Soering*.[308] The idea that the petitioner is responsible for delays in exercising remedies is a "narrow and somewhat intolerant view," expressed in *Chessman*, *Richmond*, and *Kindler*, according to Chief Justice Gubbay in *Catholic Commission*.[309] But there were a number of particular factors in the *Catholic Commission* case as well, notably the emphasis on absolutely appalling prison conditions on Zimbabwe's death row. Another court in another country might well fix on this part of the Zimbabwe court's judgment in order to distinguish its scope.

Six months after the judgment in *Catholic Commission*, Lord Diplock's view in *de Freitas* v. *Benny* was reversed by the Judicial Committee of the Privy Council. In *Pratt and Morgan*, Lord Griffiths said: "A much more difficult question is whether the delay occasioned by the legitimate resort of the accused to all available appellate procedures should be taken into account, or whether it is only delay that can be attributed to the shortcomings of the State that should be taken into account."[310] He also criticized the positions in *Richmond* and *Kindler*, and endorsed the view of Chief Justice Gubbay in *Catholic Commission* and the view of the European Court of Human Rights in *Soering*: "The European Court of Human Rights recognized that the death row phenomenon in Virginia where prisoners were held for a period of six to eight years before execution arose from repeated applications by the prisoner for a stay of execution but nevertheless held that such a long period of delay might go beyond the threshold set by Article 3."[311] Lord Griffiths concluded:

> In their Lordships' view a State that wishes to retain capital punishment must accept the responsibility of ensuring that execution follows as swiftly as practicable after sentence, allowing a reasonable time for appeal and consideration of reprieve. It is part of the human condition that a condemned man will take every opportunity to save his life through use of the appellate procedure. If the appellate procedure enables the prisoner to prolong the appellate hearings over a period of years, the fault is to be attributed to the appellate system that permits such delay and not to the prisoner who takes advantage of it. Appellate procedures that echo down the years are not compatible with capital punishment. The death row phenomenon must not become established as a part of our jurisprudence.[312]

Lord Griffiths's views in *Pratt and Morgan* concerning the death row phenomenon leave no room for ambiguity, as there is no discussion either of personal factors concerning the two applicants or of prison conditions. Given that Pratt and Morgan had been waiting fourteen years on death row, and that they had been taken to the execution cells on three occasions following reading of the death warrant, Lord Griffiths noted that "[t]he statement of these bare facts is sufficient to bring home to the mind of any person of normal sensitivity and compassion the agony of mind that these men must have suffered as they have altered between hope and despair in the fourteen years that they have been in prison facing the gallows. It is unnecessary to refer to the evidence describing the restricting conditions of imprisonment and the emotional and psychological impact of this experience."[313]

The Judicial Committee of the Privy Council's influence upon Commonwealth courts has already been felt. In a Nigerian Supreme Court case, Justice Ogwuegbu appeared to adopt the reasoning in *Pratt*: "Since capital punishment is part of our law, persons charged with capital offences and indeed all criminal cases are entitled to trial and appeal without delay. The Executive and judicial authorities must accept the responsibility of ensuring that execution follows as swiftly as practicable after sentence, allowing reasonable time for appeal and consideration of reprieve."[314] However, Chief Justice Bello, who drafted the reasons of the majority, was less impressed by the reasoning from London: "The delay in their trial, determination of their appeals and their non-execution were entirely caused by the due process of law and the appellants have not in any manner whatsoever contributed to the delay other than by the exercise of their rights to invoke judicial process."[315]

Even in the United States, the Privy Council's judgment in *Pratt and Morgan* has been influential. It was cited by Justice Stevens of the Supreme Court in *Lackey*.[316] Moreover, it has led to at least one judgment recognizing the death row phenomenon and granting a stay of execution. In *State* v. *Richmond,* an Arizona court noted that potential delay could reach three decades, something that is unprecedented even in the United States. According to the Court, citing *Pratt and Morgan,* such delayed execution would constitute cruel and unusual punishment under the Eighth Amendment of the United States Constitution and article 2, §15 of the Arizona Constitution.[317]

MITIGATING AND AGGRAVATING FACTORS

As I have already discussed, the judgment of the European Court of Human Rights in *Soering* v. *United Kingdom* generated a degree of ambiguity with respect to the issue of mitigating factors. The European Court had referred to such elements as Soering's youth and his mental instability, suggesting they were significant in assessing the existence of a breach of article 3 of the European Convention on Human Rights.[318] This reference invited some tribunals, such as the Supreme Court of Canada and the Human Rights Committee, to distinguish *Soering*, and to take the view that absent such factors mere delay in execution was not enough to constitute a breach of the norm against cruel treatment and torture. The judgment of the Privy Council in *Pratt and Morgan* is quite clearly indifferent to such elements. For their Lordships, the length of time in and of itself is clearly enough.

Nevertheless, it is surely true that factors like age and mental instability contribute to the suffering. Other issues, such as conditions of detention, would also be of obvious relevance. The better view would be to consider delay, in and of itself, to be sufficient to breach the prohibition of cruel treatment and torture, but to take account of additional mitigating and aggravating factors in assessing when delay becomes unacceptable.

The Privy Council in *Pratt and Morgan* takes some care not to suggest that there could never be mitigating or aggravating factors. Indeed, it specifically refers to the possibility of frivolous or vexatious remedies, and to escape, as matters that would change the calculation. If a prisoner flees custody and remains at large for more than five years, is he or she entitled to invoke the death row phenomenon? The Privy Council appears to answer in the negative.[319] The condemned person is thus not responsible for delay in the exercise of regular and serious remedies, including those before international human rights bodies. If he or she oversteps this, either through frivolous appeals, escape, or some other delaying technique, then any additional delay does not count. And yet, the prisoner is merely struggling to stay alive, to avoid the death sentence, and is all the while living with the torment of impending execution. Logically, even such delay should count.

In *Chessman*, the California courts took the view that the prisoner's behavior on death row, which was apparently abusive and insulting, was an aggravating factor. Admitting that such prolonged detention on death row "would be hell for most people," the Court of Appeals for the Ninth Circuit observed that Caryl Chessman was "no ordinary man," "an exhibitionist who never before had such opportunities for exhibition."[320] This passage in the decision is criticized by Chief Justice Gubbay of the Zimbabwe Supreme Court in *Catholic Commission*, who notes that there was no explanation in this "so-called reasoning" as to why Chessman's personality "would reduce the level of his mental suffering below that required for the application of the constitutional standard."[321]

In a rather unusual and quite isolated opinion, the United States District Court for Arizona has suggested there is a positive side to death row detention. While admitting that "confinement under a sentence of death would create uncertainty as to the execution and produce some fear and anxiety,"[322] the

Court noted that death row had not been completely harmful to the prisoner, who was "able to develop better skills in communicating with others," break a drug habit that he had at the time of the crime, and develop new religious beliefs.[323] Robert Johnson, in his book *Condemned to Die*, cites the case of Caryl Chessman as another one that was "paradoxically a context for growth." Johnson notes that Chessman's twelve years on death row "inspired introspection and resulted in the discovery of meaning in the experience and in his life."[324]

PHYSICAL CONDITIONS ON DEATH ROW

As with everything else accompanying the preliminaries to execution, death rows were designed with relatively short stays in mind; consequently, the surroundings are normally extremely harsh. A "death row phenomenon" argument was dismissed in Ethel Rosenberg's appeal, where the Court considered that physical conditions and treatment given the prisoner were not unacceptable.[325] The conditions were described in the judgment of the Court dismissing her application:

> The death cell block for female prisoners has three cells, each of which, according to the testimony, is identical in all respects and is about twelve feet long and four feet wide. One of these cells is occupied by the relator. There is a fourth cell in which there is a standing shower.
>
> Each cell has a cot or bunk, a chair, a small table, a toilet, and a wash stand. The cells were inspected by the United States Marshall and the Assistant Director of Prisons for the United States before the relator was transferred there and the cells were found to be sanitary and adequate.
>
> During the daytime enough sunlight enters the cells so that one in such a cell can read without the aid of artificial light. At night there are adequate lighting facilities. The relator is allowed reading periods.
>
> There is a matron in attendance at all times. The relator is allowed visitors in accordance with the rules governing state prisoners in similar circumstances.
>
> Outside the cell block is an exercise yard which is about fifty feet wide and fifty or sixty feet long. This yard is bounded by a twenty foot wall. The relator is allowed to exercise in this yard two hours every morning and two hours every afternoon.[326]

South Africa's death row, prior to its abolition in June 1995,[327] was located in Pretoria Central Prison. Lights were left on at all times. Prisoners were permitted to exercise for twenty to thirty minutes per day. As soon as an execution date was set, the prisoner was transferred from a communal cell to an isolation cell. In such a cell, the condemned person was allowed to talk with the prisoner in the neighboring cell for only four hours per day.[328] Once an official execution date had been determined, the prisoner was moved to a group of cells known as the "pot," where he or she was measured so that the hangman could adjust the noose correctly. Prisoners spent the week before execution in this solitary confinement, not even being allowed out to exercise; they were not permitted a mattress, toothbrush, toothpaste, or shoes.[329]

Death row in Zimbabwe was described in the case of Conjwayo and his co-accused, Woods and Smith, who were sentenced to death after conspiring to kill members of the African National Congress (one person actually was killed). After conviction and sentencing, they were detained on death row at Chikurubi Maximum Security Prison. The conditions were gruesome: constant supervision; cell of 4.6 meters by 1.42 meters; solid side and rear walls; windowless; self-flushing toilet; concrete sleeping platform covered with a mat; drinking water provided upon request; meals served at 8h00, 10h30 and 13h20; permitted to read the Bible and novels, but nothing else; allowed to talk to fellow inmates, and see them through a mesh screen; an electric light constantly burning in each death row cell.[330] The physical conditions of Harare Central Prison's "condemned section" (death row), as described in the *Catholic Commission* judgment, appear to be quite similar: a single cell, under constant supervision day and night; dimensions of 3.5 meters by 2 meters; single window very high up, from which only sky is visible; door of cell has a small aperture through which prison officials are able to view the inmate; an electrical bulb in the cell is the only source of light and is never extinguished; no toilet (rather, a chamber pot); thin mattress; two sets of clothing (one worn inside cell, the other outside). Prisoners are given "poor quality" food and ten cigarettes per day. They are allowed out of the cell at 6h00 for bathing and to empty the chamber pot, and permitted two thirty-minute periods of exercise outside the cell, together with other condemned prisoners. There is no exercise apparatus, and the playing of games is forbidden. Communication with other prisoners (apart from those on death row) is not permitted. A Bible and other religious literature is allowed, but no other reading material. At 15h00 all clothing must be left outside the cell, and the inmate remains naked in the cell until 6h00. The cell is "very cold" in winter months. Visits from family members of about ten minutes' duration, in the presence of prison officials, are permitted periodically.[331] Following an attempt to enable Conjwayo, Woods, and Smith to escape, conditions were tightened, and their period in the exercise yard was reduced to half an hour per day, with another half hour for various chores. This meant the prisoners spent twenty-three hours per day in their cells. Chief

Justice Gubbay noted that a policy requiring prisoners on death row to remove all clothing during the night was changed following institution of proceedings, and that "it was not in dispute that it constituted treatment of a degrading nature."[332] Death row in Tanzania is also quite comparable, with virtual solitary confinement, a small cell, limited reading material (the Bible), prisoners kept naked at night, lights never turned off, and systematic taunting by guards; delays there are said to be about four years.[333]

Florida's death row "is constructed of concrete and steel, and is painted a dull green." In winter, it is said to be cold, and in summer "unbearably hot." There is no provision for air conditioning or even fans.[334] Each condemned person is confined to a separate cell measuring 6 feet by 9 feet, containing a seatless toilet, washbowl, bed, and television.[335] Again, the prisoners are kept in strict isolation. Twice per week they are allowed into the yard for two hours of recreation; only one is permitted in the yard at a time. Once per week, the condemned are allowed to visit with other men on death row in the corridor outside their cells for two hours. Every second night, there is a five-minute shower. The food is nondescript, heavy in carbohydrates and starches, served three times every day.[336]

The European Court of Human Rights considered conditions at Virginia's death row, the Mecklenburg facility. The harsh conditions described were defended by the United Kingdom as being justified by the "necessary requirement of extra security for the safe custody of prisoners condemned to death for murder."[337] The Court, however, felt that while "it might thus well be justifiable in principle, the severity of a special regime such as that operated on death row in Mecklenburg is compounded by the fact of inmates being subject to it for a protracted period lasting on average six to eight years."[338] The Court noted that cells were 3 meters by 2.2 meters, and that prisoners were allowed to leave them for only six to seven hours per week of recreation; they could spend one hour each morning in a common area socializing with other death row inmates.[339] Jens Soering's attorneys also filed evidence showing "extreme stress, psychological deterioration and risk of homosexual abuse and physical attack" on death row.[340] This evidence was apparently contested by the state of Virginia, and the Court did not make a finding of fact on the point.[341] The Court referred to "lockdowns" that take place four times a year in order to search for contraband.[342] Fifteen days before execution, the condemned person is removed from a regular death row cell and placed in a special cell without its own lights, although the lights outside it are permanently lit. A prisoner in the death cell is watched at all times.[343]

According to a 1971 judgment, at Louisiana State Penitentiary at Angola, prisoners were kept in small cells and allowed out of them for only fifteen minutes so as to bathe. The warden told the Court that they were not allowed to exercise because he believed state law held that death row prisoners were to be kept in solitary confinement. The Court noted laconically that "[t]his statute did not contemplate an inmate spending year after year on Death Row," adding that death rows were built for stays of days and not years.[344]

Inhospitable conditions on Tennessee's death row were described in a case where the prisoner had acquiesced in the death penalty. The petitioner argued that this was due to mental disturbance brought on by conditions in death row. Harries' cell was 6 feet by 8 feet, with a toilet and a wash basin in the toilet wall. A bunk bed occupied one-third of the space in the cell. There was no window, and poor ventilation, with an average temperature of between 80 and 85 degrees Fahrenheit. Harries was confined to his cell for twenty-three hours per day. During his hour outside, he was allowed to exercise and shower. However, the exercise yard was too small for running, and the large number of inmates in the yard made even walking difficult. The Court concluded that: "the conditions of confinement inflicted on Mr. Harries are so adverse that they have caused him to waive his post-conviction remedies involuntarily."[345]

In a Massachusetts death row case, Judge Liacos described how the prisoner was generally isolated, allowed few visitors, limited in the scope of activities available, and kept under close guard. He said that on death row, "organized and controlled in grim caricature of a laboratory, the condemned prisoner's personality is subjected to incredible stress for prolonged periods of time."[346]

These various accounts of death row indicate that solitary confinement, or confinement in the prisoner's cell for twenty-three or more hours per day, is very much a common denominator. Solitary confinement may have seemed more acceptable when stays on death row rarely lasted more than a few weeks.[347] The Supreme Court of India, in *Sunil Batra* v. *Delhi Administration*, ruled that to detain a prisoner under sentence of death in solitary confinement on the alleged ground of security is a breach of fundamental rights.[348] The Human Rights Committee has considered that prolonged solitary confinement, especially if a person is kept incommunicado, may violate article 7 of the International Covenant on Civil and Political Rights,[349] which prohibits torture and cruel, inhuman, and degrading treatment or punishment. "Even such a measure as solitary confinement may, according to the circumstances, and especially when the person is kept *incommunicado*, be contrary to this article," said the committee in its first General Comment on article 7.[350] "[T]he Committee notes that prolonged solitary confinement of the detained or imprisoned person may amount to acts prohibited by article 7."[351] The Human Rights Committee has characterized prison conditions as being "inhuman" on a number of occasions;

consequently, they constitute breaches of article 7, as well as article 10§1, which states that "[a]ll persons deprived of their liberty shall be treated with humanity and with respect for the inherent dignity of the human person."[352] These violations have included solitary confinement over a period of three months, with denial of medical assistance;[353] solitary confinement for several months, with almost no natural light;[354] incommunicado detention in a cell of 1 meter by 2 meters, and solitary confinement for eighteen months;[355] and periods of incommunicado detention chained prone on bedsprings, with minimal clothing and food.[356]

The European Commission on Human Rights has made similar pronouncements on the subject of solitary confinement.[357] According to the commission, "[c]omplete sensory isolation [of a prisoner] coupled with total social isolation, can destroy the personality and constitutes a form of treatment which cannot be justified by the requirements of security or any other reason."[358] However, the commission has stated that "segregation of a prisoner from the prison community does not in itself constitute a form of inhuman or degrading treatment." Although the commission holds segregation to be undesirable, the issue of a breach of article 3 of the European Convention depends on a number of factors, including stringency of the regime, duration, and purpose, as well as its effects on the person concerned. "The removal of a prisoner from association with fellow inmates for security, disciplinary or protective reasons does not normally amount to inhuman treatment or punishment," the commission has stated.[359]

The caselaw provides little guidance as to why such harsh conditions are required on death row. This is understandable, because courts intervene only when conditions of detention are so harsh as to breach fundamental norms. The fact that they are harsh, or at least harsher than those experienced by other convicts, will not in and of itself justify judicial review. Yet even the literature on death row offers little in the way of theoretical support for the grim conditions to which condemned persons are exposed.

In its examination of the question, the United Kingdom's Royal Commission on Capital Punishment stressed that prisons where executions take place should have a separate cell block to house the execution chamber and the condemned cell, along with a separate exercise ground. "It is a standing order of the Prison Commission that condemned men shall not be exposed to the other prisoners or seen by them, and at most prisons the governors find considerable difficulty in giving the prisoner exercise without either violating this rule or imposing restrictions on the other prisoners that are a constant reminder of the presence among them of a man under sentence of death."[360]

In a 1991 case before the Supreme Court of Zimbabwe, Chief Justice Gubbay noted that since imprisonment is not part of a death sentence this becomes a factor in determining the conditions on death row.[361] "He is incarcerated pending a decision, either in the appeal to this Court, or by the President, who may exercise a prerogative of mercy, as to whether he is to be put to death," the chief justice observed. "So his punishment has not commenced."[362] This is an interesting notion, because it could be taken to imply that death row conditions should be better than those obtaining in an ordinary prison. However, the prisoner has indeed been found guilty of a heinous crime. If ever the death sentence were to be commuted, then he or she would be placed in a carceral regime appropriate to "lifers." But even those serving terms of life imprisonment are ordinarily allowed out of their cells for more than thirty minutes per day. If the objective of the authorities is to minimize any additional suffering for the condemned individual, then it would seem appropriate that the person be integrated into the general carceral population.

Chief Justice Gubbay was shocked at the conditions on death row. "I entertain no doubt that to confine a human being in a small cell over weekends for forty-seven hours (with the two daily half-hour periods out of the cell but within the condemned section itself and not in the open air), and for a much longer period where a public holiday falls on a day immediately preceding or subsequent to a weekend, is plainly offensive to one's notion of humanity and decency. It transgresses the boundaries of civilized standards and involves the infliction of unnecessary suffering."[363] Improvements in prison conditions were ordered.[364]

WHAT IS THE PROPER REMEDY?

If delay is responsible for violation of the condemned person's human rights, then the logical remedy would be to end the delay. But except in the handful of "death wish" cases,[365] it is unlikely that many individuals will be very anxious to invoke rights where the remedy is execution. This conundrum has embarrassed many lawyers (particularly in the United States), who view the issue of the death row phenomenon with some suspicion. They consider that insistence upon post-sentence delay will only become an argument in favor of procedural shortcuts and hastened executions.

In *Dhlamini's case*, before the Supreme Court of Rhodesia, Chief Justice Beadle in effect proposed that a death row prisoner "can move the Court for relief and the Court will see that the 'treatment' is stopped, but that does not affect the original 'punishment' which cannot, itself, become tainted with the inhumanity of the 'treatment' "[366] The chief justice admitted this was "something which no person sentenced to death is ever likely to [request]. Even if, therefore, in certain circumstances, delay may be considered as inhuman treatment, the remedy given an accused who is under sentence of death . . . is not one which is likely to be of much value to him, as it gives him no more than the right to ask for the delay to cease."[367]

The position of Chief Justice Beadle in *Dhlamini* has found little support in the caselaw, where there is now a fairly general consensus that the appropriate remedy for a violation of the prohibition of cruel treatment and torture is commutation. As Chief Justice Gubbay of Zimbabwe noted in *Catholic Commission*, the *Dhlamini* ruling "is out of step with more enlightened thinking."[368]

The Supreme Court of Zimbabwe has noted that "the power to 'commute' sentence of death is an executive power."[369] Where only abuse of process was alleged, the appropriate remedy would probably be a stay of execution, leaving commutation to the executive. Where constitutional issues are involved, which is most certainly the case when the international human rights norm prohibiting cruel treatment and torture is at issue, then courts are normally empowered to craft an appropriate remedy. Commutation is, of course, the solution.[370] According to Chief Justice Gubbay, "[I]t is irrelevant to the condemned prisoner's assertion that the alternative to delay may be expeditious execution. It is not his wish for a speedy death that causes due process of law, insofar as it prohibits inhuman or degrading punishment or treatment, to proscribe delay."[371] In several Indian cases, commutation has been ordered where a prisoner's stay on death row has been unconstitutionally long.[372]

METHOD OF EXECUTION

MEDIEVAL WAYS of putting people to death were expressly designed to combine killing with torture. The condemned individual was meant to suffer not only with the loss of his or her life, but the process itself was intended to be one of the most unspeakable horror. The spectacle was generally public, and it often involved grotesque mutilation of the body both before and after death. It was thus torturous, but also cruel, inhuman, and above all degrading. In England, this association of torture with the death penalty was condemned by Puritan opponents of the ecclesiastic courts.[1] Their views were taken up in Massachusetts by the settlers who drafted the 1641 Body of Liberties: "For bodily punishments we allow amongst us none that are inhumane, barbarous or cruel."[2]

Apparently the drafters of the "cruel and unusual punishment" clause in the English Bill of Rights of 1689 were not concerned with the method of punishment, but rather with its proportionality.[3] Indeed, some of the brutal punishments characterizing the Stuart era were retained until the early nineteenth century. Nevertheless, the Enlightenment reflected a growing concern with brutal methods of execution and a desire that any superfluous suffering be eliminated. This was, in fact, why the revolutionaries in France adopted the guillotine.[4] It and similar devices had existed for many years before the French Revolution, but they were reserved for aristocrats, who were to be spared the degradation and humiliation of being put to death in more barbarous, prolonged, and protracted ways. Concerns about the method of punishment appear in some of the initial drafts of the French Déclaration des droits de l'homme et du citoyen. For example, in his proposed Déclaration, the Marquis de Condorcet suggested a clause limiting the death penalty to crimes against the life of an individual or public safety, adding that capital punishment could not be associated with treatment "qui la rende plus lente ou plus douloureuse" [making it slower or more painful].[5]

If the English drafters of the 1689 Bill of Rights were indifferent to methods of imposing punishment, their American counterparts were not. When the latter included the prohibition of "cruel and unusual punishments" in the first ten amendments to the United States Constitution, they most certainly meant to encompass a prohibition of brutal methods of execution. The Eighth Amendment was adopted by Congress and by the states with the intention that it be "directed at prohibiting certain methods of punishment."[6] What the framers proclaimed has since been interpreted by the nation's courts as forbidding methods of execution that are gratuitously cruel, painful, or degrading. One recent judgment states that "[i]t is evident that the prohibitions in the Eighth Amendment evolved primarily from the concern for the manner in which individuals would be put to death."[7] For Justice William J. Brennan of the Supreme Court, "The Eighth Amendment requires that, as much as humanly possible, a chosen method of execution minimize the risk of unnecessary pain, violence and mutilation."[8] According to Judge Stephen Reinhardt of the U.S. Court of Appeals, Ninth Circuit, "[A]t the time of its adoption, the Eighth Amendment barred such punishments as embowelling alive, beheading, and quartering; public dissection; and burning alive."[9] The Supreme Court of the United States said in *Francis* v. *Resweber:*

> The traditional humanity of modern Anglo-American law forbids the infliction of unnecessary pain in the execution of the death sentence. Prohibition against the wanton infliction of pain has come into our law from the Bill of Rights of 1688. The identical words appear in our Eighth Amendment. The Fourteenth would prohibit by its due process clause execution by a state in a cruel manner.[10]

However, aside from statements of a general nature, the Supreme Court, like all other constitutional courts and international human rights bodies, has only seldom addressed whether particular methods of execution are unconstitutionally cruel.[11]

Often the courts approach the matter somewhat theoretically, declaring that techniques used in the distant past would not now pass constitutional muster. This stance implies an admission that attitudes towards punishment have evolved considerably over time, and that this evolution is germane to interpretation of the human rights norm prohibiting cruel treatment and torture. Nevertheless, jurists often use the comparison with past methods in order to justify the legality of present ones. The Indian Supreme Court, for example, has stated that stoning a person to death "is lynch law which breaches human dignity."[12] Chief Justice Bora Laskin of the Supreme Court of Canada commented, in a 1976 judgment upholding the legality of hanging, that the cruel and unusual punishment clause of the Canadian Bill of Rights prohibits "decapitation, disembowelling, and drawing and quartering."[13] For the Supreme Court of Japan,

"[I]f a law is enacted that calls for a cruel method [of imposing death] such as those used in the past—burning at the stake, crucifixion, gibbeting, or boiling in a cauldron—then that law itself must be regarded as truly in contravention of Article 36 of the Constitution [which proscribes cruel punishments]."[14] The United States Supreme Court has given burning at the stake, crucifixion, and breaking on the wheel as examples of unconstitutional methods of execution.[15]

Although courts have recognized that they have a role in considering the constitutionality of methods of execution so long as such methods are decreed by statute they will usually show a fair degree of deference to the legislature.[16] The Supreme Court of India, in a challenge to hanging as a method of execution, insisted that "[i]t is for the Courts to decide upon the constitutionality of the method prescribed by the legislature for implementing or executing a sentence."[17] It added, however, that if the Court determines a particular method to be cruel and inhuman, it will not intervene in legislative matters by recommending a satisfactory technique.[18]

International human rights bodies have also examined methods of capital punishment within the scope of the norm prohibiting torture and cruel treatment. The United Nations Human Rights Committee, in its General Comment on article 7 of the International Covenant on Civil and Political Rights,[19] noted that "when the death penalty is applied by a State party for the most serious crimes, it must not only be limited in accordance with article 6 but it must be carried out in such a way as to cause the least possible physical and mental suffering."[20] The Committee Against Torture has also expressed some mild interest in the subject.[21]

Punishments involving the intentional infliction of physical pain by the state have gradually disappeared in modern-day legal systems. Justice Albie Sachs, of the South African Constitutional Court, has described how this occurred in his country:

> [T]he British colonial administration that took over at the time of the Napoleonic wars, adopted [a position opposing the association of torture with the death penalty]. Torture was abolished. The multiple degrees of severity of capital punishment were replaced by the single relatively swift mode of hanging. The reason for this was that torture and cruel modes of execution were regarded as barbaric in themselves and degrading to the society which practised them. The incumbent judges protested that whatever might have been appropriate in Britain, in the conditions of the Cape to rely merely on hangings, corporal punishment and prison was to invite slave uprisings and mayhem. The public executioner was so distressed that he hanged himself. All this is a matter of record.[22]

Among the most significant remaining examples of such practices are the so-called Islamic punishments, involving the amputation of hands or feet, and, in the case of capital punishment, the possibility of execution by stoning or crucifixion. These traditional punishments, which find their basis in the Koran and the Shariah, were criticized by Gaspar Biro, the special rapporteur on Sudan of the Commission on Human Rights, at the commission's 1994 session.[23] This provoked a virulent reaction from the Sudanese delegation, which characterized the attack as blasphemous.[24] Punishment by whipping has largely disappeared, although it continues to exist in the military codes of some countries (e.g., Canada) and in the ordinary criminal law of others (e.g., Singapore); there are also moves to adopt it again in the United States. Corporal punishments continue to be applied to children in most countries, despite their prohibition by the Convention on the Rights of the Child,[25] which has been ratified by virtually all countries.[26]

THEORETICAL CONSIDERATIONS

Several factors have been identified in efforts to address the compatibility of various methods of execution with the norm prohibiting cruel treatment and torture. One of these is the duration of the procedure, a consideration that involves a number of possible approaches. Some have considered the lapse of time between infliction of the punishment and the moment when death is formally pronounced by a medical practitioner. The guillotine rates rather well according to this test, although there are bizarre stories of heads that continue to show signs of life after they have been severed. Other methods of execution may take considerably longer. Hanging, for example, is rapid if it causes the neck to break, but it is more drawn out when strangulation is the cause of death. Electrocution often requires more than a single "jolt" of current; in one reported case the condemned man survived, only to be submitted to the same procedure somewhat later, this time successfully.[27] In 1994, the Human Rights Committee studied evidence indicating that death in the gas chamber may take more than ten minutes after the condemned person begins to inhale cyanide. It viewed this as cruel, inhuman, and degrading punishment, running afoul of article 7 of the International Covenant on Civil and Political Rights.[28] In *Kemmler's case*, which challenged introduction of the electric chair in the State of New York, the United States Supreme Court said punishments are cruel "when they involve torture or a lingering death."[29]

It is also possible to take a somewhat larger view of the time involved, one that includes the ritual immediately preceding the imposition of punishment. "[T]he preliminaries to the act of execution should be as quick and as simple as possible, and free from anything that unnecessarily sharpens the poignancy of the prisoner's apprehension,"[30] wrote the United Kingdom's Royal Commission on Capital Punishment. It examined various methods of execution, going so far as to time (down to the minute) the different stages in the prisoner's transfer from the "death cell" to the place of execution and how long it took to set up the lethal equipment. For the commission, the fact that hanging went off more quickly than either electrocution in the electric chair or asphyxiation in the gas chamber was one of the decisive points in its favor.[31]

The Royal Commission devoted considerable attention to the issue of method of execution, and it reported that three factors are to be considered in this regard—humanity, certainty, and decency. The commission was not, strictly speaking, examining method of execution from the standpoint of the norm prohibiting cruel treatment and torture, although at least two of the three criteria, humanity and decency, fall squarely within its parameters. Like other aspects of the norm prohibiting cruel treatment and torture, a society's conception of what methods of execution are acceptable will evolve over time. Speaking on the subject of the Eighth Amendment to the United States Constitution, one judge has said that "[t]he Framers understood that our society's mores would evolve, and that some methods which had once been widely employed would become unacceptable to society, just as the torturous and barbaric punishments of the Stuarts had become unacceptable by the Framers' own time."[32]

Generally, the courts have insisted that methods of execution be instantaneous and painless, to the extent possible given the nature of the process. The United Kingdom's Royal Commission said that "the act of execution should produce immediate unconsciousness passing quickly into death."[33] According to the United States Supreme Court, "The cruelty against which the Constitution protects a convicted man is cruelty inherent in the method of punishment, not the necessary suffering involved in any method employed to extinguish life humanely."[34] The courts have also, on occasion, been critical of methods of execution that have been associated with repression, tyranny, war crimes, and crimes against humanity.[35] The use of poison gas has been singled out in this respect because of its employment in the trenches of the Somme and Verdun and in the chambers of Auschwitz and Treblinka. According to Judge Reinhardt of the United States Court of Appeals, Ninth District, assessing whether a method of punishment is cruel involves not only analyzing all of the pertinent judicial decisions but also using "the tools of philosophy, religion, logic, and history, in an effort to obtain a full understanding of the nature of a civilized society."[36] United States courts have indicated that there are three tests for determining whether punishment is cruel and unusual: historical interpretation,[37] evolving standards of decency,[38] and unnecessary or wanton infliction of pain.[39]

The Human Rights Committee, in the trio of cases where it has addressed method of execution, has not provided criteria for assessing cruelty. It has, however, condemned the gas chamber because it may provoke prolonged suffering and agony. The committee noted that asphyxiation by cyanide gas may take more than ten minutes, a stance suggesting that it adopts the criterion of instantaneity.[40]

At the same time, courts have also appeared ready to accept, up to a point, "the necessary suffering involved in any method employed to extinguish life humanely."[41] Perhaps they have been aware of the inherent difficulties in the exercise of killing, as well as the very real possibility that if too rigorous and principled a view is taken they will be compelled to find all techniques of execution to be inhumane. Such considerations appear to have inspired Christine Chanet, a member of the Human Rights Committee, who questioned the consequences of its conclusions in *Ng* v. *Canada* to the effect that the gas chamber was a breach of article 7 of the International Covenant. She declared:

> As regards article 7, I share the Committee's conclusion that the provision has been violated in the present case. However, I consider that the Committee engages in questionable discussion when, in paragraph 16.3, it assesses the suffering caused by cyanide gas and takes into consideration the duration of the agony, which it deems unacceptable when it lasts for over ten minutes. Should it be concluded, conversely, that the Committee would find no violation of article 7 if the agony lasted nine minutes?[42]

And Ms. Chanet pointed out in conclusion that "[b]y engaging in this debate, the Committee finds itself obliged to take positions that are scarcely compatible with its role as a body monitoring an international human rights instrument."[43]

Other judges have anticipated the same dilemma. Justice William J. Brennan of the United States Supreme Court, one of its die-hard abolitionists, has written: "For me, arguments about the 'humanity' and 'dignity' of *any* method of officially sponsored executions are a constitutional contradiction in terms."[44] For Judge Stephen Reinhardt, of the Court of Appeals, Ninth Circuit, "[T]he Constitution commands that we impose the death penalty in as civilized and non-brutal a manner as possible. I recognize the 'oxymoronic' quality of this directive."[45] In another decision, one reads: "[T]he physical and psychological pain associated with [the death penalty] are barbaric. . . . Such pain exists whether the death penalty is carried out by electrocution, hanging or lethal injection, and is especially barbaric when an attempted execution is bungled."[46]

Those who work to abolish the death penalty have been forced to address the same conundrum. It is obviously possible to oppose specific methods of execution, yet not oppose the death penalty as such.[47] As one author has noted, "A particular drawback of a challenge to the method of execution is the implicit approval of the death penalty itself."[48] Indeed, some abolitionist groups, such as the American Civil Liberties Union, refuse to advocate one method of execution over another for this reason.[49] Yet it is also possible to take the view, as some courts have done, that opposing a form of execution because it is cruel does not require one to propose an alternative. And some judges have seen in challenges to method of execution a kind of Trojan horse, whereby a successful attack on one technique becomes an overall assault on the death penalty.[50]

Attempts to assess the pain involved in various methods of execution are macabre, and they often reek of pseudoscience as well. Scientific assessment and study of pain, even in more banal contexts, is fraught with inherent ethical problems. In the extreme case of capital punishment, unless the execution is botched it is impossible to interview its victims. The Indian Supreme Court described the pain as only " '[i]maginable,' because in the very nature of things, there are no survivors who can give first-hand evidence of the pain involved in the execution of a death sentence."[51] Scientific research into method of execution may not even be carried out on animal subjects because of the inherent cruelty involved in strangling, asphyxiating, poisoning, and electrocuting creatures that have done no harm.[52]

The problem is an intriguing one. Unlike other aspects of the debate over cruel punishment, the courts are tempted to seek objective measures of cruelty, inhumanity, or degradation. This point has been raised before United States courts, where it has been suggested that cruelty must be measured by a purely subjective yardstick, namely, whether punishment is so cruel as to offend evolving standards of decency. But as one judge has noted, just because punishment is not deemed to be cruel by society does not mean that it will not inflict unnecessary pain and therefore run afoul of the constitutional norm.[53] He warned that to suggest such a view would mean that "even the most inhumane forms of mutilation and savagery would be permissible, so long as they inflict no more pain than necessary."[54]

Execution requires equipment, and there are commercial interests involved in promoting various methods.[55] Kemmler's 1890 challenge to the electric chair was financed by some of the young electrical companies, including Westinghouse, which were fearful of the impact on sales of state-sponsored death by electrocution.[56] In reply, Thomas Edison (a competitor) testified in favor of the technique. In a more recent example, one of the expert witnesses frequently heard before courts on the inadequacies of the electric chair happens to be the commercial promoter of equipment for lethal injection, a fact pointed out with regularity by prosecuting attorneys.[57]

One of antiquity's most celebrated victims of the death penalty, Socrates, was left to drink hemlock, in effect performing the executioner's job for him. Plato describes how Socrates prepared for the execution, and then asked that the poison be brought to him. When his friends asked why he was hastening the matter, Socrates replied that although others might postpone the time of execution he felt this was unfitting. "I do not expect any benefit from drinking the poison a little later, except to become ridiculous in my own eyes for clinging to life, and be sparing of it when there is none left," he said. "So do as I ask and do not refuse me."[58]

The idea that death row prisoners might be presented with an option between suicide and execution, as in the case of Socrates' death, was considered by the United Kingdom's Royal Commission on Capital Punishment. It was suggested that a condemned person be offered a lethal dose of some poison the night before execution, allowing him or her to escape the gallows. Although the Royal Commission considered this to be a proposal motivated by "feelings of humanity,"[59] it noted that "[t]he purpose of capital punishment is not just to rid the community of an unwanted member; it is to mark the community's denunciation of the gravest of all crimes by subjecting the perpetrator, in due form of law, to the severest of all punishments."[60] Furthermore, the commission noted that suicide was a crime, and that it was condemned by the church as a sin.[61]

Stories of prisoners attempting to "cheat" the hangman are legion. In the *Catholic Commission case,* Chief Justice Gubbay of the Zimbabwe Supreme Court referred to the affidavit of a death row prisoner describing how one man had climbed the bars to the top of his cell and then jumped to the floor head first, thereby killing himself before the executioner could do the same.[62] In 1995 in the United States, an individual took an overdose of drugs in a suicide attempt just prior to his execution date. Authorities quickly pumped his stomach and revived him so that, literally only hours later, he could be executed by a fatal quantity of state-injected drugs. Perhaps the most celebrated case of a death row suicide is that of Hermann Goering, condemned for war crimes and crimes against humanity by the International Military Tribunal at Nuremberg in 1946. Despite close surveillance, Goering was able to obtain some cyanide, probably with the connivance of an American officer, and successfully took his life the day before he was to be hanged.[63]

Method involves expertise, and there are many reports in the caselaw of "botched" executions. The likelihood of complications during execution is an important argument against the use of one or another method. One of the features of "humane" capital punishment that the United Kingdom's Royal Commission stressed was "certainty."[64] "We were told by the Home Office that there is no record during the present century of any failure or mishap in connection with an execution, and, as now carried out, execution by hanging can be regarded as speedy and certain," said the commission in its final report.[65] But according to the High Court of Tanzania in a 1994 judgment, "There are many documented cases of botched hangings in various countries including Tanzania. There are a few cases in which hangings have been messed up and the prison guards have had to pull on the prisoner's legs to speed up his death or use a hammer to hit his head."[66]

In *Francis*, an execution by the electric chair failed because the technicians responsible for connecting the wires were drunk. Willie Francis, who was sixteen years old at the time of the murder of which he was convicted,[67] petitioned the court after surviving the execution attempt, arguing that it would be cruel and unusual punishment to try again. The United States Supreme Court dismissed his petition. Justice Felix Frankfurter, whose vote was determinative in the case, told the Royal Commission some years later: "I was very much bothered by this problem, it offended my personal sense of decency to do this. Something inside of me was very unhappy, but I did not see that it violated due process."[68] In his judgment in that case, Justice Frankfurter had said he could not exclude the possibility that "a hypothetical situation, which assumes a series of abortive attempts at electrocution or even a single, cruelly willful attempt, would not raise different questions."[69] The United Kingdom's Royal Commission reviewed a report from 1885 of a condemned murderer who was reprieved after three attempts to hang him had failed.[70] The threat of bungled executions contributes to the terror in the mind of the prisoner on death row; for jurisdictions desirous of preserving the death penalty, it is also a source of discontent in public opinion.[71]

Several U.S. states now offer a choice in method of execution. A prisoner may choose between the traditional method, generally electrocution or asphyxiation, and the more modern technique of lethal injection. The idea that injection be offered as a choice was raised before the Royal Commission. It categorized such a possibility as "vacillation tormenting to [the prisoner] himself and embarrassing to the authorities"; but "[e]ven more important, we think, is the argument that it is the duty of any state that inflicts capital punishment to decide for itself what is the proper method of carrying it out, and to use that method invariably, and to take all possible means to ensure that the act is performed with dignity, solemnity, speed and certainty."[72]

The State of Washington is one locale that offers an option as to method of execution.[73] Several cases have come before the courts contesting the choice itself as a breach of the Eighth Amendment or the corresponding norm in the state constitution. According to Justice Rosellini of Washington's supreme court:

> Individual reactions to the various methods of execution and the right to choose vary greatly. In some cases, a person may be so appalled by the thought of physically hanging by the neck that the option of death by lethal injection is welcome. To others, the idea of lying strapped upon a gurney awaiting the lethal poison to seep into one's veins at an unknown time may be equally abhorrent. These individuals embrace the idea of choosing the method of their death as a way to avoid their own private terrors. But to a third type of individual, the choice itself is cruel. As they await the day of their death, they are faced not only with the terror of death itself but also with the terror of making the wrong choice on how to die. These individuals do not embrace the idea of choice; they dread its requirement that they take an active part in their own demise. To resolve this issue either way would require that, in one case or the other, the court's personal view of cruelty prevails over the views of condemned felons. But removing the choice, we impose a cruel punishment upon those who dread a particular method of execution. Retaining the right of choice, on the other hand, may impose severe psychological pressure on those who are frightened of the decision itself.[74]

Consequently, the Washington supreme court has held that the existence of a choice does not violate the Eighth Amendment.[75] In a subsequent case, petitioner Campbell argued that he was being personally involved in the choice of his means of execution, and that this violated his religious principles. The state supreme court held that "[t]he statute does not 'require' Campbell to make a decision, but only permits him to 'elect' lethal injection instead of hanging. If Campbell chooses not to participate in the decision, the statute itself will determine the method of execution."[76] This argument has a flaw. If one "chooses" not to participate in a decision, where the consequences of this choice are automatic, then one nevertheless participates in the decision. If a person is offered an apple and an orange, but can decline to eat either, then there is a choice. But if he or she must eat one or the other, then declining the apple means choosing the orange.

Campbell raised the same issue before the federal court. He argued that the legislation violated the Eighth Amendment because it forced him to assist "in the method of his own demise by electing death by intravenous injection, the less frightening method, to escape death by hanging."[77] But according to the three sitting judges of the United States Court of Appeals (Ninth Circuit),

> [n]o matter what statutory scheme is enacted, most people sentenced to death will fear their execution. Any fear that results from the prisoner's opportunity to choose the method of his execution is not unusual punishment. As for "cruelty," allowing the defendant to choose the "less frightening" method appears to us to be a more humane approach because it gives the defendant an opportunity to avoid or lessen his particular fear.[78]

Furthermore, in that judgment the Court held that a challenge to the unconstitutionality of hanging was "non-justiciable" because the condemned person had the possibility to elect lethal injection.[79] Subsequently, however, the case was heard before the court en banc. This time, the Court rejected the State's argument, noting that a case is rendered moot by an act of the parties and not by an apprehension of an act: "If the State's logic were accepted, an entire universe of claims would be foreclosed because a party might, in the future, adopt a course of action that would moot the controversy."[80] In *Campbell*, the majority concluded that the offender did not need to choose between two methods, because if he failed to choose then he would be hanged. The minority, on the other hand, noted that because it had concluded hanging to be unconstitutional, it did not need to "reach the more difficult question of whether a statute requiring a defendant to choose between two *constitutional* means of execution would violate the First or Eighth Amendments."[81]

Publicity is another feature of capital punishment that has evolved over time, no doubt because of changing perceptions about what is "decent." Making a public show of execution would at first blush seem to be fully in keeping with at least some of the objectives of capital punishment, particularly deterrence. Indeed, if such is the goal, then the more publicity the better. However, research does not bear out the conclusion that there is a relationship between deterrence, in the form of lowered homicide rates, and the publicity given to executions.[82] According to Roger Hood's 1989 study, during the course of a decade at least twenty-two countries held public executions. Several were states in the Middle East or Asia, where public execution is apparently called for under Islamic law. In China, Gabon, and Libya, executions were televised.[83] Amnesty International reported at least eighty-six public executions in Nigeria over the first eight months of 1995. On September 8 of that year, eighteen persons were executed in a sports stadium in Warri, Nigeria, for armed robbery offenses. An official who attended the execution was killed by a stray bullet from the firing squad, according to reports.[84]

The deterrence argument was invoked by the Rajasthan High Court, in India. It held that in a bride-burning case, public execution was important in order to carry "the deterrence principle to what might be called its logical conclusion."[85] However, on appeal, the Supreme Court of India said that "[t]he execution of death sentence by public hanging would be a barbaric practice clearly violative of Art. 21 of the Constitution and we are glad to note that no State in the country makes provision for execution of death sentence by public hanging which, we have no doubt, is a revolting spectacle harking back to earlier centuries. . . . [A] barbaric crime does not have to be visited with a barbaric penalty such as public hanging."[86]

Some states, such as Saudi Arabia and China, continue to carry out executions before big crowds in public squares or arenas. In the United States, executions are normally "witnessed" by a handful of journalists, state officials, clergy, and friends or relatives of the prisoner and the victim.[87] Courts have gone so far as to rule that death row prisoners may videotape executions of others in order to develop evidence of the effects of the technique, to be used eventually in their own applications challenging the method of execution.[88]

In England, executions still took place in public well into the nineteenth century. However, the practice was increasingly viewed as "a degrading form of popular entertainment, which could serve only to deprave the minds of the spectators."[89] Various studies proposed that executions no longer be held in public, including the report of a select committee of the House of Lords, in 1856. An 1868 act of Parliament decreed that henceforth executions would take place within the prison, away from public eyes.[90] The United Kingdom's Royal Commission noted the progressive trend that had put an end to public executions and rejected any attempt at reintroduction: "No doubt the ambition that prompts an average of five applications a week for the post of hangman, and the craving that draws a crowd to the prison where a notorious murderer is being executed, reveal psychological qualities of a sort that no state would wish to foster in its citizens."[91]

The question of public executions appears to have been raised only indirectly before U.S. courts. In 1994, an American judge said: "[T]here can be little doubt that the Eighth Amendment prohibits the public exhibiting of carcasses on yardarms, and the stringing up of bodies in public squares. Likewise, it prohibits the dragging by caissons of corpses through the public streets after a state-sponsored execution, and the displaying of bodies outside the homes of their former occupants or in the neighborhoods in which they lived, as a warning to allies or co-conspirators."[92]

During presentation of its initial report to the Committee Against Torture, Libya was questioned about stories of televised executions. The implication was that such public executions were a breach of the prohibition on cruel, inhuman, and degrading treatment or punishment. The representative of Libya said that a weekly television show dealing with matters of criminal justice had reported on an execution, but that the execution took place within the prison walls and was not televised.[93]

HANGING

Hanging is "a practice of great antiquity and obscure origin," according to the United Kingdom's Royal Commission on Capital Punishment.[94] The commission observed that hanging was probably invented for "its advertisement value" rather than as a method that was more effective than other forms of capital punishment known in ancient times, such as beheading, drowning, stoning, impaling, and precipitation from a height. "Hanging inflicted a signal indignity on the victim in a uniquely conspicuous fashion," the commission noted. "It displayed him to the onlookers in the most ignominious and abject of postures, and would thus be likely to enhance the deterrent effect of his punishment on anyone who might be tempted to do what he had done."[95] In 1975, the Judicial Committee of the Privy Council explained that hanging was "part of the common law."[96] The English jurist William Blackstone, who described hanging within the context of the common law, wrote that capital crimes generally compel that the offender be hanged by the neck till dead, although "in very atrocious crimes other circumstances of terror, pain, or disgrace are super-added."[97] The United States Supreme Court has cited "the custom of war" as support for the notion that individuals guilty of espionage or mutiny are traditionally hanged, whereas desertion or failure to obey orders compel shooting.[98]

Presently, hanging is generally carried out by the "long drop" method, whereby the condemned person falls through a trap door and dies out of sight beneath the scaffold.[99] The method, developed in Ireland, was introduced in England late in the nineteenth century.[100] Here is how it was set out in an 1873 Cabinet Order in Japan: "[I]n carrying out the capital punishment by hanging . . . tie both hands behind the back . . . blindfold the face . . . bring the person up onto the platform and make him stand on the centreboard . . . put the rope around his neck . . . open the trap door . . . let the convicted hang in the air."[101] The United Kingdom's Royal Commission described the procedure thus:

> [T]he chamber itself is a small room and the trap occupies a large part of the floor. The trap is formed of two hinged leaves held in position from below by bolts which are withdrawn when the lever is pulled, allowing the leaves to drop on their hinges. Above the trap a rope of a

standard length is attached to a strong chain, which is fitted to the overhead beam in such a way that it can be raised and lowered and secured at any desired height by means of a cotter slipped into one of the links and a bracket fixed on the beam. This enables the length of chain to be adjusted to make the drop accord with the height and weight of the prisoner. The executioner and his assistant arrive at the prison on the afternoon before the execution. They are told the height and weight of the prisoner and are given an opportunity to see him from a position where they themselves cannot be seen. While the prisoner is out of his cell they test the apparatus to ensure that it is working satisfactorily. For this purpose they use a sack of approximately the same weight as the prisoner, having ascertained the proper drop from a table which gives the length appropriate to a prisoner's weight. Some adjustments in the length given in the table may be necessary to allow for other physical characteristics of the prisoner, such as age and build. . . .[102]

On the morning of the execution a final check of the equipment is carried out. The rope is coiled, fitted to the chain, and secured in position by a piece of pack-thread which will be broken by the weight of the prisoner when he drops. Just before the time of execution the executioner and his assistant join the Under-Sheriff and the prison officials outside the door of the condemned cell. The Under-Sheriff gives the signal; the executioner enters the cell and pinions the prisoner's arms behind his back, and two officers lead him to the scaffold and place him directly across the division of the trap on a spot previously marked with chalk. The assistant executioner pinions his legs, while the executioner puts a white cap over his head and fits the noose round his neck with the knot drawn tight on the left lower jaw, where it is held in position by a sliding ring. The executioner then pulls the lever. The medical officer carries out an immediate inspection to assure himself that life is extinct and the body is then left to hang for an hour before being taken down.[103]

The State of Washington, one of the few remaining jurisdictions in the United States to employ hanging, now follows regulations derived from the United States Army guidelines:

Under the Washington protocol, the rope must be between three-quarters and one-and-one quarter inches in diameter. . . . The rope is boiled and then stretched to eliminate most of its elasticity. . . . The rope is then coated with wax or oil so that it will slide easily. . . . Washington employs a "long-drop" method of hanging, in which the condemned is dropped a particular distance based on the prisoner's weight. . . . The purpose of the drop . . . is to ensure that forces to the neck structures are optimized to cause rapid unconsciousness and death.[104]

The "drop" is commonly believed to break the prisoner's neck instantaneously, although contemporary expert opinion has shown this not to be true in most cases. Occlusion of the arteries is probably the most significant factor in the condemned person's loss of consciousness. Death is said to be relatively rapid, if not instantaneous. But this was not always the case. Before invention of the long drop, death resulted from suffocation and was slow and agonizing.[105] As a public spectacle, it was awesome and fearful, although this was of course the purpose of the entire exercise. "Thus," observed the Royal Commission, "hanging came to be regarded as a particularly grim and degrading form of execution, suitable for sordid criminals and crimes. Beheading, among Western peoples, used to be considered a more honorable way of suffering the death penalty, and the firing squad still is."[106] And, concluded the commission, "[w]hether or not the thought of being hanged inspires a special dread we cannot say, but there is no doubt that a stigma still attaches to it."[107] Yet the Royal Commission also claimed that the technique had a kind of dignity; for this reason, it preferred hanging over lethal injection, for example. The commission explained that "human nature is so constituted as to make it easier for a condemned man to show courage and composure in his last moments if the final act required of him is a positive one, such as walking to the scaffold, than if it is mere passivity, like awaiting the prick of a needle."[108]

Much has been made of the "art" of the hangman.[109] This generally refers to the calculations involved in adjusting the length of the rope to which the noose is attached. The condemned person must be measured and weighed in order to facilitate this. The noose may be tested beforehand with a weighted sack. If the rope is too long, then the body may be horribly mutilated during execution—there are several reports of heads being pulled off because the drop was calculated incorrectly.[110] As the Supreme Court of Zimbabwe noted, "Grim accounts exist of hangings not properly performed."[111] If the rope is too short, however, then the effect on the neck of hanging will be diminished, and the prisoner may well writhe in agony for some time, slowly suffocating. Immediately before execution the condemned person may have his or her legs and arms tied, and possibly a bag will be placed over the head.

But hanging, even with the technical improvements of the "long drop," became increasingly distasteful to many jurisdictions. The search for more palatable alternatives was begun more than a century ago. In the United States, this led to the introduction of electrocution in New York late in the nineteenth century. Quickly deemed a poor alternative to the noose, within a few years it was being passed over in other states in favor of the gas chamber. Noting the rope's steady fall from popularity not only in the United States but elsewhere in the English-speaking world, one judge concluded that "execution by hanging can hardly be compatible with 'the evolving standards of decency that mark the progress of a maturing society.' "[112] The Court of Errors and Appeals of New Jersey noted that the legislature had switched from hanging to electricity so that death "be caused as speedily as possible,"[113] adding that the statute showed "an effort by the lawmaking body to mitigate the pain and suffering of the convict."[114] In an Alabama case, where the statute providing for electrocution was judged to be inoperative, the Court considered whether earlier legislation decreeing execution by hanging was consequently revived. According to the Court, such a conclusion would violate the prohibition of cruel and unusual punishment;[115] the state's introduction of electrocution in 1940 had been "a declaration of legislative policy against a relapse into hanging by the neck until dead."[116] In 1948, the United States Supreme Court observed that Congress had abandoned hanging as the federal method, following the lead of several states that "use[d] more humane methods of execution such as electrocution, or gas."[117] However, it has been argued that in fact only a small minority of states replaced hanging because it was considered to be cruel and inhumane.[118]

Yet as late as 1953 the Royal Commission concluded, based on reports from the Home Office, that execution by hanging was "speedy and certain," something it was less inclined to conclude with respect to the electric chair and the gas chamber.[119] In 1967, the Law Commission of India made a similar finding,[120] and the same view was adopted by the country's supreme court in *Deena* v. *Union of India.*[121] In another case, the Indian Supreme Court noted that "the execution of sentence of death by hanging does involve intense physical pain and suffering, though it may be regarded by some as more humane than electrocution or application of lethal gas."[122]

One of the more astonishing findings of the United Kingdom's Royal Commission is the suggestion that hanging has some form of inherent dignity. The commission referred to "striking and unanimous testimony to the stoicism with which condemned men—and women—almost always face death on the scaffold."[123] The commission said that hanging was clearly the preferable method when assessed with respect to the criteria of humanity and certainty, although it conceded that electrocution, asphyxiation, and lethal injection rated higher on the "decency" scale.[124] The Royal Commission also admitted that "[i]f capital punishment were now being introduced into this country for the first time, we do not think it likely that this way of carrying it out [hanging] would be chosen."[125]

In the United States jurisdictions where hanging has been employed, it has been contested pursuant to the Eighth Amendment and its equivalents in the state constitutions. These attacks before the courts have never succeeded. In an early case, the Supreme Court of Oregon judged hanging to be constitutionally acceptable.[126] In Kansas, the Court summarily dismissed a challenge, supporting its views by invoking the principle of legislative deference: "The manner of inflicting the death penalty is a matter for the legislature of the state of Kansas to decide. The legislature has chosen to prescribe hanging by the neck as a means of execution in Kansas, and it is not for this court to determine the wisdom of that decree."[127] In an Iowa case, the Court held to a static view of the Eighth Amendment: "The infliction of the death penalty by hanging is of ancient origin, and is not a cruel and unusual punishment within the meaning of the constitution."[128] In Delaware, the Court was impressed by the fact that for nearly two hundred and fifty years the state legislature had consistently selected hanging as the method of execution.[129]

Washington is one of only two states (Montana is the other) that still employ hanging. In *State* v. *Frampton*, the Supreme Court of Washington reviewed the authorities, and noted that there were none that held hanging to be unconstitutional.[130] Justice Rosellini wrote that "[i]t is for the legislature, as the prescriber of the punishment for crime, to determine what method shall be used, in the absence of a definitive showing that unnecessary cruelty is involved."[131] In the late 1980s, Charles Rodman Campbell asked the Supreme Court of Washington to reconsider its precedent. The Court noted that since *Frampton*, two other states, Delaware[132] and Montana,[133] had upheld the constitutionality of hanging, and for this reason it declined to reconsider *Frampton*.[134] In fact, the Delaware decision was not settled on the merits but on a question of standing. The Delaware Court held that because there was a legislated alternative to hanging, the statute was now invulnerable to constitutional challenge: "If DeShields rejects the option to die by lethal injection, he will have waived the constitutional objection to hanging."[135]

Campbell took his case to the U.S. Court of Appeals, Ninth Circuit; in a 1994 decision, it provided far and away the most thorough examination of the question in any judicial pronouncement. In *Campbell* v. *Wood* the judges held by a six-to-five vote that execution by hanging did not violate the Eighth Amendment. An application for certiorari, to challenge the decision, was denied by the Supreme Court of the United States. The majority in the Court of Appeals relied heavily on the conclusions of fact that had been reached during a three-day evidentiary hearing by the District Court.[136] That Court had studied the "Washington Field Instruction" and determined that if its directives were followed hanging did not constitute cruel and unusual punishment. It concluded that the mechanisms causing unconsciousness and death in judicial hanging occur extremely rapidly, and that unconsciousness is likely to occur immediately or within a matter of seconds. In other words, death is not "lingering," but will follow rapidly after the moment of execution. The District Court also concluded that the risk of decapitation was negligible. The majority of the Court of Appeals said that it found no error with these findings.[137]

The Court also considered whether the virtual abandonment of hanging by other states, with the exception of Montana, was evidence that "evolving standards of decency" had now placed hanging beyond the pale of the Eighth Amendment. The majority of the Court of Appeals noted that "[t]he number of states using hanging is evidence of public perception, but sheds no light on the actual pain that may or may not attend the practice. We cannot conclude that judicial hanging is incompatible with evolving standards of decency simply because few states continue the practice."[138] However, in the opinion of the minority (five of the eleven judges), within the United States "hanging has been abandoned virtually everywhere, as states have sought less gruesome and torturous methods of execution."[139]

The Court of Appeals noted that various mechanisms are involved in death, and that the so-called hangman's fracture is one of the "less common routes to unconsciousness and death."[140] The widely held belief that "long-drop" hanging causes instant death by breaking the neck is thus not well-founded in the facts. An expert witness told the Court that one of the consequences of hanging was occlusion of the carotid arteries, which causes unconsciousness within six to eight seconds. Another possible pathway, severe trauma to the upper spinal cord, may bring about instantaneous loss of consciousness. If the cause of death is occlusion of the airway, or suffocation, "consciousness may persist for over a minute," said the witness.[141] According to the expert testimony, "[I]n general, interruption of vascular, spinal, or nervous functions by the mechanisms listed above results in rapid unconsciousness and death."[142]

There was, in the opinion of the experts, no way to determine which of the various mechanisms accounted for death in any given case. But the Court found that there exist "methods of increasing the likelihood that unconsciousness will be rapid and death comparatively painless. Chief among these is the length of the drop."[143] The majority of the Court concluded that if the drop length were calculated with some accuracy, then a combination of vascular, spinal, and nervous mechanisms would ensure loss of consciousness "within a matter of a few seconds," followed by rapid death.[144] The second important factor in ensuring swift and painless death, said the majority, was the selection and treatment of the rope. It considered that the Washington protocol, which provided for physical treatment of the rope in order to cut down on elasticity, ensured that kinetic energy generated by the drop would be transferred to the neck structures of the offender. Treatment of the rope also reduced surface friction, allowing it to slide easily and tighten around the neck.[145] The third important factor, said the majority, was the placement of the knot. Positioning it below the left ear ensured transfer of energy to the spinal structures and enhanced the possibility of occlusion of the carotid and vertebral arteries.[146]

In an earlier challenge to hanging in Washington, *State* v. *Frampton*, the Court had taken expert evidence as to the cause of death when execution is conducted by hanging. An affidavit filed on behalf of the State maintained that unconsciousness occurred within "a matter of perhaps ten seconds."[147] However, in that case the Court found the defense expert to be more persuasive. Dr. Cornelius Rosse, chairman of the anatomy department at the University of Washington School of Medicine, had concluded after reviewing the medical literature that "the common belief that death is instantaneous due to disruption of the spinal cord is incorrect in all but a very small fraction of cases. Where death is not instantaneous, its actual cause is probably strangulation or suffocation, a process that can take several minutes."[148]

In *Campbell* v. *Wood*, the District Court made several questionable evidentiary decisions in the course of hearing the evidence. For example, it excluded a great deal of testimony concerning bungled hangings on the grounds that they could not easily be compared to the Washington protocol.[149] This is a troubling conclusion, because if no reliance can be placed on proof of botched executions in other jurisdictions, the state ought to be required to experiment with methods of execution to determine whether they are humane or inhumane. The District Court had also declined to consider comparative evidence presented to show that there might be less suffering if execution were performed by lethal injection, a technique that Campbell had attempted to prove was more humane.[150] The majority of the Court of Appeals upheld these evidentiary decisions of the lower Court, although the minority judged them to be errors of law, subject to judicial review.[151]

The minority decision in *Campbell* v. *Wood* was drafted by Judge Stephen Reinhardt. In his view, "[A]lthough in the majority of hangings death is relatively painless, each time an individual is to be hanged there is a significant risk of decapitation or of a slow, lingering, and painful death."[152] He went on to observe that

[t]here is absolutely *no* question that *every* hanging involves a risk that the prisoner will not die immediately, but will instead strangle or as-

phyxiate to death. This process, which may take several minutes, is extremely painful. Not only does the prisoner experience the pain felt by any strangulation victim, but he does so while dangling at the end of a rope, after a severe trauma has been inflicted on his neck and spine. Although such slow and painful death will occur in only a comparatively small percentage of cases, every single hanging involves a significant risk that it will occur.[153]

In *Campbell*, the District Court had found that unconsciousness would result within six to twelve seconds. Judge Reinhardt responded: "In any event, six to twelve seconds must seem an exceedingly long time to a conscious prisoner dangling at the end of a rope, as he experiences the effects of severe trauma."[154]

Judge Reinhardt described judicial hanging as "an ugly vestige of earlier, less civilized times when science had not yet developed medically-appropriate methods of bringing human life to an end."[155] He continued:

Hanging is a crude, rough, and wanton procedure, the purpose of which is to tear apart the spine. It is needlessly violent and intrusive, deliberately degrading and dehumanizing. It causes grievous fear beyond that of death itself and the attendant consequences are often humiliating and disgusting.[156]

The judge also referred to hanging's historic association with lynching and frontier justice.[157] He quoted the song "Strange Fruit," made famous by Billie Holiday, which describes racially motivated extrajudicial executions in the southern United States:

Southern trees
Bear a strange fruit
Blood on the leaves
And blood at the root

Black bodies swingin'
In the Southern breeze
Strange fruit hanging
From the poplar trees.[158]

The United Nations Human Rights Committee has yet to consider whether hanging constitutes cruel, inhuman, and degrading treatment or punishment. This is difficult to understand, given the enormous number of petitions it has received from inmates on death row in Jamaica and Trinidad. In 1990, the Supreme Court of Zimbabwe asked for full argument on whether hanging was consistent with section 15(1) of the country's constitution. Specifically, the Court requested that counsel present evidence on procedures involved in hanging, and on any physical pain and mental anguish that might be attendant. But before the hearing a constitutional amendment bill was published upholding the constitutionality of executions by hanging; it later became section 15(4) of the Constitution of Zimbabwe.[159] Defending the amendment in the country's parliament, Zimbabwe's minister of justice, legal, and parliamentary affairs said any conclusion by the Court to the contrary "would be untenable to government which holds the correct and firm view . . . that Parliament makes the laws and the courts interpret them."[160] According to the minister, abolition was not a matter for the courts: "[G]overment will not and cannot countenance a situation where the death penalty is *de facto* abolished through the back door."[161] Yet the Court had proposed to do nothing more than interpret the nation's constitution, and to assess whether hanging amounted to cruel, inhuman, and degrading punishment that might be contrary to a *legislated* norm.

Justice Mwalusanya of the Tanzania High Court considered the Zimbabwe case. He declared that in *Chileya*, Zimbabwe's Supreme Court had been "about to deliver a judgment to the effect that death penalty by *hanging* was cruel and debasing punishment [but] was pre-empted by the government."[162] According to the Tanzanian judge, the Zimbabwe government "impliedly concedes that hanging is ugly and cruel and that is why they do it in secret so that the people should not witness such a cruel spectacle." Justice Mwalusanya concluded that hanging is cruel, inhuman, and degrading punishment,[163] but his judgment was overturned by the Tanzanian Court of Appeal.[164]

SHOOTING

Execution by firearms must now be the most frequently used method of capital punishment, because it is employed in China, which is far and away the greatest user of the death penalty.[165] It is still prescribed by legislation in the states of Utah and Idaho, and in a few other jurisdictions around the world.[166] The United States Supreme Court considered the constitutionality of shooting as a means of execution in *Wilkerson v. Utah*, in 1878.[167] The Court applied a "historical interpretation" test, comparing use of the firing squad to methods of execution in effect at the time of the adoption of the Bill of Rights. The Court distinguished between other methods, such as disembowelment, drawing and quartering, public dissection, and burning at the stake. It concluded that shooting was consistent with the Constitution because it was a method used traditionally under military law. In 1984 the United States District Court noted that the dicta in *Wilkerson* on shooting as a method of execution had been cited in other cases, such as *Gregg* v. *Georgia*,[168] "and will be followed by this court until more authoritative guidance is given."[169] However, the United Kingdom's Royal Commission rather summarily rejected the firing squad as an option, saying "it needs a multiplicity of executioners and it does not possess even the first requisite of an efficient method, the certainty of causing immediate death."[170]

In Utah, the condemned offender is blindfolded and then strapped to a chair. The members of the firing squad are said to wear slippers so as to muffle any sounds. One of the weapons has a blank cartridge; the members of the firing squad are not told which one, and so none of the participants can be sure if he was really an executioner. The reasoning seems bizarre, because presumably those who agree to participate have already come to terms with the moral consequences of their acts. If the firing squad does not succeed in killing the offender, it is up to the commander to deliver the coup de grâce. Apparently a notch is cut in the chair after the execution.[171] The case of Eliseo Mares, executed in Utah in 1951, suggests that the unreliability of shooting may be the way the executioners themselves voice their opposition to capital punishment. After Mares was strapped to the straight-backed chair, a heart-shaped target was pinned to his chest. Five rifles were loaded, one with a blank cartridge "so that each marksman can sleep soundly." But despite being fired from close range, not one of the four live rounds hit the target, and Mares slowly bled to death.[172]

BEHEADING

The guillotine is named for Dr. Joseph-Ignace Guillotin, a penal reformer at the time of the French Revolution. He was not the inventor of the apparatus, which had been in use in various jurisdictions for many years. But in introducing it as the sole method of execution, Guillotin intended to promote a technique that would eliminate all superfluous suffering. It takes little imagination to understand how death by guillotine is instantaneous and perhaps, for all practical purposes, painless. France abolished capital punishment in 1981. The last use of the guillotine was during the late 1970s. Execution by decapitation, or beheading, continues to be practiced in several countries, however, including Saudi Arabia, the United Arab Emirates, Yemen, Qatar, Mauritania, and Congo. Where decapitation is performed by the sword, as in Saudi Arabia, the absence of suffering is proportional to the skill of the swordsman.[173] Because of the toughness of the muscles, skin, and vertebrae in the neck, the first blow is not always successful and repeated efforts may be required.[174]

The horror of beheading, even with the eminently reliable guillotine, is the mutilation that it causes to the human body. The United Kingdom's Royal Commission conceded that the guillotine was effective, quick, and foolproof. "But we are sure," said the commissioners, "that the mutilation it produces would be shocking to public opinion in this country."[175] In his evaluation of different methods of execution, Judge Reinhardt of the U.S. Court of Appeals, Ninth Circuit, concluded that "any court faced with the issue today would certainly hold that, whatever the state of the law in 1789, beheading is inconsistent with our current standards of decency, both because every state has rejected that form of execution *and* because there is a savagery to the extreme bodily mutilation and the outpouring of blood that is simply inconsistent with human dignity."[176] Justice Brennan of the United States Supreme Court considered that basic notions of human dignity, enshrined in the Eighth Amendment, "command that the state minimize 'mutilation' and 'distortion' of the condemned prisoner's body."[177]

There have been frequent suggestions that a severed head remains alive for a short time after the execution, even that it is capable of showing sensation and emotion.[178] In animal experiments, unconsciousness results some twelve to fourteen seconds after severance or occlusion of the carotid arteries.[179] The human brain has sufficient oxygen for metabolism to continue for about seven seconds after the flow of blood to the head has ended. A study from 1993 concludes that "[i]t may be presumed that the prisoner becomes unconscious within a few seconds, but not immediately after, the spinal cord is severed."[180]

ELECTROCUTION

Execution by electricity is normally effected by strapping the condemned person in a wooden chair and connecting electrodes to his or her body. The head and the right leg will have previously been shaved in order to facilitate attaching electrodes. Between 2000 and 2200 volts at an amperage of 7 to 12 is then applied. The current is subsequently reduced and reapplied a series of times[181] until the prisoner is declared dead.[182] Execution by electrocution appears to have remained a purely American phenomenon. New York State introduced the method in 1888, following a study by the governor on the best method of inflicting capital punishment.[183] Several other states soon followed suit: Ohio in 1896; Massachusetts in 1898; New Jersey in 1907; Virginia in 1908; North Carolina in 1909; Kentucky in 1910; and Arkansas, Indiana, Pennsylvania, and Nebraska in 1913. They were apparently motivated by "a well-grounded belief that electrocution is less painful and more humane than hanging."[184] Legislation in Texas declared that hanging "is antiquated and has been supplanted in many states by the more modern and humane system of electrocution."[185] When Louisiana abandoned hanging for electrocution, it was stated that "electrocution is recognized as a more humane and less painful manner or means of carrying out the death penalty than by hanging."[186] Following the revival of capital punishment in the United States after the Supreme Court's decision in *Gregg* v. *Georgia* in 1976, the electric chair enjoyed a rather brief vogue as the favored method of execution.[187] It is now used in only a few states, notably Florida, and has been replaced in most jurisdictions with lethal injection, reflecting the will to develop more humane methods of execution.[188] The United Kingdom's Royal Commission rejected suggestions that electrocution be introduced in that country as a replacement for hanging. However, the commissioners seemed relatively impressed with the electric chair, noting that "unconsciousness is apparently instantaneous"[189] and that "[t]he leg is sometimes slightly burned, but the body is not otherwise marked or mutilated."[190]

New York State's introduction of electrocution as a method of execution was challenged immediately in a case that went all the way to the United States Supreme Court.[191] As the Court was later to note, New York was seeking a "humane and practical" alternative to hanging.[192] The first person condemned to the electric chair, William Kemmler, attacked the method of execution as a breach of the Eighth Amendment. New York State designated a commission to study the matter,[193] at which Thomas Edison and other experts on electricity testified. At considerable expense, the industrialist George Westinghouse supported Kemmler's judicial challenges to electrocution, fearing that its adoption might encourage the public to think that electricity was dangerous.[194] After considering the commission's report, a county court judge ruled electrocution to be consistent with the Eighth Amendment. The method was still untried at the time, and the evidence presented was insufficient to convince the Court that the electric chair was unconstitutionally cruel.[195] The Supreme Court rejected Kemmler's challenge on the grounds that the Eighth Amendment did not apply to the states, a position it subsequently reversed. Therefore, it never really ruled on whether the execution of Kemmler by electrocution constituted cruel and unusual punishment, although the case has since been widely cited as authority for the acceptability of the electric chair.[196]

The *New York Times* covered Kemmler's execution (which took place on August 7, 1890, at Auburn Penitentiary) in a front-page piece bearing the headline "Far Worse Than Hanging":

> Simultaneously, with the click of the lever the body of the man in the chair straightened. Every muscle of it seemed to be drawn to its highest tension. It seemed as though it might have been thrown across the chamber were it not for the straps which held it. There was no move-

ment of the eyes. The body was as rigid as though cast in bronze, save for the index finger of the right hand, which closed up so tightly that the nail penetrated the flesh on the first joint, and the blood trickled out on the arm of the chair. . . .

After the first convulsion there was not the slightest movement of Kemmler's body. . . . Then the eyes that had been momentarily turned from Kemmler's body returned to it and gazed with horror on what they saw. The men rose from their chairs impulsively and groaned at the agony they felt. "Great God! He is alive!" some one said; "[T]urn on the current," said another. . . .

Again came that click as before, and again the body of the unconscious wretch in the chair became as rigid as one of bronze. It was awful, and the witnesses were so horrified by the ghastly sight that they could not take their eyes off it. The dynamo did not seem to run smoothly. The current could be heard sharply snapping. Blood began to appear on the face of the wretch in the chair. It stood on the face like sweat. . . . An awful odor began to permeate the death chamber, and then, as though to cap the climax of this fearful sight, it was seen that the hair under and around the electrode on the head and the flesh under and around the electrode at the base of the spine was singeing. The stench was unbearable.[197]

Since 1890, when the United States Supreme Court dismissed Kemmler's application contesting the constitutionality of the electric chair, judicial challenges to execution by electrocution have been rejected on several occasions.[198] A West Virginia court, in what may have been an inadvertent admission of the cruelty of electrocution, described it as "not as cruel as hanging, which is surely not prohibited."[199] Addressing the issue of cruelty, Chief Justice Oliver Wendell Holmes of the Supreme Judicial Court of Massachusetts took the view that electrocution was unimpeachable precisely because it was adopted with a view to eliminating any pain attendant on execution: "[W]hen, as here, the means adopted are chosen with just the contrary intent, and are devised for the purpose of reaching the end proposed as swiftly and painlessly as possible, we are of opinion that they are not forbidden by the constitution."[200] Some courts have adopted a historical approach, noting that the Eighth Amendment is aimed at punishments imposed by the Stuarts.[201] For obvious reasons, the Stuart kings had not considered replacing hanging with the electric chair. But such an argument only highlights the absurdity of an "original intent" view of the prohibition of cruel treatment and torture. Just as standards of decency will evolve, so too will innovative new methods of execution be developed. They cannot escape judicial scrutiny merely because they employ new technology.

Although the constitutionality of the electric chair has been maintained consistently since *Kemmler,* there have been important dissenting opinions. In a 1985 challenge to the infliction of death by electrocution, Justice Brennan of the United States Supreme Court maintained that

> death by electrical current is extremely violent and inflicts pain and indignities far beyond the "mere extinguishment of life." Witnesses routinely report that, when the switch is thrown, the condemned prisoner "cringes," "leaps," and "fights the straps with amazing strength." "The hands turn red, then white, and the cords of the neck stand out like steel bands." The prisoner's limbs, fingers, toes and face are severely contorted. The force of the electrical current is so powerful that the prisoner's eyeballs sometimes pop out and "rest on [his] cheeks." The prisoner often defecates, urinates, and vomits blood and drool. "The body turns bright red as its temperature rises," and the prisoner's "flesh swells and his skin stretches to the point of breaking." Sometimes the prisoner catches on fire, particularly "if [he] perspires excessively." Witnesses hear a loud and sustained sound "like bacon frying," and the "sickly smell of frying human flesh in the immediate neighborhood of the chair is sometimes bad enough to nauseate even the Press representatives who are present." In the meantime, the prisoner almost literally boils: "the temperature in the brain itself approaches the boiling point of water," and when the postelectrocution autopsy is performed "the liver is so hot that doctors have said that it cannot be touched by the human hand." The body frequently is badly burned and disfigured.[202]

Justice Brennan claimed that it would be wrong to assume the electric chair brings about death in a manner that is instantaneous and painless. Expert opinion is sharply divided on the point, and there is serious evidence to suggest that electrocution "causes unspeakable pain and suffering," he said.[203] "Although it is an open question whether and to what extent an individual feels pain upon electrocution, there can be no serious dispute that in numerous cases death is far from instantaneous."[204]

Justice Peter D. Cory of the Supreme Court of Canada, in *Kindler* v. *Canada,* referred to an account of death in the electric chair:

> Electrocution has been described by one medical doctor as "a form of torture [that] rivals burning at the stake." Electrocutions have been known to drag on interminably, literally cooking the prisoners. In one instance a man's brain "was found to be 'baked hard,' the blood on his

head had turned to charcoal, and his entire back was burnt black." One man somehow survived electrocution and was returned months later, with the approval of the Supreme Court, for a second (and unsuccessful) encounter with the chair. More recently, John Spenkelink's electrocution lasted over six minutes and required three massive surges of electricity before he finally died. Although we have no accounts of the damage to Spenkelink's body caused by his execution, allegations that Florida prison officials stuffed his anus with cotton and taped his mouth shut suggest that they may have anticipated the forbidding spectacle typically provided by electrocution, and made every effort to make the sanction cosmetically acceptable.[205]

The electric chair has been prone to malfunction, and there are reports in the cases of "botched" executions.[206] As Justice Brennan noted in 1985, "It is an inescapable fact that the ninety-five-year history of electrocution in this country has been characterized by repeated failures swiftly to execute and the resulting need to send recurrent charges into condemned prisoners to ensure their deaths."[207] The most famous case of botched electrocution is the attempted execution of Willie Francis by the State of Louisiana,[208] mentioned in Justice Cory's comments above. When electrocution failed a first time, Francis petitioned the courts arguing that to try again would breach his rights under the Eighth Amendment to the Constitution.[209] The two executioners responsible for connecting the cables to the chair had apparently been drunk at the time; they passed a flask back and forth while preparing the apparatus.[210] And faulty wiring was not the only problem; the current was not applied continuously, as was specified in the governor's death warrant. Several witnesses to the execution testified that Francis received multiple jolts of electricity.[211] One, Harold Resweber, described in an affidavit the failed attempt to kill Francis:

> Then the electrocutioner turned on the switch and when he did Willie Francis' lips puffed out and he groaned and jumped so that the chair came off the floor. Apparently the switch was turned on twice and then the condemned man yelled: "Take it off. Let me breath" [sic].[212]

Another eyewitness, Ignace Doucet, described the execution as follows:

> I saw the electrocutioner turn on the switch and I saw his lips puff out and swell, his body tensed and stretched. I heard the one in charge yell to the man outside for more juice when he saw that Willie Francis was not dying and the one on the outside yelled back he was giving him all he had. Then Willie Francis cried out "Take it off. Let me breath" [sic]. Then they took the hood from his eyes and unstrapped

him. . . . This boy really got a shock when they turned that machine on.[213]

The official chaplain, Rev. Maurice L. Rosseve, was also present:

After he was strapped in the chair the Sheriff of St. Martin Parish asked him if he had anything to say about anything and he said nothing. Then the hood was placed before his eyes. Then the officials in charge of the electrocution were adjusting the mechanisms and when the needle of the meter registered to a certain point on the dial, the electrocutioner pulled down on the switch and at the same time said: "Goodby Willie." At that very moment, Willie Francis' lips puffed out and his body squirmed and tensed and he jumped so that the chair rocked on the floor. Then the condemned man said: "Take it off. Let me breath" [*sic*].[214]

Governor Jimmie Davis, within a week of the botched electrocution, sought to make a second try at executing the offender.[215] Francis challenged this move in the United States Supreme Court. Although four judges considered that a second attempt at electrocution would violate the Eighth Amendment, five did not; Justice Felix Frankfurter cast the deciding vote. Justice Stanley F. Reed, writing for the plurality, said that "we must and do assume that the state officials carried out their duties under the death warrant in a careful and humane manner" and that the affair was an accident. In Justice Reed's view, Francis had suffered an "amount of mental anguish and physical pain" identical to what might be felt in "any other occurrence, such as, for example, a fire in the cell block."[216] There could be no suggestion that a second attempt had an "element of cruelty," as "[t]here is no purpose to inflict unnecessary pain nor any unnecessary pain involved in the proposed execution."[217]

The dissenting justices confronted the issue of intent: "Although the failure of the first attempt, in the present case, was unintended, the reapplication of the electric current will be intentional."[218] In any event, "The intent of the execution cannot lessen the torture or excuse the result."[219] They noted that it was unthinkable that any modern legislature would enact a capital punishment statute authorizing "repeated application of an electrical current separated by intervals of days or hours until finally death shall result."[220] Indeed, the electric chair had been introduced in Louisiana precisely in order to eliminate extraneous pain and suffering associated with other methods, notably hanging. For the dissenters, "The all-important consideration is that the execution shall be so instantaneous and substantially painless that the punishment shall be reduced, as nearly as possible, to no more than that of death itself."[221]

Although there has apparently not been a case of multiple attempts at electrocution since the execution of Willie Francis, evidence that the electric chair does not bring instant death has continued to mount. In 1984, when Alpha Otis Stephens was executed in Georgia, the *New York Times* reported that the first charge failed to kill him and he "struggled to breathe for eight minutes. . . . His body slumped when the current stopped . . . but shortly afterward witnesses saw him struggle to breathe. In the six minutes allowed for the body to cool before doctors could examine it, Mr. Stephens took about twenty-three breaths."[222] Terrible and lingering pain would appear to have been inflicted upon Horace Dunkins when the Alabama electric chair malfunctioned on July 14, 1989.[223] The two technicians who connected the chair for the prisoner's electrocution admitted they had plugged it into the wrong receptacles. A doctor who witnessed the execution said that Dunkins was "literally burned to death after receiving a painful electric shock that was inadequate to kill him."[224]

The botched execution of Horace Dunkins was invoked by petitioner Wallace Norrell Thomas, who sought a stay of his execution until Alabama obtained its new electric chair. At an evidentiary hearing, the district judge held that "in a properly performed judicial electrocution the initial application of electricity is meant to cause instant brain death."[225] Evidence led by Thomas challenging the State's submission that brain death was instant was dismissed by the District Court judge as being founded on "incorrect assumptions of fact."[226] The judge said that "although [Alabama's] electric chair is old, it is in proper working condition . . . and . . . the likelihood of an error similar to that which occurred during the Dunkins execution is remote."[227] He said that there was no "credible evidence that prison inmates, including Thomas, who are to be executed in this electric chair in the foreseeable future will suffer any pain."[228]

In another case, *Ritter* v. *Smith*,[229] the offender challenged his execution because the chair had earlier malfunctioned in the case of John Louis Evans.[230] The Court, relying incorrectly on the Supreme Court's judgment in *Francis*,[231] held that the possibility it might malfunction in the future was not enough to make the method of execution contrary to the Constitution.[232] *Francis* had only established that an electric chair expected to function properly in the future, even if it had malfunctioned in the past, could be used. There had been no suggestion in that case that the chair was improperly constructed or defective, merely that human error had botched the execution. A description of Evans's death was subsequently quoted by Justice Brennan of the United States Supreme Court, in *Glass* v. *Louisiana*, partly to show that botched electrocutions are "by no means confined to bygone decades":

At 8:30 P.M. the first jolt of 1900 volts of electricity passed through Mr. Evans' body. It lasted thirty seconds. Sparks and flames erupted from the electrode tied to Mr. Evans' left leg. His body slammed against the straps holding him in the electric chair and his fist clenched permanently. The electrode apparently burst from the strap holding it in place. A large puff of greyish smoke and sparks poured out from under the hood that covered Mr. Evans' face. An overpowering stench of burnt flesh and clothing began pervading the witness room. Two doctors examined Mr. Evans and declared that he was not dead. The electrode on the left leg was refastened. At 8:30 [*sic*] P.M. Mr. Evans was administered a second thirty-second jolt of electricity. The stench of burning flesh was nauseating. More smoke emanated from his leg and head. Again, the doctors examined Mr. Evans. The doctors reported that his heart was still beating, and that he was still alive. At that time, I asked the prison commissioner, who was communicating on an open telephone line to Governor George Wallace to grant clemency on the grounds that Mr. Evans was being subjected to cruel and unusual punishment. The request for clemency was denied. At 8:40 P.M., a third charge of electricity, thirty seconds in duration, was passed through Mr. Evans' body. At 8:44, the doctors pronounced him dead. The execution of John Evans took fourteen minutes.[233]

Justice Brennan concluded: "[E]ven if electrocution does not invariably produce pain and indignities, the apparent century-long pattern of 'abortive attempts' and lingering deaths suggests that this method of execution carries an unconstitutionally high risk of causing such atrocities."[234]

At Jesse Tafero's execution, in Florida on May 4, 1990, witnesses said that flames, sparks, and smoke emanated from the hood on his head and that four jolts of power were required to kill him.[235] After this episode, Judy Buenoano challenged her pending execution in the same electric chair. Following a two-day hearing, the United States District Court for the Middle District of Florida found that a defective sponge, which had since been replaced, was responsible for the malfunction during Tafero's electrocution.[236] Apparently, a synthetic instead of a natural sponge had been placed on his head to assist in conducting the electricity. The sponge caught fire and caused the flames and smoke that so horrified witnesses to the execution. Two physicians testified that Tafero lost consciousness with the first surge of electricity. The Court accepted testimony from the Florida Department of Corrections claiming that Tafero did not suffer any unusual or prolonging effects during the execution, and that most such executions do not last longer than seven minutes.[237] Once again relying on the

United States Supreme Court's ruling in *Francis*, the District Court refused to intervene, and its judgment was upheld on appeal. According to a dissenting justice of the Florida Supreme Court, "The majority simply proclaims that the state may choose any method of death, and the method cannot be challenged, because we 'presume' that the state cannot be wrong."[238]

Another dissenter, Justice Kogan, said it was possible that the flames resulted "from Tafero's own body tissue being superheated by an inefficient flow of electricity through his body."[239] The justice questioned the account provided by the Florida Department of Corrections (DOC):

> DOC presents this Court with a paradox. DOC asks us to believe that *120 volts* [applied in an experiment] caused the sponge to shrink by two-thirds in a mere ten seconds, but that three separate *2,000-volt* surges over a six-to seven-minute period had two inconsistent results: (1) The sponge in the skull cap burst into profuse flames that literally danced around the head of Tafero during all three jolts of electricity; and yet (2) the sponge remained sufficiently intact that a piece could be removed for testing. Indeed, the fact that the sponge reduced its volume by two-thirds after being placed in the kitchen toaster for ten seconds indicates not only that the sponge survived the electrical jolts, but that portions of it had not even *melted* to any significant extent.[240]

Justice Kogan said that Buenoano's explanations "make scientific sense"; he found support for this in the autopsy report, which

> indicated a large area of charred and blackened flesh on the top and left-hand side of the head. Surrounding the blackened flesh were patches of browned and reddened skin and a few places in which skin appeared to be peeling away from the skull. In addition, most of Tafero's eyebrows and eyelashes had been burned away, curled or singed by the flames, especially on the side of the head showing the most serious charring.[241]

According to the justice, one eyewitness to the execution had said that Tafero continued to move and breathe *after* his head had caught fire.[242] Another witness testified that the entire top of the dead prisoner's head was covered with wounds:

> There is one dominant charred area and a myriad of smaller gouged, raw areas to the upper right side and lower right of the large burned area. The dominant charred area is on the top left side of the head. It is larger than my hand. . . . The funeral director said that this was a third degree burn.[243]

In the Tafero execution, Florida authorities had connected the electrode to the prisoner's leg using what was described as a "homemade" Army-boot electrode. This prompted Justice Kogan to observe that, "[t]he Court thus is faced with a ghastly possibility: A homemade electrode fashioned out of a used Army boot, spare parts and roofing material may sometimes result in flames, smoke, and extensive charring of flesh during an execution."[244]

Other prisoners besides Judy Buenoano challenged execution in the Florida chair following Tafero's death.[245] In one of these cases, which in effect demonstrates a refusal to intervene, the judge said that "[a] federal court is particularly ill-suited to fill the role of the office of master electrician for the electrocution chamber at the Florida State Prison. . . . The Eighth Amendment . . . does not license the court to practice the electrician's trade."[246]

As in the case of hanging, one must conclude that judicial challenges to execution have generally been unsuccessful. However, the judgments are generally accompanied by exhaustive dissenting opinions that indicate how divided the judiciary really is on such questions. Furthermore, legislative reforms appear to be motivated by a recognition that such methods of execution as the electric chair are unsatisfactory.

ASPHYXIATION BY LETHAL GAS

Like use of the electric chair, employment of the gas chamber to impose the death penalty is essentially restricted to the United States (where both techniques were first developed). Its adoption falls within an unequivocal trend in the United States towards execution that minimizes pain, suffering, and above all mutilation of the body.[247] With the aptly named Humane Death Bill of 1921, Nevada became the first state to introduce asphyxiation by lethal gas as a method of execution. According to the original protocol, the condemned individual was to be placed in a special cell for one week; at an unspecified moment during this period the valves would be opened while the prisoner was asleep and the individual would die without awakening. A challenge to this law under the Eighth Amendment to the United States Constitution was unsuccessful.[248] At the time, the Court praised introduction of the technique as an initiative by states that "sought to provide a method of inflicting the death penalty in the most humane manner known to modern science."[249]

The approach proposed originally by Nevada was abandoned in favor of a special killing cell known as the gas chamber; execution was effected rapidly while the prisoner was conscious. Execution by cyanide gas was subsequently adopted in nine other states: Arizona, California, Colorado, Maryland, Mississippi, Missouri, New Mexico, North Carolina, and Wyoming. Several petitions in the courts of these states were dismissed.[250] In a California challenge in 1953, the Court concluded: "We think it fair to assume that our Legislature, in enacting the law in question, sought to provide a method of inflicting the death penalty in the most humane manner known to modern science."[251] However, the United States Supreme Court has only considered the issue obliquely, in denying applications for judicial review.[252]

Like hanging and the electric chair, the gas chamber has steadily been abandoned in favor of lethal injection—no jurisdiction now recognizes it as an exclusive method of execution. California, North Carolina, and Maryland allow for death by lethal gas, unless the prisoner chooses to be executed by lethal injection.[253] Mississippi and Arizona use gas in executions for sentences imposed before a specified date; they will execute solely by lethal injection in the future.[254] Judge Marilyn H. Patel of the United States District Court for the Northern District of California noted that "the abandonment of the gas chamber as a means of execution [has occurred at a rate] dramatically higher than the abandonment of other means of execution."[255]

The execution business is rife with symbolism, and proponents of the death penalty will point out that a similar method is used to put domestic animals "to sleep." The Supreme Court of Nevada, in hearing an early challenge to the gas chamber, also commented on the use of gas by dental surgeons to extract teeth painlessly.[256] Yet the gas chamber also has its stigmas. The use of lethal gas in warfare is now prohibited by international humanitarian law.[257] Poison gas was the method chosen by the Nazis to carry out their mass murders of Jews, Gypsies, and others during World War II. The connection with war crimes and crimes against humanity remains to this day. A leading proponent of "humane" execution technology in the United States, Fred Leuchter, has also provided "expert" testimony on behalf of those who deny the Holocaust.[258] Attempting to bolster his credibility by citing knowledge and experience gained in the death rows of U.S. penitentiaries, Leuchter has claimed, in pamphlets and in testimony, that it was impossible that the gas chambers of Auschwitz were used in committing genocide.[259]

The California gas chamber, located at San Quentin State Prison, is a modified octagon, approximately seven and one-half feet in diameter.[260] There are two chairs; a condemned inmate is strapped in by the legs and arms before execution. A reservoir is located under the chair to hold a mixture of sulfuric acid and distilled water. There is also a bedpan to catch the excretions of the prisoner. A cheesecloth bag of sodium cyanide crystals is suspended over the reservoir. There are holes in the seat so that the gas may rise.[261] Five of the eight sides of the chamber have windows, and chairs are placed outside for witnesses. The United Kingdom's Royal Commission heard testimony describing the operation of the gas chamber, and the methodology does not appear to have changed substantially since then.

> Twenty minutes before execution three pints of U.S.P. sulfuric acid and six pints of water are carefully mixed in a lead container. The container is covered with a lid of similar material and is placed under the chair in a position to receive the pellets when dropped. There are two copper pipes adjacent to the chair which lead under the floor outside the physician's stand. At the end of the pipe in the chamber is rubber hose which is to be connected to the head of a Bowles stethoscope strapped to the prisoner's chest. Attached to the other end of the copper pipes at the physician's stand are the earpieces of a stethoscope for determining the time of the prisoner's death.[262]

The offender is strapped into a chair in the chamber, with all clothes except shorts removed in order to eliminate the possibility of pockets of gas remaining in items of clothing.[263] When the order is given to commence execution, a lever is pushed and the sodium cyanide crystals are dropped into the acid. This produces hydrocyanic gas, which is inhaled by the prisoner. After the inmate is pronounced dead, ammonia gas is forced into the chamber until the cyanide has been neutralized; then the ammonia gas is removed by a specially constructed exhaust fan.[264] In its deliberations, the Royal Commission also considered the possibility of using lethal gas without a chamber. The idea, proposed by the British Medical Association, was to administer carbon monoxide through a mask. But the commission noted that the onset of unconsciousness would take at least a minute and that a struggle might be involved in putting on the mask. Since the only way to avoid this would be to render the prisoner unconscious first, the Royal Commission felt that if this step was to be taken the State might just as well go directly to lethal injection.[265]

Execution by asphyxiation normally makes use of hydrogen cyanide, or hydrocyanic, gas.[266] Expert testimony concerning its effects on humans was considered in 1994, in *Fierro v. Gomez*. In that case, Judge Patel noted that cyanide, the lethal ingredient, affects many systems within the body. Where the experts differ is on how quickly unconsciousness occurs; as with other examinations of method of execution, one of the difficulties is the absence of survivors to study. Cyanide that is inhaled binds to an enzyme system (the cytochrome oxidase system), thereby blocking transfer of oxygen to cells.[267] Deprived of oxygen and thus unable to produce energy, the cells cease functioning and then die, leading to unconsciousness and death for the person in question. The process is similar to what happens when someone drowns or is strangled.[268]

There is no question that cyanide inhalation has a number of other consequences, many of which can be very painful to the prisoner. Being deprived of oxygen forces cells to attempt to generate energy by other means. One consequence of this is the production of lactic acid, which causes acidosis; the resulting pain is said to be similar to that experienced by a person undertaking intense physical activity or having a heart attack.[269] Cyanide inhalation may also result in tetany, a painful sustained muscular contraction or spasm; other types of spasm are possible, as well. That these occur during gas execution is corroborated by witnesses. Judge Patel cited a number of eyewitness accounts of executions at San Quentin's gas chamber where prisoners were conscious for three to five minutes and where they appeared to writhe in pain, struggling with the straps, clenching their fists, and showing other signs of consciousness and pain.[270]

Justice Peter D. Cory of Canada's supreme court, in *Kindler* v. *Canada*, described killing by gas in a graphic report of the execution of Eddie Daniels, written by Reverend Myer Tobey:

> In the chamber now, he was strapped to the chair. The cyanide had been prepared, and was placed beneath his chair, over a pan of acid that would later react with the cyanide to form the deadly gas. Electrocardiographic wires were attached to Daniels' forearms and legs, and connected to a monitor in the observation area. This lets the doctor know when the heart stops beating.
>
> This done, the prison guards left the room, shutting the thick door, and sealing it to prevent the gas from leaking. I took my place at one of the windows, and looked at Eddie, and he looked at me. We said the prayer together, over and over.
>
> At a motion of the warden, a prison guard then pulled a lever releasing the cyanide crystals beneath the chair. Eddie heard the chemical pellets drop, and he braced himself. We did not take our eyes off each other.
>
> In an instant, puffs of light white smoke began to rise. Daniels saw the smoke, and moved his head to try to avoid breathing it in. As the gas continued to rise he moved his head this way and that way, thrashing as much as his straps would allow still in an attempt to avoid breathing. He was like an animal in a trap, with no escape, all the time being watched by his fellow humans in the windows that lined the chamber. He could steal only glimpses of me in his panic, but I continued to repeat "My Jesus I Love You," and he too would try to mouth it.

Then the convulsions began. His body strained as much as the straps would allow. He had inhaled the deadly gas, and it seemed as if every muscle in his body was straining in reaction. His eyes looked as if they were bulging, much as a choking man with a rope cutting off his windpipe. But he could get no air in the chamber.

Then his head dropped forward. The doctor in the observation room said that that was it for Daniels. This was within the first few minutes after the pellets had dropped. His head was down for several seconds. Then, as we had thought it was over, he again lifted his head in another convulsion. His eyes were open, he strained and he looked at me. I said one more time, automatically, "My Jesus I Love You." And he went with me, mouthing the prayer. He was still alive after those several minutes, and I was horrified. He was in great agony. Then he strained and began the words with me again. I knew he was conscious, this was not an automatic response of an unconscious man. But he did not finish. His head fell forward again.

There were several more convulsions after this, but his eyes were closed. I could not tell if he were conscious or not at that point. Then he stopped moving, approximately ten minutes after the gas began to rise, and was officially pronounced dead.[271]

As I have mentioned, where experts on the gas chamber differ is on how quickly unconsciousness occurs. Defenders of judicial asphyxiation claim it comes on very quickly and any painful side effects occur after the prisoner has lost consciousness. Cyanide is also said to create a sudden drop in phosphocreatinine, bringing on unconsciousness within ten to thirty seconds.[272] Critics of the gas chamber, on the other hand, claim that the prisoner is conscious considerably longer, and may also lapse out of and into consciousness for several minutes. In *Fierro v. Gomez*, Judge Patel found as a question of fact, after hearing a battery of expert witnesses, that loss of consciousness took considerably longer than thirty seconds, and that prisoners experienced intense pain while they were still awake. She said:

> Although the precise dose delivered at San Quentin cannot be reliably determined, the court finds it is well in excess of a lethal dose. Although this finding tends to support defendants' view that death in the gas chamber occurs relatively quickly, it is far from dispositive. Compared to a very small dose of cyanide, which may not cause death until 30 minutes to one hour of exposure, a large dose of cyanide does produce relatively rapid unconsciousness and death. However, the time increments crucial to this litigation are small—the difference be-

tween several seconds and several minutes—and defendants' evidence does not demonstrate that the dose administered at San Quentin is so strong as to produce immediate unconsciousness and/or death.[273]

Judge Patel concluded:

> In sum, based on the evidence presented at trial, the testimony of the experts and the scientific literature introduced as exhibits, the court finds that inmates who are put to death in the gas chamber at San Quentin do not become immediately unconscious upon the first breath of lethal gas. The court further finds that an inmate probably remains conscious anywhere from 15 seconds to one minute, and that there is a substantial likelihood that consciousness, or a waxing and waning of consciousness, persists for several additional minutes. During this time, the court finds that inmates suffer intense, visceral pain, primarily as a result of lack of oxygen to the cells. The experience of "air hunger" is akin to the experience of a major heart attack, or to being held under water. Other possible effects of the cyanide gas include tetany, an exquisitely painful contraction of the muscles, and painful build-up of lactic acid and adrenaline. Cyanide-induced cellular suffocation causes anxiety, panic, terror, and pain.[274]

In *Gray* v. *Lucas*, decided in 1983 by the United States Court of Appeals, Fifth Circuit, the constitutionality of the gas chamber was upheld.[275] The Court refused to conclude that "as a matter of law or fact, the pain and terror resulting from death by cyanide is so different in degree or nature from that resulting from other traditional modes of execution as to implicate the eighth amendment right."[276] The Court conceded that "[t]raditional deaths by execution, such as by hanging, have always involved the possibility of pain and terror for the convicted person."[277] Certiorari was denied by the majority of the United States Supreme Court, although three justices would have heard the appeal. Chief Justice Burger referred to affidavits filed by Gray challenging the constitutionality of the gas chamber, but he opposed even an evidentiary hearing on the matter because "they do not as a matter of law establish an Eighth Amendment violation."[278] The chief justice endorsed the comment of the Court of Appeals, cited above. Justice Thurgood Marshall called this an error, noting that the Court of Appeals had admitted that execution by lethal gas involved "extreme pain over a span of ten to twelve minutes," and said this must surely be characterized as "lingering."[279] Justice Marshall also referred to the legislative abandonment of the gas chamber as demonstrating "awareness of the trauma associated with the lethal-gas method."[280] In his view, "This evolving consensus against compulsory use of the lethal-gas method buttresses the conclusion that the procedure must now be considered 'cruel.' "[281]

Gray v. *Lucas* has been followed in a number of challenges before the state courts.[282] However, the legislatures continued to eliminate the gas chamber in favor of lethal injection; in 1992, one judge noted that of the states relied upon by the Court in *Gray* as having approved of lethal gas, only California still used it.[283] Judge Patel chose not to follow *Gray* v. *Lucas*, and she concluded that execution in the gas chamber was a form of cruel and unusual treatment or punishment. The judge wrote that "the eyewitness descriptions of executions by lethal gas provided in plaintiff's memoranda are comparable to the descriptions of hanging in *State* v. *Frampton*, a case in which the court found hanging to be an unconstitutional method of execution."[284]

California's continued use of the gas chamber came before the Supreme Court of the United States in 1992, in a death row petition lodged by Robert Alton Harris. A stay was ordered when ten judges of the District Court had called for a vote on rehearing the case en banc,[285] but this was overturned by the United States Supreme Court. The Court noted that the petitioner's claim that the gas chamber violated the Eighth Amendment "could have been brought more than a decade ago," and that it was merely another of his "last minute attempts to manipulate the judicial process."[286] However, Justice John Paul Stevens (with whom Justice Harry A. Blackmun was in agreement) said that "[i]n light of all that we know today about the extreme and unnecessary pain inflicted by execution by cyanide gas, and in light of the availability of more humane and less violent methods of execution, Harris' claim has merit."[287] He also said, "To my mind, the gas chamber is nothing more than a chemical garotte."[288]

Justice Stevens cited exhibits that were part of the record, including findings presented in a declaration by a medical expert:

> Following inhalation of cyanide gas, a person will first experience hypoxia, a condition defined as a lack of oxygen in the body. The hypoxic state can continue for several minutes after the cyanide gas is released in the execution chamber. During this time a person will remain conscious and immediately may suffer extreme pain throughout his arms, shoulders, back, and chest. The sensation may be similar to pain felt by a person during a massive heart attack.[289]

He added, quoting another expert: "Execution by gas . . . produces prolonged seizures, incontinence of stool and urine, salivation, vomiting, retching, ballistic writhing, flailing, twitching of extremities, [and] grimacing."[290]

Justice Stevens noted that California's gas chamber statute had been introduced in 1937 and that at the time it was considered to provide for a humane method of execution. However, "fifty-five years of history and moral development have superseded that judgment." The justice pointed to the use of cyanide gas in the Nazi death camps, the development of cyanide agents for use as chemical weapons, enhanced knowledge about the processes involved in execution by lethal gas, and "the development of less cruel methods of execution." All of this led him to believe that use of the gas chamber was "unnecessarily cruel."[291] Justice Stevens noted that of twenty states to adopt new methods of execution since the Supreme Court authorized the death penalty again in *Gregg* v. *Georgia*, not one had chosen gas, and that "one by one" the states are abandoning gas as "inhumane and torturous." Writing in 1992, he observed that only 6 of the 168 persons executed since 1977 had been put to death by gas.[292]

This emphasis on the evolving attitudes to the gas chamber and its inhumanity was an answer to the majority's claim that Harris's application was tardy. As early as 1983 seven states still authorized execution by poison gas. At the time, three members of the Court were prepared to grant certiorari in *Gray* v. *Lucas;* since then, noted Justice Stevens, four states (Colorado, Mississippi, Oregon, and Wyoming) had abandoned cyanide gas.[293]

Fierro's case was tried in 1994 before Judge Patel of the United States District Court for the Northern District of California. She was concerned about the impact of the recent decision of the Ninth Circuit Court of Appeals, *Campbell* v. *Wood*, which addressed the constitutionality of hanging.[294] Observing that "[i]t is difficult at times to decipher the Campbell opinion," Judge Patel said that it did clarify the point that the key question in challenges to method of execution is how much pain the inmate suffers.[295] Noting that unconsciousness during hanging set in within a matter of seconds, she recalled that the Court had held in *Campbell* that persistence of consciousness for one or two minutes might breach the Constitution, although no precise threshold was established.[296] On this wing of the *Campbell* precedent, Judge Patel considered that the gas chamber had probably failed the test.[297] Furthermore, she invoked legislative trends in favor of suppressing the gas chamber as evidence that it was no longer consistent with "evolving standards of decency."[298]

Use of execution by poison gas was attacked by Charles Ng in a petition before the United Nations Human Rights Committee. Fighting extradition to California from Canada on a murder charge, Ng argued that use of the gas chamber might expose him to torture or to cruel, inhuman, and degrading treatment or punishment, in breach of article 7 of the International Covenant on Civil and Political Rights.[299] The committee agreed, concluding rather laconically:

> In the present case, the author has provided detailed information that execution by gas asphyxiation may cause prolonged suffering and agony and does not result in death as swiftly as possible, as asphyxiation by cyanide gas may take over ten minutes. The State party had the opportunity to refute these allegations on the facts; it has failed to do so. Rather, the State party has confined itself to arguing that in the absence of a norm of international law which expressly prohibits asphyxiation by cyanide gas, "it would be interfering to an unwarranted degree with the internal laws and practices of the United States to refuse to extradite a fugitive to face the possible imposition of the death penalty by cyanide gas asphyxiation."
>
> In the instant case and on the basis of the information before it, the Committee concludes that execution by gas asphyxiation, should the death penalty be imposed on the author, would not meet the test of "least possible physical and mental suffering," and constitutes cruel and inhuman treatment, in violation of article 7 of the Covenant. . . .
>
> The Committee need not pronounce itself on the compatibility, with article 7, of methods of execution other than that which is at issue in this case.[300]

But Canada apparently did contest the issue of the gas chamber on the facts, stating that "none of the methods currently in use in the United States is of such a nature as to constitute a violation of the Covenant or any other norm of international law."[301]

Two members of the Human Rights Committee, Andreas Mavrommatis and Waleed Sadi, dissented from the majority view, stating that the evidence before the committee did not justify a conclusion that execution by gas asphyxiation constituted cruel and inhuman treatment within the meaning of article 7. In their opinion:

> Every known method of judicial execution in use today, including execution by lethal injection, has come under criticism for causing prolonged pain or the necessity to have the process repeated. We do not believe that the Committee should look into such details in respect of execution such as whether acute pain of limited duration or less pain of longer duration is preferable and could be a criterion for a finding of violation of the Covenant.[302]

A similar opinion was expressed by Kurt Herndl: "To attempt to establish categories of methods of judicial executions, as long as such methods are not manifestly arbitrary and grossly contrary to the moral values of a democratic society, and as long as such methods are based on a uniformly applicable legislation adopted by democratic processes, is futile, as it is futile to attempt to quantify the pain and suffering of any human being subjected to capital punishment."[303] Nisuke Ando dissented along the same lines, confessing that he was unable to determine the kind of suffering that was inadmissible under article 7 of the Covenant.[304] Such positions are very hard to understand, because they seem to open the door to all kinds of abuse in imposition of the death penalty. Even the conservative courts of the United States have departed from such a view for more than a century.

The committee member Fausto Pocar, in his individual reasons, took a more radical position. He said he agreed that there was a violation of article 7 of the Covenant, but because "by definition, every execution of a sentence of death may be considered to constitute cruel and inhuman treatment within the meaning of article 7 of the Covenant."[305] Francisco José Aguilar Urbina said that he too considered the death penalty to constitute cruel, inhuman, and degrading treatment, in violation of article 7 of the Covenant.[306] I agree with this conclusion; however, it is not correct to say, as did the South African Constitutional Court, that it constitutes the position of the majority of the Human Rights Committee.[307]

LETHAL INJECTION

Execution by injecting lethal drugs was introduced in the United States by legislation in 1977 and was first carried out in Texas in 1983. It has very quickly replaced hanging, electrocution, and lethal gas in most jurisdictions. The condemned person is strapped to a gurney, and a small tube, or cannula, is inserted into the vein on one arm at the angle of the elbow. Once the cannula is passed into the vein, a series of substances are injected. The first, the barbiturate sodium thiopentone, is a rapid acting anesthetic. The second, pancuronium bromide, is a muscle relaxant that paralyzes respiration. Last, potassium chloride is injected, and this stops the heart. Prisoners are said to become unconscious within ten to fifteen seconds; death results from anesthetic overdose and from respiratory and cardiac arrest.[308] Justice Antonin Scalia of the United States Supreme Court has spoken of the merits of what he calls "a quiet death by lethal injection."[309] A lower court has said that "[t]here is general agreement that lethal injection is at present the most humane type of execution available and is far preferable to the sometimes barbaric means employed in the past."[310] Another judge has said that there is a national consensus that "lethal injection does not violate the American society's evolving standards of decency."[311]

The technique is not, however, without its flaws. Frequent problems arise in cannulating the vein—inserting the tube involves a degree of expertise, and it cannot be performed by medical professionals because of ethical considerations.[312] Some prisoners are simply not able to receive the injection. Others have scarred arms, resulting from suicide attempts or drug abuse. Veins may be invisible, covered with layers of fat, or so flat that a needle which pierces one wall goes through the opposite one as well.[313] There are numerous reports of executions in the United States where such problems arose and where there were excruciating delays while prison personnel endeavored to connect the apparatus. In two recent cases, prisoners waited hours while technicians struggled to administer the "medication."[314]

There is also evidence that lethal injection is accompanied by pain and suffering for the prisoner. In one recent case, a judge described execution by lethal injection as painful. He cited in this context the description by Ellen Goodman, a syndicated columnist, of the 1984 execution of James David Autry.[315] According to *Newsweek*, when Autry was executed in Texas on March 14, 1984, he "took at least ten minutes to die and throughout much of that time was conscious, moving about and complaining of pain."[316] Justice William J. Brennan of the United States Supreme Court has noted that injection using barbiturates has its "own risks of pain, indignity, and prolonged suffering."[317] The United Kingdom's Royal Commission, which studied injection as an alternative to hanging, noted that intravenous injection required a high degree of skill and that for this reason intramuscular injection ought not to be ruled out. However, the commission observed that this technique is considerably slower and that injection of the poison into muscles might cause superfluous pain.[318] There have also been unsuccessful challenges to lethal injection in the United States on the grounds that there is a violation of food and drug legislation, in that the offender is forced to become an unwilling consumer of drugs whose safeness and efficacy have not been demonstrated in approved tests.[319]

The Human Rights Committee has held that execution by lethal injection is not a breach of article 7 of the International Covenant on Civil and Political Rights.[320] The committee's conclusions are unsatisfactory, however. In the first case, *Kindler* v. *Canada*,[321] it rejected the argument but noted that Kindler's attorney had not led evidence of cruel and inhuman treatment. In the second, *Cox* v. *Canada*,[322] the committee rejected the argument by citing *Kindler*, despite the presentation in *Cox* of substantial evidence pointing to suffering during execution by injection. An affidavit—supplied by Professor Michael Radelet of the University of Florida, an authority on the subject—described several "botched" executions using lethal injection:

> *January 24, 1992. Arkansas. Rickey Ray Rector.* It took medical staff more than 50 minutes to find a suitable vein in Rector's arm. Witnesses were

not permitted to view this scene, but reported hearing Rector's loud moans throughout the process. During the ordeal Rector (who suffered serious brain damage from a lobotomy) tried to help the medical personnel find a vein. The administrator of the State's Department of Corrections medical programs said (paraphrased by a newspaper reporter) "the moans did come as a team of two medical people that had grown to five worked on both sides of his body to find a vein." The administrator said that may have contributed to his occasional outbursts. [The order to execute Rector was given by the governor at the time, Bill Clinton.]

March 10, 1992. Oklahoma. Robyn Lee Parks. Parks had a violent reaction to the drugs used in the lethal injection. Two minutes after the drugs were administered, the muscles in his jaw, neck and abdomen began to react spasmodically for approximately 45 seconds. Parks continued to gasp and violently gag. Death came eleven minutes after the drugs were administered. Said *Tulsa World* reporter Wayne Greene, "The death looked scary and ugly."

May 7, 1992. Texas. Justin Lee May. May had an unusually violent reaction to the lethal drugs. According to Robert Wernsman, a reporter for the *Item* (Huntsville), May "gasped, coughed and reared against his heavy leather restraints, coughing once again before his body froze. . . ." Associated Press reporter Michael Braczyk wrote, "He went into a coughing spasm, groaned and gasped, lifted his head from the death chamber gurney and would have arched his back if he had not been belted down. After he stopped breathing, his eyes and mouth remained open."[323]

Canada had argued that death by lethal injection could not be inhuman, because it was the same method proposed by advocates of euthanasia.

In *Ng.* v. *Canada*, in partially concurring reasons, Bertil Wennergren supported the committee's conclusion with respect to article 7. He compared the gas chamber, which he considered unacceptable, with lethal injection, which seemed to him to be less offensive from the standpoint of article 7:

[T]he State of California, in August 1992, enacted a statute law that enables an individual under sentence of death to choose lethal injection as the method of execution, in lieu of the gas chamber. The statute law went into effect on 1 January 1993. Two executions by lethal gas had taken place during 1992, approximately one year after the extradition of Mr. Ng. By amending its legislation in the way described above, the State of California joined twenty-two other States in the United States. The purpose of the legislative amendment was not, however, to eliminate an allegedly cruel and unusual punishment, but to forestall last-minute appeals by condemned prisoners who might argue that execution by lethal gas constitutes such punishment. Not that I consider execution by lethal injection acceptable either from a point of view of humanity, but—at least—it does not stand out as an unnecessarily cruel and inhuman method of execution, as does gas asphyxiation.[324]

CONCLUSION

There is evidence to support the affirmation that all methods used to execute are likely to cause some degree of pain. In distinction with earlier times, there appears to be virtually unanimous agreement in modern systems of criminal law that the method should attempt to avoid undue suffering. The question that courts have contemplated is not so much whether execution causes pain as at what point the process reaches a threshold of unacceptability. Different procedures are frequently compared, although only in the United States is there ongoing experimentation in the search for a more humane method. This development has resulted in the abandonment in recent years of hanging, electrocution, and gassing in favor of lethal injection.

But courts, particularly those in the United States, have also considered a more subjective element, the "evolving standards of decency" that compel abandoning one form of punishment simply because society deems it unacceptable.[325] The guillotine and other methods of beheading may well fall into this category. Ostensibly instantaneous, with little or no suggestion of suffering, decapitation is at the same time brutal and grotesque and leaves the body unspeakably mutilated.

Albert Camus complained, ironically, "that in an atomic age we kill as we did in the age of steelyards . . . [;] science, which has taught us too much about killing, could at least teach us to kill decently."[326] He meant, of course, that there is no way to kill decently. It is uncontested that the method of capital punishment may be challenged in court subject to constitutional or international norms prohibiting torture and cruel punishment. With some important exceptions, however, the caselaw tends to uphold the technique chosen by the legislature. These judgments are unconvincing. The much-vaunted and increasingly popular technique of lethal injection may well improve upon hanging, electrocution, and the gas chamber, in the same way as these improved upon burning at the stake, disembowelling, and drawing and quartering. But such improvement, if it exists, is only incremental. Can it be of no significance that the United Kingdom, after a thorough analysis of methods of execution, rejected the newer techniques in favor of hanging—but then abolished the death penalty altogether? The horror of the entire discussion must surely have influenced members of Parliament. Once the courts admit that the means of capital punishment may be suspect, it seems impossible to find a method of killing that is humane, certain, and decent.

CONCLUSION

THIS BOOK is about the death penalty, but it is also about contemporary human rights law. Never before has law evolved and developed in such an international context, pushed forward by a synergy between national and international tribunals wrestling with similar facts and essentially identical norms. The first issue to come before this new international law system is the death penalty—specifically, the death penalty examined from the perspective of the prohibition of cruel treatment and torture.

Those who originally conceived the modern enumerations of fundamental rights and freedoms approached capital punishment from the standpoint of the right to life. Unlike the prohibition of cruel treatment and torture—which had been expressed as early as 1641 in the Massachusetts Body of Liberties, and reiterated in such instruments as the English Bill of Rights of 1689, the French Déclaration des droits de l'homme et du citoyen of 1789, and the American Bill of Rights of 1791—the right to life was very much a new idea. It was included in the Universal Declaration of Human Rights of 1948, although its scope was unclear and its eventual ramifications unknown. The drafters of the Universal Declaration believed the death penalty to be an implied limit on the right to life, one that was dictated by existing circumstances and one that would be only temporary. They envisaged its limitation and eventual abolition as interpretation of the Universal Declaration—humanity's common standard of achievement—evolved over time.

What the drafters of the document never foresaw is that a great deal of death penalty litigation would focus not on the right to life but on the prohibition of cruel treatment and torture. When the norms promulgated in the Universal Declaration were fleshed out, in a series of regional and universal human rights treaties, the death penalty was explicitly declared to be a limitation on the right to life. Attempts to argue that dynamic or evolutive interpretation of human rights norms may permit courts to set aside this textual recognition of the legitimacy of the death penalty, in favor of an expansive view of both the right to life and the prohibition of cruel treatment and torture, have thus far met with limited success.

The June 1995 judgment of the South African Constitutional Court crystallizes these paradoxes. It is a sign of the progressive development of human rights law that when the South African drafters prepared their interim constitution they proclaimed a right to life that was not subject to any explicit limitations. The text was in many ways analogous to the broad declaration of principle set out by the United Nations General Assembly in the Universal Declaration of Human Rights, almost half a century earlier. Yet the members of the Constitutional Court were not able to reach a consensus on whether the death penalty could be sustained as an implied limitation on the right to life. They dwelt, rather, on the prohibition of cruel, inhuman, and degrading treatment or punishment. The justices found the death penalty to be an arbitrary and unequal punishment, in practice endorsing a judgment rendered two decades earlier by the United States Supreme Court (but one whose effects it later neutralized).

The South African Constitutional Court's decision is the latest in a series of celebrated cases that have focussed the death penalty debate on the prohibition of cruel treatment and torture. It goes the furthest of them all by declaring judicial execution to be unconstitutional, but that is because nothing in the country's interim constitution explicitly secures capital punishment from judicial control. Other courts have directed their attentions to the modalities of the death penalty. Thus, the United Nations Human Rights Committee has held that a particular method of execution, asphyxiation by gas, unnecessarily prolongs the suffering of the offender and thereby breaches article 7 of the International Covenant on Civil and Political Rights. Similarly, the Inter-American Commission on Human Rights, the European Court of Human Rights, and the Judicial Committee of the Privy Council have all determined that a prolonged wait on "death row" prior to execution constitutes cruel treatment in breach of the prisoner's fundamental rights.

For human rights law, the death penalty is an enigma. Its use was widely accepted in the early years of this new body of law. When the international community set up its first criminal court, at Nuremberg in 1945, the death penalty was contemplated as an appropriate sanction and, in many cases, actually carried out. The early human rights instruments recognized it as an exception to the right to life, and the death penalty was then still a punishment widely accepted in domestic legal systems. Times have clearly changed. More than half of the world's countries have abolished capital punishment, and the new international protocols expressly exclude it. Thus, the law is in transition. It is, to be sure, too early to say that capital punishment is deemed contrary to customary international human rights law, although specialized treaties now exist to accommodate the growing number of abolitionist countries. But no longer can one affirm that capital punishment is compatible with human rights law. In this legal twilight zone, which may endure for years and perhaps decades, recent judicial attention has been concentrated not so much on the right to life (where it has traditionally been thought that the issue of capital punishment was most properly situated) as on the prohibition of cruel treatment and torture. Yet when the drafters of the Universal Declaration of Human Rights declared the prohibition of "cruel, inhuman, and degrading treatment or punishment" in 1948, nobody felt that the death penalty came within the scope of that norm.

This result is something of a theoretical aberration, and more than one critic has noted that judges are merely trying to do indirectly what they cannot do directly. The suspicion has been that although judges in human rights tribunals are personally committed to abolition, they are unable to give full effect to their views because the law itself still seems to recognize explicitly or implicitly the legality of capital punishment. Consequently, as the European Court of Human Rights decided in the *Soering case*, extradition to a state where the death penalty may be applied did not offend the European Convention on Human Rights, but the death row phenomenon did.

The problem, of course, is with the inherent contradictions in implementing the death penalty. Death row exists because human rights norms require states to provide condemned offenders with thorough appeal and review mechanisms, including recourse to international bodies like the Human Rights Committee and the Inter-American Commission on Human Rights. It is virtually impossible to facilitate appropriate review of death sentences while ensuring that execution is carried out in a "reasonable" time. Similarly, when one turns to the method of execution, the futility of a search for "humane" ways to murder an individual becomes apparent. Precisely because the right to life is at the very core of human rights, "the mere extinguishment of life"[1] may be impossible without attendant physical and mental suffering.

In the first part of this book, I traced the development of the norm prohibiting cruel treatment and torture, and its relationship to the issue of the death penalty. Long before human rights law ever existed in the modern sense, jurists had determined that disproportionate punishments were anathema to criminal law. The social purposes that were sought by appropriate punishment could only be achieved when "the punishment fit the crime." This was the original of the biblical stricture of "an eye for an eye, a tooth for a tooth." Later, cruel treatment came to include notions relating to the inhumanity of the process itself. Even a penalty that was felt to be proportionate to the crime might be administered cruelly. This more modern view has come to dominate judicial thinking on the nature of cruel treatment. .

It is quite clear that when the revolutionaries of the seventeenth and eighteenth centuries proscribed cruel and unusual punishments, they in no way meant to exclude the death penalty (even though the more enlightened thinkers of the time had called into question whether it should ever be used). It is only in the second half of the twentieth century, with the development of human rights law, that the compatibility of the death penalty with the prohibition of cruel treatment has come to be disputed. I have examined this debate, which involves consideration of basic premises of criminal law, in the third chapter of this book. Punishment endeavors to fulfill a number of precise aims, foremost among them being deterrence and retribution. Attempts to reconcile these goals of criminal law with the sacred principles of human rights law can be difficult. Criminal law, by its very nature, depends on public sentiments; it aims to mold behavior and is, consequently, molded by it. This is a slippery slope, often made even more hazardous by demagogic appeals to "public opinion"—it is doubtful, for instance, that the Universal Declaration of Human Rights would score well in a public opinion poll. And so jurists, politicians, and intellectuals must help to develop and inform public attitudes. A marvelous example of what can happen is the June 1995 judgment of the South African Constitutional Court overturning the death penalty.

In the final chapters, I have examined in detail two very specific issues relating to implementation of the death penalty, the death row phenomenon and the method of execution. Both have been dealt with in a large number of judgments from national and international tribunals, with sometimes contradictory results. Yet here too a degree of consensus can be discerned, at least with respect to the direction the decisions are taking. Many courts have now recognized the death row phenomenon as a breach of the norm prohibiting cruel treatment. Those that have yet to do so, notably the United States Supreme Court and the Human Rights Committee, are clearly wrestling with the issue. Their own disquiet on the question is a most direct consequence of the judgments of other jurisdictions, such as the European Court of Human Rights and the Judicial Committee of the Privy Council. As for the method of execution, here there seems to be an important element of cultural relativism. Yet a pattern is also present, one of a constant if ephemeral search for a technique of killing that is free of gratuitous pain, suffering, humiliation, and mutilation.

"Time works changes, [and] brings into existence new conditions and purposes," said the United States Supreme Court in one of its very first judgments dealing with the Eighth Amendment. "Therefore a principle to be vital must be capable of wider application than the mischief which gave it birth."[2] This fascinating ferment of evolving human rights norms has generated the rich body of international and comparative caselaw, most of it produced in the first half of the final decade of the millennium, that has been the subject of this book. The judicial debate continues to advance, more rapidly than many had ever thought possible, as international human rights norms carve out their place within the sphere that states have, at least historically, sought jealously to preserve as their sovereign domain.

NOTES

INTRODUCTION

1. *Makwanyane and Mchunu* v. *The State*, (1995) 16 *H.R.L.J.* 154. See: William A. SCHABAS, "South Africa's Constitutional Court Outlaws the Death Penalty," (1995) 16 *H.R.L.J.* 133.
2. Constitution of the Republic of South Africa, Act 200 of 1993, assented to 25 January 1994, date of commencement 27 April 1994, *Government Gazette*, Vol. 343, No. 15466, s. 11§2.
3. *Ng* v. *Canada* (no. 469/1991), (1994) 15 *H.R.L.J.* 149. However, later in the year it rejected an argument claiming that execution by intravenous injection of a lethal substance constituted a violation of article 7 of the Covenant: *Cox* v. *Canada* (no. 539/1993), (1995) 15 *H.R.L.J.* 410.
4. International Covenant on Civil and Political Rights, (1976) 999 U.N.T.S. 171.
5. *Pratt et al.* v. *Attorney General for Jamaica et al.*, [1993] 4 All E.R. 769, [1993] 2 L.R.C. 349, [1994] 2 A.C. 1, [1993] 3 W.L.R. 995, 43 W.I.R. 340, 14 *H.R.L.J.* 338, 33 I.L.M. 364 (J.C.P.C.), at p. 788 (All E.R.), 35 (A.C.).
6. Constitution of Jamaica, s. 17§1.
7. *Catholic Commission for Justice and Peace in Zimbabwe* v. *Attorney-General et al.*, (1993) 1 Z.L.R. 242 (S), 4 S.A. 239 (Z.S.C.), 14 *H.R.L.J.* 323.
8. *Soering* v. *United Kingdom et al.*, July 7, 1989, Series A, Vol. 161, 11 E.H.R.R. 439.
9. Convention for the Protection of Human Rights and Fundamental Freedoms (the "European Convention on Human Rights"), (1955) 213 U.N.T.S. 221, E.T.S. 5, art. 3.
10. Universal Declaration of Human Rights, G.A. Res. 217A (III), U.N. Doc. A/810 (1948), art. 5.
11. Geneva Convention of August 12, 1949 For the Amelioration of the Condition of the Wounded and Sick in Armed Forces in the Field, (1950) 75 U.N.T.S. 135, art. 3; Geneva Convention of August 12, 1949 For the Amelioration of the Condition of Wounded, Sick and Shipwrecked Members of Armed Forces at Sea, (1950) 75 U.N.T.S. 135, art. 3; Geneva Convention of August 12, 1949 Relative to the Treatment of Prisoners of War, (1950) 75 U.N.T.S. 135, art. 3; Geneva Convention of August 12, 1949 Relative to the Protection of Civilians, (1950) 75 U.N.T.S. 135, art. 3.
12. *Supra* note 4, art. 7.
13. *Supra* note 9, art. 3.
14. American Declaration of the Rights and Duties of Man, O.A.S. Doc. OEA/Ser.L/V/I.4, art. 26.
15. American Convention on Human Rights, (1979) 1144 U.N.T.S. 123, O.A.S.T.S. 36, art. 5§2.
16. African Charter of Human and Peoples' Rights, O.A.U. Doc. CAB/LEG/67/3 rev. 5, 4 E.H.R.R. 417, 21 *I.L.M.* 58, art. 5.
17. Declaration on the Protection of All Persons from Being Subjected to Torture and Other Cruel, Inhuman or Degrading Treatment or Punishment, G.A. Res. 3452 (XXX), art. 1.2.
18. Yoram DINSTEIN, "The right to life, physical integrity and liberty," in Louis HENKIN, ed.,

The International Bill of Rights: The Covenant on Civil and Political Rights, New York: Columbia University Press, 1981, p. 122; Rosalyn HIGGINS, "Derogations under human rights treaties," (1976–77) 48 *B.Y.I.L.* 281, at p. 282.

19. *Supra* note 11.
20. Theodor MERON, *Human Rights and Humanitarian Norms as Customary International Law,* Oxford: Clarendon Press, 1986, at p. 33.
21. *Id.,* at p. 34.
22. Vienna Declaration and Programme of Action, U.N. Doc. A/CONF.157/24 (Part I), chap. III (1993), 14 *H.R.L.J.* 352, §5.
23. *Id.,* §§54–61.
24. Jack DONNELLY, "Human rights and human dignity: An analytical critique of non-Western conceptions of human rights," (1982) 76 *Am. Pol. Sci. Rev.* 303; Abdullahi Ahmed AN-NA'IM, "Problems and prospects of universal cultural legitimacy for human rights," in Abdullahi Ahmed AN-NA'IM, Francis DENG, eds., *Human Rights in Africa: Cross-cultural Perspectives,* Washington: Brookings Institution, 1990, pp. 31–67.
25. Speech of Liu Huauqiu, head of the Chinese Delegation, Vienna, June 15, 1993, quoted in Pieter VAN DIJK, "A common standard of achievement: About universal validity and uniform interpretation of international human rights norms," (1995) 13 *N.Q.H.R.* 105.
26. Jack DONNELLY, *Universal Human Rights in Theory and Practice,* Ithaca and London: Cornell University Press, 1989, at p. 6.
27. On the right to life, see: B. G. RAMCHARAN, ed., *The Right to Life in International Law,* Boston: Martinus Nijhoff, 1985; Daniel PRÉMONT, ed., *Essais sur le concept de "droit de vivre" en mémoire de Yougindra Khushalani,* Brussels: Bruylant, 1988; William A. SCHABAS, *The Abolition of the Death Penalty in International Law,* Cambridge: Cambridge University Press (Grotius Publications), 1993; Thomas DESCH, "The concept and dimensions of the right to life—as defined in international standards and in international and comparative jurisprudence," (1985–86) 36 *Österreichische Zeitschrift für Öffentliches Recht und Volkerrecht* 77.
28. Abdullahi Ahmed AN-NA'IM, "The meaning of cruel, inhuman or degrading treatment or punishment," in Abdullahi Ahmed AN-NA'IM, ed., *Human Rights in Cross-Cultural Perspectives: A Quest for Consensus,* Philadelphia: University of Pennsylvania Press, 1992, pp. 19–43, at p. 31.
29. *Tyrer* v. *United Kingdom,* April 25, 1978, Series A, No. 26, 2 E.H.R.R. 1, 59 I.L.R. 339.
30. U.N. Doc. E/CN.4/1994/48.
31. *Supra* note 4.
32. "Statement by H.E. Mr Abdelaziz Shiddo, Minister of Justice and Attorney-General of the Republic of the Sudan and Leader of Sudan Delegation to the 50th Session of the Commission on Human Rights, Commenting on the report of Dr. Gaspar Biro, Special Rapporteur on Human Rights situation in the Sudan under agenda item (12)," Geneva, February 25, 1994. See also: U.N. Doc. E/CN.4/1994/122, §58-64.
33. U.N. Doc. A/BUR/49/SR.5, §13.
34. AN-NA'IM, *supra* note 28, at p. 33. On capital punishment in Islamic law, see: Frédéric SUDRE, *Droit international et européen des droits de l'homme,* Paris: Presses universitaires de France, 1989, at pp. 85–87; A. WAZIR, "Quelques aspects de la peine de mort en droit pénal islamique," (1987) 58 *Revue internationale de droit pénal* 421; CENTRE DES ÉTUDES DE SÉCURITÉ (ARABIE SAOUDITE), "L'égalité et commodité de la peine de mort en droit musulman," (1987) 58 *Revue internationale de droit pénal* 431; N. HOSNI, "La peine de mort en droit égyptien et en droit islamique," (1987) 58 *Revue internationale de droit pénal* 407. In an interesting twist on this debate, an individual challenged Malaysia's mandatory death penalty for drug trafficking as being unconstitutional because it was contrary to Islamic law and, consequently, in breach of the Constitution of Malaysia, art. 3: *Che Omar bin Che Soh* v. *Public Prosecutor,* [1988] L.R.C. (Const.) 95 (Supreme Court of Malaysia).

35. The phrase was coined by Chief Justice Warren of the United States Supreme Court in *Trop v. Dulles,* 356 U.S. 86, 101, 78 S.Ct. 590, 598, 2 L.Ed.2d 630 (1958).
36. *People* v. *Anderson,* 6 Cal.3d 628, 647, 100 Cal.Rptr. 152, 493 P.2d 880, 893 (1972), *cert. denied,* 406 U.S. 958, 92 S.Ct. 2060, 32 L.Ed.2d 344 (1972) (Wright, C.J.).
37. *Weems* v. *United States,* 217 U.S. 349, 378, 30 S.Ct. 544, 553, 54 L.Ed. 793 (1910).
38. R. St. J. MACDONALD, "The margin of appreciation," in R. St. J. MACDONALD et al., eds., *The European System for the Protection of Human Rights,* Dordrecht, London, and Boston: Martinus Nijhoff, 1993, pp. 83–124.
39. 1 WM. & MARY, 2d Sess. (1689), c. 2. See: Anthony F. GRANUCCI, " 'Nor cruel and unusual punishments inflicted': The original meaning," (1969) 57 *Cal. L. Rev.* 839.
40. Lilly E. LANDERER, "Capital punishment as a human rights issue before the United Nations," (1971) 4 *H.R.J.* 511; Alfred VERDOODT, *Naissance et signification de la Déclaration universelle des droits de l'homme,* Louvain and Paris: Nauwelaerts, 1963, at pp. 99–100; SCHABAS, *supra* note 27, at pp. 30–45.
41. U.N. Doc. A/C.3/265.
42. The Fifth and Fourteenth Amendments affirm that nobody shall be deprived of life "without due process of law." In *Furman* v. *Georgia,* 408 U.S. 238, 92 S.Ct. 2726, 33 L.Ed.2d 346 (1972), the United States Supreme Court found that existing death penalty statutes were unconstitutional because they breached the Eighth Amendment, which prohibits "cruel and unusual punisment." However, the majority did not consider that the death penalty per se was unconstitutional.
43. *Supra* note 9. Article 2§1 of the Convention recognizes the death penalty as an exception or limitation to the right to life. In *Soering* v. *United Kingdom et al., supra* note 8, the majority of the European Court of Human Rights concluded that the death penalty as such could not violate the prohibition of "inhuman and degrading treatment" found in art. 3 because of the existence of article 2§1.
44. *Supra* note 4. Article 6§2 of the Covenant recognizes the death penalty as a limitation to the right to life, subject to a series of restrictions on its use found in paragraphs 2, 4, and 5.
45. A majority of justices of the South African Constitutional Court considered that capital punishment violated the constitutional norm protecting the right to life: *Makwanyane and Mchunu* v. *The State, supra* note 1. The same conclusion was reached, in 1990, by the Hungarian Constitution Court: Decision No. 23/1990 (X.31.) AB, unreported. See also: Tibor HORVATH, "L'abolition de la peine de mort en Hongrie," [1992] 2 *Revue internationale de criminologie et de police technique* 167. For a detailed analysis of the "right-to-life" norm in international law, as it relates to the question of capital punishment, see: SCHABAS, *supra* note 27.
46. South African Constitutional Court: *Makwanyane and Mchunu* v. *The State, supra* note 1, at p. 158 (*per* Chaskalson, P.); Supreme Court of Canada: *Kindler* v. *Canada,* [1991] 2 S.C.R. 779, 67 C.C.C. (3d) 1, 84 D.L.R. (4th) 438, 6 C.R.R. (2d) 193 (*per* Cory, J., dissenting).
47. Again, this phrase is borrowed from Chief Justice Warren in *Trop* v. *Dulles, supra* note 35.
48. Protocol No. 6 to the Convention for the Protection of Human Rights and Fundamental Freedoms Concerning the Abolition of the Death Penalty, E.T.S. 114; Second Optional Protocol to the International Covenant on Civil and Political Rights Aimed at Abolition of the Death Penalty, G.A. Res. 44/128, (1990) 29 I.L.M. 1464; Additional Protocol to the American Convention on Human Rights to Abolish the Death Penalty, O.A.S.T.S. 73, 29 I.L.M. 1447.
49. "Capital punishment and implementation of the safeguards guaranteeing the protection of the rights of those facing the death penalty, Report of the Secretary-General," U.N. Doc. E/ 1995/78, §32.
50. *Soering* v. *United Kingdom* et al., *supra* note 8, at pp. 51–52 (Series A), 484 (E.H.R.R.).
51. *Murakami* v. *Japan. Hanrieshu* II, No. 3, 191 (Criminal), in John M. MAKI, *Court and Constitution in Japan: Selected Supreme Court Decisions 1948–60,* Seattle: University of Washington Press, 1964, at pp. 156–64.
52. *Supra* note 42.

53. *Gregg* v. *Georgia*, 428 U.S. 153, 96 S.Ct. 2909, 49 L.Ed.2d 859 (1976).

54. *Supra* note 1.

55. *Pratt et al.* v. *Attorney General for Jamaica et al.*, *supra* note 5, at pp. 783 (All E.R.), 29 (A.C.).

56. David PANNICK, *Judicial Review of the Death Penalty*, London: Duckworth, 1983.

THE PROHIBITION OF CRUEL TREATMENT AND TORTURE

1. Geneva Convention of August 12, 1949 For the Amelioration of the Condition of the Wounded and Sick in Armed Forces in the Field, (1950) 75 U.N.T.S. 135, art. 3; Geneva Convention of August 12, 1949 For the Amelioration of the Condition of Wounded, Sick and Shipwrecked Members of Armed Forces at Sea, (1950) 75 U.N.T.S. 135, art. 3; Geneva Convention of August 12, 1949 Relative to the Protection of Civilians, (1950) 75 U.N.T.S. 135, art. 3.

2. Among general works on the issue of cruel treatment and torture in international law, see: Nigel RODLEY, *The Treatment of Prisoners Under International Law*, Paris: Unesco, Oxford: Clarendon Press, 1987; Steven ACKERMAN, "Torture and other forms of cruel and unusual punishment in international law," (1978) 11 *Vand. J. Int'l L.* 653; Barry KLAYMAN, "The definition of torture in international law," (1978) 51 *Temple L.Q.* 460.

3. *Genesis* 9:6.

4. *Exodus* 21:24.

5. *Leviticus* 24:19–20. In the Koran, see verses 5:32 and 17:33.

6. ARISTOTLE, *Ethics*, trans. John Warrington, London: Dent, 1963, at pp. 99–101.

7. Anthony F. GRANUCCI, " 'Nor cruel and unusual punishments inflicted': The original meaning," (1969) 57 *Cal. L. Rev.* 839, at pp. 844–45.

8. Frederick POLLOCK, Frederic William MAITLAND, *The History of English Law*, 2d ed., Cambridge: Cambridge University Press, 1952, at pp. 449–62, 513–18.

9. Magna Carta, chapters 20–22. On the early common law and proportionality in the determination of punishment, see the comments of Justice Peter D. Cory in *Kindler* v. *Canada*, [1991] 2 S.C.R. 779, 67 C.C.C. (3d) 1, 84 D.L.R. (4th) 438, 6 C.R.R. (2d) 193.

10. John L. BOWERS Jr., J. L. BUREN Jr., "The constitutional prohibition against cruel and unusual punishment—its present significance," (1950–51) 4 *Vand. L. Rev.* 680; "Recent Cases," (1950) 34 *Minn. L. Rev.* 134; GRANUCCI, *supra* note 7, at pp. 846–47. For an early case citing the Magna Carta, see: *Hodges* v. *Humkin, Mayor of Liskerret*, in The Reports of Edward Bulstrode (Cases in King's Bench, 1609–26), pp. 139–40.

11. Sir William BLACKSTONE's *Commentaries on the Laws of England*, Book 4, 9th ed., London: Strahen, Cadell and Prince, 1783 (rpt, London: Garland, 1978), at p. 92.

12. *Id.*, at p. 327.

13. GRANUCCI, *supra* note 7, at pp. 848–49.

14. John STRYPE, *The Life and Acts of John Whitgift*, Oxford: Clarendon Press, 1822; Powell Mills DAWLEY, *John Whitgift and the English Reformation*, New York: Scribner's, 1954.

15. Massachusetts Body of Liberties, clause 46, in Richard L. PERRY, John C. COOPER, *Sources of Our Liberties*, Washington: American Bar Association, 1952, at p. 153. On the influence of the Massachusetts Body of Liberties on other colonial codes, see Stefan A. RIESENFELD, "Lawmaking and legislative precedent in American legal history," (1949) 33 *Minn. L. Rev.* 103, at pp. 123–34.

16. *Kindler* v. *Canada*, *supra* note 9, at p. 802 (S.C.R.).

17. Robert ZALLER, "The debate on capital punishment during the English Revolution," (1987) 31 *Am. J. Legal Hist.* 126, at p. 141.

18. 1 WM. & MARY, 2d Sess. (1689), c. 2; See: Irving BRANT, *The Bill of Rights, Its Origin and Meaning*, Indianapolis: Bobbs-Merrill, 1965.

19. 1 WM. & MARY, 2d Sess. (1689), c. 2.

20. George William KEETON, *Lord Chancellor Jeffreys and the Stuart Cause*, London: Macdonald, 1965, at pp. 301–31; BRANT, *supra* note 18.

21. GRANUCCI, *supra* note 7, at pp. 855–56.

22. *Id.*, at p. 860.
23. Sir James Fitzjames STEPHEN, *History of the Criminal Law in England*, vol. 1, London: Macmillan, 1883, at p. 490; GRANUCCI, *supra* note 7, at p. 859.
24. 10 H.C. Jour. 15 (1688–89).
25. GRANUCCI, *supra* note 7, at p. 855.
26. See: Hugo Adam BEDAU, ed., *The Death Penalty in America*, Garden City, N.Y.: Aldine, 1964, at pp. 6–7.
27. *Louisiana ex rel. Francis* v. *Resweber*, 329 U.S. 459, 473, 67 S.Ct. 374, 381, 91 L.Ed. 422 (1947) (Burton, J., dissenting).
28. W. R. RIDDEL, "The first British courts in Canada," (1923–24) 33 *Yale L.J.* 577; André MOREL, "La réception du droit criminel anglais au Québec (1760–1892)," (1978) 13 *Revue juridique Thémis* 449.
29. *Gregg* v. *Georgia*, 428 U.S. 153, 169–70, 96 S.Ct. 2909, 2923, 49 L.Ed.2d (1976) (Stewart, J.). Justice Stewart endorsed the conclusions of Anthony Granucci, *supra* note 7, pp. 859–60, stating: "The English version appears to have been directed against punishments unauthorized by statute and beyond the jurisdiction of the sentencing court, as well as those disproportionate to the offense." Granucci's conclusions were also endorsed in *Furman* v. *Georgia*, 408 U.S. 238, 261, 92 S.Ct. 2726, 2737, 33 L.Ed.2d 346 (1972).
30. *Riley* v. *Attorney-General of Jamaica*, [1983] 1 A.C. 719, [1982] 3 All E.R. 469, 35 W.I.R. 279 (J.C.P.C.), at p. 734 (A.C.), 478 (All E.R.) (*per* Lords Scarman and Brightman, dissenting).
31. *Id.*, at pp. 734–35 (A.C.), 479 (All E.R.) (*per* Lords Scarman and Brightman, dissenting). The judgment of the majority in *Riley* was overruled by the Judicial Committee of the Privy Council in *Pratt et al.* v. *Attorney General for Jamaica et al.*, [1993] 4 All E.R. 769, [1993] 2 L.R.C. 349, [1994] 2 A.C. 1, [1993] 3 W.L.R. 995, 43 W.I.R. 340, 14 *H.R.L.J.* 338, 33 I.L.M. 364 (J.C.P.C.), at pp. 784–85 (All E.R.), 31 (A.C.), where a panel of seven judges expressly adopted the dissenting opinion of Lords Scarman and Brightman.
32. *Gregg* v. *Georgia*, *supra* note 29, at pp. 169–70 (U.S.), 2923 (S.Ct.); *Harmelin* v. *Michigan*, 501 U.S. 957, 966, 111 S.Ct. 2686, 2687, 115 L.Ed.2d 836 (1991) (Scalia, J., concurring).
33. Canadian Bill of Rights, R.S.C. (1985), App. III.
34. Canadian Charter of Rights and Freedoms, R.S.C. (1985), App. II, no. 44, Schedule B, Part I.
35. Universal Declaration of Human Rights, G.A. Res. 217A (III), U.N. Doc. A/810 (1948).
36. Cesare BECCARIA, *On Crimes and Punishments*, trans. Henry Paolucci, Indianapolis: Bobbs-Merrill, 1963.
37. Steven LYNN, "Locke and Beccaria: Faculty psychology and capital punishment," in William B. THESING, *Executions and the British Experience from the 17th to the 20th Century: A Collection of Essays*, Jefferson, N.C.: McFarland, 1990, at pp. 29–44; Robert BADINTER, "Beccaria, l'abolition de la peine de mort et la révolution française," [1989] *Revue de science criminelle et de droit pénal comparé* 245; Mireille DELMAS-MARTY, "Le rayonnement international de la pensée de Cesare Beccaria," [1989] *Revue de science criminelle et de droit pénal comparé* 252; Jean IMBERT, *La peine de mort*, Paris: Presses universitaires de France, 1989.
38. Marcello MAESTRO, *Cesare Beccaria and the Origins of Penal Reform*, Philadelphia: Temple University Press, 1972; Leon RADZINOWICZ, *A History of English Criminal Law and Its Administration from 1750*, vol. 1, London: Stevens and Sons, 1948, at pp. 290–93.
39. See, for example, the reasons of Justice Cory of the Supreme Court of Canada, in *Kindler* v. *Canada*, *supra* note 9, at p. 793 (S.C.R.).
40. Robert Allen RUTLAND, *The Birth of the Bill of Rights, 1776–1791*, Chapel Hill: University of North Carolina Press, 1955, at pp. 35–36, 232.
41. Virginia Constitution, Bill of Rights, par. 9 (1776).
42. The Northwest Territorial Government, art. II, U.S.C. Vol. I, p. xxxiv.
43. GRANUCCI, *supra* note 7, at p. 840.
44. Solicitor General Robert Bork, arguing in defense of death penalty legislation in *Jurek* v. *Texas*, 428 U.S. 262, 96 S.Ct. 2950, 49 L.Ed.2d 929 (1976), said: "[W]e know as a fact that the men who framed the Eighth Amendment did not mean—did not intend as an original matter to

outlaw capital punishment because, as has been mentioned, they prescribed the procedures that must be used in inflicting it in the Fifth Amendment. We know that the men who framed and ratified the Fourteenth Amendment did not intend to outlaw capital punishment, because they also discussed and framed the procedures which must be followed inflicting it. So we know that as an original matter, as a matter of original intention, it is quite certain that the Eighth Amendment was not intended to bar the death penalty and that the Constitution contemplates its infliction." Quoted in Randall COYNE, Lyn ENTZEROTH, *Capital Punishment and the Judicial Process*, Durham, N.C.: Carolina Academic Press, 1994, at p. 104.

45. Jonathan ELLIOT, *The Debates in the Several State Conventions on the Adoption of the Federal Constitution, as recommended by the General Convention at Philadelphia*, vol. 2, Washington: Taylor & Maury, 1854, at p. 111.

46. *Id.*, at pp. 447–48. These comments call to mind a paragraph in Blackstone's *Commentaries*, which follows a gruesome description of methods of capital punishment and torture then in use in England: "Disgusting as this catalogue may seem, it will afford pleasure to an English reader, and do honour to the English law, to compare it with that shocking apparatus of death and torment, to be met with in the criminal codes of almost every other nation in Europe." BLACKSTONE, *supra* note 11, at p. 377.

47. ELLIOT, *supra* note 45, at p. 452.

48. *Furman* v. *Georgia*, *supra* note 29, at pp. 268 (U.S.), 2737 (S.Ct.).

49. 1 Annals of Cong. 754 (1789). Quoted in: *Weems* v. *United States*, 217 U.S. 349, 30 S.Ct. 544, 550, 54 L.Ed. 793 (1910); see also: Helen E. VEIT et al., *Creating the Bill of Rights*, Baltimore: Johns Hopkins University Press, 1991, at pp. 180, 187.

50. GRANUCCI, *supra* note 7, at p. 860.

51. See: *Furman* v. *Georgia*, *supra* note 29, at pp. 263–64 (U.S.), 2738–39 (S.Ct.) (Brennan, J.).

52. *Id.*, at pp. 319–20 (U.S.), 2767 (S.Ct.) (Marshall, J.).

53. *Pervear* v. *Commonwealth*, 5 Wall. 475, 479–80, 18 L.Ed. 608 (1867).

54. *Wilkerson* v. *Utah*, 99 U.S. 130, 134, 25 L.Ed. 345 (1878).

55. *In re Kemmler*, 136 U.S. 436, 10 S.Ct. 930, 34 L.Ed. 519 (1890).

56. *Id.*, at pp. 447 (U.S.), 933 (S.Ct.).

57. Hugo Adam BEDAU, *The Courts, the Constitution, and Capital Punishment*, Lexington, Mass.: Lexington Books, 1977, at p. 35.

58. *Weems* v. *United States*, *supra* note 49. For contemporary academic comment on *Weems* see: NOTE, "What is cruel and unusual punishment," (1910) 24 *Harv. L. Rev.* 54.

59. "*Weems* is a landmark case because it represents the first time that the Court invalidated a penalty prescribed by a legislature for a particular offense. The Court made it plain beyond any reasonable doubt that excessive punishments were as objectionable as those that were inherently cruel." *Per* Justice Marshall in *Furman* v. *Georgia*, *supra* note 29, at pp. 326 (U.S.), 2770 (S.Ct.).

60. *Supra* note 54.

61. *Supra* note 55.

62. Arthur GOLDBERG, Allen DERSHOWITZ, "Declaring the death penalty unconstitutional," (1970) 83 *Harv. L. Rev.* 1773, at p. 1782.

63. *Furman* v. *Georgia*, *supra* note 29, at pp. 268 (U.S.), 2741 (S.Ct.).

64. *Trop* v. *Dulles*, 356 U.S. 86, 101, 78 S.Ct. 590, 598, 2 L.Ed.2d 630 (1958).

65. But he did not put an end to use of the "original intent" argument: see the recent opinion of Justice Antonin Scalia in *Harmelin* v. *Michigan*, *supra* note 32, at p. 2686 (S.Ct.).

66. *Trop* v. *Dulles*, *supra* note 64, at pp. 125 (U.S.), 611 (S.Ct.) (Frankfurter, J., dissenting).

67. *Id.*, at pp. 101 (U.S.), 598 (S.Ct.).

68. *Furman* v. *Georgia*, *supra* note 29. The Eighth Amendment had also been successfully invoked in a 1962 case where the Supreme Court held that imprisonment for narcotics addiction was unconstitutional: *Robinson* v. *California*, 370 U.S. 660, 82 S.Ct. 1417 (1962).

69. Only a year earlier, in *McGautha* v. *California*, 402 U.S. 183, 91 S.Ct. 1454, 28 L.Ed.2d 711

(1971), it had dismissed a petition relying on the equivalent formulation in the Fourteenth Amendment. In *Furman,* some of the dissenting justices refused to budge, arguing that they were "imprisoned in the *McGuatha* holding": *Furman* v. *Georgia, supra* note 29, at pp. 2726, 2731 (Douglas, J., dissenting).

70. For example, the South African Constitutional Court in 1995: *Makwanyane and Mchunu* v. *The State,* (1995) 16 *H.R.L.J.* 154 (*per* Chaskalson, P.).
71. The Fourteenth Amendment, adopted in 1868, makes the "cruel and unusual punishment" clause applicable to legislation enacted by the states: *Robinson* v. *California, supra* note 68.
72. *Furman* v. *Georgia, supra* note 29, at pp. 256 (U.S.), 2735 (S.Ct.).
73. *Id.,* at pp. 286 (U.S.), 2750 (S.Ct.) (Brennan, J., concurring); *id.,* at pp. 369 (U.S.), 2793 (S.Ct.) (Marshall, J., concurring). The contradictions within the majority camp were stressed by the dissenters in the first paragraph of their reasons: *id.,* at pp. 375 (U.S.), 2796 (S.Ct.) (Burger, C.J., dissenting).
74. *Id.,* at pp. 406 (U.S.), 2809 (S.Ct.) (Burger, C.J., dissenting).
75. *Id.,* at pp. 257–58 (U.S.), 2735 (S.Ct.) (Douglas, J.); *id.,* at pp. 307 (U.S.), 2760 (S.Ct.) (Stewart, J.); *id.,* at pp. 315 (U.S.), 2764–65 (S.Ct.) (White, J.).
76. *Rockwell* v. *Superior Court,* 18 Cal.3d 420, 134 Cal. Rptr. 650, 556 P.2d 1101 (1976); *State* v. *Spence,* 367 A.2d 983 (Del.Supr. 1976).
77. *Gregg* v. *Georgia, supra* note 29; *Proffitt* v. *Florida,* 428 U.S. 242, 96 S.Ct. 2960, 49 L.Ed.2d 913 (1976); *Jurek* v. *Texas, supra* note 44; *Woodson* v. *North Carolina,* 428 U.S. 280, 96 S.Ct. 2978, 49 L.Ed.2d 944 (1976); *Roberts (Stanislaus)* v. *Louisiana,* 428 U.S. 325, 96 S.Ct. 3001, 49 L.Ed.2d 974 (1976).
78. *Gregg* v. *Georgia, supra* note 29, at pp. 177 (U.S.), 2927 (S.Ct.) (Stewart, J.).
79. *Id.,* at p. 183 (U.S.) (Stewart, J.).
80. *Id.,* at pp. 195 (U.S.), 2929–30 (S.Ct.) (Stewart, J.).
81. *Stanford* v. *Kentucky; Wilkins* v. *Missouri,* 492 U.S. 361, 109 S.Ct. 2969, 106 L.Ed.2d 306 (1989).
82. *Penry* v. *Lynaugh,* 492 U.S. 302, 109 S.Ct. 2934 (1989).
83. *McCleskey* v. *Kemp,* 481 U.S. 279, 107 S.Ct. 1756 (1987).
84. *Robinson* v. *California, supra* note 68.
85. *District Atty. for Suffolk Dist.* v. *Watson,* 381 Mass. 648, 411 N.E.2d 1274, 1289 (1980) (Liacos, J., concurring).
86. *Doe* v. *Maher,* 40 Conn.Sup. 394, 419, 515 A.2d 134 (1986).
87. *Miller* v. *State,* 584 S.W.2d 758, 760 (Tenn. 1979). See: J. ACKER, E. WALSH, "Challenging the death penalty under state constitutions," (1989) 42 *Vand. L. Rev.* 1299.
88. *People ex rel. Kemmler* v. *Durston,* 24 N.E. 6, 7 (N.Y.1890).
89. See, for example: *Commonwealth* v. *O'Neil,* 327 N.E.2d 662 (Mass.1975); *Commonwealth* v. *O'Neil II,* 369 Mass. 242, 339 N.E.2d 676 (1975).
90. *District Atty. for Suffolk Dist.* v. *Watson, supra* note 85, at p. 1289 (N.E.2d) (Liacos, J., concurring). See also: NOTE, "The death penalty in Massachusetts," (1974) 8 *Suffolk U. L. Rev.* 632.
91. *District Atty. for Suffolk Dist.* v. *Watson, supra* note 85, at p. 1300 (N.E.2d) (Quirico, J., dissenting). Other courts have also examined whether such clauses are "disjunctive" or "conjunctive": *R. V. Miller and Cockriell* v. *The Queen,* [1977] 2 S.C.R. 680, 31 C.C.C. (2d) 177, 38 C.R.N.S. 139, 70 D.L.R. (3d) 324, [1976] 5 W.W.R. 711, 11 N.R. 386; *Makwanyane and Mchunu* v. *The State, supra* note 70.
92. *People* v. *Anderson,* 6 Cal.3d 628, 634, 100 Cal.Rptr. 152, 493 P.2d 880, 883 (1972), *cert. denied,* 406 U.S. 958, 92 S.Ct. 2060, 32 L.Ed.2d 344 (1972) (Wright, C.J.). The Court cited: NOTE, "The death penalty cases," (1968) 56 *Cal. L. Rev.* 1268.
93. *People* v. *Anderson, supra* note 92, at pp. 641 (Cal.3d), 888 (P.2d) (Wright, C.J.).
94. *Id.,* at pp. 636 (Cal.3d), 885 (P.2d) (Wright, C.J.).
95. Claude FOHLEN, "La filiation américaine de la Déclaration des droits de l'homme," in Claude-Albert COLLIARD, et al., eds., *La Déclaration des droits de l'homme et du citoyen de 1789, Ses origines–Sa pérennité,* Paris: Documentation française, 1990, pp. 21–29; Gabriel LEPOINTE, *His-*

toire des institutions du droit public français, Paris: Éditions Domat Montchrestien, 1953, at p. 35; V. MARCAGGI, *Les origines de la Déclaration des droits de l'homme de 1789*, Paris: Fontemoing, 1912, at pp. 11–44.

96. Stéphane RIALS, *La déclaration des droits de l'homme et du citoyen*, Paris: Hachette, 1988, at pp. 528, 567, 590; Thomas JEFFERSON, *The Papers of Thomas Jefferson*, ed. Julian P. BOYD, vol. 14, Princeton: Princeton University Press, 1958, at pp. 438–40; and vol. 15, at pp. 230–33.

97. Georges LEVASSEUR, "Les grands principes de la Déclaration des droits de l'homme et le droit répressif français," in COLLIARD et al., eds., *supra* note 95, pp. 233–45, at p. 237. See also: Mireille DELMAS-MARTY, "La jurisprudence du Conseil constitutionnel et les principes fondamentaux du droit pénal proclamés par la Déclaration de 1979," in *La déclaration des droits de l'homme et du citoyen et la jurisprudence*, Paris: Presses universitaires de France, 1989, at pp. 151–69.

98. For the drafting history, see: Monique CAVERIVIÈRE, "Article 8," in Gérard CONAC et al., eds., *La déclaration des droits de l'homme et du citoyen de 1789*, Paris: Economica, 1993, pp. 173–86; Gérard CONAC, "L'élaboration de la déclaration des droits de l'homme et du citoyen," in CONAC et al., eds., *id.*, pp. 7–52, at pp. 28–30.

99. LEVASSEUR, *supra* note 97, pp. 233–45, at p. 237.

100. Maximilien ROBESPIERRE, *Œuvres, VII*, Paris: Presses universitaires de France, 1952, at pp. 432–37. See: Paul SAVEY-CASARD, *La peine de mort: esquisse historique et juridique*, Geneva: Droz, 1968, at pp. 70–75; Jacques GOULET, *Robespierre, la peine de mort et la terreur*, Paris: Les Castor Astral, 1983, at p. 13.

101. Maximilien ROBESPIERRE, *Œuvres, IX*, Paris: Presses universitaires de France, 1952, at p. 130.

102. Thomas PAINE, "Preserving the Life of Louis Capet," in Michael FOOT, Isaac KRAMNICK, eds., *The Thomas Paine Reader*, London: Penguin, 1987, at pp. 394–98.

103. *Annuaire de l'Institut de droit international*, 1929, vol. II, Brussels: Goemaere, 1929, at pp. 118–20; an English version was published some years later: INSTITUT DE DROIT INTERNATIONAL, "Declaration of Inernational Rights of Man," (1941) 35 *A.J.I.L.* 663.

104. Louis B. SOHN, "How American international lawyers prepared for the San Francisco bill of rights," (1995) 89 *A.J.I.L.* 540.

105. Hersh LAUTERPACHT, *An International Bill of the Rights of Man*, New York: Columbia University Press, 1945, at p. 70.

106. U.N.C.I.O. Doc. 2G/14(g); U.N.C.I.O. Doc. 2G/7/(2).

107. The First Committee did, on June 1, 1945, resolve that the General Assembly should examine the Panamanian text and give it an effective form (U.N.C.I.O. Doc. 944, I-I, 34); see also Lilly E. LANDERER, "Capital punishment as a human rights issue before the United Nations," (1971) 4 *H.R.J.* 511, at p. 513.

108. U.N. Doc. A/125, §47.

109. U.N. Doc. E/CN.4/W.4.

110. U.N. Doc. E/CN.4/W.8.

111. U.N. Doc. E/CN.4/W.13.

112. U.N. Doc. E/CN.4/AC.1/3.

113. U.N. Doc. E/CN.4/AC.1/3/Add.1, art. 4; reprinted in U.N.Doc. E/CN.4/21, Annex A.

114. U.N. Doc. E/CN.4/AC.1/3/Add.1.

115. U.N. Doc. E/CN.4/AC.1/3/Add.1, pp. 20–24.

116. U.N. Doc. A/C.3/271, p. 1.

117. U.N. Doc. E/CN.4/SR.91, at pp. 16–17; U.N. Doc. E/CN.4/SR.182, §49.

118. Upon a proposal from Panama: U.N. Doc. A/C.3/220.

119. KLAYMAN, *supra* note 2, at p. 460.

120. Albert VERDOODT, *Naissance et signification de la Déclaration universelle des droits de l'homme*, Louvain and Paris: Éditions Nauwelaerts, 1963, at p. 107.

121. Barry PHILLIPS, *"Pratt and Morgan v. Attorney-General for Jamaica,"* (1994) 88 *A.J.I.L* 775, at p. 778.

122. LANDERER, *supra* note 107; VERDOODT, *supra* note 120, at pp. 99–100; William A. SCHABAS, *The Abolition of the Death Penalty in International Law*, Cambridge: Cambridge University Press (Grotius Publications), 1993, at pp. 30–45.
123. G.A. Res. 2200A (XXI).
124. International Covenant on Civil and Political Rights, (1976) 999 U.N.T.S. 171.
125. John P. HUMPHREY, "The Universal Declaration of Human Rights: Its history, impact and judicial character," in B. G. RAMCHARAN, ed., *Human Rights: Thirty Years After the Universal Declaration*, The Hague: Martinus Nijhoff, 1984. See also the dissent of Judge Tanaka in *South West Africa Cases, Second Phase (Ethiopia* v. *South Africa, Liberia* v. *South Africa)*, [1966] I.C.J. Reports 6, at pp. 288–93; and *United States Diplomatic and Consular Staff in Tehran (United States of America* v. *Iran)*, [1980] I.C.J. Reports 3, at p. 42.
126. U.N. Doc. E/CN.4/L.1013 and Add. 1, sponsored by Austria, Italy, Sweden, Venezuela.
127. G.A. Res. 2393 (XXIII) (1969). U.N. Doc. A/PV.1727, by ninety-four votes to none, with three abstentions. Adoption in the Third Committee: U.N. Doc. A/C.3/SR.1559, §34.
128. U.N. Doc. A/C.3/SR.1560, §1.
129. G.A. Res. 2394 (XXIII) (1968).
130. "Capital punishment," E.S.C. Res. 1574(L) (1971), §2.
131. For example, G.A. Res. 32/61 (1982), E.S.C. Res. 1930 (LVIII) (1975).
132. G.A. Res. 44/128 (1989).
133. U.N. Doc. CAT/C/SR.11, §14.
134. *Supra* note 124.
135. International Covenant on Economic, Social and Cultural Rights, (1976) 993 U.N.T.S. 3. See: Matthew CRAVEN, *The International Covenant on Economic, Social and Cultural Rights*, Oxford: Clarendon Press, 1995; Lucie LAMARCHE, *Perspectives occidentales du droit international des droits économiques de la personne*, Brussels: Éditions Bruylant, 1995.
136. Optional Protocol to the International Covenant on Civil and Political Rights, (1976) 999 U.N.T.S. 171 (providing for an individual petition mechanism to the Human Rights Committee); Second Optional Protocol to the International Covenant on Civil and Political Rights, G.A. Res. 44/128, (1990) 29 I.L.M. 1464 (abolition of the death penalty).
137. International Covenant on Civil and Political Rights, *supra* note 124, art. 48§1.
138. *Id.*, art. 28. See: Dominic MCGOLDRICK, *The Human Rights Committee*, Oxford: Clarendon Press, 1991; Manfred NOWAK, *CCPR Commentary*, Kehl, Germany: Engel, 1993.
139. International Covenant on Civil and Political Rights, *supra* note 124, art. 40.
140. *Id.*, art. 41.
141. Optional Protocol to the International Covenant on Civil and Political Rights, *supra* note 136.
142. Subsequent practice is to be taken into account in establishing the context of treaties, for the purposes of their interpretation: Vienna Convention on the Law of Treaties, (1979) 1155 U.N.T.S. 331, art. 31§3(a).
143. International custom, as evidence of a general practice accepted as law, is one of the sources of international law: Statute of the International Court of Justice, art. 38§1(b).
144. *Kindler* v. *Canada* (No. 470/1991), (1993) 14 *H.R.L.J.* 307, 6 R.U.D.H. 165, §17, §6.5; also *Ng* v. *Canada* (No. 469/1991), (1994) 15 *H.R.L.J.* 149, §16.1.
145. On article 6 of the Covenant, see: MCGOLDRICK, *supra* note 138, at pp. 328–61; NOWAK, *supra* note 138, at pp. 103–25; SCHABAS, *supra* note 122, at pp. 92–135.
146. As was noted by several delegates to the Commission on Human Rights: U.N. Doc. E/CN.4/SR.37, at pp. 4, 5; U.N. Doc. E/CN.4/SR.91, at pp. 14, 15.
147. U.N. Doc. E/CN.4/193; U.N. Doc. E/CN.4/SR.192, at p. 5. For discussion of the drafting history of article 7 of the Covenant, see: KLAYMAN, *supra* note 2, at pp. 462–68.
148. For adoption of draft article 7, see: U.N. Doc. A/C.3/SR.855, §27.
149. U.N. Doc. A/C.3/L.675.
150. U.N. Doc. A/4045, §15.
151. G.A. Res. 2393(XXIII) (1968).

152. For example: G.A. Res. 2857(XXVI); G.A. Res. 32/61; G.A. Res. 44/128.
153. *Kindler* v. *Canada, supra* note 144, §6.7.
154. "General Comment 7/16," U.N. Doc. CCPR/C/21/Add.1, §2.
155. "General Comment 20/44," U.N. Doc. CCPR/C/21/Rev.1/Add.3, §1.
156. "General Comment 6/16," U.N. Doc. CCPR/C/21/Add.1 (1984).
157. "General Comment 20/44," *supra* note 155, §5.
158. *Id.*
159. E.S.C. Res. 663C(XXIV); as amended, E.S.C. Res. 2076(LXII).
160. "General Comment 20/44," *supra* note 155, §10.
161. NOWAK, *supra* note 138, at p. 134.
162. *Ng* v. *Canada, supra* note 144.
163. *Id.*, §16.1.
164. *Kindler* v. *Canada, supra* note 144; *Cox* v. *Canada* (No. 539/1993), (1995) 15 *H.R.L.J.* 410.
165. *Pratt and Morgan* v. *Jamaica* (Nos. 210/1986, 225/1987), U.N. Doc. A/44/40, p. 222, *Reid* v. *Jamaica* (No. 250/1987), U.N. Doc. A/45/40, Vol. II, p. 85, (1990) 11 *H.R.L.J.* 319; *Cox* v. *Canada, supra* note 164.
166. *Pratt and Morgan* v. *Jamaica, supra* note 165.
167. *Soering* v. *United Kingdom et al.*, July 7, 1989, Series A, Vol. 161, 11 E.H.R.R. 439.
168. *Pratt et al.* v. *Attorney General for Jamaica et al., supra* note 31.
169. See my detailed discussion of the Human Rights Committee's attitude towards the "death row phenomenon" in "The Death Row Phenomenon" in this volume.
170. "General Comment 7/16," *supra* note 154, §1.
171. *Id.*, §2; "General Comment 20/44," *supra* note 155, §4.
172. NOWAK, *supra* note 138, at p. 129.
173. MCGOLDRICK, *supra* note 138, at p. 371.
174. *Id.*, at pp. 371–72.
175. "General Comment 24/52," U.N. Doc. CCPR/C/21/Rev.1/Add.6 (1994), §8.
176. Vienna Convention on the Law of Treaties, *supra* note 142, art. 19. See also: Reservations to the Convention on the Prevention of Genocide (Advisory Opinion), [1951] I.C.J. Reports 16; Restrictions to the Death Penalty (Arts. 4§2 and 4§4 American Convention on Human Rights), Advisory Opinion OC-3/83 of September 8, 1983, Series A No. 3, 4 *H.R.L.J.* 352, 70 I.L.R. 449; *Loizidou* v. *Turkey (Preliminary objections)*, March 23, 1995, Series A, No. 310.
177. "Multilateral Treaties deposited with the Secretary-General, Status as at 31 December 1994," U.N. Doc. ST/LEG/SER.E/13 (1995), p. 125. A similar reservation was formulated in 1994 at the time of the ratification by the United States of the Convention Against Torture and Other Cruel, Inhuman and Degrading Treatment or Punishment, G.A. Res. 39/46: "That the United States considers itself bound by the obligation under article 16 to prevent 'cruel, inhuman or degrading treatment or punishment,' only insofar as the term 'cruel, inhuman or degrading treatment or punishment' means the cruel, unusual and inhumane treatment or punishment prohibited by the Fifth, Eighth or Fourteenth Amendments to the Constitution of the United States." "Multilateral Treaties deposited with the Secretary-General, Status as at 31 December 1994," *id.*, at p. 179.
178. Marian NASH (LEICH), "U.S. Presentation Before Human Rights Committee (1995)," (1995) 89 *A.J.I.L.* 589, at p. 591. The reference is to a 1989 judgment of the European Court of Human Rights, *Soering* v. *United Kingdom et al., supra* note 167.
179. "Multilateral Treaties deposited with the Secretary-General, Status as at 31 December 1994," *supra* note 177, at pp. 127–30. Although Belgium and France objected to other reservations formulated by the United States, they made no comment on the reservation to article 7. See: William A. SCHABAS, "Invalid Reservations to the International Covenant on Civil and Political Rights: Is the United States Still a Party?" (1995) 21 *Brook. J. Int'l L.* 277.
180. "Consideration of reports submitted by states parties under article 40 of the Covenant, Comments of the Human Rights Committee," U.N. Doc. CCPR/C/79/Add.50 (1995), §14.

181. International Covenant on Civil and Political Rights, *supra* note 124, art. 4§2.
182. Convention for the Protection of Human Rights and Fundamental Freedoms (the "European Convention on Human Rights"), (1955) 213 U.N.T.S. 221, E.T.S. 5, art. 15§1; American Convention on Human Rights, (1979) 1144 U.N.T.S. 123. O.A.S.T.S. 36, art. 27.
183. Canadian Charter of Rights and Freedoms, *supra* note 34, s. 33; Constitution of the Republic of South Africa, Act 200 of 1993, assented to 25 January 1994, date of commencement 27 April 1994, *Government Gazette*, Vol. 343, No. 15466, art. 34.
184. International Covenant on Civil and Political Rights, *supra* note 124, art. 4; European Convention on Human Rights, *supra* note 182, art. 15.
185. Vienna Convention on the Law of Treaties, *supra* note 142, art. 54.
186. NOWAK, *supra* note 138, at. p. 126.
187. *Id.*
188. European Convention on Human Rights, *supra* note 182.
189. American Convention on Human Rights, *supra* note 182.
190. African Charter of Human and Peoples' Rights, O.A.U. Doc. CAB/LEG/67/3 rev. 5, 4 E.H.R.R. 417, 21 *I.L.M.* 58.
191. *Supra* note 182. A number of important works analyze the European Convention: J. E. S. FAWCETT, *The Application of the European Convention on Human Rights*, 2d ed., Oxford: Clarendon Press, 1987; Francis G. JACOBS, *The European Convention of Human Rights*, Oxford: Clarendon Press, 1975; P. VAN DIJK, G. J. H. VAN HOOF, *Theory and Practice of the European Convention on Human Rights*, Deventer: Kluwer, 1984; Gérard COHEN-JONATHAN, *La Convention européenne des droits de l'homme*, Paris: Economica-PUAM, 1989; Frédéric SUDRE, *La Convention européenne des droits de l'homme*, Paris: Presses universitaires de France, 1990; Jacques VELU, Rusen ERGEC, *La Convention européenne des droits de l'homme*, Brussels: Bruylant, 1990; R. St. J. MACDONALD, et al., eds., *The European System for the Protection of Human Rights*, Dordrecht, London, and Boston: Martinus Nijhoff, 1993; L.-E. PETTITI, et al., eds., *La Convention européenne des droits de l'homme, Commentaire article par article*, Paris: Economica, 1995.
192. On article 3 of the Convention, see: Antonio CASSESE, "Prohibition of torture and inhuman or degrading treatment or punishment," in MACDONALD et al., eds., *supra* note 191, pp. 225–61; Peter J. DUFFY, "Article 3 of the European Convention on Human Rights," (1983) 32 *I.C.L.Q.* 316; Louise DOSWALD-BECK, "What does the prohibition of 'Torture or Inhuman or Degrading Treatment or Punishment' mean? The interpretation of the European Commission and Court of Human Rights," (1978) 25 *Neth. Int'l L. Rev.* 24; Frédéric SUDRE, "Article 3," in PETTITI et al., eds., *supra* note 191, pp. 155–75; Frédéric SUDRE, "La notion de 'peines et traitements inhumains ou dégradants' dans la jurisprudence de la Commission et de la Cour européennes des droits de l'homme," (1984) 88 *R.G.D.I.P.* 825; Alphonse SPIELMAN, "La Convention européene des droits de l'homme et la peine de mort," in *Présence du droit public et les droits de l'homme, Mélanges offerts à Jacques Vélu*, Brussels: Bruylant, 1992, p. 1503.
193. In fact, the first draft provision simply referred to article 5 of the Universal Declaration: CASSESE, *supra* note 192, at p. 226.
194. *Collected Edition of the* Travaux Préparatoires *of the European Convention on Human Rights*, vol. 3, Dordrecht: Martinus Nijhoff, 1985, at pp. 204–6.
195. Hans DANELIUS, "Torture and cruel, inhuman or degrading treatment or punishment," (1989) 58 *Nordic J. Int'l. L.* 172, at pp. 172–73. Professor Cassese says simply that the reasons "cruel" was dropped are "not recorded": CASSESE, *supra* note 192, at p. 228.
196. SUDRE, "Article 3," *supra* note 192, at p. 157.
197. *Collected Edition of the* Travaux Préparatoires *of the European Convention on Human Rights*, vol. 1, Strasbourg: Council of Europe, 1975, at p. 253; *Collected Edition of the* Travaux Préparatoires *of the European Convention on Human Rights*, vol. 2, Strasbourg: Council of Europe, 1975, at p. 36.
198. *Collected Edition of the* Travaux Préparatoires *of the European Convention on Human Rights*, vol. 1, Strasbourg: Council of Europe, 1975, p. 254.

199. European Convention on Human Rights, *supra* note 182, arts. 25 and 46.
200. Pursuant to Protocol No. 9 to the Convention for the Protection of Human Rights and Fundamental Freedoms, E.T.S. 140, in the case of states that have ratified this instrument.
201. *Denmark* v. *Greece* (App. no. 3321/67), *Norway* v. *Greece* (App. no. 3322/67), *Sweden* v. *Greece* (App. no. 3323/67), *Netherlands* v. *Greece* (App. no. 3344/67), (1969) 12 *Yearbook of the European Convention on Human Rights* 186.
202. *Id.;* see also: *Ireland* v. *United Kingdom* (App. no. 5310/71), (1976) 19 *Yearbook of the European Convention on Human Rights* 512; *Ireland* v. *United Kingdom*, January 18, 1978, Series A, No. 25, 2 E.H.R.R. 25, pp. 66–67 (Series A), 80 (E.H.R.R.); *Tyrer* v. *United Kingdom*, April 25, 1978, Series A, No. 26, 2 E.H.R.R. 1, 59 I.L.R. 339, at pp. 14 (Series A), 8 (E.H.R.R.); *Campbell and Cosans* v. *United Kingdom*, February 23, 1982, Series A, No. 48, 4 E.H.R.R. 293, at pp. 12 (Series A), 300 (E.H.R.R.).
203. *Denmark, Norway, Sweden, and the Netherlands* v. *Greece, supra* note 201.
204. PHILLIPS, *supra* note 121, at p. 779.
205. *Ireland* v. *United Kingdom* (App. no. 5310/71), *supra* note 202, at pp. 750, 752. See: RODLEY, *supra* note 2, at pp. 74–78.
206. *Ireland* v. *United Kingdom*, January 18, 1978, *supra* note 202, at p. 65.
207. *Supra* note 124.
208. European Convention on Human Rights, *supra* note 182, art. 2§1.
209. Protocol No. 6 to the Convention for the Protection of Human Rights and Fundamental Freedoms Concerning the Abolition of the Death Penalty, E.T.S. 114.
210. *Kirkwood* v. *United Kingdom* (App. no. 10479/83), (1984) 37 D.R. 158, 6 E.H.R.R. 373, at pp. 184 (D.R.), 381 (E.H.R.R.). For the judgment before the English courts, see: *R.* v. *Secretary of State for the Home Department, ex parte Kirkwood*, [1984] 2 All E.R. 390 (H.L.).
211. *Soering* v. *United Kingdom et al., supra* note 167, at pp. 31 (Series A), 463–64 (E.H.R.R.).
212. *Id.*
213. On the "death row phenomenon" in general, see "The Death Row Phenomenon" in this volume.
214. Extradition Treaty Between the Government of the United Kingdom of Great Britain and Northern Ireland and the Government of the United States of America, (1977) 1049 U.N.T.S. 167, art. IV: If the offence for which extradition is requested is punishable by death under the relevant law of the requesting Party, but the relevant law of the requested Party does not provide for the death penalty in a similar case, extradition may be refused unless the requesting Party gives assurance satisfactory to the requested party that the death penalty will not be carried out.
215. European Convention on Extradition, (1960) 359 U.N.T.S. 273, E.T.S. 24. Similar provisions can be found as early as 1889 in the South American Convention, in the 1892 extradition treaty between the United Kingdom and Portugal, in the 1908 extradition treaty between the United States and Portugal, and in the 1912 draft treaty prepared by the International Commission of Jurists. On these early versions, see: J. S. REEVES, "Extradition treaties and the death penalty," (1924) 18 *A.J.I.L.* 290; "American Institute of International Law, Project No. 17," (1926) 20 *A.J.I.L. Supplement* 331; "Harvard Law School Draft Extradition Treaty," (1935) 29 *A.J.I.L.* 228. The Italian Constitutional Court has ruled that article 11 of the European Convention on Extradition does not codify a customary rule of international law: *Re Cuillier, Ciamborrani and Vallon*, (1988) 78 I.L.R. 93 (Constitutional Court, Italy). A provision similar to that of the European Convention on Extradition appears in the Inter-American Convention on Extradition, (1981) 20 *I.L.M.* 723, art. 9. The "Model Treaty on Extradition" proposed by the Eighth United Nations Congress on the Prevention of Crime and Treatment of Offenders, 1990, contains the following text: "Article 4. Extradition may be refused in any of the following circumstances: . . . (c) If the offence for which extradition is requested carries the death penalty under the law of the requesting State, unless that State gives such assurance

as the requested State considers sufficient that the death penalty will not be imposed or, if imposed, will not be carried out." (U.N. Doc. A/CONF. 14/28/Rev. 1, p. 68).

See also: Sharon A. WILLIAMS, "Extradition and the death penalty exception in Canada: Resolving the Ng and Kindler cases," (1991) 13 *Loy. L.A. Int'l & Comp. L.J.* 799; Sharon A. WILLIAMS, "Extradition to a state that imposes the death penalty," [1990] *C.Y.I.L.* 117; Sharon A. WILLIAMS, "Nationality, double jeopardy, prescription and the death sentence as bases for refusing extradition," (1991) 62 *Int'l Rev. Penal L.* 259; Sharon A. WILLIAMS, "Human rights safeguards and international cooperation in extradition: Striking the balance," (1992) 3 *Crim. L.F.* 191; Donald K. PIRAGOFF, Marcia V. J. KRAN, "The impact of human rights principles on extradition from Canada and the United States: The role of national courts," (1992) 3 *Crim. L.F.* 191; William A. SCHABAS, "Extradition et la peine de mort: le Canada renvoie deux fugitifs au couloir de la mort," (1992) 4 *R.U.D.H.* 65; William A. SCHABAS, "Kindler and Ng: Our supreme magistrates take a frightening step into the court of public opinion," (1991) 51 *Revue du Barreau* 673.

216. As a result of the court's decision in *Soering*, the United Kingdom sought and obtained more thorough assurances that the death penalty would not be imposed, as was noted by the Committee of Ministers of the Council of Europe on March 12, 1990 (Council of Europe, *Information Sheet No. 26*, Strasbourg, 1990, p. 116). Soering was subsequently extradited, tried, and sentenced to life imprisonment. See: Richard B. LILLICH, "The *Soering* case," (1991) 85 *A.J.I.L.* 128.

217. *Soering* v. *United Kingdom et al., supra* note 167, at pp. 43 (Series A), 476 (E.H.R.R.).

218. JACOBS, *supra* note 191, p. 23.

219. It is clear from the judgment that the argument had been made that the United Kingdom had not rejected capital punishment unequivocally because it had failed to ratify Protocol No. 6 to the European Convention, *supra* note 209. The European Commission on Human Rights, in the same case, held that Protocol No. 6 had "no relevance" to the obligations of the United Kingdom under the Convention because it had neither signed nor ratified it (at p. 56 in Series A). In his concurring view, Judge De Meyer observed that the failure to ratify Protocol No. 6 was not in any way determinative of the matter, because the "unlawfulness" of capital punishment had already been recognized by the Committee of Ministers of the Council of Europe in opening the instrument for signature (at p. 52 in Series A).

220. *Soering* v. *United Kingdom et al., supra* note 167, at pp. 51 (Series A), 484 (E.H.R.R.).

221. *Id.*, at pp. 52 (Series A), 485 (E.H.R.R.).

222. *Id.*, §103. This view was taken by the minority of the Supreme Court of Canada: *Kindler* v. *Canada, supra* note 9. See also: Hugo Adam BEDAU, "Thinking of the death penalty as cruel and unusual punishment," (1985) 18 *U.C. Davis L. Rev.* 873.

223. JACOBS, *supra* note 191, at p. 23. The Turkish courts have invoked article 2§1 of the European Convention to support a decision upholding the constitutionality of that country's death penalty, which is set out in article 11 of the penal code: (1963) 6 *Yearbook of the European Convention on Human Rights* 821.

224. One distinguished scholar, Yoram Dinstein, has suggested that "there is a general practice amounting to customary international law, in the conditional and presumptive sense indicated, that when a State (like the United States) which has not abolished capital punishment seeks extradition from a State which has (like the United Kingdom), the requesting State must guarantee that the extraditee would not be executed." Yoram DINSTEIN, "General report," (1991) 62 *Int'l Rev. Penal L.* 31, at p. 36.

225. *Soering* v. *United Kingdom et al., supra* note 167, §103.

226. "Opinion of the Steering Committee on Human Rights," November 12–16, 1979.

227. *Riley* v. *Attorney-General of Jamaica, supra* note 30, at pp. 727 (A.C.), 473 (All E.R.) (*per* Lords Scarman and Brightman, dissenting).

228. *Minister of Home Affairs* v. *Fisher*, [1980] A.C. 319 (J.C.P.C.), at p. 328 (*per* Lord Wilberforce).

See also: *Maharaj* v. *Attorney-General of Trinidad and Tobago (No. 2)*, [1979] A.C. 385 (J.C.P.C.), at p. 402 (*per* Lord Hailsham of St. Marylebone, dissenting).

229. *Canadian Charter of Rights and Freedoms*, *supra* note 34, s. 12. See: *Kindler* v. *Canada*, *supra* note 9, at p. 793 (S.C.R.) (*per* Cory, J., dissenting); p. 839 (S.C.R.) (*per* McLachlin, J.); p. 830 (S.C.R.) (*per* La Forest, J.).

230. American Declaration of the Rights and Duties of Man, O.A.S. Doc. OEA/Ser.L/V/II.23, doc. 21, rev. 6, art. 26.

231. *Supra* note 182.

232. Robert NORRIS, "The individual petition procedure of the inter-American system for the protection of human rights," in Hurst HANNUM, ed., *Guide to International Human Rights Law Practice*, Philadelphia: University of Pennsylvania Press, 1984, at p. 104.

233. The United States has not ratified the American Convention on Human Rights, and cannot therefore be attacked before the commission or the court for alleged violations of that instrument. However, several petitions have come before the Inter-American Commission directed against the United States for breaches of the American Declaration of the Rights and Duties of Man. The United States has replied, unsuccessfully, by contesting the commission's jurisdiction: *White and Potter* v. *United States* (Case No. 2141), Resolution No. 23/81, O.A.S. Doc. OEA/Ser.L/V/II.52 doc. 48, O.A.S. Doc. OEA/Ser.L/V/II.54 doc 9 rev. 1, at pp. 25–54, INTER-AMERICAN COMMISSION ON HUMAN RIGHTS, *Ten Years of Activities, 1971–1981*, Washington: Organization of American States, 1982, at pp. 186–209, (1981) 1 *H.R.L.J.* 110. See: D. T. FOX, "Inter-American Commission on Human Rights finds United States in violation," (1988) 82 *A.J.I.L.* 601. Canada, which is in a position similar to that of the United States, has been named in several petitions since joining the O.A.S. in 1990, and has chosen not to contest the commission's jurisdiction: William A. SCHABAS, "Canada and the American Convention on Human Rights: Will we ever ratify?" in *A New Policy for a Changing Hemisphere*, Ottawa: Carleton University Press, 1996 (forthcoming).

234. *Supra* note 230.

235. *Roach and Pinkerton* v. *United States* (Case No. 9647), Resolution No. 3/87, reported in: O.A.S. Doc. OEA/Ser.L/V/II.71 doc. 9 rev. 1, p. 147, *Inter-American Yearbook on Human Rights, 1987*, Dordrecht, London, and Boston: Martinus Nijhoff, 1990, p. 328, 8 *H.R.L.J.* 345; *Celestine* v. *United States* (Case No. 10,031), Resolution No. 23/89, reported in O.A.S. Doc. A/Ser.L./V/II.76 doc. 44, O.A.S. Doc. A/Ser.L/V/II.77 rev. 1, doc. 7, p. 62.

236. *Godinez Cruz Case*, Judgment of January 20, 1989, Series C, No. 5, §164.

237. *Pratt and Morgan* v. *Jamaica*, report of July 9, 1987. This decision of the Inter-American Commission followed an October 1984 ruling that dismissed Pratt and Morgan's petition: *Pratt* v. *Jamaica* (Case No. 9054), Resolution No. 13/84, reported in O.A.S. Doc. OEA/Ser.L/V/II.66 doc. 10 rev. 1, at pp. 111–13. The 1987 report of the commission was never published, and only came to light when it was referred to in the 1993 judgment of the Judicial Committee of the Privy Council in *Pratt et al.* v. *Attorney General for Jamaica et al.*, *supra* note 31, at p. 778 (All E.R.), 23 (A.C.).

238. O.A.U. Doc. CAB/LEG/67/3 Rev. 5. See: Fatsah OUGUERGOUZ, *La Charte africaine des droits de l'homme et des peuples*, Geneva: Presses universitaires de France, 1993; Keba MBAYE, *Les droits de l'homme en Afrique*, Paris: Pedone, 1992; E. KODJO, "La Charte africaine des droits de l'homme et des peuples," (1989) 1 *R.U.D.H.* 29; M. G. AHANHANZO, "Introduction à la Charte africaine des droits de l'Homme et des Peuples," in *Mélanges Colliard*, Paris: Pedone, 1984, at p. 511.

239. "Draft Protocol to the African Charter on Human and Peoples' Rights on the Establishment of an African Court on Human and Peoples' Rights," O.A.U. Doc. OAU/LEG/EXP/AFC/HPR (I); *Constitutional Rights Project (in respect of Nabab Akama, G. Adega et al.)* (Comm. no. 69/91), (1996) 3 I.H.R.R. 132; *Constitutional Rights Project (in respect of Zamani Lakwot et al.)* (Comm. no. 87/93), (1996) 3 I.H.R.R. 137.

240. Etienne-Richard MBAYA, "À la recherche du noyau intangible dans la Charte africaine," in *Le*

noyau intangible des droits de l'homme, Fribourg: Éditions universitaires Fribourg Suisse, 1991, pp. 207–26, at p. 221. See also: MBAYE, *supra* note 238, at p. 197.

241. *Nemi* v. *The State*, [1994] 1 L.R.C. 376 (Supreme Court, Nigeria), at p. 386 (Bello, C.J.N.); also at p. 400 (Uwais, J.S.C.). On the death penalty in Nigeria, see: Mike IKHARIALE, "Death penalty in Nigeria: A constitutional aberration," (1991) 1 *J. Hum. Rts. L. Prac.* 40.

242. *Makwanyane and Mchunu* v. *The State, supra* note 70.

243. Geneva Convention of August 12, 1949 Relative to the Protection of Civilians, *supra* note 1, art. 68§4; Protocol Additional I to the 1949 Geneva Conventions and Relating to the Protection of Victims of International Armed Conflicts, (1979) 1125 U.N.T.S. 3, arts. 76§3, 77§5; Protocol Additional II to the 1949 Geneva Conventions and Relating to the Protection of Victims of Non-International Armed Conflicts, (1979) 1125 U.N.T.S. 609, art. 6§4.

244. Geneva Convention of August 12, 1949 Relative to the Treatment of Prisoners of War, *supra* note 1, art. 101; Geneva Convention of August 12, 1949 Relative to the Protection of Civilians, *supra* note 1, art. 75. A draft provision providing for a moratorium on executions during all non-international armed conflicts was eventually dropped from Protocol Additional II. On humanitarian law provisions dealing with the death penalty, see William A. SCHABAS, *supra* note 122, at pp. 179–207.

245. Geneva Convention of August 12, 1949 For the Amelioration of the Condition of the Wounded and Sick in Armed Forces in the Field, *supra* note 1, art. 3; Geneva Convention of August 12, 1949 For the Amelioration of the Condition of Wounded, Sick and Shipwrecked Members of Armed Forces at Sea, *supra* note 1, art. 3; Geneva Convention of August 12, 1949 Relative to the Treatment of Prisoners of War, *supra* note 1, art. 3; Geneva Convention of August 12, 1949 Relative to the Protection of Civilians, *supra* note 1, art. 3.

246. *Military and Paramilitary Activities in and Against Nicaragua (Nicaragua* v. *United States)*, [1986] I.C.J. Reports 14, §§218, 255, 292 (9).

247. Convention Against Torture and Other Cruel, Inhuman and Degrading Treatment or Punishment, G.A. Res. 39/46.

248. Declaration on the Protection of All Persons from Being Subjected to Torture and Other Cruel, Inhuman or Degrading Treatment or Punishment, G.A. Res. 3452 (XXX).

249. *Supra* note 123, at p. 177.

250. "Initial Report of Bulgaria," U.N. Doc. CAT/C/5/Add. 28, §§50–54; "Initial Report of Ukraine," U.N. Doc. CAT/C/17/Add.4, §§13–14; "Initial Report of Libya," U.N. Doc. CAT/C/9/Add.7, §§28, 40; "Initial Report of Libya," U.N. Doc. CAT/C/9/Add.12, pp. 19–20; "Initial Report of Libya," U.N. Doc. CAT/C/9/Add.12/Rev.1, §§89–92; "First Supplementary Report of China," U.N. Doc. CAT/C/7/Add.14, §§38–42, 123–29; "Initial Report of Cyprus," U.N. Doc. CAT/C/16/Add.2, §23; "Initial Report of Senegal," U.N. Doc. CAT/C/5/Add.19, §§4–6; "First Supplementary Report of Belarus," U.N. Doc. CAT/C/17/Add.6, §3; "Initial Report of Netherlands (Aruba)," U.N. Doc. CAT/C/25/Add.5, §51; "Initial Report of Mauritius," U.N. Doc. CAT/C/24/Add.3, §36; U.N. Doc. CAT/C/SR.28, §§41, 74 (Soviet Union); U.N. Doc. CAT/C/SR.52, §11 (Ukrainian S.S.R.); U.N. Doc. CAT/C/SR.77, §§7, 12 (Chile).

251. "Initial Report of Panama," U.N. Doc. CAT/C/17/Add.7, §23k; "Initial Report of Italy," U.N. Doc. CAT/C/9/Add.9, §24; "Initial Report of Argentina," U.N. Doc. CAT/C/17/Add.2, §23; "Initial Report of Portugal," U.N. Doc. CAT/C/15, §61; "Initial Report of Canada," U.N. Doc. CAT/C/17/Add.5, §§17–19; U.N. Doc. CAT/C/SR.64, §42 (Netherlands); "Initial Report of Mexico," U.N. Doc. CAT/C/5/Add.7, §§19–20; "Initial Report of Czech Republic," U.N. Doc. CAT/C/21/Add.2, §41; U.N. Doc. CAT/C/SR.63, §91, U.N. Doc. CAT/C/SR.64, §41 (Netherlands (Netherlands Antilles)); U.N. Doc. CAT/C/SR.96, §40 (Australia). When Canada was questioned by the Committee Against Torture about the extradition of Kindler and Ng, government spokesperson Martin Low informed the committee that the matter was pending before the Human Rights Committee and expressed his hope that the committee would appreciate the "impropriety" of further discussion. He added that "some delay was inevitable when, following conviction, a person had invoked legal procedures that were in-

tended to ensure that the execution could not take place before the most exhaustive review and legal scrutiny": U.N. Doc. CAT/C/SR.140, §36.

252. "Initial Report of Romania," U.N. Doc. CAT/C/16/Add.1, §7; U.N. Doc. CAT/C/SR.167, §20 (Portugal); "Initial Report of Hungary," U.N. Doc. CAT/C/17/Add.8, §§6–8; "Initial Report of Uruguay," U.N. Doc. CAT/C/12/Add.3, §4; "Initial Report of Poland," U.N. Doc. CAT/C/9/Add. 13, §6; "Initial Report of Switzerland," U.N. Doc. CAT/C/17/Add.12, §§27–28; "Initial Report of Senegal," U.N. Doc. CAT/C/5/Add.19, §6; "Initial Report of Philippines," U.N. Doc. CAT/C/5/Add.18, §29.

253. "Initial Report of Uruguay," U.N. Doc. CAT/C/5/Add.30, p. 25; U.N. Doc. CAT/C/SR.62, §5 (Turkey); U.N. Doc. CAT/C/SR.98, §54 (Bulgaria); U.N. Doc. CAT/C/SR.161, §8 (Poland); U.N. Doc. CAT/C/SR.146/Add.2, §19 (China); U.N. Doc. CAT/C/SR.169, §25 (Cyprus); U.N. Doc. CAT/C/SR.160, §17 (Poland); U.N. Doc. CAT/C/SR.130, §15, U.N. Doc. CAT/C/SR.135, §26 (Libya); U.N. Doc. CAT/C/SR.133, §18 (Belarus); U.N. Doc. CAT/C/SR.107, §§31, 45 (Luxembourg); U.N. Doc. CAT/C/SR.140, §36 (Canada); U.N. Doc. CAT/C/SR.80, §25 (Algeria); U.N. Doc. CAT/C/SR.76, §22 (Panama); U.N. Doc. CAT/C/SR.14, §65, U.N. Doc. CAT/C/SR.14, §44 (Philippines); U.N. Doc. CAT/C/SR.28, §27 (Switzerland); U.N. Doc. CAT/C/SR.32, §29, U.N. Doc. CAT/C/SR.33, §14 (Byelorussian S.S.R.); U.N. Doc. CAT/C/SR.34, §35 (Cameroon); U.N. Doc. CAT/C/SR.34, §§60, 67, U.N. Doc. CAT/C/SR.35, §59 (Hungary); U.N. Doc. CAT/C/SR.46, §§43, 57, U.N. Doc. CAAT/C/SR.47, §29 (Tunisia); U.N. Doc. CAT/C/SR.50, §15, U.N. Doc. CAT/C/SR.51, §§18–19, 37, 41, 46 (China); U.N. Doc. CAT/C/SR.52, §§30, 43, U.N. Doc. CAT/C/SR.53, §8 (Ukrainian S.S.R.); U.N. Doc. CAT/C/SR.79, §§24, 27 U.N. Doc. CAT/C/SR.80, §25 (Algeria); U.N. Doc. CAT/C/SR.79, §34 (Chile); U.N. Doc. CAT/C/SR.93, §88 (Libya).

254. Lillich, *supra* note 216.

255. "Multilateral Treaties deposited with the Secretary-General, Status as at 31 December 1994," *supra* note 177, at p. 180.

256. Convention Against Torture and Other Cruel, Inhuman and Degrading Treatment or Punishment, *supra* note 247, art. 3.

257. Human Rights Committee: *Kindler* v. *Canada*, *supra* note 144; *Ng* v. *Canada*, *supra* note 144; *Cox* v. *Canada*, *supra* note 164. European Court of Human Rights: *Soering* v. *United Kingdom et al.*, *supra* note 167. European Commission on Human Rights: *Kirkwood* v. *United Kingdom*, *supra* note 210; *Soering* v. *United Kingdom et al.*, *supra* note 167; *Aylor-Davis* v. *France* (No. 22742/93), (1994) 76A *D.R.* 164, *H.* v. *Sweden* (App. no. 22408/93/91), (1994) 79 A D.R. 85. France: *Fidan*, (1987) II *Receuil Dalloz-Sirey* 305 (Conseil d'État); *Gacem*, (1988) I *Semaine juridique* IV-86 (Conseil d'État); *Dame Joy Davis-Aylor*, C.E., req. no 144590, 15/10/93, D. 1993, IR, 238; J.C.P. 1993, Actualités no 43, [1993] *Revue française de droit administratif* 1166, conclusions C. Vigoreux. Netherlands: *Short* v. *Netherlands*, (1990) 76 Rechtspraak van de Week 358, (1990) 29 *I.L.M.* 1378. Canada: *Kindler* v. *Canada*, *supra* note 9; *Reference: Re Ng Extradition (Can.)*, [1991] 2 S.C.R. 858, 84 D.L.R. (4th) 498, 67 C.C.C. (3d) 61.

258. But see: *Khan* v. *Canada*, (1995) 15 *H.R.L.J.* 426, where the committee found that expulsion of an individual to a country that had not ratified the Convention and where there was a risk of torture constituted a breach of the Convention.

259. ECOSOC Res. 663C (XXIV); as amended, ECOSOC Res. 2076 (LXII). See also: United Nations Body of Principles for the Protection of All Persons Under any Form of Detention or Imprisonment, G.A. Res. 43/197.

260. A number of similar instruments are also of relevance: Code of Conduct for Law Enforcement Officials, G.A. Res. 34/169 (1979); Principles of Medical Ethics relevant to the role of Health Personnel, Particularly Physicians, in the Protection of Prisoners and Detainees against Torture and Other Cruel, Inhuman or Degrading Treatment or Punishment, G.A. Res. 37/194 (1982).

261. E.T.S. 126.

262. Inter-American Convention to Prevent and Punish Torture, O.A.S.T.S. 67, 25 I.L.M. 519.

263. For discussions of the history of capital punishment in India, see: Nishtha JASWAL, *Role of the Supreme Court with Regard to the Right to Life and Personal Liberty,* New Delhi: Ashish Publishing House, 1990; Jill COTTRELL, "Wrestling with the death penalty in India," (1991) 7 *South African J. Hum. Rts.* 185.

264. The term "torture" appears in several other international instruments: American Declaration of the Rights and Duties of Man, *supra* note 230, art. I; European Convention on Human Rights, *supra* note 182, art. 3; International Covenant on Civil and Political Rights, *supra* note 124, art. 7; American Convention on Human Rights, *supra* note 182, art. 5§2; African Charter of Human and People's Rights, *supra* note 190, art. 5; Code of Conduct for Law Enforcement Officials, *supra* note 260; Principles of Medical Ethics relevant to the role of Health Personnel, Particularly Physicians, in the Protection of Prisoners and Detainees against Torture and Other Cruel, Inhuman or Degrading Treatment or Punishment, *supra* note 260; American Convention to Prevent and Punish Torture, *supra* note 259, art. 2.

265. *Denmark, Norway, Sweden, and the Netherlands* v. *Greece, supra* note 201.

266. Convention Against Torture and Other Cruel, Inhuman and Degrading Treatment or Punishment, *supra* note 247.

267. See the similar but not identical definition in article 2 of the Inter-American Convention to Prevent and Punish Torture, *supra* note 262: "Any act intentionally performed whereby physical or mental pain or suffering is inflicted on a person for purposes of criminal investigation, as means of intimidation, as personal punishment, as a preventive measure, as a penalty, or for any other purpose. Torture shall also be understood to be the use of methods upon a person intended to obliterate the personality of the victim or to diminish his physical or mental capacities, even if they do not cause physical pain or mental anguish. The concept of torture shall not include physical or mental pain or suffering that is inherent in or solely the consequence of lawful measures, provided that they do not include the performance of the acts or use of the methods referred to in this article."

268. The Declaration on the Protection of All Persons from Being Subjected to Torture and Other Cruel, Inhuman or Degrading Treatment or Punishment, *supra* note 248, from which the Convention is largely derived, says: "It does not include pain or suffering arising only from, inherent in or incidental to, lawful sanctions to the extent consistent with the Standard Minimum Rules for the Treatment of Prisoners."

269. NOWAK, *supra* note 138, at p. 134 n. 45.

270. J. H. BURGERS, H. DANELIUS, *The United Nations Convention against Torture—A Handbook,* Dordrecht, London, and Boston: Martinus Nijhoff, 1988, at p. 122.

271. Pnina Baruh SHARVIT, "The definition of torture in the United Nations Convention Against Torture and Other Cruel, Inhuman and Degrading Treatment or Punishment," (1993) 23 *Israel Yearbook on Human Rights* 147, at p. 169. See also: RODLEY, *supra* note 2, at pp. 29–30; BURGERS, DANELIUS, *supra* note 270, at pp. 42–47; H. HANG, "Efforts to eliminate torture through international law," (1989) 29 *Int'l Rev. Red Cross* 9.

272. Declaration Against Torture and Other Cruel, Inhuman and Degrading Treatment or Punishment, *supra* note 248.

273. *Denmark, Norway, Sweden, and the Netherlands* v. *Greece, supra* note 201, at p. 186.

274. *Ireland* v. *United Kingdom,* January 18, 1978, *supra* note 202, at pp. 66 (Series A), 80 (E.H.R.R.).

275. *People* v. *Anderson, supra* note 92, at pp. 646 (Cal.3d), 892 (P.2d) (Wright, C.J.).

276. *District Atty. for Suffolk Dist.* v. *Watson, supra* note 85, at p. 1281 (N.E.2d).

277. *Campbell* v. *Wood,* 18 F.3d 662, 702 (9th Cir. 1994) (Reinhardt, J., dissenting), *cert. denied,* 114 S.Ct. 2125 (1994).

278. *Denmark, Norway, Sweden, and the Netherlands* v. *Greece, supra* note 201.

279. *Ireland* v. *United Kingdom,* January 18, 1978, *supra* note 202, at pp. 66 (Series A), 79–80 (E.H.R.R.).

280. *Denmark, Norway, Sweden, and the Netherlands* v. *Greece, supra* note 201.

281. *East African Asians* v. *United Kingdom*, (1970) 13 *Yearbook of the European Convention on Human Rights* 994, (1981) 3 E.H.R.R. 76.

282. *Soering* v. *United Kingdom et al.*, *supra* note 167, at p. 472 (E.H.R.R.).

283. *Vuolanne* v. *Finland* (No. 265/1987), U.N. Doc. A/44/40, at p. 249, §9.2.

284. *Supra* note 230.

285. U.N. Doc. A/C.3/L.675.

286. U.N. Doc. A/C.3/SR.290, §64; U.N. Doc. A/C.3/SR.851, §§20, 26, 40; U.N. Doc. A/C.3/SR.852, §§16, 23; U.N. Doc. A/C.3/SR.853, §3. It was withdrawn by the Philippine representative: U.N. Doc. A/C.3/SR.853.

287. *Supra* note 33, s. 2b.

288. Canadian Charter of Rights and Freedoms, *supra* note 34, s. 12.

289. William A. SCHABAS, *International Human Rights Law and the Canadian Charter*, Toronto: Carswell, 1991.

290. *Trop* v. *Dulles*, *supra* note 64, at pp. 99–100 (U.S.), 598 (S.Ct.).

291. *Furman* v. *Georgia*, *supra* note 29, at pp. 376 (U.S.), 2797 (S.Ct.) (Burger, C.J., dissenting).

292. *Trop* v. *Dulles*, *supra* note 64, at pp. 100 (U.S.), 597 (S.Ct.); cited in *Gregg* v. *Georgia*, *supra* note 29, at pp. 173 (U.S.), 2925 (S.Ct.).

293. *Gregg* v. *Georgia*, *supra* note 29. On dignity and the Eighth Amendment, see also: *Furman* v. *Georgia*, *supra* note 29, at pp. 282 (U.S.), 2748 (S.Ct.) (Brennan, J., concurring); *Jackson* v. *Bishop*, 414 F.2d 571 (8th Cir. 1968).

294. *Gregg* v. *Georgia*, *supra* note 29, at p. 230 (U.S.).

295. *Conjwayo* v. *Minister of Justice, Legal & Parliamentary Affairs*, [1991] 1 Z.L.R. 105, [1992] 2 S.A. 56 (S.C.), at p. 63 (S.A.) (Gubbay, C.J.).

296. *People* v. *Anderson*, *supra* note 92, at pp. 650 (Cal.3d), 895 (P.2d) (Wright, C.J.).

297. *District Atty. for Suffolk Dist.* v. *Watson*, *supra* note 85, at p. 1294 (N.E.2d) (Liacos, J., concurring).

298. Clarence DARROW, *Attorney for the Damned*, New York: Simon & Schuster, 1957, at p. 92. Also William J. BOWERS, "The effect of executions is brutalization, not deterrence," in Kenneth A. HAAS, James A. INCIARDI, eds., *Challenging Capital Punishment: Legal and Social Science Approaches*, Beverly Hills, Cal: Sage Publications, 1988, pp. 49–89.

299. *District Atty. for Suffolk Dist.* v. *Watson*, *supra* note 85, at p. 1286 (N.E.2d 1274) (Hennessey, C.J., concurring).

300. *Pratt and Morgan* v. *Jamaica*, *supra* note 165.

301. *Ng.* v. *Canada*, *supra* note 144, at p. 34.

302. *Denmark, Norway, Sweden, and the Netherlands* v. *Greece*, *supra* note 201, at p. 186 (Yearbook). In the *Irish case*, the commission and the court concluded that certain treatments were not unacceptable because they were "the result of a lack of judgment rather than an intention to hurt or degrade": *Ireland* v. *United Kingdom* (App. no. 5310/71), *supra* note 202, at p. 472; *Ireland* v. *United Kingdom*, January 18, 1978, *supra* note 202, at p. 60. Antonio Cassese criticizes both the commission and the court because of their insistence on an element of intent, noting that "although the intention to cause suffering *may* be one of the constituent elements of inhuman treatment or punishments, *it is not indispensable*": CASSESE, *supra* note 192, at p. 246.

303. PHILLIPS, *supra* note 121, at pp. 779–80.

304. *Id.*, at p. 780.

305. *Louisiana ex rel. Francis* v. *Resweber*, *supra* note 27, at pp. 464 (U.S.), 376 (S.Ct.). See: Lonny J. HOFFMAN, "The madness of the method: The use of electrocution and the death penalty," (1992) *Tex. L. Rev.* 1039, at p. 1048.

306. *Louisiana ex. rel. Francis* v. *Resweber*, *supra* note 27, at pp. 471 (U.S.), 380 (S.Ct.).

307. *In re Storti*, 60 N.E. 210, 210 (Mass.1901) (Holmes, C.J.).

308. *Campbell* v. *Wood*, *supra* note 277, at p. 687.

309. *Campbell and Cosans* v. *United Kingdom*, *supra* note 202, at pp. 13 (Series A), 302 (E.H.R.R.).

310. *Tyrer* v. *United Kingdom*, *supra* note 202, at p. 20 (Series A). See also the separate opinion of

President Fawcett in *Ireland* v. *United Kingdom*, January 18, 1978, *supra* note 202, at p. 502 (Series B).

311. *Soering* v. *United Kingdom et al.*, *supra* note 167, at p. 780.
312. David PANNICK, *Judicial Review of the Death Penalty*, London: Duckworth, 1982, at p. 74.
313. *Tyrer* v. *United Kingdom*, *supra* note 202, §12.
314. *Denmark, Norway, Sweden, and the Netherlands* v. *Greece*, *supra* note 201, at p. 501 (Yearbook).
315. International Covenant on Civil and Political Rights, *supra* note 124, art. 2§1.
316. International Covenant on Economic, Social and Cultural Rights, *supra* note 135, art. 2§1.
317. Albert BECKMAN, Michael BOTHE, "General report on the theory of limitations on human rights," in Armand DE MESTRAL et al., eds., *The Limitations of Human Rights in Comparative Constitutional Law*, Cowansville, Qué.: Éditions Yvon Blais, 1986, at pp. 105–12.
318. *Supra* note 35.
319. For example: International Covenant on Civil and Political Rights, *supra* note 124, arts. 12§3, 18§3, 19§3, 21 22§2, 25; European Convention on Human Rights, *supra* note 182, arts. 8§2, 9§2, 10§2, 11§2; American Convention on Human Rights, *supra* note 182, arts. 12§3, 13§2, 15, 16§2, 22§§3–4; African Charter of Human and Peoples' Rights, *supra* note 190, arts. 8, 11, 12§§2, 14.
320. *Ireland* v. *United Kingdom* (App. no. 5310/71), *supra* note 202, at p. 502 (Series B).
321. *Id.*
322. *Tyrer* v. *United Kingdom*, *supra* note 202, §5.
323. *Makwanyane and Mchunu* v. *The State*, *supra* note 70, at p. 170 (*per* Chaskalson, P.).
324. *Supra* note 124. See also: European Convention on Human Rights, *supra* note 182, arts. 2 and 3; American Convention on Human Rights, *supra* note 182, arts. 4 and 5§2.
325. *Callins* v. *Collins, cert. denied*, 114 S.Ct. 1127, 1127, 127 L.Ed. 435 (1994) (Scalia, J.). See also: *Gregg* v. *Georgia*, *supra* note 29, at pp. 177 (U.S.), 2927 (S.Ct.) (Stewart, J.). See also: *State* v. *Ross*, 230 Conn. 183, 646 A.2d 1318, 1356 (1994).
326. *Bachan Singh* v. *State of Punjab*, A.I.R. 1980 S.C. 898, (1980) 2 S.C.C. 684, at p. 930 (A.I.R.) (Sarkaria, J.). See also: *Jagmohan Singh* v. *State of U.P.*, A.I.R. 1973 S.C. 947, at pp. 958–59.
327. *Riley* v. *Attorney-General of Jamaica*, *supra* note 30, at pp. 472 (All E.R.), 726 (A.C.) (Lord Bridge of Harwich). See also: *Runyowa* v. *The Queen*, [1967] A.C. 26 (J.C.P.C.), at pp. 46–47.
328. NOWAK, *supra* note 138, at p. 134.
329. *Soering* v. *United Kingdom et al.*, *supra* note 167.
330. *People* v. *Anderson*, *supra* note 92, at pp. 637–38 (Cal.3d), 886 (P.2d) (Wright, C.J.).
331. *Id.*, at pp. 639 (Cal.3d), 887 (P.2d (Wright, C.J.).
332. *Soering* v. *United Kingdom et al.*, *supra* note 167, at pp. 50–51 (Series A), 475–84 (E.H.R.R.).
333. Dennis DAVIS, "Democracy—its influence upon the process of constitutional interpretation," (1994) 10 *South African J. Hum. Rts.* 103, at p. 108.
334. International Covenant on Civil and Political Rights, *supra* note 124, art. 6§6.

ARBITRARINESS AND INEQUALITY

1. Universal Declaration of Human Rights, G.A. Res. 217A (III), U.N. Doc. A/810 (1948).
2. International Covenant on Civil and Political Rights, (1976) 999 U.N.T.S. 171.
3. Convention for the Protection of Human Rights and Fundamental Freedoms (the "European Convention on Human Rights"), (1955) 213 U.N.T.S. 221, E.T.S. 5.
4. American Declaration of the Rights and Duties of Man, O.A.S. Doc. OEA/Ser.L/V/II.23, doc. 21, rev. 6, art. 26.
5. American Convention on Human Rights, (1979) 1144 U.N.T.S. 123, O.A.S.T.S. 36.
6. African Charter of Human and Peoples' Rights, O.A.U. Doc. CAB/LEG/67/3 rev. 5, 4 E.H.R.R. 417, 21 *I.L.M.* 58.
7. *Furman* v. *Georgia*, 408 U.S. 238, 312, 92 S.Ct. 2726, 2764, 33 L.Ed.2d 346 (1972) (White, J., concurring).
8. *Id.*, at pp. 313 (U.S.), 2764 (S.Ct.) (White, J., concurring).

9. *Id.*

10. *Id.*, at pp. 309 (U.S.), 2762 (S.Ct.) (Stewart, J., concurring).

11. *Id.*, at pp. 293 (U.S.), 2754 (S.Ct.) (Brennan, J., concurring).

12. See "The Death Row Phenomenon" in this volume.

13. *Callins* v. *Collins, cert. denied,* 114 S.Ct. 1127, 127 L.Ed. 435 (1994) (Blackmun, J., dissenting).

14. *Id.*, at p. 1131.

15. *Id.*, at p. 1132.

16. *Godfrey* v. *Georgia,* 446 U.S. 420, 442, 100 S.Ct. 1759, 1772, 64 L.Ed.2d 398 (1980) (Marshall, J., concurring).

17. *Makwanyane and Mchunu* v. *The State,* (1995) 16 *H.R.L.J.* 154, at p. 180 (*per* Ackerman, J.).

18. *People* v. *Anderson,* 6 Cal.3d 628, 651, 100 Cal.Rptr. 152, 493 P.2d 880, 895 (1972), *cert. denied,* 406 U.S. 958, 92 S.Ct. 2060, 32 L.Ed.2d 344 (1972) (Wright, C.J.).

19. *Makwanyane and Mchunu* v. *The State, supra* note 17, at pp. 194–95 (Mahomed, J., concurring), at p. 200 (Mokgoro, J., concurring).

20. *Id.*, at p. 192 (Madala, J., concurring).

21. Jill COTTRELL, "Wrestling with the death penalty in India," (1991) 7 *South African J. Hum. Rts.* 185, at p. 195; also Jill COTTRELL, "The Supreme Court of India and the supreme penalty," [1985] *Lawasia* 75.

22. *Babugowda* v. *Karnataka,* [1988] 18 Ind. Jud. Reps. (Karn) 96.

23. U.N. Doc. CAT/C/SR.146/Add.2, §19; see also, "Initial Report of China," U.N. Doc. CAT/C/7/Add.14, §38; U.N. Doc. CAT/C/SR.51, §18. See: Alan W. LEPP, "Note: The death penalty in late-imperial, modern and post-Tiananmen China," (1990) 11 *Mich. J. Int'l. L.* 987, at pp. 1033–36.

24. International Covenant on Civil and Political Rights, *supra* note 2, art. 14§7; Protocol No. 7 to the Convention for the Protection of Human Rights and Fundamental Freedoms, E.T.S. 117, art. 4§1; American Convention on Human Rights, *supra* note 5, art 8§4.

25. *Gregg* v. *Georgia,* 428 U.S. 153, 183 n.28, 96 S.Ct. 2909, 2930 n.28, 49 L.Ed.2d 859 (1976) (Stewart, J.). Also: *People* v. *Anderson, supra* note 18, at pp. 651 (Cal.3d), 896 (P.2d); *Commonwealth* v. *O'Neil* II, 369 Mass. 242, 339 N.E. 2d 676 (1975).

26. *Capital Punishment,* U.N. Doc. ST/SOA/SD/9, U.N. Doc. ST/SOA/SD/10 (1968), Vol. II, p. 123. The volume is a consolidation of two reports, the first by the French criminologist Marc Ancel and the second by Norval Morris. It was cited by Justice Marshall in: *Furman* v. *Georgia, supra* note 7, at p. 353 (U.S.); *Gregg* v. *Georgia, supra* note 25, at p. 233 (U.S.).

27. G. PIERCE, M. RADELET, "The role and consequences of the death penalty in American politics," (1990–91) 18 *N.Y.U. Rev. L. & Soc. Change* 771, at pp. 715–16. The literature on the subject of deterrence is vast: Hugo Adam BEDAU, "The question of deterrence," in Hugo Adam BEDAU, ed., *The Death Penalty in America,* Garden City, N.Y.: Aldine, 1964, pp. 258–332; William F. GRAVES, "The deterrent effect of capital punishment in California," in BEDAU, ed., *supra,* pp. 322–32; John K. PECK, "The deterrent effect of capital punishment: Ehrlich and his critics," (1976) 85 *Yale L.J.* 359; Leonard D. SAVITZ, "The deterrent effect of capital punishment in Philadelphia," in BEDAU, ed., *supra,* pp. 315–21; Thorsten SELLIN, "Homicides in retentionist and abolitionist states," in T. SELLIN, ed., *Capital Punishment,* New York: Harper and Row, 1967, pp. 135–37; K. L. AVIO, "Capital punishment in Canada: A time-series analysis of the deterrent hypothesis," (1979) 12 *Can. J. Econ.* 647; William C. BAILEY, "Imprisonment v. the death penalty as a deterrent for murder," (1977) 1 *Law and Hum. Behav.* 239; D. C. BALDUS, J. COLE, "A comparison of the work of Thorsten Sellin and Isaac Ehrlich on the deterrent effect of capital punishment," (1975) 85 *Yale L.J.* 170; William J. BOWERS, Glenn L. PIERCE, "The illusion of deterrence in Isaac Ehrlich's research on capital punishment," (1975) 85 *Yale L.J.* 187; Isaac EHRLICH, "The deterrent effect of capital punishment: A question of life and death," (1975) 65 *Am. Econ. Rev.* 397; William J. BOWERS, Glenn L. PIERCE, "Deterrence or brutalization: What is the effect of executions?" (1980) 26 *Crime & Delinq.* 453; Edward MILLER, "Executing minors and the mentally retarded: The retribution

and deterrence rationales," (1990) 43 *Rutgers L. Rev.* 15; P. PASSELL, "The deterrent effect of the death penalty: A statistical test," (1975) 28 *Stan. L. Rev.* 61; David P. PHILLIPS, "The deterrent effect of capital punishment: New evidence on an old controversy," (1980) 86 *Am. J. Soc.* 139; Hans ZEISEL, "The deterrent effects of the death penalty: Facts v. faith," (1976) *Sup. Ct. Rev.* 317.

28. EHRLICH, *supra* note 27.
29. PASSELL, *supra* note 27; BALDUS, COLE, *supra* note 27; BOWERS, PIERCE, "The illusion of deterrence in Isaac Ehrlich's research on capital punishment," *supra* note 27; PECK, *supra* note 27.
30. *Gregg* v. *Georgia, supra* note 25, at pp. 236 (U.S.), 2975 (S.Ct.) (Marshall, J., dissenting).
31. *Furman* v. *Georgia, supra* note 7, at pp. 359 (U.S.), 2787 (S.Ct.).
32. *Id.,* at pp. 354, 362 (U.S.).
33. *Opinion of the Justices,* 364 N.E.2d 184, 187–88 (Mass.1977). Also: *Commonwealth* v. *O'Neil, supra* note 25 (Tauro, C.J., concurring).
34. *Gregg* v. *Georgia, supra* note 25, at pp. 185 (U.S.), 2931 (S.Ct.) (Stewart, J.).
35. *Id.* at pp. 186–87 (U.S.), 2931 (S.Ct.) (Stewart, J.).
36. *Id.* at pp. 186 (U.S.), 2930 (S.Ct.) (Stewart, J.).
37. COTTRELL, "Wrestling with the death penalty in India," *supra* note 21, at p. 195. Professor Cottrell cites *Triveniben* v. *State of Gujarat,* A.I.R. 1989 S.C. 142, [1989] 1 S.C.J. 383; *Asharfi Lal* v. *Rajasthan,* [1987] 1 Ind. Jud. Reps. (S.C.) 636, at p. 674.
38. *Furman* v. *Georgia, supra* note 7, at pp. 312 (U.S.), 2763–64 (S.Ct.) (White, J., concurring).
39. *People* v. *Anderson, supra* note 18, at pp. 652 (Cal.3d), 896 (P.2d) (Wright, C.J.).
40. *Coleman* v. *Balkcom,* 451 U.S. 949, 960, 101 S.Ct. 2994, 2996, 68 L.Ed.2d 334 (1981).
41. *Furman* v. *Georgia, supra* note 7, at pp. 303 (U.S.), 2758–59 (S.Ct.).
42. President Chaskalson discusses the relevance of Canadian caselaw to the construction of the limitation clause in *Makwanyane and Mchunu* v. *The State, supra* 17, §§105–7, 110. See also the reasons of Acting Justice Kentridge in *S.* v. *Zuma and Two Others,* Case No. CCT/5/94, judgment of April 5, 1995, unreported, §35. German caselaw and legal scholarship is reviewed by President Chaskalson in *Makwanyane and Mchunu* v. *The State, supra* 17, at p. 171 (*per* Chaskalson, P.).
43. President Chaskalson points out that the European Convention on Human Rights, *supra* note 3, is also subject to limitation following the principle of the "margin of appreciation." He concludes that this is not a "safe guide" to interpretation of the South African Constitution, because the European approach is the result of "an international agreement which has to accommodate the sovereignty of the member states" (*Makwanyane and Mchunu* v. *The State, supra* 17, at pp. 171–72 (*per* Chaskalson, P.)).
44. *Makwanyane and Mchunu* v. *The State, id.,* at p. 170 (*per* Chaskalson, P.).
45. *Id.,* at p. 169 (*per* Chaskalson, P.).
46. *Mbushuu and Another* v. *The Republic,* Court of Appeal of Tanzania, Criminal Appeal No. 142 of 1994, unreported judgment of January 30, 1995.
47. *Id.*
48. *Makwanyane and Mchunu* v. *The State, supra* note 17, at p. 173 (*per* Chaskalson, P.).
49. *Id.* Also: Langa, J., *id.,* at p. 190.
50. *Id.* at p. 183. Also: Mahomed, J., *id.,* at p. 197.
51. *Id.* at p. 173 (*per* Chaskalson, P.).
52. *Id.* See also: Mahomed, J., *id.,* at p. 196.
53. *Id.,* at p. 173 (*per* Chaskalson, P.).
54. *Id.,* at p. 174 (*per* Chaskalson, P.). Acting Justice Kentridge added to this the comment that it cannot be shown that the death penalty is not a deterrent: *id.,* at p. 188; also O'Regan, J., *id.,* at p. 203.
55. *Id.,* at p. 189 (*per* Kreigler, J.).
56. *Id.*
57. *Williams* v. *New York,* 337 U.S. 241, 248, 69 S.Ct. 1079, 1084, 93 L.Ed.2d 1337 (1949).

58. UNITED KINGDOM, *Royal Commission on Capital Punishment, 1949–1953, Minutes of Evidence,* Dec. 1, 1949, p. 207 (1950). This excerpt from Lord Denning's testimony is cited in *Gregg* v. *Georgia, supra* note 25, at pp. 184 (U.S.), 2930 (S.Ct.); *Coleman* v. *Balkcom, supra* note 40, at pp. 960 (U.S.), 2996 (S.Ct.).

59. *Pratt et al.* v. *Attorney General for Jamaica et al.,* [1993] 4 All. E.R. 769, [1993] 2 L.R.C. 349, [1994] 2 A.C. 1, [1993] 3 W.L.R. 995, 43 W.I.R. 340, 14 *H.R.L.J.* 338, 33 I.L.M. 364 (J.C.P.C.).

60. *Wallen* v. *Baptiste (no. 2),* (1994) 45 W.I.R. 405 (Court of Appeal, Trinidad and Tobago), at p. 443 (Hamel-Smith, J.A.).

61. *Coleman* v. *Balkcom, supra* note 40, at pp. 961 (U.S.), 2996 (S.Ct.).

62. *Furman* v. *Georgia, supra* note 7, at pp. 308 (U.S.), 2761 (S.Ct.) (Stewart, J., concurring).

63. *Gregg* v. *Georgia, supra* note 25, at pp. 183 (U.S.), 2930 (S.Ct.).

64. *Furman* v. *Georgia, supra* note 7, at pp. 303 (U.S.), 2758 (S.Ct.) (Brennan, J., concurring).

65. *Gregg* v. *Georgia, supra* note 25, at pp. 238 (U.S.), 2976 (S.Ct.) (Marshall, J., dissenting).

66. *Id.,* at pp. 238–39 (U.S.), 2976 (S.Ct.) (Marshall, J., dissenting).

67. *Id.,* at pp. 240–41 (U.S.), 2977 (S.Ct.) (Marshall, J., dissenting).

68. *Id.,* at pp. 238–41 (U.S.), 2976–77 (S.Ct.) (Marshall, J., dissenting).

69. *Rajendra Prasad* v. *State of Uttar Pradesh,* A.I.R. 1979 S.C. 916, at p. 938 (Krishna Iyer, J.).

70. *Catholic Commission for Justice and Peace in Zimbabwe* v. *Attorney-General et al.,* [1993] 4 S.A. 239, 270 (Z.S.C.), [1993] 1 Z.L.R. 242 (S), 14 *H.R.L.J.* 323 (Gubbay, C.J.).

71. *People* v. *Anderson, supra* note 18, at pp. 651 (Cal.3d), 896 (P.2d) (Wright, C.J.).

72. *Makwanyane and Mchunu* v. *The State, supra* note 17, at pp. 174–75 (*per* Chaskalson, P.); see also: Mahomed, J., *id.,* at pp. 197–98; O'Regan, J., *id.,* at pp. 203–4.

73. *Id.,* at pp. 174–75 (*per* Chaskalson, P.).

74. *Id.*

75. *Id.,* at p. 175 (*per* Chaskalson, P.).

76. *Id.,* at p. 186 (*per* Kentridge, A.J.).

77. *Id.,* at p. 191 (Langa, J.). See also Mokgoro, J., *id.,* at pp. 200–201.

78. *Id.,* at p. 184 (Didcott, J.).

79. *Coleman* v. *Balkcom, supra* note 40, at pp. 960 (U.S.), 2996 (S.Ct.).

80. *Furman* v. *Georgia, supra* note 7.

81. *Gregg* v. *Georgia, supra* note 25, at pp. 195 (U.S.), 2936–37 (S.Ct.) (Stewart, J.).

82. *Lockett* v. *Ohio,* 438 U.S. 586, 602, 98 S.Ct. 2954, 2963, 57 L.Ed.2d 973 (1978); *Williams* v. *New York, supra* note 57; *Pennsylvania ex rel. Sullivan* v. *Ashe,* 302 U.S. 51, 58 S.Ct. 59 (1937).

83. *Roberts (Stanislaus)* v. *Louisiana,* 428 U.S. 325, 333, 96 S.Ct. 3001, 49 L.Ed.2d 974 (1976).

84. *Lockett* v. *Ohio, supra* note 82, at pp. 605 (U.S.), 2965 (S.Ct.). See also: *Woodson* v. *North Carolina,* 428 U.S. 280, 304, 96 S.Ct. 2978, 49 L.Ed.2d 944 (1976); *Skipper* v. *South Carolina,* 476 U.S. 1, 106 S.Ct. 1669, 90 L.Ed.2d 1 (1986).

85. *Lockett* v. *Ohio, supra* note 82, at pp. 605 (U.S.), 2965 (S.Ct.).

86. *Callins* v. *Collins, supra* note 13, at pp. 1132–33 (S.Ct.) (Blackmun, J., dissenting).

87. *Lockett* v. *Ohio, supra* note 82, at pp. 604 (U.S.), 2964 (S.Ct.). On mandatory death sentences, see: *Woodson* v. *North Carolina, supra* note 84; *Roberts (Stanislaus)* v. *Louisiana, supra* note 83.

88. K. DAVIS, *Discretionary Justice,* Urbana: University of Illinois Press, 1976, at p. 170, quoted in *McCleskey* v. *Kemp,* 481 U.S. 279, 312, 107 S.Ct. 1756, 1778, 95 L.Ed.2d 262 (1987). However, in *McGautha* v. *California,* 402 U.S. 183, 91 S.Ct. 1454, 28 L.Ed.2d 711 (1971), the Supreme Court dismissed an argument that statutes allowing the death penalty to be imposed at the discretion of the jury violated the Fourteenth Amendment.

89. *Callins* v. *Collins, supra* note 13, at p. 1136 (S.Ct.) (Blackmun, J., dissenting). See: Scott E. SUNBY, "The *Lockett* paradox: Reconciling guided discretion and unguided mitigation in capital sentencing," (1991) 38 *UCLA L. Rev. 1147.*

90. *Callins* v. *Collins, supra* note 13, at p. 1129 (S.Ct.) (Blackmun, J., dissenting).

91. *McCleskey* v. *Kemp, supra* note 88, at pp. 313 n. 37 (U.S.), 1778 (S.Ct.).

92. *Id.*, at pp. 320 (U.S.), 1782 (S.Ct.) (Brennan, J., dissenting). See also: *State* v. *Ross*, 230 Conn. 183, 646 A.2d 1318, 1384 (1994) (Berdon, A.J., dissenting in part).
93. J. JEFFRIES, "A change of mind that came too late," *New York Times*, June 23, 1994, p. A23, col. 1.
94. *District Atty. for Suffolk Dist.* v. *Watson*, 381 Mass. 648, 411 N.E.2d, at p. 1286 (Hennessey, C.J., concurring). Justice Quirico disagreed, stating that although he was prepared to recognize the phenomenon of racial prejudice in Massachusetts the statistics were "unconvincing" and did not meet the court's standards for review: *id.*, at p. 1302 (N.E.2d) (Quirico, J., dissenting).
95. *Callins* v. *Collins, supra* note 13, at p. 1135 (S.Ct.) (Blackmun, J., dissenting).
96. *Rajendra Prasad* v. *State of Uttar Pradesh, supra* note 69, at p. 936 (Krishna Iyer, J.).
97. *Makwanyane and Mchunu* v. *The State, supra* note 17, at p. 163 (*per* Chaskalson, P.).
98. *Callins* v. *Collins, supra* note 13, at p. 1129 (S.Ct.) (Blackmun, J., dissenting).
99. *Id.*, at pp. 1128–29 (S.Ct.) (Blackmun, J., dissenting).
100. *Makwanyane and Mchunu* v. *The State, supra* note 17, at p. 163 (*per* Chaskalson, P.).
101. International Covenant on Civil and Political Rights, *supra* note 2, art. 14§3(d).
102. "General Comment 6/16," U.N. Doc. CCPR/C/21/Add.1 (1984), §7.
103. *Reid* v. *Jamaica* (No. 250/1987), U.N. Doc. A/45/40, Vol. II, p. 85, (1990) 11 *H.R.L.J.* 319, §11.4.
104. *Id.*, §13. See also: *Campbell* v. *Jamaica* (No. 248/1987), U.N. Doc. CCPR/C/44/D/248/1987, §6.6; *Pratt and Morgan* v. *Jamaica* (Nos. 210/1986, 225/1987), U.N. Doc. A/44/40, p. 222, §13.2; *Little* v. *Jamaica* (No. 283/1988), U.N. Doc. CCPR/C/43/D/283/1988, §8.4; *Kelly* v. *Jamaica* (No. 253/1987), U.N. Doc. A/46/40, p. 241, §5.10.
105. *Kelly* v. *Jamaica, supra* note 104.
106. Stephen BRIGHT, "Counsel for the poor: The death sentence not for the worst crime but for the worst lawyer," (1994) 103 *Yale L.J.* 1835.
107. *Reid* v. *Jamaica, supra* note 103, §13.
108. *Pinto* v. *Trinidad and Tobago* (No. 232/1987), U.N. Doc. A/45/40, Vol. II, p. 69, §12.5.
109. *Supra* note 2.
110. *Id.*, §13.2. Release was also declared to be the appropriate remedy in *Kelly* v. *Jamaica, supra* note 104, §7; *Campbell* v. *Jamaica, supra* note 104, §8. Not all members of the committee have concurred in proposing release, and some have suggested what they feel to be more appropriate remedies, such as further judicial review or a declaration of mistrial. See: *Kelly* v. *Jamaica, supra* note 104, at p. 250 (*per* Sadi).
111. *Reid* v. *Jamaica, supra* note 103, §4.
112. *Id.*, §11.3.
113. *Little* v. *Jamaica, supra* note 104, §3.2.
114. *Id.*, §3.3.
115. *Id.*, §8.4.
116. *Thomas* v. *Jamaica* (No. 272/1988), U.N. Doc. CCPR/C/44/D/272/1988, §11.4. See also: *Kelly* v. *Jamaica, supra* note 104, §5.9; *Sawyers and Mclean* v. *Jamaica* (Nos. 226/1987 and 256/1987), U.N. Doc. A/46/40, p. 226, §13.6; *Henry* v. *Jamaica* (No. 230/1987), U.N. Doc. CCPR/C/43/D/230/1987, §8.2; *Campbell* v. *Jamaica, supra* note 104, §6.5; *Robinson* v. *Jamaica* (No. 223/1987), U.N. Doc. A/44/40, p. 241, §10.4.
117. *Collins* v. *Jamaica* (No. 240/1987), U.N. Doc. CCPR/C/43/D/240/1987, §8.5; also *Henry* v. *Jamaica, supra* note 116, §8.3.
118. *Gregg* v. *Georgia, supra* note 25, at pp. 199 (U.S.), 2937 (S.Ct.).
119. *Supra* note 2, art. 14§5.
120. *Gregg* v. *Georgia, supra* note 25, at pp. 207 (U.S.), 2940 (S.Ct.) (Stewart, J.); also White, J., at pp. 212 (U.S.), 2943 (S.Ct.). See also: *Callins* v. *Collins, supra* note 13, at p. 1129 (S.Ct.) (Blackmun, J., dissenting).
121. *Lockett* v. *Ohio, supra* note 82, at pp. 621 (U.S.), 2973 (S.Ct.).
122. *State* v. *Ross, supra* note 92, at p. 1382 (Berdon, A.J., dissenting in part).

123. *DiGarmo* v. *Texas*, 474 U.S. 973, 975, 106 S.Ct. 337, 338–39, 88 L.Ed.2d 322 (1985) (Brennan, J., dissenting).

124. *Corbitt* v. *New Jersey*, 439 U.S. 212, 99 S.Ct. 492, 58 L.Ed.2d 466 (1978); *Bardenkircher* v. *Hayes*, 434 U.S. 357, 98 S.Ct. 663, 54 L.Ed.2d 604 (1978).

125. On plea bargaining generally in capital cases, see: Welsh S. WHITE, *The Death Penalty in the Nineties: An Examination of the Modern System of Capital Punishment*, Ann Arbor: University of Michigan Press, 1991, at pp. 53–72.

126. *United States* v. *Jackson*, 390 U.S. 570, 99 S.Ct. 1209, 20 L.Ed.2d 138 (1968). But see also: *Brady* v. *United States*, 397 U.S. 742, 90 S.Ct. 1463, 25 L.Ed. 747 (1970); *Parker* v. *North Carolina*, 397 U.S. 790, 90 S.Ct. 1458, 25 L.Ed.2d 785 (1970); *North Carolina* v. *Alford*, 400 U.S. 25, 91 S.Ct. 160, 27 L.Ed.2d 162 (1970); *Corbitt* v. *New Jersey*, *supra* note 124, at pp. 219 (U.S.), 493 (S.Ct.).

127. *United States* v. *Jackson*, *supra* note 126, at pp. 570, 581 (U.S.), 1209, 1216 (S.Ct.).

128. 1 WM. & MARY, 2d Sess. (1689), c. 2.

129. Sir William BLACKSTONE, *Commentaries on the Laws of England*, vol. 4, *92.

130. George William KEETON, *Lord Chancellor Jeffreys and the Stuart Cause*, London: Macdonald, 1965, at pp. 320–31.

131. *State* v. *McMurtrey*, 726 P.2d 202, 151 Ariz. 105 (1986).

132. *Brady* v. *United States*, *supra* note 126.

133. *Blackmon* v. *Wainwright*, 608 F.2d 183 (5th Cir.1979), *cert. denied*, 449 U.S. 852, 101 S.Ct. 143, 66 L.Ed.2d 64 (1980); *Adamson* v. *Ricketts*, 758 F.2d 441 (9th Cir. 1985), *rev'd on other grounds*, 789 F.2d 722 (9th Cir. 1986).

134. *Supra* note 2.

135. *Cox* v. *Canada* (No. 539/1993), (1995) 15 *H.R.L.J.* 410, at p. 416.

136. *Lockett* v. *Ohio*, *supra* note 82, at pp. 613–14 (U.S.), 2969 (S.Ct.). But see the comments of Burger, C.J., *id.*, at pp. 610 n. 16 (U.S.), 2967 n. 16 (S.Ct.).

137. *Supra* note 2, art. 6§2.

138. U.N. Doc. A/C.3/SR.814, §12.

139. Daniel D. NSEREKO, "Arbitrary deprivation of life: Controls on permissible deprivations," in B. G. RAMCHARAN, ed., *The Right to Life in International Law*, Boston: Martinus Nijhoff, 1985, pp. 245–83, at pp. 254–55.

140. *Supra* note 5.

141. Charte arabe des droits de l'homme, (1995) 7 *R.U.D.H.* 212, art. 10.

142. E.S.C. Res. 1984/50. Subsequently endorsed by G.A. Res. 39/118.

143. Geneva Convention of August 12, 1949 Relative to the Protection of Civilians, (1950) 75 U.N.T.S. 135, art. 68§2.

144. "Initial Report of Bulgaria," U.N. Doc. CCPR/C/SR.131, §30, U.N. Doc. CCPR/C/SR.132, §37; "Initial Report of Mali," U.N. Doc. CCPR/C/1/Add.49, U.N. Doc. CCPR/C/SR.283, §11.

145. "Initial Report of Sudan," U.N. Doc. CCPR/C/45/Add.3, U.N. Doc. CCPR/C/SR.1065–67, U.N. Doc. A/46/40, §509.

146. "Initial Report of Bulgaria," *supra* note 144, §14.

147. "Initial Report of Jordan," U.N. Doc. CCPR/C/1/Add.56; "Initial Report of Iraq," U.N. Doc. CCPR/C/1/Add.45; U.N. Doc. CCPR/C/SR.200, §19, §42; "Initial Report of Japan," U.N. Doc. CCPR/C/10/Add.1; "Initial Report of Libyan Arab Jamahiriya," U.N. Doc. CCPR/C/1/Add.3*, U.N. Doc. CCPR/C/1/Add.20.

148. "Initial Report of Iran," U.N. Doc. CCPR/C/1/Add.58, U.N. Doc. CCPR/C/SR.365, §§7, 8.

149. *Id.*

150. "Initial Report of Sudan," *supra* note 145.

151. "Initial Report of Iran," *supra* note 148.

152. "Initial Report of Togo," U.N. Doc. CCPR/C/36/Add.5, U.N. Doc. CCPR/C/SR.870, 871, 874, 875, U.N. Doc. A/44/40, §259.

153. "Third Periodic Report of the Union of the Soviet Socialist Republics," U.N. Doc. CCPR/

C/52/Add.2 and 6, U.N. Doc. CCPR/C/SR.928–32, U.N. Doc. A/45/40, §93; U.N. Doc. CCPR/C/SR.119, §14 (Bulgaria).

154. "Second Periodic Report of Iraq," U.N. Doc. CCPR/C/46/Add.4, U.N. Doc. CCPR/C/SR.1077–79, U.N. Doc. A/46/40, §632.

155. "Initial Report of Kenya," U.N. Doc. CCPR/C/1/Add.47, U.N. Doc. CCPR/C/SR.271, §29.

156. "Initial Report of Romania," U.N. Doc. CCPR/C/1/Add.33, U.N. Doc. CCPR/C/SR.135, §37.

157. U.N. Doc. CCPR/C/SR.136, §§39–40.

158. "General Comment 6/16," *supra* note 102, §7.

159. U.N. Doc. CCPR/C/SR.362, §43. See also: "Initial Report of Madagascar," U.N. Doc. CCPR/C/1/Add.14, U.N. Doc. CCPR/C/SR.87, §19; U.N. Doc. A/33/40*, §282; "Initial Report of Democratic Yemen," U.N. Doc. CCPR/C/50/Add.2, U.N. Doc. CCPR/C/SR.927, SR.932, U.N. Doc. A/45/40, §45; "Initial Report of Viet Nam," U.N. Doc. CCPR/C/26/Add.3, U.N. Doc. CCPR/C/SR.982, SR.983, SR.986, SR.987, U.N. Doc. A/45/40, §465.

160. "Third Periodic Report of Tunisia," U.N. Doc. CCPR/C/52/Add.5, U.N. Doc. CCPR/C/SR.990–92, U.N. Doc. A/45/40, §§513–14.

161. "Initial Report of Algeria," U.N. Doc. CCPR/C/62/Add.1, §84.

162. *Bachan Singh* v. *State of Punjab*, A.I.R. 1980 S.C. 898, (1980) 2 S.C.C. 684, at p. 931 (*per* Sarkaria, J.). See also: *Allauddin Mian* v. *State of Bihar*, [1991] L.R.C. (Crim.) 573 (Supreme Court of India), at p. 583 (Ahmadi, J.).

163. Z. P. SEPARAVIC, "Political crimes and the death penalty," (1987) 58 *Revue internationale de droit pénal* 755; Marc ANCEL, "Le crime politique et le droit pénal au XXᵉ siècle," [1938] *Revue d'histoire politique et constitutionnelle* 87.

164. U.N. Doc. E/CN.4/82/Add.2; U.N. Doc. E/CN.4/85, at p. 60; U.N. Doc. E/CN.4/SR.97, at p. 4; U.N. Doc. A/C.3/L.460.

165. *Supra* note 5, art. 4§4. Resolutions of the General Assembly have criticized politically motivated executions: G.A. Res. 35/172; G.A. Res. 36/22. The Sub-Commission on Prevention of Discrimination and Protection of Minorities has called for the abolition of the death penalty for political offenses: S.-C.H.R. Res. I(XXXIV), U.N. Doc. E/CN.4/1512, U.N. Doc. E/CN.4/Sub.2/495.

166. *Supra* note 141, art. 11.

167. Execution of opponents to apartheid has been denounced in a number of Security Council resolutions: S.C. Res. 191 (1964); S.C. Res. 253 (1968); S.C. Res. 503 (1982).

168. U.N. Doc. CCPR/C/SR.200, §19 (1980).

169. "Initial Report of Mali," U.N. Doc. CCPR/C/SR.284, §20; U.N. Doc. CCPR/C/SR.284, §6 (Tarnopolsky).

170. "Initial Report of Mongolia," U.N. Doc. CCPR/C/1/Add.38; U.N. Doc. CCPR/C/SR.197, §6 (Janca); U.N. Doc. CCPR/C/SR.198, §21 (Koulishev); U.N. Doc. CCPR/C/SR.198, §32 (Sadi).

171. U.N. Doc. CCPR/C/SR.258, §10 (Tomuschat).

172. *Id.*

173. U.N. Doc. CCPR/C/SR.200, §42 (Prado Vallejo).

174. "Initial Report of Democratic Yemen," *supra* note 159.

175. "Initial Report of Viet Nam," *supra* note 159.

176. U.N. Doc. CCPR/C/SR.378, §54.

177. U.N. Doc. A/33/40, §153.

178. U.N. Doc. CCPR/C/1/Add.3, §7; Also: "Initial Report of Democratic Yemen," *supra* note 159; "Initial Report of Viet Nam," *supra* note 159; "Initial Report of Algeria," *supra* note 161.

179. "Initial Report of Mongolia," *supra* note 170; U.N. Doc. CCPR/C/SR.197, §17 (Evans); U.N. Doc. CCPR/C/SR.198, §32 (Sadi).

180. *Id.*; U.N. Doc. CCPR/C/SR.197, §6 (Janca); U.N. Doc. CCPR/C/SR.198, §21 (Koulishev); U.N. Doc. CCPR/C/SR.198, §32 (Sadi).

181. "Second Periodic Report of Mauritius," U.N. Doc. CCPR/C/28/Add.12, at p. 113; see also "Initial Report of Bolivia," U.N. Doc. A/44/40, at p. 95; U.N. Doc. A/44/40, §508.

182. The matter of execution for drug trafficking was also raised by the Committee Against Torture when Mauritius presented its periodic report on April 26, 1995: U.N. Doc. HR/4134. See on this subject: Ezzat A. FATTAH, "The use of the death penalty for drug offences and for economic crimes—a discussion and a critique," (1987) 58 *Revue internationale de droit pénal* 723; S. L. HARRING, "Death, drugs and development: Malaysia's mandatory death penalty for traffickers and the international war on drugs," (1991) 29 *Columb. J. Transnat'l L.* 364; A. DESTRÉE, "Opium et peine de mort en Iran," (1972) 52 *Revue de droit pénal et de criminologie* 568.

183. U.N. Doc. CAT/C/SR.130, §15.

184. U.N. Doc. CAT/C/SR.133, §18 (Belarus).

185. U.N. Doc. E/1990/38, §41.

186. *Gregg* v. *Georgia, supra* note 25, at pp. 187 (U.S.), 2932 (S.Ct.) (Stewart, J.).

187. *Coker* v. *Georgia,* 433 U.S. 584, 97 S.Ct. 2861, 53 L.Ed.2d 282 (1977). But this had not always been the case in the United States. In *Dutton* v. *State (No. 2),* 91 A. 418, 422 (Md.1914) (Boyd, C.J.), a Maryland court held that its discretionary death penalty for the crime of "assault with intent to rape," under Code Pub. Gen. Laws 1904, art. 27, §17 of Maryland, was not unconstitutional and was not a cruel and unusual punishment in breach of art. 16 of the state's Declaration of Rights.

188. *Lockett* v. *Ohio, supra* note 82, at pp. 619–20 (U.S.), 2972 (S.Ct.). Also: *Enmund* v. *Florida,* 458 U.S. 782, 102 S.Ct. 3368, 73 L.Ed.2d 1140 (1982); *Tison* v. *Arizona,* 481 U.S. 137, 107 S.Ct. 1676, 95 L.Ed.2d 127 (1987). See also *R.* v. *Vaillancourt,* [1987] 2 S.C.R. 636, in which the Supreme Court of Canada held a felony murder provision to violate a constitutional guarantee of substantive due process.

189. *Lockett* v. *Ohio, supra* note 82, at p. 2983 (S.Ct.).

190. *Id.,* at p. 2967 (S.Ct.).

PUBLIC OPINION

1. See: Roger HOOD, *The Death Penalty: A Worldwide Perspective,* Oxford: Clarendon Press, 1989, at pp. 148–58.

2. International Covenant on Civil and Political Rights, (1976) 999 U.N.T.S. 171.

3. U.N. Doc. CCPR/C/81/Add.4, §139.

4. S/RES/955 (1994).

5. U.N. Doc. S/PV.3453, p. 16.

6. E.T.S. no. 114.

7. In a 1985 letter to the International Federation of Human Rights, Prime Minister Margaret Thatcher explained why the United Kingdom refused to ratify Protocol No. 6: "This Protocol presents the United Kingdom with an unusual difficulty. Successive governments have taken the view that capital punishment is an issue of conscience which should be decided by the vote of individual members of Parliament and that this should not be influenced by the Government. In these circumstances I am sure you will appreciate that it would be inconsistent for the Government to take a policy to sign and ratify the Protocol; and that it would be difficult to sign and ratify on the basis of a particular vote bearing in mind that the issue is tested in Parliament at not infrequent intervals": *Lettre de la Fédération internationale des droits de l'homme,* nos. 123–24, September 10, 1985.

   A 1985 resolution of the European Parliament held that the death penalty was "a cruel and inhuman form of punishment and a violation of the right to life" and called on the United Kingdom to sign the Protocol (*Official Journal of the European Communities, Debates of the European Parliament,* No. 2-334, Annex, pp. 300–303). Note that the United Kingdom had opposed adoption of Protocol No. 6 for the same reasons, taking the view that this was a question for Parliament and not a matter to be settled by international treaty: see William A. SCHABAS, *The Abolition of the Death Penalty in International Law,* Cambridge University Press (Grotius Publications), 1993, at pp. 228–38.

8. *Supra* note 2, art. 6§5.
9. *Id.*, art. 14.
10. *Id.*, art. 4.
11. *Weems* v. *United States*, 217 U.S. 349, 378, 30 S.Ct. 544, 553, 54 L.Ed. 793 (1910).
12. *Trop* v. *Dulles*, 356 U.S. 86, 101, 78 S.Ct. 590, 598, 2 L.Ed.2d 630 (1958).
13. For example: *Catholic Commission for Justice and Peace in Zimbabwe* v. *Attorney-General et al.*, [1993] 4 S.A. 239 (Z.S.C.), [1993] 1 Z.L.R. 242 (S), 14 *H.R.L.J.* 323 (*per* Gubbay, C.J.).
14. On method of execution, see generally "Method of Execution" in this volume.
15. *State* v. *Ross*, 230 Conn. 183, 646 A.2d 1318, 1376 (1994) (Berdon, A.J., dissenting in part).
16. *Makwanyane and Mchunu* v. *The State*, Case No. CCT/3/94, (1995) 16 *H.R.L.J.* 154, at p. 187 (*per* Kentridge, A.J.).
17. *Pratt et al.* v. *Attorney General for Jamaica et al.*, [1993] 4 All E.R. 769, [1993] 2 L.R.C. 349, [1994] 2 A.C. 1, [1993] 3 W.L.R. 995, 43 W.I.R. 340, 14 *H.R.L.J.* 338, 33 I.L.M. 364 (J.C.P.C.), at p. 783 (All E.R.).
18. See, for example, the judgment of Justice Beverley McLachlin of the Supreme Court of Canada in *Kindler* v. *Canada*, [1991] 2 S.C.R. 779, 67 C.C.C. (3d) 1, 84 D.L.R. (4th) 438, 6 C.R.R. (2d) 193, at p. 839 (S.C.R.) (*per* McLachlin, J., concurring). See: William A. SCHABAS, "Kindler and Ng: Our supreme magistrates take a frightening step into the court of public opinion," (1991) 51 *Revue du Barreau* 673.
19. William J. BOWERS et al., "A new look at public opinion on capital punishment: What citizens and legislators prefer," (1994) 22 *Am. J. Crim. L.* 77.
20. *Trop* v. *Dulles*, *supra* note 12, at pp. 101 (U.S.), 598 (S.Ct.) (plurality opinion); *People* v. *Anderson*, 6 Cal.3d 628, 647, 100 Cal.Rptr. 152, 493 P.2d 880, 893 (1972), *cert. denied*, 406 U.S. 958, 92 S.Ct. 2060, 32 L.Ed.2d 344 (1972) (Wright, C.J.).
21. *State* v. *Ross*, *supra* note 15, 1381 (Conn. 1994) (Berdon, A.J., dissenting in part).
22. *Furman* v. *Georgia*, 408 U.S. 238, 92 S.Ct. 2726, 33 L.Ed.2d 346 (1972).
23. J. H. ELY, *Democracy and Distrust: A Theory of Judicial Review*, Cambridge: Harvard University Press, 1980, at p. 65 (quoted in *District Atty. for Suffolk Dist.* v. *Watson*, 381 Mass. 648, 411 N.E.2d 1274, 1301 (1980) (Quirico, J., dissenting)).
24. *Gregg* v. *Georgia*, 428 U.S. 153, 96 S.Ct. 2909, 49 L.Ed.2d 859 (1976).
25. *Id.*, at pp. 175–76 (U.S.), 2926 (S.Ct.).
26. *Furman* v. *Georgia*, *supra* note 22, at pp. 268 (U.S.), 2741 (S.Ct.) (Brennan, J.), quoting from Arthur GOLDBERG, Allen DERSHOWITZ, "Declaring the death penalty unconstitutional," (1970) 83 *Harv. L. Rev.* 1773, at p. 1782.
27. *Makwanyane and Mchunu* v. *The State*, *supra* 16, at p. 168 (*per* Chaskalson, P.). Among the articles examining public opinion and the death penalty in South Africa are H. MORSBACH, G. MORSBACH, "Attitudes towards capital punishment in South Africa," (1967) 7 *Brit. J. Crim. Just.* 402; J. MIDGLEY, "Public opinion and the death penalty in South Africa," (1974) 14 *Brit. J. Criminology* 347; Keith I. SMITH, "The penalty of death: Public attitudes in South Africa," (1989) 2 *South African J. Crim. Just.* 256; and Barend VAN NIEKERK, "Hanged by the neck until you are dead: The death penalty in South Africa," (1969) 86 *S.A.L.J.* 457, (1970) 87 *S.A.L.J.* 60.
28. *Makwanyane and Mchunu* v. *The State*, *supra* note 16.
29. *Id.* See also: Didcott, J., *id.*, at pp. 185–85; Kentridge, A. J., *id.*, at p. 186.
30. *Furman* v. *Georgia*, *supra* note 22, at pp. 443 (U.S.), 2831 (S.Ct.); cited in *id.*, §89 (*per* Chaskalson, P.).
31. *People* v. *Anderson*, *supra* note 20, at pp. 648 (Cal.3d), 893–94 (P.2d). Note that the judgment of the California Supreme Court abolishing the death penalty was immediately neutralized by a constitutional amendment, Cal. Const. art. 1, §27. *People* v. *Frierson*, 25 Cal.3d 142, 184, 599 P.2d 587, 158 Cal.Rptr. 281 (1979).
32. *Republic* v. *Mbushuu et al.*, [1994] 2 L.R.C. 335 (High Court of Tanzania), at p. 349.
33. *Dudgeon* v. *United Kingdom*, September 23, 1981, Series A, Vol. 45, 4 E.H.R.R. 149, 67 I.L.R.

345, at p. 184 (E.H.R.R.). But see: *Tyrer* v. *United Kingdom*, April 25, 1978, Series A, No. 26, 2 E.H.R.R. 1, 59, I.L.R. 339, §31.

34. *Gregg* v. *Georgia, supra* note 24, at pp. 175 (U.S.), 2926 (S.Ct.) (Stewart, J.). Other examples of the recognition of need for judicial restraint and deference to legislative judgment in the evaluation of evolving standards of decency include: *Roberts (Stanislaus)* v. *Louisiana*, 428 U.S. 325, 350–56, 96 S.Ct. 3001, 49 L.Ed.2d 974 (1976) (White, J., dissenting); *Furman* v. *Georgia, supra* note 22, at pp. 383–84 (U.S.) (Burger, C.J., dissenting), 410 (U.S.) (Blackmun, J., dissenting), 428–33, 451–56 (U.S.) (Powell, J., dissenting), 465–70 (U.S.) (Rehnquist, J., dissenting).

35. R. St. J. MACDONALD, "The margin of appreciation," in R. St. J. MACDONALD et al., eds., *The European System for the Protection of Human Rights*, Dordrecht, London, and Boston: Martinus Nijhoff, 1993, pp. 83–124.

36. *Dennis* v. *United States*, 341 U.S. 494, 525, 71 S.Ct. 857, 875 (1951) (Frankfurter, J., concurring in affirmance of judgment).

37. *Furman* v. *Georgia, supra* note 22, at pp. 383 (U.S.), 2800 (S.Ct.) (Burger, C.J., dissenting).

38. *Gore* v. *United States*, 357 U.S. 386, 393, 78 S.Ct. 1280, 1285, 2 L.Ed.2d 1405 (1958). See also: *District Atty. for Suffolk Dist.* v. *Watson, supra* note 23, at p. 1299 (N.E.2d) (Quirico, J., dissenting); *Roberts (Stanislaus)* v. *Louisiana, supra* note 34, at pp. 355 (U.S.), 3016 (S.Ct.) (White, J., dissenting).

39. *Bachan Singh* v. *State of Punjab*, A.I.R. 1980 S.C. 898, at p. 900 (Sarkaria, J.).

40. See Laws of New York, 1995, Ch. 1, §§60.05 and ff.

41. Charles Kenneth ELDRED, "The new federal death penalties," (1994) 22 *Am. J. Crim. L.* 293.

42. *Supra* note 22.

43. *Supra* note 24.

44. *Id.*, at pp. 180–81 (U.S.), 2928 (S.Ct.).

45. *Id.*, at pp. 174 n. 19 (U.S.), 2925 n. 19 (S.Ct.) (Stewart, J.).

46. *Furman* v. *Georgia, supra* note 22, at pp. 411 (U.S.), 2815 (S.Ct.).

47. *Id.*, at pp. 413 (U.S.), 2816 (S.Ct.). See also the comments of Justice Powell, *id.*, at pp. 436–37 (U.S.), 2827–28 (S.Ct.).

48. *Stanford* v. *Kentucky*, 492 U.S. 361, 370, 109 S.Ct. 2969, 2975, 106 L.Ed.2d 306 (1989) (Scalia, J.).

49. *Penry* v. *Lynaugh*, 492 U.S. 302, 331, 109 S.Ct. 2934, 2953, 106 L.Ed.2d 256 (1989) O'Connor, J.).

50. *State* v. *Ramseur*, 106 N.J. 123, 173, 524 A.2d 188, 212 (1987) (Wilentz, J.).

51. *Gregg* v. *Georgia, supra* note 24, at pp. 233 (U.S.), 2973 (S.Ct.) (Marshall, J., dissenting), quoting: Austin SARAT, Neil VIDMAR, "Public opinion, the death penalty and the Eighth Amendment: Testing the Marshall hypothesis," (1976) 1 *Wis. L. Rev.* 171.

52. *Gregg* v. *Georgia, supra* note 24, at pp. 232 (U.S.), 2973 (S.Ct.) (Marshall, J., dissenting).

53. *Id.*, at pp. 233 (U.S.), 2973–74 (S.Ct.).

54. *People* v. *Anderson, supra* note 20, at pp. 640–41 (Cal.3d), 888 (P.2d) (Wright, C.J.). See also: *McKenzie* v. *Osborne*, 640 P.2d 368, 431 (Mont.1981) (Sheehy, J.).

55. *Kindler* v. *Canada, supra* note 18, at p. 789 (S.C.R.) (*per* Sopinka, J., dissenting).

56. *Id.*, at p. 793 (S.C.R.) (*per* Cory, J., dissenting).

57. *Id.*, at p. 839 (S.C.R.) (*per* McLachlin, J.).

58. Note the comments of President Bush when he sought approval from Congress for ratification of the International Covenant on Civil and Political Rights, *supra* note 2. Among the limitations imposed by the Covenant on use of the death penalty is the stricture that it only be employed for the "most serious crimes." Bush proposed a reservation to the provision, noting "the sharply differing view taken by many of our future treaty partners on the issue of the death penalty (including what constitutes 'serious crimes' under article 6(2))": (1992) 31 I.L.M. 645, at p. 653.

59. *Coker* v. *Georgia*, 433 U.S. 584, 593–96, 97 S.Ct. 2861, 2866–68, 53 L.Ed.2d 982 (1977).

60. *Enmund* v. *Florida*, 458 U.S. 782, 792, 102 S.Ct. 3368, 3374, 73 L.Ed.2d 1140 (1982).

61. *Id.*, at pp. 789–93 (U.S.), 3372–74 (S.Ct.).
62. International Covenant on Civil and Political Rights, *supra* note 2, art. 6§5; American Convention on Human Rights, (1979), 1144 U.N.T.S. 123, O.A.S.T.S. 36, art. 4§5; Geneva Convention of August 12, 1949 Relative to the Protection of Civilians, (1950) 75 U.N.T.S. 135, art. 68§4; Protocol Additional I to the 1949 Geneva Conventions and Relating to the Protection of Victims of International Armed Conflicts, (1979) 1125 U.N.T.S. 3, art. 77§5; Protocol Additional II to the 1949 Geneva Conventions and Relating to the Protection of Victims of Non-International Armed Conflicts, (1979) 1125 U.N.T.S. 609, art. 6§4; Convention on the Rights of the Child, G.A. Res. 44/25, art. 37*a*). See: Victor L. STREIB, *Death Penalty for Juveniles*, Bloomington and Indianapolis: Indiana University Press, 1987; Victor L. STREIB, "Capital punishment for children in Ohio," (1984) 18 *Akron L. Rev.* 51; Victor L. STREIB, "Death penalty for children: The American experience with capital punishment for crimes committed while under age eighteen," (1983) 36 *Okla. L. Rev.* 613; William A. SCHABAS, "The death penalty for crimes committed by persons under eighteen years of age," in E. VERHELLEN, ed., *Monitoring Children's Rights*, Dordrecht, London, and Boston: Martinus Nijhoff, 1995, at pp. 603–9.
63. *Thompson* v. *Oklahoma*, 487 U.S. 815, 826–29, 108 S.Ct. 2687, 2694–96, 101 L.Ed.2d 702 (1988) (plurality).
64. *Id.*, at pp. 850 (U.S.), 2707 (S.Ct.) (O'Connor, J., concurring); also 826–29 (U.S.), 2694–96 (S.Ct.).
65. J. D. FELTHAM, "The common law and the execution of insane criminals," (1964) 4 *Melb. U. L. Rev* 434; Geoffrey C. HAZARD, Jr., David W. LOUISELL, "Death, the state, and the insane: Stay of execution," (1962) 9 *U.C.L.A. L. Rev.* 381; George G. GROVER, "Execution of insane persons," (1950) 23 *S. Cal. L. Rev.* 246; William A. SCHABAS, "International norms on execution of the insane and the mentally retarded," (1993) 4 *Crim. L.F.* 95.
66. *Ford* v. *Wainwright*, 477 U.S. 399, 408–10, 416–18, 106 S.Ct. 2595, 2601–2, 2605–6, 91 L.Ed.2d 335 (1986).
67. *Campbell* v. *Wood*, 18 F.3d 662, 707 n. 29 (9th Cir. 1994) (Reinhardt, J., dissenting), *cert. denied*, 114 S.Ct. 2125 (1994).
68. *Glass* v. *Louisiana*, 471 U.S. 1080, 1089, 105 S.Ct 2159 (1985) (Brennan, J., dissenting from denial of certiorari).
69. *Fierro* v. *Gomez*, 865 F.Supp. 1387, 1406 (N.D.Cal. 1994).
70. *Campbell* v. *Wood*, *supra* note 67, at pp. 696–97.
71. *Id.*, at p. 682 (Beerer, C.J.).
72. Protocol No. 6 to the Convention for the Protection of Human Rights and Fundamental Freedoms Concerning the Abolition of the Death Penalty, *supra* note 6 (in peacetime); Second Optional Protocol to the International Covenant on Civil and Political Rights Aimed at Abolition of the Death Penalty, G.A.Res. 44/128, (1990) 29 *I.L.M.* 1464; Additional Protocol to the American Convention on Human Rights to Abolish the Death Penalty, O.A.S.T.S. 73, 29 *I.L.M.* 1447; American Convention on Human Rights, (1979) 1144 U.N.T.S. 123, O.A.S.T.S. 36, art. 4§4 (in states that have previously abolished the death penalty). According to an interpretation favored by some members of the Human Rights Committee, the International Covenant on Civil and Political Rights is also an abolitionist instrument for states that have already abolished the death penalty: *Ng* v. *Canada* (no. 469/1991), (1994) 15 *H.R.L.J.* 149 (*per* Francisco José Aguilar Urbina and Fausto Pocar).
73. Jean-Bernard MARIE, "International Human Rights Instruments: Ratifications as of January 1, 1995," (1995) 15 *H.R.L.J.* 75.
74. "Statute of the International Tribunal for the Former Yugoslavia," S/RES/827, annex, art. 24(1); "Statute of the International Tribunal for Rwanda," S/RES/955, annex, art. 23(1).
75. U.N. Doc. A/49/10, art. 47.
76. *Trop* v. *Dulles*, *supra* note 12, at pp. 102 (U.S.), 599 (S.Ct.).
77. *People* v. *Anderson*, *supra* note 20, at pp. 654 (Cal.3d), 898 (P.2d) (Wright, C.J.).

78. *Kindler* v. *Canada, supra* note 18, at pp. 804–7 (S.C.R.) (*per* Cory, J.). See also: *Makwanyane and Mchunu* v. *The State, supra* 16, at p. 187 (*per* Kentridge, A.J.).
79. *Bachan Singh* v. *State of Punjab, supra* note 39, at pp. 900, 929.
80. *Makwanyane and Mchunu* v. *The State, supra* note 16, at p. 187 (*per* Kentridge, A.J.); also p. 160 (*per* Chaskalson, P.).
81. *Kindler* v. *Canada, supra* note 18, at p. 834 (S.C.R.) (*per* La Forest, J.).
82. *Id.,* at p. 833 (S.C.R.) (*per* La Forest, J.).
83. *Id.*
84. *Supra* note 2.
85. *People* v. *Anderson, supra* note 20, at pp. 648 (Cal.3d), 894 (P.2d) (Wright, C.J.).
86. *Id.*
87. *District Atty. for Suffolk Dist.* v. *Watson, supra* note 23, at p. 1282 (N.E.2d).
88. *State* v. *Ross, supra* note 15, at pp. 1377–78.
89. *District Atty. for Suffolk Dist.* v. *Watson, supra* note 23, at pp. 662 (Mass), 1282 (N.E.2d).
90. See my more detailed discussion of the question of moratoria in "The Death Row Phenomenon" in this volume.
91. *Makwanyane and Mchunu* v. *The State, supra* note 16, at p. 187 (*per* Kentridge, A.J., concurring).
92. Thirty-three of the United States provide for jury participation in capital sentencing. In only four (Alabama, Delaware, Florida, and Indiana) may the judge overrule the jury's decision. This may even involve ordering sentence of death where the jurors have been more clement: *Harris* v. *Alabama,* 115 S.Ct. 1031 (1995).
93. *Harris* v. *Alabama, supra* note 92, at pp. 1039–41 (Stevens, J., dissenting).
94. *Witherspoon* v. *Illinois,* 391 U.S. 510, 519 n. 15, 88 S.Ct. 1770, 1775 n. 15, 20 L.Ed.2d 776 (1968), quoting *Trop* v. *Dulles, supra* note 12, at pp. 101 (U.S.), 598 (S.Ct.) (plurality opinion). This citation is referred to approvingly in *Gregg* v. *Georgia, supra* note 24, at pp. 191 (U.S.), 2933 (S.Ct.) (Stewart, J.).
95. *People* v. *Anderson, supra* note 20, at p. 893 (P.2d) (Wright, C.J.).
96. *Gregg* v. *Georgia, supra* note 24, at pp. 181 (U.S.), 2929 (S.Ct.) (Powell, J., dissenting).
97. *Kindler* v. *Canada, supra* note 18, at p. 800 (S.C.R.) (Cory, J., dissenting), citing B. W. MCLANE, "Juror attitudes toward local disorder: The evidence of the 1328 Lincolnshire Trailbaston proceedings," in J. S. COCKBURN, T. A. GREEN, eds., *Twelve Good Men and True: The Criminal Trial Jury in England, 1200–1800,* Princeton: Princeton University Press, 1988, p. 36, at pp. 54–55.
98. *Id.,* citing D. HAY, "Property, authority and the criminal law," in D. HAY et al., *Albion's Fatal Tree: Crime and Society in Eighteenth-Century England,* London: Allen Lane, 1975, p. 17, at p. 22; Michel FOUCAULT, *Discipline and Punish: The Birth of the Prison,* New York: Pantheon, 1977.
99. *Kindler* v. *Canada, supra* note 18.
100. *Id.*
101. *Gregg* v. *Georgia, supra* note 24, at pp. 181–82 (U.S.), 2929 (S.Ct.) (Stewart, J.).
102. *Furman* v. *Georgia, supra* note 22, at pp. 402 (U.S.), 2810 (S.Ct.) (Burger, C.J., dissenting).
103. See, for example, *Makwanyane and Mchunu* v. *The State, supra* note 16, at p. 168 (*per* Chaskalson, P.).
104. *Republic* v. *Mbushuu et al., supra* note 32, at p. 351.
105. *Gregg* v. *Georgia, supra* note 24, at pp. 233 (U.S.), 2973 (S.Ct.) (Marshall, J., dissenting); also, *Furman* v. *Georgia, supra* note 22, at pp. 360–69 (U.S.), 2788–92 (S.Ct.) (Marshall, J., concurring).
106. BOWERS et al., *supra* note 19.
107. *State* v. *Ross, supra* note 15, at p. 1380 n. 16 (A.2d) (Berdon, A.J., dissenting in part).
108. *Id.*
109. *Simmons* v. *South Carolina,* 114 S.Ct. 2187, 2191, 129 L.Ed.2d 133 (1994) (Blackmun, J.).
110. *People* v. *Anderson, supra* note 20, at pp. 648 (Cal.3d), 894 (P.2d) (Wright, C.J.).
111. *State* v. *Ross, supra* note 15, at p. 1377 (A.2d) (Berdon, A.J., dissenting in part).
112. *Gregg* v. *Georgia, supra* note 24, at pp. 181 n. 25 (U.S.), 2929 n.25 (S.Ct.) (Stewart, J.).
113. *Kindler* v. *Canada, supra* note 18, at p. 852 (S.C.R.) (*per* McLachlin, J., concurring).

114. *Id.*, at p. 832 (S.C.R. (*per* La Forest, J.).
115. *Furman* v. *Georgia, supra* note 22, at pp. 268–69 (U.S.), 2741 (S.Ct.) (Brennan, J., concurring).
116. *Thompson* v. *Oklahoma, supra* note 63, at pp. 865 (U.S.), 2714–15 (S.Ct.); cited in *Makwanyane and Mchunu* v. *The State, supra* note 16, at p. 187 (*per* Kentridge, A.J.).
117. *Pratt et al.* v. *Attorney General for Jamaica et al., supra* note 17.

THE DEATH ROW PHENOMENON

1. Among works on the "death row phenomenon" see: Stephen M. GETTINGER, *Sentenced to Die: The People, the Crimes and the Controversy*, New York: Macmillan, 1979; Bruce JACKSON, Diane CHRISTIAN, *Death Row*, Boston: Beacon Press, 1980; J. ALEXIS, M. DE MERIEUX, "Inordinately delayed hanging: Whether an inhuman punishment," (1987) 29 *J. Indian L. Inst.* 356; Johnnie L. GALLEMORE Jr., James H. PANTON, "Inmate responses to lengthy death row confinement," (1972) 129 *Am. J. Psychiatry* 167; Nancy HOLLAND, "Death row conditions: Progression toward constitutional protections," (1985) 2 *Akron L. Rev.* 293; Robert JOHNSON, *Condemned to Die: Life Under Sentence of Death*, New York: Elsevier, 1981; COMMENT, "The death penalty cases," (1968) 56 *Cal. L. Rev.* 1270; NOTE, "The Eighth Amendment and our evolving standards of decency: A time for re-evaluation," (1969) 3 *Suffolk U. L. Rev.* 616.
2. See Helen PREJEAN, *Dead Man Walking*, New York: Random House, 1993. Sister Helen describes how death row guards at the Louisiana State Penitentiary shout "dead man walking" whenever a person sentenced to be executed moves about the prison.
3. JOHNSON, *supra* note 1, at p. 47, quoted in *Sher Singh* v. *State of Punjab*, [1983] 2 S.C.R. 582, A.I.R. 1983 S.C. 465, at p. 470 (A.I.R.) (*per* Chaskalson, P.).
4. Albert CAMUS, "Réflexions sur la guillotine," in Albert CAMUS, Arther KOESTLER, *Réflexions sur la peine capitale*, Paris: Clamann-Lévy, 1957, at p. 153.
5. *People* v. *Anderson*, 6 Cal.3d 628, 649, 100 Cal.Rptr. 152, 493 P.2d 880, 894 (1972), *cert. denied*, 406 U.S. 958, 92 S.Ct. 2060, 32 L.Ed.2d 344 (1972) (Wright, C.J.).
6. *Commonwealth* v. *O'Neil II*, 369 Mass. 242, 339 N.E.2d 676, 680–81 (1975) (Tauro, C.J., concurring).
7. *Coleman* v. *Balkcom*, 451 U.S. 949, 952, 101 S.Ct. 2031, 2022, 68 L.Ed.2d (1981), (Stevens, J., concurring in denial of certiorari).
8. For just one example of the progressive increase in stays on death row, see: Janos MIHALIK, "The death penalty in Bophuthatswana: A new deal for condemned prisoners?" (1990) 107 *South African L.J.* 465, at pp. 471–473.
9. *Riley* v. *Attorney-General of Jamaica*, [1983] 1 A.C. 719, 3 All E.R. 469, 35 W.I.R. 279 (J.C.P.C.), at pp. 479 (All E.R.), 734–35 (A.C.) (*per* Lords Scarman and Brightman, dissenting).
10. UNITED KINGDOM, *Royal Commission on Capital Punishment, 1949–1953, Report*, London: Her Majesty's Stationery Office, 1953, at p. 264.
11. David PANNICK, *Judicial Review of the Death Penalty*, London: Duckworth, 1983, at p. 84.
12. *Furman* v. *Georgia*, 408 U.S. 238, 288–89, 92 S.Ct. 2726, 33 L.Ed.2d (1972) (Brennan, J., concurring). See also: *Ex parte Medley*, 134 U.S. 160, 172 (1890).
13. *Solesbee* v. *Balkcom*, 339 U.S. 9, 14, 70 S.Ct. 457, 460, 94 L.Ed. 604 (1950) (Frankfurter, J., dissenting). However, in a California case it was argued unsuccessfully that death row drove inmates mad or to suicide; although evidence had been led on the subject, the court said there were no percentage figures on the issue; *In re Anderson*, 69 Cal.2d 613, 447 P.2d 117, 73 Cal.Rptr. 21 (1968); see also: NOTE, "Mental suffering under sentence of death: A cruel and unusual punishment," (1972) 57 *Iowa L. Rev.* 814.
14. Oscar WILDE, *Plays, Prose Writings and Poems*, London: Everyman's Library, 1930, at p. 524.
15. H. BLUESTONE, C. L. MCGAHEE, "Reaction to extreme stress: Impending death by execution," (1962) 119 *Am. J. Psychiatry* 393; Robert JOHNSON, "Under sentence of death: The psychology of death row confinement," (1979) 5 *Law Psychol. Rev.* 141; William D. KENNER, "Competency on death row," (1986) 8 *Int'l. J. L. Psychiatry* 253; GALLEMORE, PANTON, *supra* note 1.

16. *Rajendra Prasad* v. *State of Uttar Pradesh*, [1979] 3 S.C.R. 78, A.I.R. 1979 S.C. 916, at pp. 130 (S.C.R.), 943 (A.I.R.) (Krishna Iyer, J.).
17. *Abbot* v. *A.-G. of Trinidad and Tobago*, [1979] 1 W.L.R. 1342, 32 W.I.R. 347 (J.C.P.C.), at p. 1345 (W.L.R.) (*per* Lord Diplock).
18. *Riley* v. *Attorney-General of Jamaica, supra* note 9, at pp. 479 (All E.R.), 735 (A.C.) (*per* Lords Scarman and Brightman, dissenting).
19. The death cells in the Nicosia Central Prison are accessible to the public. They have been maintained as a shrine to those hanged by the British during the 1950s. I made this observation during a visit in August 1995.
20. Lloyd VOGELMAN, "The living dead: Living on death row," (1989) 5 *South African J. Hum. Rts.* 183, at p. 192.
21. *Francis* v. *Jamaica* (No. 606/1994), U.N. Doc. CCPR/C/54/D/606/1994, §9.2.
22. *Leonard* v. *Wolff*, 444 U.S. 807, 811 n. 2, 100 S.Ct. 29, 30–31 n. 2, 62 L.Ed.2d 20 (1979) (Marshall, J., dissenting).
23. *District Atty. for Suffolk Dist.* v. *Watson*, 381 Mass. 648, 411 N.E.2d 1274, 1291 n. 5 (1980) (Liacos, J., concurring).
24. *Pratt et al.* v. *Attorney General for Jamaica et al.*, [1993] 4 All E.R. 769, [1993] 2 L.R.C. 349, [1994] 2 A.C. 1, [1993] 3 W.L.R. 995, 43 W.I.R. 340, 14 *H.R.L.J.* 338, 33 I.L.M. 364 (J.C.P.C.).
25. *Pratt and Morgan* v. *Jamaica* (Nos. 210/1986, 225/1987), U.N. Doc. A/44/40, p. 222.
26. *Id.*, at §13.7.
27. *Pratt et al.* v. *Attorney General for Jamaica et al.*, *supra* note 24.
28. *Guerra* v. *Baptiste*, [1995] 4 All E.R. 583 (J.C.P.C.), at p. 596.
29. *Andrews* v. *Shulsen*, 600 F.Supp. 408, 431 (D.Utah 1984), *aff'd*, 802 F.2d 1256 (10th Cir.1986), *cert. denied*, 485 U.S. 919, 108 S.Ct. 1091, 99 L.Ed.2d 253, *reh'g denied*, 485 U.S. 1015, 108 S.Ct. 1491, 99 L.Ed.2d 718 (1988).
30. *Catholic Commission for Justice and Peace in Zimbabwe* v. *Attorney-General et al.*, [1993] 4 S.A. 239 (Z.S.C.), [1993] 1 Z.L.R. 242 (S), 14 *H.R.L.J.* 323, at pp. 245–246 (S.A.) (*per* Gubbay, C.J.). See: Laurel ANGUS, "Delay before execution: Is it inhuman and degrading treatment," (1993) 9 *South African J. Hum. Rts.* 432.
31. See: *Arsenault* v. *Commonwealth*, 353 Mass, 575, 233 N.E.2d 730, *rev'd*, 393 U.S. 5, 89 S.Ct. 35, 21 L.Ed.2d 5 (1968).
32. *District Atty. for Suffolk Dist.* v. *Watson, supra* note 23, at p. 1290 (N.E.2d) (Liacos, J., concurring); Justice Quirico, dissenting, contested the admissibility of this "unverified 'brief' ": *id.*, at p. 1302 (N.E.2d).
33. *Id.*, at p. 1290 (N.E.2d) (Liacos, J., concurring).
34. See, for example: *Leonard* v. *Wolff, supra* note 22, at pp. 1306 (U.S.), 3 (S.Ct.) (Rehnquist, Circuit J.), and 807, 811 n. 2 (U.S.), 29 (S.Ct.) (Marshall, J., and Brennan, J., dissenting from denial of stay); *Hopper* v. *Evans*, 456 U.S. 605, 607–8 (1982) (Burger, C.J.).
35. *Gilmore* v. *Utah*, 429 U.S. 1012, 1013 n. 1, 96 S.Ct. 436, 437 n. 1, 50 L.Ed.2d 632 (1976) (Burger, C.J., concurring); *id.*, at pp. 1015 n. 4 (U.S.), 438 n. 4 (S.Ct.) (Burger, C.J., concurring).
36. Melvin I. UROFKSY, *Letting Go: Death, Dying and the Law*, New York: Charles Scribner's Sons, 1993, at pp. 76–96; Melvin I. UROFSKY, "A right to die: Termination of appeal for condemned prisoners," (1984) 75 *J. Crim. L. & Criminology* 553; Welsh S. WHITE, "Defendants who elect execution," (1987) 48 *U. Pitt. L. Rev.* 853; G. Richard STRAFER, "Volunteering for execution: Competency, voluntariness and the propriety of the third party intervention," (1983) 74 *J. Crim. L. & Criminology* 860; Jane L. MCCLELLAN, "Stopping the rush to the death house: Third-Party standing in death-row volunteer cases," (1994) 26 *Ariz. St. L.J.* 201; Kathleen L. JOHNSON, "The death row right to die: Suicide or intimate decision," (1981) 54 *S. Cal. L. Rev.* 575; Tim KAINE, "Capital punishment and the waiver of sentence review," (1983) 18 *Harv. C.R.-C.L. L. Rev.* 483.
37. *United States ex rel. Townsend* v. *Twomey*, 322 F.Supp. 158, 174–75 (N.D. Ill.1971) (Perry, J.).

38. "An Eye for an Eye," *Time*, January 24, 1983, at p. 32.
39. Robert Lee MASSIE, "Death by degrees," *Esquire*, April 1971, at p. 179. See also: *Massie v. Sumner*, 624 F.2d 72 (9th Cir. 1980), *cert. denied*, 449 U.S. 1103 (1981).
40. *People* v. *Stanworth*, 71 Cal.2d 820, 830 nn. 12–13, 457 P.2d 889, 896 nn. 12–13, 80 Cal.Rptr. 49, 46 nn. 12–13 (1969).
41. *Smith by and through Smith* v. *Armontrout*, 632 F.Supp. 503, 515 (W.D.Mo. 1986). See also: *State* v. *Dodd*, 120 Wash.2d 1, 838 P.2d 86 (1992); *Clark* v. *Blackburn*, 524 F.Supp. 1248 (1981).
42. Hugo Adam BEDAU, *The Courts, the Constitution and Capital Punishment*, Lexington, Mass.: Lexington Books, 1977, at pp. 121–25.
43. *Evans* v. *Vennett*, 467 F. Supp. 1108, 1110 (1979).
44. *Pratt et al.* v. *Attorney General for Jamaica et al.*, *supra* note 24, at pp. 774, 782 (All E.R.), 19, 28 (A.C.).
45. In 1995, the Court showed some interest in hearing a case on the subject (*Lackey* v. *Texas*, 115 S.Ct. 1421, 63 L.W. 3705, 131 L.Ed.2d 304 (1995)). Lackey's application for a stay of execution, presented to Justice Antonin Scalia and subsequently referred by him to the Court, was granted pending consideration of his application for a writ of habeas corpus before the district court. Since then, the matter has apparently stalled in the lower courts, and it is unlikely to return to the Supreme Court.
46. A. L. WIRIN, Paul M. POSNER, "A decade of appeals," (1961) 8 *U.C.L.A. L. Rev.* 768.
47. *People* v. *Chessman*, 52 Cal.2d 467, 341 P.2d 679, 699 (1959), *cert. denied*, 361 U.S. 925, *petition for rehearing denied*, 361 U.S. 941 (1959).
48. *In re Anderson*, *supra* note 13, at p. 130 (P.2d).
49. *Chessman* v. *Dickson*, 275 F.2d 604, 608 (9th Cir.1960). The district court judge was taken to task for this statement on appeal.
50. *Id.*
51. *Id.*, at pp. 607–8.
52. WIRIN, POSNER, *supra* note 46. On the Chessman case, see also: NOTE, "The Caryl Chessman case: A legal analysis," (1960) 44 *Minn. L. Rev.* 941.
53. *Brown* v. *State*, 6 Div. 128, 264 So.2d 529, 534 (1971).
54. *Id.*, at p. 538 (1971).
55. *People* v. *Anderson*, *supra* note 5, at pp. 649 (Cal.3d), 894 (P.2d) (Wright, C.J.).
56. *Id.*, at pp. 650 (Cal.3d), 895 (P.2d) (Wright, C.J.).
57. *United States ex rel. Townsend* v. *Twomey*, *supra* note 37. See also: *In re Anderson*, *supra* note 13, at pp. 129–30 (P.2d).
58. Convention for the Protection of Human Rights and Fundamental Freedoms (the "European Convention on Human Rights"), (1955) 213 U.N.T.S. 221, E.T.S. 5.
59. *Dhlamini et al.* v. *Carter N.O. et al.*, [1968] 1 R.L.R. 136(A.), 1968 (2) S.A. 445, at pp. 154–55 (R.L.R.), 454 (S.A.) (*per* Beadle, C.J.).
60. *Id.*, at pp. 155 (R.L.R.), 455 (S.A.) (*per* Beadle, C.J.).
61. Philip JOSEPH, "Towards abolition of Privy Council appeals: The Judicial Committee and the Bill of Rights," (1985) 2 *Canterbury L. Rev.* 273.
62. *De Freitas* v. *Benny*, [1976] A.C. 239, [1975] 3 W.L.R. 388, 27 W.I.R. 318 (J.C.P.C.), at p. 246 (A.C.).
63. *Id.*
64. *Pratt et al.* v. *Attorney General for Jamaica et al.*, *supra* note 24, at pp. 783 (All E.R.), 29 (A.C.) (*per* Lord Griffiths).
65. *Abbott* v. *A.-G. of Trinidad and Tobago*, *supra* note 17, at p. 1345 (W.L.R.) (*per* Lord Diplock).
66. *Id.*
67. *Id.*
68. *Id.*
69. *Riley* v. *Attorney-General of Jamaica*, *supra* note 9, at pp. 469 (All E.R.), 719 (A.C.).
70. *Supra* note 58.

71. *Riley* v. *Attorney-General of Jamaica, supra* note 9, at pp. 472–73 (All E.R.), 726 (A.C.) (*per* Lord Bridge of Harwich).
72. *Id.*
73. *Id.*, at pp. 478 (All E.R.), 735 (A.C.) (*per* Lords Scarman and Brightman, dissenting).
74. *Id.*, at pp. 478–79 (All E.R.), 735 (A.C.) (*per* Lords Scarman and Brightman, dissenting).
75. *Id.*
76. *Abbott* v. *A.-G of Trinidad and Tobago, supra* note 17, at p. 1345 (W.L.R.) (*per* Lord Diplock).
77. *Riley* v. *Attorney-General of Jamaica, supra* note 9, at pp. 479 (All E.R.), 735 (A.C.) (*per* Lords Scarman and Brightman, dissenting).
78. *Id.*, at pp. 480 (All E.R.), 736 (A.C.) (*per* Lords Scarman and Brightman, dissenting).
79. *Re Applications by Thomas and Paul*, [1986] L.R.C. (Const.) 285 (High Court of Trinidad and Tobago), at p. 295.
80. *Id.*
81. *Id.*
82. *Id.*, at p. 292.
83. *Id.*
84. *Kitson Branche* v. *Attorney-General*, unreported judgment of the High Court of Trinidad and Tobago, Civil Appeal No. 63 of 1977 (Hyatali, C.J.), quoted in *Re Applications by Thomas and Paul, supra* note 79, at p. 296. For discussion of *Branche*, see: PANNICK, *supra* note 11, at pp. 87–88.
85. *Richards* v. *Attorney-General of St. Kitts & Nevis*, (1992) 44 W.I.R. 141 (Court of Appeal of the Eastern Caribbean States), at p. 147 (*per* Sir Vincent Floissac, C.J.).
86. *Id.*, at p. 148 (*per* Matthew, acting J.A.).
87. *Clark (Stafford)* v. *Attorney-General*, (1992) 45 W.I.R. 1 (Supreme Court of the Bahamas) (*per* Gonsalves-Sabola, C.J.). Also: *Jurisingh* v. *Attorney-General* (unreported) civil appeals 151 to 153 of 1992, Trinidad and Tobago Court of Appeal.
88. International Covenant on Civil and Political Rights, (1976) 999 U.N.T.S. 171.
89. *Supra* note 58.
90. American Declaration of the Rights and Duties of Man, O.A.S. Doc. OEA/Ser.L/V/I.4.
91. American Convention on Human Rights, (1979) 1144 U.N.T.S. 123, O.A.S.T.S. 36.
92. *Pratt* v. *Jamaica* (Case No. 9054), Resolution No. 13/84, reported in O.A.S. Doc. OEA/Ser.L/V/II.66 doc. 10 rev. 1, at pp. 111–13.
93. *Id.* Similar conclusions were reached in other death penalty cases considered by the commission: *Champagne* v. *Jamaica* (Case No. 7505), Resolution No. 27/86, reported in O.A.S. Doc. OEA/Ser.L/V/II.68 doc. 8 rev. 1, at pp. 51–55; *Cuthbert* v. *Jamaica* (Case No. 9190), Resolution No. 28/86, reported in O.A.S. Doc. OEA/Ser.L/V/II.68 doc. 8 rev. 1, at pp. 55–57; *Riley* v. *Jamaica* (Case No. 3102), Resolution No. 25/81, reported in O.A.S. Doc. OEA/Ser.L/V/II.57 doc. 6 rev. 1, at pp. 89–91; *Thomas* v. *Jamaica* (Case No. 3115), Resolution No. 24/81, reported in O.A.S. Doc. OEA/Ser.L/V/II.57 doc. 6 rev. 1, at pp. 91–93; *Wright* v. *Jamaica* (Case No. 9260), Resolution 29/88, reported in O.A.S. Doc. OEA/Ser.L/V/II.74 doc. 10 rev 1, at p. 154.
94. *Pratt et al.* v. *Attorney General for Jamaica et al., supra* note 24, at pp. 778 (All E.R.), 23–24 (A.C.).
95. *Pratt and Morgan* v. *Jamaica, supra* note 25.
96. On July 17, 1986, the Judicial Committee of the Privy Council dismissed Pratt's application for leave to appeal, although it expressed grave misgivings about the delay in the Court of Appeal between dismissal of the appeal and the issuing of written reasons. This, it said, could be a source of grave injustice and possibly constitute inhuman and degrading treatment: *Pratt et al.* v. *Attorney General for Jamaica et al., supra* note 24, at pp. 777 (All E.R.), 22 (A.C.).
97. *Supra* note 88.
98. *Pratt and Morgan* v. *Jamaica, supra* note 25, §9.3. There is no rule of *res judicata*, and the committee may examine a matter that has already been adjudicated by another international tribunal or other body: M. TARDU, "The Protocol to the United Nations Covenant on Civil

and Political Rights and the Inter-American system: A study of coexisting petition procedures," (1976) 70 *A.J.I.L.* 778; A. A. CANÇADO TRINDADE, "Co-existence and co-ordination of mechanisms of international protection of human rights (at global and regional levels)," (1987) 202 *R.C.A.D.I.* 9.

99. *Supra* note 91, art. 5§2.
100. *Pratt and Morgan* v. *Jamaica, supra* note 25, §13.2.
101. *Id.*, §13.7.
102. *Id.*, §15.
103. *Id.*, §13.6. See also: *Reid* v. *Jamaica* (No. 250/1987), U.N. Doc. A/45/40, Vol. II, p. 85, (1990) 11 *H.R.L.J.* 319, §11.6.
104. The committee was subsequently reminded of its poor record in this area by the Judicial Committee of the Privy Council: *Pratt et al.* v. *Attorney General for Jamaica et al., supra* note 24, at pp. 777–78 (All E.R.).
105. *Pratt and Morgan* v. *Jamaica, supra* note 25, §§13.6, 13.7.
106. *Supra* note 58.
107. *Altun* v. *Federal Republic of Germany* (App. no. 10308/83), (1983) 36 D.R. 209, 5 E.H.R.R. 611.
108. *Kirkwood* v. *United Kingdom* (App. no. 10479/83), (1984) 37 D.R. 158.
109. *Soering* v. *United Kingdom* (App. no. 14038/88), Series A, Vol. 161, at p. 54, 11 E.H.R.R. 439, at p. 485.
110. *Soering* v. *United Kingdom et al.*, July 7, 1989, Series A., Vol. 161, 11 E.H.R.R. 439.
111. Protocol No. 6 to the Convention for the Protection of Human Rights and Fundamental Freedoms Concerning the Abolition of the Death Penalty, E.T.S. no. 114. The United Kingdom is one of only a few members of the Council of Europe that have not ratified Protocol No. 6. The European Commission on Human Rights has said that it will "not exclude the possibility that a Contracting State's responsibility might be engaged under Article 1 of Protocol No. 6 where a fugitive is extradited to a State where he is seriously at risk of being sentenced to death and executed": *Aylor-Davis* v. *France* (App. no. 22742/93), (1994) 76A *D.R.* 164, at p. 170.
112. For scholarly comment on the *Soering* case, see: NOTE, "European Court on Human Rights—extradition—inhuman or degrading treatment or punishment, Soering Case," (1990) 20 *Ga. J. Int'l. & Comp. L.* 463; S. BREITENMOSER, G. E. WILMS, "Human rights v. extradition: The Soering case," (1990) 11 *Mich. J. Int'l L.* 845; V. COUSSIRAT-COUSTÈRE, "Jurisprudence de la Cour européene des droits de l'homme de 1989 à 1991," [1991] *A.F.D.I.* 583; W. Ganshof VAN DER MEERSCH, "L'extradition et la Convention européenne des droits de l'homme: L'affaire Soering," (1990) *Revue trimestrielle des droits de l'homme* 5; Frédéric SUDRE, "Extradition et peine de mort—arrêt Soering de la Cour européenne des droits de l'homme du 7 juillet 1989," (1990) *Revue générale de droit international public* 103; Michael O'BOYLE, Extradition and expulsion under the European Convention on Human Rights: Reflections on the *Soering* case," in James O'REILLY, ed., *Human Rights and Constitutional Law: Essays in Honour of Brian Walsh*, Dublin: Round Hall Press, 1992, p. 93; Ann SHERLOCK, "Extradition, death row and the Convention," (1990) 15 *European L. Rev.* 87; H. WATTENDORFF, E. du PERRON, "Human Rights v. Extradition: The Soering case," (1990) 11 *Mich. J. Int'l L.* 845; C. WARBRICK, "Coherence and the European Court of Human Rights: The adjudicative background to the Soering case," (1990) 11 *Mich. J. Int'l L.* 1073; J. QUIGLEY, J. SHANK, "Death row as a violation of human rights: Is it illegal to extradite to Virginia?" (1989) 30 *Va. Int'l L.J.* 251; Richard B. LILLICH, "The *Soering* case," (1991) 85 *A.J.I.L.* 128; Christine VAN DEN WYNGAERT, "Applying the European Convention on Human Rights to extradition: Opening Pandora's box?" (1990) 39 *I.C.L.Q.* 757; Susan MARKS, "Yes, Virginia, extradition may breach the European Convention on Human Rights," (1990) 49 *Cambridge L.J.* 194; Henri LABAYLE, "Droits de l'homme, traitement inhumain et peine capitale: Réflexions sur l'édification d'un ordre public européen en matière d'extradition par la Cour européenne des droit de l'homme," (1990) 64 *Semaine juridique* 3452; P. ROLLAND, P. TAVERNIER, "Chronique de jurisprudence de la Cour

européenne des droits de l'homme," [1990] *J.D.I.* 734; F. C. PALAZZO, "La pena di morte dinanzi alla Corte europea di Strasburgo," [1990] *Rivista italiana di diritto e procedura penale* 367; L. E. PETTITI, "Arrêt Soering c./Grande-Bretagne du 8 juillet 1989," [1989] *Revue de science criminelle et de droit pénal comparé* 786; Vincent BERGER, *Jurisprudence de la Cour européenne des droits de l'homme*, 4th ed., Paris: Sirey, 1994, at pp. 12–17.

113. Convention Against Torture and Other Cruel, Inhuman and Degrading Treatment or Punishment, G.A. Res. 39/46.

114. *Supra* note 88.

115. "Multilateral Treaties deposited with the Secretary-General, Status as at 31 December 1994," U.N. Doc. ST/LEG/SER.E/13 (1995), at p. 125.

116. "Consideration of reports submitted by States parties under article 40 of the Covenant, Comments of the Human Rights Committee," U.N. Doc. CCPR/C/79/Add.50 (1995), §14. For a discussion of this issue, see "The Prohibition of Cruel Treatment and Torture," earlier in this volume.

117. "Multilateral Treaties deposited with the Secretary-General, Status as at 31 December 1994," *supra* note 115, at pp. 179–80 (italics mine).

118. *Kindler* v. *Canada*, [1991] 2 S.C.R. 779, 67 C.C.C. (3d) 1, 84 D.L.R. (4th) 438, 6 C.R.R. (2d) 193; *Reference: Re Ng Extradition (Can.)*, [1991] 2 S.C.R. 858, 84 D.L.R. (4th) 498, 67 C.C.C. (3d) 61. See: William A. SCHABAS, "Kindler and Ng: Our supreme magistrates take a frightening step into the court of public opinion," (1991) 51 *Revue du barreau* 673; William A. SCHABAS, "Extradition et la peine de mort: le Canada renvoie deux fugitifs au couloir de la mort," (1992) 4 *R.U.D.H.* 65; William A. SCHABAS, "*Kindler* v. *Canada*," (1993) 87 *A.J.I.L.* 128; John PAK, "Canadian extradition and the death penalty: Seeking a constitutional assurance of life," (1993) 26 *Cornell Int'l L.J.* 239.

119. Extradition Treaty Between Canada and the United States of America, [1976] C.T.S. 3: "When the offense for which extradition is requested in punishable by death under the laws of the requesting State and the laws of the requested State do not permit such punishment for that offense, extradition may be refused unless the requesting State provides such assurances as the requested State considers sufficient that the death penalty shall not be imposed, or, if imposed, shall not be executed," The provision is of no real significance in extradition towards Canada, which has not carried out the death penalty since 1962, and which in 1976 abolished capital punishment except in a limited number of military offenses: Criminal Law Amendment Act (No. 2), 1976, S.C. 1974-75-76, c. 105; National Defence Act, R.S.C. 1985, c.N-4, ss. 63–66, 68–70 and 95; also s. 55.

120. R.S.C. 1985, App. II, no 44, Schedule B, Part I.

121. *Kindler* v. *Canada*, *supra* note 118, at p. 835 (*per* La Forest, J.). See also: LILLICH, *supra* note 112, at p. 145. But see: Michael SHEA, "Expanding judicial scrutiny of human rights in extradition cases after *Soering*," (1992) 17 *Yale J. Int'l L.* 110.

122. *Canada* v. *Schmidt*, [1987] 1 S.C.R. 500, 33 C.C.C. (3d) 193, 28 C.R.R. 280, 20 O.A.C. 161, 76 N.R. 12.

123. *Pratt and Morgan* v. *Jamaica*, *supra* note 25.

124. The beatings raised issues under another provision of the International Covenant on Civil and Political Rights, *supra* note 88, art. 10§1, which states: "All persons deprived of their liberty shall be treated with humanity and with respect for the inherent dignity of the human person."

125. *Barrett and Sutcliffe* v. *Jamaica* (Nos. 270/1988 and 271/1988) U.N. Doc. CCPR/C/44/D/1988 and 271/1988, U.N. Doc. A/47/40, p. 246, §§3.4, 3.5.

126. *Id.*, §8.4.

127. *Soering* v. *United Kingdom et al.*, *supra* note 110, at pp. 42 (Series A), 475 (E.H.R.R.).

128. *Barrett and Sutcliffe* v. *Jamaica*, *supra* note 125, at p. 252 (*per* Chanet, dissenting).

129. *Supra* note 118,

130. Pursuant to Rule 86: U.N. Doc. CCPR/C/SR.17, §§25, 26, U.N. Doc. CCPR/C/3/Rev.1;

CCPR/C/OP/1, Annex II, p. 155. In its views in *Kindler* v. *Canada* (No. 470/1991), U.N. Doc. CCPR/C/48/D/470/1991, (1993) 14 *H.R.L.J.* 307, 6 *R.U.D.H.* 165, §17, the committee "expresses its regret that the State party did not accede to the Special Rapporteur's request."

131. *Kindler* v. *Canada,* (No. 470/1991), U.N. Doc. CCPR/C/45/D/470/1991, unreported.
132. *Kindler* v. *Canada, supra* note 130. See: William A. SCHABAS, "Soering's legacy: The Human Rights Committee and the Judicial Committee of the Privy Council take a walk down death row," (1994) 43 *I.C.L.Q.* 913.
133. *Kindler* v. *Canada, supra* note 130, §15.2.
134. *Id.,* §15.3.
135. Although materials showing the intolerable conditions on death row in Pennsylvania are readily available: see, for example, *Peterkin* v. *Jeffes,* 661 F.Supp. (E.D.Pa.1987).
136. *Kindler* v. *Canada, supra* note 130, §15.3.
137. *Id.,* §3.
138. *Id.,* at p. 315 *(H.R.L.J.).* See also the concurring views of Herndl and Sadi in *Cox* v. *Canada* (No. 539/1993), (1995) 15 *H.R.L.J.* 410, at p. 419.
139. *Kindler* v. *Canada, supra* note 130.
140. *Id.,* at p. 316.
141. *Id.,* at pp. 318, 323.
142. *Catholic Commissioon for Justice and Peace in Zimbabwe* v. *Attorney-General et al., supra* note 30, at pp. 263–64 (S.A.) (*per* Gubbay, C.J.).
143. *Id.,* at pp. 239, 270 (S.A.).
144. *Id.,* at pp. 244, 245, 250, 264, 270 (S.A.).
145. *Id.,* at p. 268 (S.A.). The phrase "living dead" was apparently coined by Robert Johnson: JOHNSON, *supra* note 1, at p. 110, quoted in *Sher Singh* v. *State of Punjab, supra* note 3, at p. 470 (A.I.R.) (*per* Chandrachud, C.J.).
146. Constitution of Zimbabwe Amendment (No. 13) Act 1993.
147. *Nkomo et al.* v. *Attorney-General, Zimbabwe et al.,* [1994] (3) S.A. 34 (Z.S.C.) (*per* Gubbay, C.J.).
148. There were already precedents for judicial recognition of the death row phenomenon in India. In a 1974 case, the Supreme Court of India considered, among a number of humanitarian grounds for commutation, "an extrinsic factor [, one nevertheless] recognized by the Court as of human significance in the sentencing context [,] the brooding horror of 'hanging' which has been haunting the prisoner in her condemned cell for over two years": *Ediga Anamma* v. *State of Andhra Pradesh,* [1974] 2 S.C.R. 329, A.I.R. 1794 S.C. 799, at p. 335 (S.C.R.). See also: *State of U.P.* v. *Lalla Singh,* A.I.R. 1978 S.C. 368.
149. *Vatheeswaran* v. *State of Tamil Nadu,* (1983) 2 S.C.R. 348, A.I.R. 1983 S.C. 361, 1983 Cri. L.J. 481, at p. 364 (A.I.R.) (*per* Chinnappa Reddy, J.). See also: *Javed Ahmed Abdul Hamid Pawala* v. *State of Maharashtra,* [1985] 2 S.C.R. 9, A.I.R. 1985 S.C. 231; *Madhu Mehta* v. *Union of India,* [1989] 3 S.C.R. 775, A.I.R. 1989 S.C. 2299 (*per* Sabyasachi Mukharji, J.).
150. *Vatheeswaran* v. *State of Tamil Nadu, supra* note 149, at p. 366 (A.I.R.) (*per* Chinnappa Reddy, J.). See: Nishtha JASWAL, *Role of the Supreme Court with Regard to the Right to Life and Personal Liberty,* New Delhi: Ashish Publishing House, 1990; Jill COTTRELL, "Wrestling with the death penalty in India," (1991) 17 *South African J. Hum. Rts.* 185.
151. *Mullin* v. *Administration, Union Territory of Delhi,* A.I.R. 1993 S.C. 746.
152. *Sunil Batra* v. *Delhi Administration,* [1979] 1 S.C.R. 392, A.I.R. 1978 S.C. 1675.
153. *Sher Singh* v. *State of Punjab, supra* note 3, at pp. 591 (S.C.R.), 472 (A.I.R.) (*per* Chandrachud, C.J.).
154. *Catholic Commission for Justice and Peace in Zimbabwe* v. *Attorney-General et al., supra* note 30, at p. 253 (S.A.). Also: *Javed Ahmed Abdul Hamid Pawala* v. *State of Maharashtra, supra* note 149, at p. 236 (A.I.R.) (*per* Chinnappa Reddy, J.). Also: *State of U.P.* v. *Lalloo,* A.I.R. 1986 S.C. 576.
155. *Sher Singh* v. *State of Punjab, supra* note 3, at p. 471 (A.I.R.) (*per* Chandrachud, C.J.).
156. *Id.,* at p. 470 (*per* Chandrachud, C.J.).
157. COTTRELL, *supra* note 150, at p. 194.

158. *Javed Ahmed Abdul Hamid Pawala* v. *State of Maharashtra, supra* note 149, at p. 236 (A.I.R.) (*per* Chinnappa Reddy, J.).
159. *Id.,* at p. 234 (A.I.R.) (*per* Chinnappa Reddy, J.).
160. *Id.,* at p. 236 (A.I.R.) (*per* Chinnappa Reddy, J.).
161. *Sawai Singh* v. *Rajasthan,* [1988] 2 *Rajasthan Law Weekly* 106 (Jaipur High Court). See also: *Madhu Mehta* v. *Union of India, supra* note 149.
162. *Triveniben* v. *State of Gujarat,* A.I.R. 1989 S.C. 142, [1989] 1 S.C.J. 383, [1992] L.R.C. (Const.) 425 (*per* Oza, J.). See, however, the concurring judgment of Justice Shetty, *id.,* at p. 410 (S.C.J.), who considered that the court could take into account excessive delay at trial.
163. COTTRELL, *supra* note 150, at pp. 194–95.
164. *Triveniben* v. *State of Gujarat, supra* note 162, at p. 410 (S.C.J.) (Shetty, J.).
165. *Daya Singh* v. *Union of India,* [1992] L.R.C. (Const) 452 (Supreme Court of India) (*per* Sharma, J.).
166. *Pratt et al.* v. *Attorney General for Jamaica et al., supra* note 24, at pp. 783–84 (All E.R.), 30 (A.C.). A companion case, dealing with the scope of judicial review in death penalty matters in Jamaica, was decided the same day: *Walker* v. *R.,* [1993] 3 W.L.R. 1087, [1993] 2 L.R.C. 371, [1994] 2 A.C. 36. See J. A. COUTTS, "Effect of long delay in execution," (1994) 58 *J. Crim. L.* 177; William A. SCHABAS, "Case Comment: Pratt and Morgan v. Jamaica," (1994) 5 *Crim. L.F.* 180; William A. SCHABAS, *supra* note 132; Barry PHILLIPS, "Pratt and Morgan v. Attorney-General for Jamaica," (1994) 88 *A.J.I.L.* 775; Lovemore MADHUKU, "Delay before execution: More on it being inhuman and degrading," (1994) 10 *South African J. Hum. Rts.* 276.
167. *Abbott* v. *A.-G. of Trinidad and Tobago, supra* note 17.
168. *Riley* v. *Attorney-General of Jamaica, supra* note 9.
169. For a post-*Pratt* example of a prisoner's escape being discounted from the relevant period of delay, because "[d]uring his escape from custody for a period of some two months and seventeen days it cannot be said that he was subject to cruel and unusual punishment, nor exposed to the alleged condition of the condemned cells," see: *Wallen* v. *Baptiste (no. 2),* (1994) 45 W.I.R. 405 (Court of Appeal, Trinidad and Tobago), at p. 436 (Hamel-Smith, J.A.).
170. Since *Pratt,* the Judicial Committee of the Privy Council has reiterated the point that frivolous or vexatious applications for delay are not to be counted, precisely because "the postponement of the carrying out of the death penalty can have a profound effect on the question whether it would be inhuman or degrading treatment or punishment to execute the convicted man given the lapse of time since conviction and sentence." See: *Reckley* v. *Minister of Public Safety and Immigration,* [1995] J.C.J. No. 26, at §8 (*per* Lord Browne-Wilkinson).
171. *Pratt et al.* v. *Attorney General for Jamaica et al., supra* note 24, at pp. 774, 782 (All E.R.), 19, 28 (A.C.).
172. In a 1944 case, *Piare Dusadh* v. *Emperor,* (1944) 6 F.C.R. 61, A.I.R. 1944 F.C. 1, the Federal Court of India addressed circumstances where death sentences had been imposed "several months ago" and were followed by lengthy debate on constitutional points in the higher courts. The court stated: "We do not doubt that this court has power, where there has been inordinate delay in executing death sentences in cases which come before it, to allow the appeal in so far as the death sentence is concerned and substitute a sentence of transportation for life on account of the time factor alone, however right the death sentence was at the time when it was originally imposed." The court added, however, that this jurisdiction closely entrenched on the power and duties of the executive, and that consequently the court would intervene with great caution. In *Piare Dusadh,* the court had been told that in England, where capital cases were brought to the House of Lords due to an important point of law, the consequential delay in finally disposing of the case was treated as a ground for the commutation of the death sentence. Note, however, that the doctrine of abuse of process is not a part of human rights law, and that it is not principally destined at the protection of the rights of the individual. This can be seen in the judgment of Lord Diplock of the Privy Council in

Abbott v. *A.-G of Trinidad and Tobago, supra* note 17, who dismissed the significance of suffering by the prisoner on death row, but acknowledged that delayed execution "brings the administration of criminal justice into disrepute among law-abiding citizens." See also *Guerra* v. *Baptiste, supra* note 28, at p. 589.

173. *Pratt et al.* v. *Attorney General for Jamaica et al., supra* note 24, at pp. 788–89 (All E.R.), 35 (A.C.).

174. *Id.,* at pp. 783 (All E.R.), 29 (A.C.).

175. PHILLIPS, *supra* note 166, at p. 781.

176. *Id.,* at p. 788.

177. *Bradshaw* v. *Attorney General,* [1995] J.C.J. No. 23, at §20 (*per* Lord Slynn of Hadley).

178. *Pratt et al.* v. *Attorney General for Jamaica et al., supra* note 24, at p. 785.

179. *Id.,* at p. 784, referring to the reasons of Judge O'Scannlain in *Richmond* v. *Lewis,* 948 F.2d. 1473 (9th Cir. 1990), *rev'd on other grounds,* 113 S.Ct. 528, 121 L.Ed.2d 411 (1992), *vacated,* 986 F.2d 1583 (9th Cir.1993), and Justice La Forest in *Kindler* v. *Canada, supra* note 118, at p. 830 (S.C.R.).

180. There is, however, some isolated resistance. See the July 1994 judgment of the Trinidad and Tobago Court of Appeal, which refuses to follow *Pratt* and which indicates its unhappiness with *Pratt* and tends to favor the approach endorsed by the Indian courts whereby only delay subsequent to exhaustion of all appeal remedies may be counted: *Wallen* v. *Baptiste (no. 2), supra* note 169.

181. *Nemi* v. *The State,* [1994] 1 L.R.C. 376 (Supreme Court of Nigeria), at p. 405 (*per* Ogwuegbu, J.S.C.).

182. *Makwanyane and Mchunu* v. *The State,* (1995) 16 *H.R.L.J.* 154, at p. 186 (*per* Kentridge, A.J.).

183. *Gregg* v. *Georgia,* 428 U.S. 153, 96 S.Ct. 2909, 49 L.Ed.2d 859 (1976).

184. *Lackey* v. *Texas, supra* note 45. Justice Breyer agreed with Justice Stevens's opinion. But since *Lackey,* the Court of Appeals, Ninth Circuit, has referred to *Pratt, Catholic Commission,* and *Soering,* stating that "[w]ith all due respect to our colleagues abroad, we do not believe this view will prevail in the United States." *McKenzie* v. *Day,* 57 F.3d 1461, 1466 (9th Cir.1995) (Kozinski, J.). See Also: *McKenzie* v. *Day,* 57 F.3d 1493 (9th Cir.1995).

185. *In re Medley,* 134 U.S. 160 (1890).

186. *Id.,* at p. 172 (Miller, J.).

187. *Lackey* v. *Texas, supra* note 45.

188. *Lackey* v. *Scott,* 115 S.Ct. 1818, 131 L.Ed.2d 741 (1995).

189. *Stafford* v. *Ward,* 59 F.3d 1025, 1028 (10th Cir.1995).

190. *McKenzie* v. *Day,* 57 F.3d 1461, 1468 (9th Cir.1995) (Kozinski, J.).

191. *Id.,* at p. 1488 (Norris, J., dissenting). Also: *McKenzie* v. *Day,* 57 F.3d 1493 (9th Cir.1995) (Browning, J., dissenting).

192. *Cox* v. *Canada, supra* note 138, at p. 417.

193. *Id.,* at p. 418.

194. *Id.,* at p. 421.

195. *Id.,* at p. 419.

196. *Francis* v. *Jamaica, supra* note 21, §9.2.

197. *Pratt et al.* v. *Attorney General for Jamaica et al., supra* note 24, at pp. 788–89 (All E.R.), 35 (A.C.). See also: *Bradshaw* v. *Attorney General, supra* note 177, §22 (*per* Lord Slynn of Hadley).

198. *Pratt et al.* v. *Attorney General for Jamaica et al., supra* note 24, pp. 772 (All E.R.), 17 (A.C.).

199. *Id.,* at pp. 789 (All E.R.), 27 (A.C.).

200. *Vatheeswaran* v. *State of Tamil Nadu, supra* note 149, at p. 364 (A.I.R.) (*per* Chinnappa Reddy, J.). See also: *Ediga Anamma* v. *State of Andhra Pradesh, supra* note 148 (two years); *State of U.P.* v. *Sahai,* A.I.R. 1981 S.C. 1442; *State of Bihar* v. *Uma Sankar Kotriwal,* A.I.R. 1981 S.C. 641, (1981) Cri. L.J. 159.

201. *Bhagwan Bux Singh* v. *State of U.P.,* A.I.R. 1978 S.C. 34 (two and a half years).

202. *Sadhu Singh* v. *State of U.P.,* A.I.R. 1978 S.C. 1506 (three and a half years).

203. *Sher Singh* v. *State of Punjab, supra* note 3, at p. 591 (S.C.R.), 469 (A.I.R.) (*per* Chandrachud, C.J.). See also: *Triveniben* v. *State of Gujarat, supra* note 162, at p. 143 (A.I.R.).

204. *Catholic Commission for Justice and Peace in Zimbabwe* v. *Attorney-General et al., supra* note 30.

205. *Soering* v. *United Kingdom et al., supra* note 110, at p. 42 (Series A), 475 (E.H.R.R.).

206. *Pratt et al.* v. *Attorney General for Jamaica et al., supra* note 24, at p. 783 (All E.R.), 29 (A.C.).

207. *Makwanyane and Mchunu* v. *The State, supra* 182, at p. 186 (*per* Kentridge, A.J.).

208. *District Atty. for Suffolk Dist.* v. *Watson, supra* note 23, at p. 1291 n. 5 (N.E.2d) (Liacos, J., concurring).

209. *Wallen* v. *Baptiste (no. 2), supra* note 169, at p. 444 (*per* Hamel-Smith, J.A.).

210. *Reckley* v. *Minister of Public Safety and Immigration, supra* note 170, §10 (*per* Lord Browne-Wilkinson).

211. *Guerra* v. *Baptiste, supra* note 28, at p. 592.

212. *Id.*

213. *Id.*, at p. 593.

214. *Soering* v. *United Kingdom et al., supra* note 110.

215. *An Act for better preventing the horrid Crime of Murder*, 25 Geo. 2, c. 37; also *Offences against the Person Act 1828*, 9 Geo 4, c. 31.

216. UNITED KINGDOM, *supra* note 10, at pp. 261–62.

217. *Id.*, at pp. 241, 262.

218. *Pratt et al.* v. *Attorney General for Jamaica et al., supra* note 24, at pp. 773 (All E.R.), 18 (A.C.)

219. 434 H.C. Deb. 5 s., p. 490.

220. *Id.*, at pp. 788 (All E.R.), 34–35 (A.C.).

221. *Vatheeswaran* v. *State of Tamil Nadu, supra* note 149.

222. *Pratt et al.* v. *Attorney General for Jamaica et al., supra* note 24, at pp. 788 (All E.R.), 35 (A.C.)

223. *Catholic Commission for Justice and Peace in Zimbabwe* v. *Attorney-General et al., supra* note 30, at p. 269 (S.A.) (*per* Gubbay, C.J.).

224. *Vatheeswaran* v. *State of Tamil Nadu, supra* note 149, at 367 (A.I.R.) (*per* Chinnappa Reddy, J.).

225. *Catholic Commission for Justice and Peace in Zimbabwe* v. *Attorney-General et al., supra* note 30, at pp. 269, 270 (S.A.) (*per* Gubbay, C.J.).

226. *Pratt et al.* v. *Attorney General for Jamaica et al., supra* note 24, at pp. 774, 782 (All E.R.).

227. *Connelly* v. *Director of Public Prosecutions*, [1964] A.C. 1254, [1964] 2 All E.R. 401, 48 Cr.App.R. 183 (H.L.).

228. International Covenant on Civil and Political Rights, *supra* note 88, art. 14§3(c).

229. *Dickey* v. *Flordia*, 298 U.S. 30, 42, 90 S.Ct. 1564, 1571 (1970) (Brennan, J.); *Barker* v. *Wingo*, 407 U.S. 514, 532, 92 S.Ct. 2182, 2193, 33 L.Ed.2d 101 (1972) (Powell, J.).

230. *Pratt et al.* v. *Attorney General for Jamaica et al., supra* note 24, at pp. 786–87 (All E.R.), 33 (A.C.).

231. *Lackey* v. *Texas, supra* note 45.

232. *Reference: Re Ng Extradition (Can.), supra* note 118; *Ng* v. *Canada* (No. 469/1991), (1994) 15 *H.R.L.J.* 149.

233. *Cox* v. *Canada, supra* note 138.

234. See: International Covenant on Civil and Political Rights, *supra* note 88, art. 14§3(c); European Convention on Human Rights, *supra* note 58, art. 6§1; American Convention on Human Rights, *supra* note 91, art. 8§1.

235. Roger HOOD, *The Death Penalty: A World-wide Perspective*, Oxford: Clarendon Press, 1989, at pp. 74–75.

236. Geneva Convention of August 12, 1949 Relative to the Treatment of Prisoners of War, (1950) 75 U.N.T.S. 135.

237. The earlier International Convention Concerning the Treatment of Prisoners of War, (1932–33) 118 L.N.T.S. 343, established a moratorium of three months.

238. Geneva Convention of August 12, 1949 Relative to the Protection of Civilians, (1950) 75 U.N.T.S. 135, art. 75.

239. William A. SCHABAS, *The Abolition of the Death Penalty in International Law*, Cambridge: Cambridge University Press (Grotius Publications), 1993, at pp. 199–207.
240. International Covenant on Civil and Political Rights, *supra* note 88, art. 6§4.
241. HOOD, *supra* note 235, at pp. 76–77.
242. U.N. Doc. CAT/C/SR.146/Add.2, §19; see also, "Initial Report of China," U.N. Doc. CAT/C/7/Add.14, §38; U.N. Doc. CAT/C/SR.51, §18. See: Alan W. LEPP, "Note: The death penalty in late-imperial, modern and post-Tiananmen China," (1990) 11 *Mich. J. Int'l L.* 987, at pp. 1033–36.
243. U.N. Doc. CAT/C/SR.51, §37. See also the comments of Peter Burns: "Initial Report of China," Annex, U.N. Doc. CAT/C/7/Add.14, §51.
244. U.N. Doc. CAT/C/SR.51, §41.
245. LEPP, *supra* note 42, at pp. 1033–34.
246. *Id.*, at p. 1035. According to Lepp, in a 1956 speech Mao Zedong had suggested that capital punishment should be suppressed because it had no real advantages, it was prone to error, and it eliminated potential sources of labor. The 1957 criminal law provision suggested that China intended to abolish the death penalty eventually.
247. This was the case in South Africa, between the February 1990 moratorium and the judgment of the South African Constitutional Court in June 1995: *Makwanyane and Mchunu* v. *The State, supra* note 182. Also, for Zimbabwe: *Catholic Commission for Justice and Peace in Zimbabwe* v. *Attorney-General et al., supra* note 30; Jamaica: *Riley* v. *Attorney-General of Jamaica, supra* note 9, at pp. 479 (All E.R.), 735 (A.C.) (*per* Lords Scarman and Brightman, dissenting).
248. *Catholic Commission for Justice and Peace in Zimbabwe* v. *Attorney-General et al., supra* note 30.
249. *Riley* v. *Attorney-General of Jamaica, supra* note 9, at p. 724 (A.C.) (*per* Lord Bridge of Harwich), at p. 735 (A.C.) (*per* Lords Scarman and Brightman, dissenting).
250. *Id.*, at p. 735 (A.C.) (*per* Lords Scarman and Brightman, dissenting).
251. U.N. Doc. CAT/C/SR.161, §8.
252. For example: *Gilmore* v. *Utah, supra* note 35.
253. *Pratt et al.* v. *Attorney General for Jamaica et al., supra* note 24, at pp. 775 (All E.R.), 20 (A.C.).
254. *Id.*, at pp. 776 (All E.R.), 21 (A.C.).
255. *Id.*
256. *Id.*, at pp. 781 (All E.R.), 27 (A.C.).
257. *Id.*, at pp. 774 (All E.R.), 19 (A.C.).
258. *Id.*, at pp. 775 (All E.R.), 20 (A.C.).
259. *Id.*, at pp. 777 (All E.R.), 22 (A.C.).
260. *Id.*, at pp. 776 (All E.R.), 22 (A.C.).
261. *Id.*, at pp. 777 (All E.R.), 22 (A.C.).
262. *Id.*
263. *Id.*
264. Quoted in *id.*, at pp. 778 (All E.R.), 23–24 (A.C.).
265. *Pratt* v. *Jamaica, supra* note 92.
266. *Pratt and Morgan* v. *Jamaica, supra* note 25.
267. *Supra* note 88.
268. *Connelly* v. *Director of Public Prosecutions, supra* note 227.
269. *Pratt et al.* v. *Attorney General for Jamaica et al., supra* note 24, at pp. 774, 782 (All E.R.), 19–28 (A.C.).
270. *United States ex rel. Townsend* v. *Twomey, supra* note 37, at p. 174 (Perry, J.).
271. *Richmond* v. *Ricketts*, 640 F.Supp. 767, 803 (D.Ariz.1986).
272. *Id.*
273. *Richmond* v. *Lewis, supra* note 179, at p. 1491 n. 14.
274. In 1995, in *Lackey* v. *Texas, supra* note 45, Justice Stevens of the United States Supreme Court opened the door to such a case.

275. *Andrews* v. *Shulsen, supra* note 29; *Chessman* v. *Dickson, supra* note 49; *Harrison* v. *United States,* 392 U.S. 219, 88 S.Ct. 2008, 20 L.Ed.2d 1047 (1968).
276. *Richmond* v. *Lewis, supra* note 179, at p. 1491.
277. *Id.,* at pp. 1491–92.
278. *Andrews* v. *Shulsen, supra* note 29. And for yet another attempt by Andrews to litigate the matter, this time after fourteen years on death row: *State* v. *Andrews,* 843 P.2d 1027 (Utah 1992).
279. *District Atty. for Suffolk Dist.* v. *Watson, supra* note 23, at p. 1302 (N.E.2d) (Quirico, J., dissenting).
280. *Kindler* v. *Canada, supra* note 118, at p. 838 (S.C.R.).
281. *Id.*
282. See, for example: *Cox* v. *Canada, supra* note 138; *Francis* v. *Jamaica, supra* note 21.
283. *Sher Singh* v. *State of Punjab, supra* note 3, at p. 472 (A.I.R.) (*per* Chandrachud, C.J.).
284. *Pratt et al.* v. *Attorney General for Jamaica et al., supra* note 24, at pp. 783 (All E.R.), 29–30 (A.C.).
285. *Bradshaw* v. *Attorney General, supra* note 177, at §26 (*per* Lord Slynn of Hadley).
286. *Triveniben* v. *State of Gujarat, supra* note 162, at p. 143 (*per* Oza, J.). Even before *Triveniben,* there are suggestions of this approach in some Indian cases: *State* v. *Chempalal,* A.I.R. 1981 S.C. 1675.
287. *Catholic Commission for Justice and Peace in Zimbabwe* v. *Attorney-General et al., supra* note 30, at p. 266 (S.A.) (*per* Gubbay, C.J.).
288. *Tyrer* v. *United Kingdom,* April 25, 1978, Series A, No. 26, 2 E.H.R.R. 1, 59 I.L.R. 339, §9.
289. *Id.,* §9.
290. *Id.,* §33.
291. *Soering* v. *United Kingdom et al., supra* note 110, §56.
292. *Id.,* §106.
293. *Id.*
294. *Id.,* §111.
295. *De Freitas* v. *Benney, supra* note 62, at p. 243 (A.C.).
296. As was noted by Chief Justice Gubbay in *Catholic Commission for Justice and Peace in Zimbabwe* v. *Attorney-General et al., supra* note 30, at p. 267 (S.A.).
297. *Abbot* v. *A.-G of Trinidad and Tobago, supra* note 17, at p. 1345 (W.L.R.) (*per* Lord Diplock).
298. PANNICK, *supra* note 11, at p. 85.
299. *Riley* v. *Attorney-General of Jamaica, supra* note 9, at pp. 479 (All E.R.), 735 (A.C.) (*per* Lords Scarman and Brightman, dissenting).
300. Lord Griffiths felt that there was a degree of ambiguity in their reasons: "Their Lordships are therefore doubtful whether Lord Scarman and Lord Brightman would have regarded delay caused by appeals made within the time scale permitted by the State as time to be left out of account in computing the total period of delay." *Pratt et al.* v. *Attorney General for Jamaica et al., supra* note 24, at pp. 785 (All E.R.), 31 (A.C.).
301. *Vatheeswaran* v. *State of Tamil Nadu, supra* note 149, at p. 364 (A.I.R.) (*per* Chinnappa Reddy, J.)
302. *Sher Singh* v. *State of Punjab, supra* note 3, at p. 472 (A.I.R.).
303. *District Atty. for Suffolk Dist.* v. *Watson, supra* note 23, at p. 1283 (N.E.2d) (Hennessey, C.J., concurring).
304. *Catholic Commission for Justice and Peace in Zimbabwe* v. *Attorney-General et al., supra* note 30, at p. 259 (S.A.) (*per* Gubbay, C.J.).
305. *Id.,* at p. 267 (S.A.) (*per* Gubbay, C.J.).
306. *Richmond* v. *Lewis, supra* note 179.
307. *Kindler* v. *Canada, supra* note 118.
308. *Soering* v. *United Kingdom et al., supra* note 110.
309. *Catholic Commission for Justice and Peace in Zimbabwe* v. *Attorney-General et al., supra* note 30, at p. 264 (S.A.) (*per* Gubbay, C.J.).

310. *Pratt et al.* v. *Attorney General for Jamaica et al.*, *supra* note 24, at pp. 783 (All E.R.), 30 (A.C.).
311. *Id.*, at pp. 785 (All E.R.), 32 (A.C.).
312. *Id.*, at pp. 786 (All E.R.), 33 (A.C.).
313. *Id.*, at pp. 772 (All E.R.), 17 (A.C.).
314. *Nemi* v. *The State*, *supra* note 181, at p. 405 (*per* Ogwuegbu, J.S.C.).
315. *Id.*, at p. 381 (*per* Bello, C.J.N.).
316. *Lackey* v. *Texas*, *supra* note 45.
317. *State* v. *Richmond*, 886 P.2d 1329, 1333 (Ariz.1994) (Zlaket, J.).
318. *Soering* v. *United Kingdom et al.*, *supra* note 110, §§108–9, 111.
319. *Pratt et al.* v. *Attorney General for Jamaica et al.*, *supra* note 24, at pp. 783 (All E.R.), 29–30 (A.C.).
320. *Chessman* v. *Dickson*, *supra* note 49, at pp. 607–8.
321. *Catholic Commission for Justice and Peace in Zimbabwe* v. *Attorney-General et al.*, *supra* note 30, at p. 255 (S.A.) (*per* Gubbay, C.J.). Chief Justice Gubbay cites NOTE, (1959–60) 44 *Minn. L. Rev.* 994.
322. *Richmond* v. *Ricketts*, *supra* note 71, at p. 803.
323. *Id.*
324. JOHNSON, *supra* note 1, at p. 5.
325. *Rosenberg* v. *Carroll*, 99 F.Supp. 630 (S.D.N.Y.1951).
326. *Id.*, at pp. 632–33.
327. *Makwanyane and Mchunu* v. *The State*, *supra* note 182.
328. Nathan V. HOLT, "Human rights and capital punishment: The case of South Africa," (1989) 30 *Va. J. Int'l L.* 273, at pp. 315–16.
329. VOGELMAN, *supra* note 20, at pp. 191–94.
330. *Conjwayo* v. *Minister of Justice, Legal & Parliamentary Affairs*, [1991] 1 Z.L.R. 105, [1992] 2 S.A. 56 (S.C.), at p. 59 (*per* Gubbay, C.J.).
331. *Catholic Commission for Justice and Peace in Zimbabwe* v. *Attorney-General et al.*, *supra* note 30, at pp. 244, 245 (S.A.) (*per* Gubbay, C.J.); also *id.*, at pp. 268–69 (Z.L.R.).
332. *Conjwayo* v. *Minister of Justice, Legal & Parliamentary Affairs*, *supra* note 330, at p. 60 (S.A.) (*per* Gubbay, C.J.).
333. *Republic* v. *Mbushuu et al.*, [1994] 2 L.R.C. 335 (High Court of Tanzania), at p. 345.
334. Peter W. LEWIS, "Killing the killers: A post-*Furman* profile of Florida's condemned," (1975) 25 *Crime & Delinq.* 200, at p. 208.
335. *Id.*, at p. 209.
336. *Id.*
337. *Soering* v. *United Kingdom et al.*, *supra* note 110, §107.
338. *Id.*, §100.
339. *Id.*, §63.
340. *Id.*, §64.
341. *Id.*, §107.
342. *Id.*, §67.
343. *Id.*, §68.
344. *Sinclair* v. *Henderson*, 331 F.Supp. 1123, 1129–30 (E.D.La.1971).
345. *Groseclose ex rel. Harries* v. *Dutton*, 594 F.Supp. 949, 959–62 (M.D. Tenn.1984).
346. *District Atty. for Suffolk Dist.* v. *Watson*, *supra* note 23, at p. 1293 (N.E.2d) (Liacos, J., concurring).
347. *State* v. *Tomasi*, 75 N.J.L. 739, 769 A. 214, 218 (1908); *McElvaine* v. *Brush*, 142 U.S. 155, 12 S.Ct. 156, 35 L.Ed. 971 (1891). See: Richard G. SINGER, "Confining solitary confinement: Constitutional arguments for a new penology," (1971) 56 *Iowa L. Rev.* 1251.
348. *Sunil Batra* v. *Delhi Administration*, *supra* note 152. Also: *Vatheeswaran* v. *State of Tamil Nadu*, *supra* note 149, at p. 362 (A.I.R.) (*per* Chinnappa Reddy, J.).
349. *Supra* note 88.

350. "General Comment 7/16," U.N. Doc. CCPR/C/21/Add.1, §2.
351. "General Comment 20/44," U.N. Doc. CCPR/C/21/Rev.1/Add.3, §6.
352. See: "General Comment 7/16," *supra* note 350, §2. Also, "General Comment 9/16," U.N. Doc. CCPR/C/21/Add.1, §3.
353. *Antonaccio v. Uruguay* (No. R.14/63), U.N. Doc. A/37/40, at p. 114.
354. *De Voituret v. Uruguay* (No. 109/1981), U.N. Doc. A/39/40, at p. 164.
355. *Marais v. Madagascar* (No. 49/179, U.N. Doc. A/38/40, at p. 141.
356. *Wight v. Madagascar* (No. 115/1982), U.N. Doc. A/40/40, at p. 171.
357. J. E. S. FAWCETT, *The Application of the European Convention on Human Rights*, 2d ed., Oxford: Clarendon Press, 1987, at pp. 47–48; *Hilton v. United Kingdom* (App. no. 5613/72), (1976) 4 D.R. 177, 3 E.H.R.R. 104; *Bonzi v. Switzerland* (App. no. 7854/77), (1978) 12 D.R. 185, at p. 189.
358. *Ireland v. United Kingdom* (App. no. 5310/71), (1976) 19 *Yearbook of the European Convention on Human Rights* 794; *Ensslin, Baader, Raspe v. Germany* (App. no. 7587/76), (1978) 14 D.R. 109; *McFeeley et al.* v. *United Kingdom* (App. no. 8317/78), (1980) 20 D.R. 82. For a critique of the European Commission's caselaw, see: Antonio CASSESE, "Prohibition of torture and inhuman or degrading treatment or punishment," in R. St. J. MACDONALD et al., eds., *The European System for the Protection of Human Rights*, Dordrecht, London, and Boston: Martinus Nijhoff, 1993, pp. 225–61, at pp. 237–41.
359. *Koskinen v. Finland* (App. no. 20560/92), (1994) 14 E.H.R.R. CD146, at p. CD158; *Kröcher et al.* v. *Switzerland* (App. no. 8463/78), (1982) 34 D.R. 24, at p. 53.
360. UNITED KINGDOM, *supra* note 10, at p. 265.
361. *Conjwayo v. Minister of Justice, Legal & Parliamentary Affairs*, *supra* note 330, at pp. 63–64 (S.A.) (*per* Gubbay, C.J.).
362. *Id.*
363. *Id.*, at p. 64 (S.A.) (*per* Gubbay, C.J.).
364. John HATCHARD, "Capital punishment in southern Africa: Some recent developments," (1994) 43 *I.C.L.Q.* 923, at p. 933.
365. *Supra* notes 34–43 and corresponding text.
366. *Dhlamini et al.* v. *Carter N.O. et al.*, *supra* note 59, at pp. 154–55 (R.L.R.), 454 (S.A.) (*per* Beadle, C.J.).
367. *Id.*, at pp. 155 (R.L.R.), 455 (S.A.) (*per* Beadle, C.J.).
368. *Catholic Commission for Justice and Peace in Zimbabwe* v. *Attorney-General et al.*, *supra* note 30, at p. 252 (S.A.) (*per* Gubbay, C.J.).
369. *Id.*, at p. 271 (S.A.) (*per* Gubbay, C.J.).
370. *Id.*
371. *Id.*, at p. 252 (S.A.) (*per* Gubbay, C.J.). See also PANNICK, *supra* note 11, at pp. 84–85.
372. *Javed Ahmed Abdul Hamid Pawala* v. *State of Maharashtra*, *supra* note 149, at p. 236 (A.I.R.) (*per* Chinnappa Reddy, J.); *Sher Singh* v. *State of Punjab*, *supra* note 3, at pp. 469, 472 (A.I.R.) (*per* Chandrachud, C.J.).

METHOD OF EXECUTION

1. *A Book against Oaths Ministered in the Courts of Ecclesiastical Commission*, quoted in Anthony F. GRANUCCI, " 'Nor cruel and unusual punishments inflicted': The original meaning," (1969) 57 *Cal. L. Rev.* 839, at pp. 848–49.
2. Richard L. PERRY, John C. COOPER, *Sources of Our Liberties*, Washington: American Bar Association, 1952, at p. 148.
3. GRANUCCI, *supra* note 1, at pp. 859–60.
4. Simon SCHAMA, *Citizens: A Chronicle of the French Revolution*, Toronto: Vintage Books, 1989, at pp. 619–24; John LAURENCE, *A History of Capital Punishment*, New York: Citadel Press,

1960, at pp. 28–40; Daniel ARASSE, *La Guillotine et l'imaginaire de la terreur*, Paris: Flammarion, 1987.

5. Stéphane RIALS, *La déclaration des droits de l'homme et du citoyen*, Paris: Hachette, 1988, at p. 548.

6. GRANUCCI, *supra* note 1, at pp. 841–42.

7. *Groseclose* v. *Dutton*, 609 F.Supp. 1432, 1440 (M.D.Tenn.1985).

8. *Glass* v. *Louisiana*, 471 U.S. 1080, 1086, 105 S.Ct. 2159, 2163 (1985) (Brennan, J., dissenting from denial of certiorari).

9. *Campbell* v. *Wood*, 18 F.3d 662, 695 (9th Cir. 1994) (Reinhardt, J., dissenting), *cert. denied*, 114 S.Ct. 2125 (1994) citing *Wilkerson* v. *Utah*, 99 U.S. 130, 135, 25 L.Ed. 345 (1878).

10. *Louisiana ex rel. Francis* v. *Resweber*, 329 U.S. 459, 463, 67 S.Ct. 374, 376, 91 L.Ed. 422 (1947).

11. *Campbell* v. *Wood*, *supra* note 9 (Beezer, J.).

12. *Rajendra Prasad* v. *State of Uttar Pradesh*, A.I.R. 1979 S.C. 916, 932 (Krishna Iyer, J.).

13. *R.* v. *Miller and Cockriell*, [1977] 2 S.C.R. 680, 31 C.C.C. (2d) 177, 38 C.R.N.S. 139, 70 D.L.R. (3d) 324, [1976] 5 W.W.R. 711, 11 N.R. 386, at p. 330 (D.L.R.).

14. *Murakami* v. *Japan. Hanriesbu* II, No. 3, 191 (Criminal), in John M. MAKI, ed., *Court and Constitution in Japan: Selected Supreme Court Decisions 1948–60*, Seattle: University of Washington Press, 1964, at pp. 156–64.

15. *In re Kemmler*, 136 U.S. 436, 446, 10. S.Ct. 930, 933, 34 L.Ed. 519 (1890), *affirming* 119 N.Y. 569, 7 L.R.Q. 715, 16 Am.St.Rep. 859, 24 N.E. 6 (1890).

16. *Glass* v. *Louisiana*, *supra* note 8, at p. 1083 (U.S.) (Brennan, J., dissenting from denial of certiorari); *Fierro* v. *Gomez*, 790 F.Supp. 966, 970 (N.D.Cal. 1992) (Patel, J.); *State* v. *Kilpatrick*, 439 P.2d 99, 110 (Kan. 1968).

17. *Deena* v. *Union of India*, A.I.R. 1983 S.C. 1155, [1983] Cri. L.J. 1602, at p. 1173 (A.I.R.) (Chandrachud, C.J.).

18. *Id.*

19. International Covenant on Civil and Political Rights, (1976) 999 U.N.T.S. 171.

20. "General Comment 20/44," U.N. Doc. CCPR/C/21/Rev.1/Add.3, §6. The committee also took the occasion to reiterate that "article 6 of the Covenant refers generally to abolition of the death penalty in terms that strongly suggest that abolition is desirable." The committee's position has been expressly endorsed by at least one state party, Canada, which has said: "It may be that certain forms of execution are contrary to article 7. Torturing a person to death would seem to fall into this category as torture is a violation of article 7. Other forms of execution may be in violation of the Covenant because they are cruel, inhuman or degrading." *Kindler* v. *Canada* (No. 470/1991), (1993) 14 *H.R.L.J.* 307, 6 *R.U.D.H.* 165, §9.6.

21. "Initial Report of China," U.N. Doc. CAT/C/7/Add.14, §126. See also: "Initial Report of China," Annex, U.N. Doc. CAT/C/7/Add.14, §51.

22. *Makwanyane and Mchunu* v. *The State*, (1995) 16 *H.R.L.J.* 154, at p. 207 (*per* Sachs, J.) (references omitted).

23. U.N. Doc. E/CN.4/1994/48.

24. "Statement by H.E. Mr Abdelaziz Shiddo, Minister of Justice and Attorney-General of the Republic of the Sudan and Leader of Sudan Delegation to the 50th Session of the Commission on Human Rights, Commenting on the report of Dr. Gaspar Biro, Special Rapporteur on Human Rights situation in the Sudan under agenda item (12)," Geneva, February 25, 1994. See also: U.N. Doc. E/CN.4/1994/122, §§58–64.

25. G.A. Res. 44/25, 28 I.L.M. 1448.

26. One of the few exceptions is the United States, which signed the Convention only in February 1995, and has yet to ratify it.

27. *Louisiana ex rel. Francis* v. *Resweber*, *supra* note 10.

28. *Ng* v. *Canada* (No. 469/1991), (1994) 15 *H.R.L.J.* 149.

29. *In re Kemmler*, *supra* note 15, at p. 447 (U.S.).

30. UNITED KINGDOM, *Royal Commission on Capital Punishment, 1949–1953, Report,* London: Her Majesty's Stationery Office, 1953, at p. 253.
31. *Id.*
32. *Campbell* v. *Wood, supra* note 9, at p. 695 (Reinhardt, J., dissenting).
33. UNITED KINGDOM, *supra* note 30, at p. 253.
34. *Louisiana ex rel. Francis* v. *Resweber, supra* note 10, at pp. 464 (U.S.), 381 (S.Ct.) (Reed, J.).
35. *Campbell* v. *Wood, supra* note 9, at p. 697 (Reinhardt, J., dissenting).
36. *Id.*
37. *Furman* v. *Georgia,* 408 U.S. 238, 261, 92 S.Ct. 2726, 2737, 33 L.Ed.2d 346 (1972); *Thompson* v. *Oklahoma,* 487 U.S. 815, 108 S.Ct. 2687, 101 L.Ed.2d 702 (1988); *Stanford* v. *Kentucky,* 492 U.S. 361, 109 S.Ct. 2969, 106 L.Ed.2d 306 (1989); *Harmelin* v. *Michigan,* 501 U.S. 957, 111 S.Ct. 2686, 115 L.Ed.2d 836 (1991).
38. *Trop* v. *Dulles,* 356 U.S. 86, 101, 78 S.Ct. 590, 598, 2 L.Ed.2d 630 (1958); *Stanford* v. *Kentucky, supra* note 37, at pp. 369 (U.S.), 2974 (S.Ct.).
39. *Louisiana ex rel. Francis* v. *Resweber, supra* note 10; *Rhodes* v. *Chapman,* 452 U.S. 337, 101 S.Ct. 23, 69 L.Ed.2d 59 (1981); *Campbell* v. *Wood, supra* note 9, at p. 668.
40. *Ng* v. *Canada, supra* note 28. In the dissenting opinion of members A. Mavrommatis and W. Sadi, who were not offended by the gas chamber, lapidation is given as an example of a method of execution that violates article 7: *ibid.,* at p. 25.
41. *Louisiana ex rel. Francis* v. *Resweber, supra* note 10, at pp. 464 (U.S.), 376 (S.Ct.).
42. *Ng* v. *Canada, supra* note 28, at pp. 162–63.
43. *Id.*
44. *Glass* v. *Louisiana, supra* note 8, at pp. 1093–94 (U.S.) (Brennan, J., dissenting from denial of certiorari).
45. *Campbell* v. *Wood, supra* note 9, at p. 702, citing *Wilkerson* v. *Utah, supra* note 9, at pp. 135–36 (U.S.).
46. *State* v. *Ross,* 230 Conn. 183, 646 A.2d 1318, 1378–79 (1994) (Berdon, A.J., dissenting in part).
47. Lonny J. HOFFMAN, "The madness of the method: The use of electrocution and the death penalty," (1992) 70 *Tex. L. Rev.* 1039, at p. 1041.
48. Linda J. NORRIS, "Constitutional law: The death penalty as punishment for murder does not violate the eighth amendment," (1976) 8 *Tex. Tech. L. Rev.* 515, at p. 523 n. 62.
49. HOFFMAN, *supra* note 47, at p. 1041.
50. *Hamblen* v. *Dugger,* 748 F.Supp. 1498, 1504–5 (M.D.Fla.1990), *cert. denied,* 110 S.Ct. 3289 (1990).
51. *Deena* v. *Union of India, supra* note 17, at p. 1186 (A.I.R.) (Chandrached, C.J.).
52. As was noted by an expert witness in *State* v. *Frampton,* 95 Wash.2d 469, 627 P.2d 922, 935 (1981) (Dolliver, J.)
53. *Campbell* v. *Wood, supra* note 9, at p. 693 n. 3 (Reinhardt, J., dissenting), citing *Hudson* v. *McMillian,* 112 S.Ct. 995, 1001, 117 L.Ed.2d 156 (1992); *Estelle* v. *Gamble,* 429 U.S. 97, 102–3, 97 S.Ct. 285, 290, 50 L.Ed.2d 251 (1976).
54. *Campbell* v. *Wood, supra* note 9, at p. 694.
55. Robert JOHNSON, *Death Work: A Study of the Modern Execution Process,* Pacific Grove, Cal.: Brooks/Cole, 1990.
56. HOFFMAN, *supra* note 47, at p. 1043.
57. Stephen TROMBLEY, *The Execution Protocol,* New York: Random House, 1992, at pp. 51–63, 71.
58. PLATO, *The Trial and Death of Socrates,* trans. G. M. A. Grube, Indianapolis: Hackett, 1988, at p. 57.
59. UNITED KINGDOM, *supra* note 30, at p. 266.
60. *Id.*
61. *Id.* In many jurisdictions suicide is not a crime, although assisting suicide usually remains subject to criminal sanctions. See, for example: *Rodriguez* v. *British Columbia* [1993] 3 S.C.R.

519, 79 C.C.C. (3d) 1, [1993] 3 W.W.R. 553, 76 B.C.L.R. (2d) 145; Joan M. GILMOUR, "Withholding and withdrawing life support from adults at common law," (1993) 31 *Osgoode Hall L.J.* 473; Ian DUNDAS, "Case comment: *Rodriguez* and assisted suicide in Canada," (1994) 32 *Alta. L. Rev.* 811; Mark E. CHOPKO, Michael F. MOSES, "Assisted suicide: Still a wonderful life," (1995) 70 *Notre Dame L. Rev.* 519.

62. *Catholic Commission for Justice and Peace in Zimbabwe* v. *Attorney-General et al.*, [1993] 4 S.A. 239 (Z.S.C.), [1993] 1 Z.L.R. 242 (S), 14 *H.R.L.J.* 323.

63. Telford TAYLOR, *The Anatomy of the Nuremberg Trials*, New York: Alfred A. Knopf, 1992, at p. 609.

64. UNITED KINGDOM, *supra* note 30, at p. 253.

65. *Id.*, at p. 247.

66. *Republic* v. *Mbushuu et al.*, [1994] 2 L.R.C. 335 (High Court of Tanzania), at p. 343.

67. At least one work suggests that Francis was not resposible for the crime: Arthur S. MILLER, Jeffrey H. BOWMAN, *Death by Installments: The Ordeal of Willie Francis*, Westport (Conn.), New York, and London: Greenwood Press, 1988. Use of capital punishment for crimes committed while under the age of eighteen is prohibited by several international conventions, and furthermore, according to the United Nations Human Rights Committee, violates customary international human-rights law: "General Comment No. 24/52," U.N. Doc. CCPR/C/21/ Rev.1/Add.6 (1994), 15 *H.R.L.J.* 464, §8.

68. Felix FRANKFURTER, *Of Law and Men*, New York: Harcourt Brace, 1956, at p. 98. See the chapter "Frankfurter's Extrajudicial Machinations" in MILLER, BOWMAN, *supra* note 67, at pp. 123–30.

69. *Louisiana ex rel. Francis* v. *Resweber*, *supra* note 10, at pp. 471 (U.S.), 380 (S.Ct.).

70. UNITED KINGDOM, *supra* note 30, at p. 247.

71. *Id.*

72. *Id.*, at p. 259.

73. Washington Revised Code § 10.95.180. "The punishment of death . . . shall be inflicted either by hanging by the neck or, at the election of the defendant, by intravenous injection of a substance or substances in a lethal quantity."

74. *State* v. *Rupe*, 101 Wash.2d 664, 683 P.2d 571, 594 (1984) (Rosellini, J.).

75. *Id.*

76. *State* v. *Campbell*, 770 P.2d 620, 623 (Wash.1989).

77. *Campbell* v. *Blodgett*, 978 F.2d 1502, 1517 (9th Cir.1992) (Hug, Poole, and Hall, JJ.).

78. *Id.*, at pp. 1517–18 (Hug, Poole, and Hall, JJ.).

79. *Id.*, at p. 1518 (Hug, Poole, and Hall, JJ.).

80. *Campbell* v. *Wood*, *supra* note 9, at p. 680 (en banc). Followed in *Hunt* v. *Nuth*, 57 F.3d 1327 (4th Cir. 1995).

81. *Campbell* v. *Wood*, *supra* note 9, at p. 681 (Reinhardt, J., dissenting).

82. Steven STACK, "Publicized executions and homicide, 1950–1980," (1987) 52 *Am. Soc. Rev.* 532; W. C. BAILEY, "Murder, capital punishment, and television: Execution publicity and homicide rates," (1990) 55 *Am. Soc. Rev.* 628; Steven STACK, "The impact of publicized executions on homicide," (1995) 22 *Crim. Just. & Behav.* 172; Jef I. RICHARDS, R. Bruce EASTER, "Televising executions: The high-tech alternative to public hangings," (1992) 40 *U.C.L.A. L. Rev.* 381.

83. Roger HOOD, *The Death Penalty: A Worldwide Perspective*, Oxford: Clarendon Press, 1989, pp. 77–79.

84. "Nigeria: 32 prisoners convicted of armed robbery," AI Index: AFR 44/17/95.

85. Jill COTTRELL, "Wrestling with the death penalty in India," (1991) 7 *South African J. Hum. Rts.* 185, at p. 188.

86. *Attorney General of India* v. *Lachma Devi*, A.I.R. 1986 S.C. 467, [1986] L.R.C. (Crim.) 1, at p. 468 (A.I.R.) (Bhagwata, C.J.; Madon and Oza, JJ.).

87. *Garrett* v. *Estelle*, 424 F.Supp. 468, 470 (N.D.Tex.), *rev'd*, 556 F.2d 1274 (5th Cir.1977), *cert.*

denied, 438 U.S. 914 (1978). Also: *KQED Inc.* v. *Vasquez*, No. C-90-1383 RHS, 1991 U.S. Dist. LEXIS 19791 (N.D. Cal. 1991).

88. *Fierro* v. *Gomez*, No. C-92-1482 MHP, 1992 WL 566298 (N.D. Cal. April 21, 1992); *In re Donald Thomas*, 155 FRD (D.Md.1994). See also: Marcia COYLE, "Inmate wants execution taped," *National Law Journal*, February 21, 1994.

89. UNITED KINGDOM, *supra* note 30, at p. 246. See: David C. COOPER, *The Lesson of the Scaffold: The Public Execution Controversy in Victorian England*, Athens: Ohio University Press, 1974.

90. *An Act to provide for the carrying out of capital punishment within prisons*, 31 VICT. c. 24.

91. UNITED KINGDOM, *supra* note 30, at p. 256.

92. *Campbell* v. *Wood, supra* note 9, at p. 702 (Reinhardt, J., dissenting).

93. U.N. Doc. CAT/C/SR.135, §26.

94. UNITED KINGDOM, *supra* note 30, at p. 246.

95. *Id.*, at p. 246.

96. *De Freitas* v. *Benny*, [1976] A.C. 239, [1975] 3 W.L.R. 388 (J.C.P.C.), at p. 246 (A.C.).

97. William BLACKSTONE, *Commentaries on the Laws of England*, IV, at p. 377.

98. *Wilkerson* v. *Utah, supra* note 9, at p. 134.

99. UNITED KINGDOM, *supra* note 30, at p. 247.

100. *Campbell* v. *Wood, supra* note 9, at p. 684 (Beezer, J.).

101. *Ichikawa* v. *Japan*, 15 Keishu 7, at p. 1106 (July 19, 1961), in Horoshi ITOH, Lawrence Ward BEER, eds., *The Constitutional Case Law of Japan: Selected Supreme Court Decisions 1961–70*, Seattle: University of Washington Press, 1978, at pp. 161–63.

102. UNITED KINGDOM, *supra* note 30, at p. 249.

103. *Id.*, at p. 250.

104. *Campbell* v. *Wood, supra* note 9, at p. 683 (Beezer, J.).

105. Martin R. GARDNER, "Executions and indignities—An eighth amendment assessment of methods of inflicting capital punishment," (1978) 39 *Ohio State L.J.* 96, at p. 120.

106. UNITED KINGDOM, *supra* note 30, at p. 246.

107. *Id.*, at p. 248.

108. *Id.*, at p. 261.

109. I have found no reports of women who serve as executioners, and it seems unnecessary to coin a gender-neutral term.

110. CANADA, HOUSE OF COMMONS, SPECIAL COMMITTEE ON THE CRIMINAL CODE (DEATH PENALTY), *Minutes of Proceedings and Evidence*, March 4, 1937, at p. 46.

111. *Catholic Commission for Justice and Peace in Zimbabwe* v. *Attorney-General et al., supra* note 62, at p. 268 (S.A.) (Gubbay, CJ.).

112. *State* v. *Frampton, supra* note 52, at p. 934 (P.2d) (Dolliver, J.). See also: *Campbell* v. *Wood, supra* note 9, at p. 700 (Reinhardt, J., dissenting).

113. *State* v. *Tomasi*, 75 N.J.L. 739, 69 A. 214, 217 (1908) (Pitney, J.).

114. *Id.*, at pp. 217–18 (Pitney, J.).

115. *Brown* v. *State*, 6 Div. 128, 264 So.2d 529, 534 (1971).

116. *Id.*, at pp. 538–39 (So.2d).

117. *Andres* v. *United States*, 333 U.S. 740, 745 n. 6, 68 S.Ct. 880, 883 n. 6, 92 L.Ed. 1055 (1948), quoting H.R. Rep No. 164, 75th Cong., 1st Sess, at 1.

118. Gary E. HOOD, "*Campbell* v. *Wood*: The death penalty in Washington State: 'Hanging' on to a method of execution," (1994–95) 30 *Gonz. L. Rev.* 163, at p. 177.

119. UNITED KINGDOM, *supra* note 30, at p. 247.

120. *Deena* v. *Union of India, supra* note 17, at p. 1177 (A.I.R.) (Chandrachud, C.J.).

121. *Id.*

122. *Bachan Singh* v. *State of Punjab*, A.I.R. 1982 S.C. 1325, at p. 1347 (Bhagwati, J.).

123. UNITED KINGDOM, *supra* note 30, at p. 260.

124. *Id.*, at p. 256.

125. *Id.*, at p. 248.

126. *State* v. *Butchek*, 253 P. 367, 370 (Or.1927). See also: *State* v. *Finch*, 54 Or. 482, 103 P. 505 (1909).

127. *State* v. *Kilpatrick*, 201 Kan. 6, 439 P.2d 99, 110 (1968).

128. *State* v. *Burris*, 190 N.W. 38, 43 (Iowa 1922).

129. *DeShields* v. *State*, 534 A.2d 630, 640 (Del.1987), *cert. denied*, 486 U.S. 1017, 108 S.Ct. 1754, 100 L.Ed.2d 217 (1988). See also: *State* v. *Cannon*, 190 A.2d 514, 516–18 (Del.1963).

130. *State* v. *Frampton, supra* note 52, at p. 933 (P.2d) (Dolliver, J.). Also: *State* v. *Rupe, supra* note 74, at p. 701 (Wash.2d), 593 (P.2d).

131. *State* v. *Frampton, supra* note 52, at p. 944 (P.2d) (Rosellini, J., concurring in part, dissenting in part).

132. *DeShields* v. *State, supra* note 129, at p. 639 (A.2d).

133. *McKenzie* v. *Osborne*, 195 Mont. 26, 640 P.2d 368 (1981). See also: *State* v. *Coleman*, 185 Mont. 299, 605 P.2d 1000, 1059 (1979), *cert. denied*, 446 U.S. 970, 100 S.Ct. 2952, 64 L.Ed.2d 831; *Fitzpatrick* v. *State*, 638 P.2d 1002, 1011 (Mont.1981).

134. *State* v. *Campbell*, 112 Wash.2d 186, 770 P.2d 620, 623 (1989).

135. *DeShields* v. *State, supra* note 129, at p. 639 (A.2d).

136. HOOD, *supra* note 118.

137. *Campbell* v. *Wood, supra* note 9, at p. 685 (Beezer, J.).

138. *Id.*, at p. 682 (Beezer, J.). For the minority view, see p. 698.

139. *Id.*, at p. 697 (Reinhardt, J., dissenting).

140. *Id.*, at pp. 683–84 (Beezer, J.), citing Ryk JAMES, Rachel NASMYTH-JONES, "The occurrence of cervical fractures in victims of judicial hanging," (1992) 54 *Forensic Sci. Int'l* 81.

141. *Id.*, at p. 684 (Beezer, J.).

142. *Id.*

143. *Id.*

144. *Id.*

145. *Id.*, at p. 685 (Beezer, J.).

146. *Id.*

147. *State* v. *Frampton, supra* note 52, at p. 934 (P.2d) (Dolliver, J.).

148. *Id.*

149. *Campbell* v. *Wood, supra* note 9, at pp. 685–86. In an earlier case, a Washington court had observed: "Incidents in which the victims of judicial hanging have not died instantaneously, but have suffered lingering and at times violent deaths are numerous in Washington history." *State* v. *Frampton, supra* note 52, at p. 935 (P.2d) (Dolliver, J.).

150. *Campbell* v. *Wood, supra* note 9, at pp. 686–87.

151. *Id.*, at p. 694 (Reinhardt, J., dissenting).

152. *Id.*

153. *Id.*, at p. 712 (Reinhardt, J., dissenting).

154. *Id.*, at p. 712 n. 38 (Reinhardt, J., dissenting).

155. *Id.*, at p. 701 (Reinhardt, J., dissenting).

156. *Id.*

157. *Id.*

158. *Id.*

159. *Chileya* v. *S.*, S.C. 64/90 (unreported). See: John HATCHARD, "Capital punishment in southern Africa: Some recent developments," (1994) 43 *I.C.L.Q.* 923, at pp. 924–25.

160. ZIMBABWE, *Parliamentary Debates*, 6 Dec. 1990.

161. *Id.*

162. *Republic* v. *Mbushuu et al., supra* note 66, at p. 345.

163. *Id.*, at p. 351.

164. *Mbushuu and Another* v. *The Republic*, Court of Appeal of Tanzania, Criminal Appeal No. 142 of 1994, unreported judgment of January 30, 1995.

165. "Initial Report of China," Annex, U.N. Doc. CAT/C/7/Add.14, §51.

166. Utah: Utah Code Ann. §77-19-10 (1973), although recent amendments also provide for lethal injection: *id.*, §77-19-10(2) (Supp.1983); and Belarus: "Initial Report of the Byelorussian Soviet Socialist Republic," U.N. Doc. CCPR/C/1/Add.27.
167. *Wilkerson* v. *Utah, supra* note 9.
168. *Gregg* v. *Georgia*, 428 U.S. 153, 96 S.Ct. 2909, 49 L.Ed.2d 859 (1976).
169. *Andrews* v. *Shulsen*, 600 F.Supp. 408, 431 (D.Utah 1984), *aff'd*, 802 F.2d 1256 (10th Cir.1986), *cert. denied*, 485 U.S. 919, 108 S.Ct. 1091, 99 L.Ed.2d 253, *reh'g denied*, 485 U.S. 1015, 108 S.Ct. 1491, 99 L.Ed.2d 718 (1988).
170. UNITED KINGDOM, *supra* note 30, at p. 249.
171. Negley K. TEETERS, Jack H. HEDBLOM, ". . . *Hang by the Neck* . . .": *The Legal Use of Scaffold and Noose, Gibbet, Stake, and Firing Squad from Colonial Times to the Present*, Springfield, Ill.: Charles C. Thomas, 1967, at pp. 445–46; Charles P. LARROWE, "Notches on a chair: Utah firing squad," *Nation*, vol. 182, no. 15 (April 14, 1956), p. 291.
172. Michael V. DISALLE, Lawrence G. BLOCHMAN, *The Power of Life or Death*, New York: Random House, 1965, at pp. 20–21.
173. AMNESTY INTERNATIONAL, *"When the State Kills* . . . , *The Death Penalty: A Human Rights Issue*, New York: Amnesty International, 1989, at p. 60.
174. Harold HILLMAN, "The possible pain experienced during execution by different methods," (1993) 22 *Perception* 745, at p. 747.
175. UNITED KINGDOM, *supra* note 30, at p. 249.
176. *Campbell* v. *Wood, supra* note 9, at p. 706 (Reinhardt, J., dissenting).
177. *Glass* v. *Louisiana, supra* note 8, at pp. 1085 (U.S.), 2162–63 (S.Ct.) (Brennan, J., dissenting from denial of certiorari).
178. Albert CAMUS, "Réflexions sur la guillotine," in Albert CAMUS, Arthur KOESTLER, *Réflexions sur la peine capitale*, Paris: Clamann-Lévy, 1957, at pp. 134–35.
179. N. G. GREGORY, S. B. WOOTON, "Sheep slaughtering procedures: Time to loss of brain responsiveness after exsanguination or cardiac arrest," (1984) 140 *Brit. Veterinary J.* 354.
180. HILLMAN, *supra* note 174, at p. 747.
181. "[E]lectrocution almost never results in *instantaneous* death," and the need for recurrent shocks is commonplace: HOFFMAN, *supra* note 47, at p. 1055.
182. *Glass* v. *Louisiana, supra* note 8, at p. 1086 n. 13 (U.S.) (Brennan, J., dissenting from denial of certiorari), quoting Lewis Edward LAWES, *Life and Death in Sing Sing*, New York: Doubleday, 1928, at p. 170.
183. New York, *Laws* (1888), c. 489, sec. 505; "Note," (1890–91) 4 *Harv. L. Rev.* 287; Carlos F. MACDONALD, "The infliction of the death penalty by means of electricity: Being a report of seven cases," (1892) *Transactions of the Medical Society of New York* 400; Larry Charles BERKSON, *The Concept of Cruel and Unusual Punishment*, Lexington, Mass.: D. C. Heath, 1975, at pp. 23–29; James W. GARNER, "Infliction of the death penalty by electrocution," (1910) 1 *J. Crim. L. & Criminology* 626; E. A. SPIZKA, H. E. RADASCH, "The brain lesions produced by electricity as observed after legal execution," (1912) 44 *Am. J. Med. Sci.* 341; S. P. KLEIN, "Capital punishment in the electric chair," (1914) 49 *N.Y. Med. J.* 1089; LAURENCE, *supra* note 4, at pp. 63–68.
184. *Malloy* v. *South Carolina*, 237 U.S. 180, 185, 35 S.Ct. 507, 509, 59 L.Ed. 905 (1915).
185. Tex. Gen. Laws ch 51, §§1, 14.
186. *State ex rel. Pierre* v. *Jones*, 200 La. 808, 9 So.2d 42, 43 (1942).
187. *Glass* v. *Louisiana, supra* note 8, at p. 1081 (U.S.) (Brennan, J., dissenting from denial of certiorari).
188. GARDNER, *supra* note 105, at p. 126 n. 228.
189. UNITED KINGDOM, *supra* note 30, at p. 251.
190. *Id.*
191. *Kemmler's case* was based on the state constitution and was not, strictly speaking, an Eighth

Amendment case, although it has been viewed as such since then: NOTE, (1980–91) 4 *Harv. L. Rev.* 287.

192. *In re Kemmler, supra* note 15, at pp. 442–43 (U.S.)

193. In *Glass* v. *Louisiana, supra* note 8, at p. 1082 (U.S.) (Brennan, J., dissenting from denial of certiorari), Justice Brennan cites the *Report of the Commission to Investigate and Report the Most Humane and Practical Method of Carrying into Effect the Sentence of Death in Capital Cases* (Jan. 17, 1888).

194. Deborah W. DENNO, "Is electrocution an unconstitutional method of execution? The engineering of death over the century," (1994) 35 *Wm. & Mary L. Rev.* 551, at p. 577.

195. HOFFMAN, *supra* note 47, at p. 1044.

196. See, for a review of *Kemmler*, as well as an exhaustive treatment of the constitutionality of electrocution in United States law: DENNO, *supra* note 194.

197. *New York Times*, August 7, 1890, at p. 1.

198. *McElvaine* v. *Brush*, 142 U.S. 155, 12 S.Ct. 156, 35 L.Ed. 971 (1891); *Hart* v. *Commonwealth*, 109 S.E. 582, 587 (Va.1921); *Dix* v. *Newsome*, 584 F.Supp. 1052, 1068 (N.D.Ga.1984).

199. *State* v. *Woodward*, 68 W.Va. 66, 30 L.R.A. (N.S.) 1004, 69 S.E. 385, 388 (W.Va.1910).

200. *In re Storti*, 60 N.E. 210, 210 (Mass.1901) (Holmes, C.J.).

201. *Hobbs* v. *State*, 133 Ind. 404, 32 N.E. 1019, 1021, 18 L.R.A. 774 (1893).

202. *Glass* v. *Louisiana, supra* note 8, at pp. 1086–88 (U.S.) (Brennan, J., dissenting from denial of certiorari) (references omitted).

203. *Id.*, at p. 1088 (U.S.) (Brennan, J., dissenting from denial of certiorari).

204. *Id.*, at p. 1089 (U.S.) (Brennan, J., dissenting from denial of certiorari).

205. *Kindler* v. *Canada*, [1991] 2 S.C.R. 779, 67 C.C.C. (3d) 1, 84 D.L.R. (4th) 438, 6 C.R.R. (2d) 193, at p. 816 (S.C.R.) (*per* Cory, J., dissenting), citing Robert JOHNSON, *Condemned to Die: Life Under Sentence of Death*, New York: Elsevier, 1981, at pp. 86–87.

206. *Glass* v. *Louisiana, supra* note 8, at pp. 1089–92 (U.S.) (Brennan, J., dissenting from denial of certiorari).

207. *Id.*, at p. 1089 (U.S.) (Brennan, J., dissenting from denial of certiorari).

208. Francis committed his crime at the age of sixteen. A book on the case suggests he was wrongly convicted: see MILLER, BOWMAN, *supra* note 67.

209. *Louisiana ex rel. Francis* v. *Resweber, supra* note 10.

210. MILLER, BOWMAN, *supra* note 67, at p. 7.

211. *Louisiana ex rel. Francis* v. *Resweber, supra* note 10, at p. 480 n. 2 (U.S.) (Burton, J., dissenting).

212. *Id.*

213. *Id.*

214. *Id.*

215. MILLER, BOWMAN, *supra* note 67, at pp. 10–11.

216. *Louisiana ex rel. Francis* v. *Resweber, supra* note 10, at p. 462 (U.S.), 375 (S.Ct.) (Reed, J.).

217. *Id.*, at pp. 464 (U.S.), 376 (S.Ct.) (Reed, J.). Justice Reed's reliance on "purpose to inflict unnecessary pain" is an original contribution to Eighth Amendment jurisprudence. This had not previously been decided, and no precedent was cited to support such an affirmation: HOFFMAN, *supra* note 47, at p. 1048.

218. *Louisiana ex rel. Francis* v. *Resweber, supra* note 10, at pp. 476 (U.S.), 382 (S.Ct.) (Burton, J., dissenting).

219. *Id.*, at pp. 477 (U.S.), 382 (S.Ct.) (Burton, J., dissenting).

220. *Id.*, at pp. 474 (U.S.), 381 (S.Ct.) (Burton, J., dissenting).

221. *Id.*

222. *New York Times*, December 13, 1984, p. A18, col. 1; December 17, 1984, p. A22, col. 1.

223. *Thomas* v. *Jones*, 742 F.Supp. 598, 605 (S.D.Ala.1990).

224. *Id.*

225. *Id.*

226. *Id.*

227. *Id.*, at p. 606.
228. *Id.*, at p. 607.
229. *Ritter* v. *Smith*, 568 F.Supp. 1499 (S.D.Ala.1983), *aff'd in part, rev'd in part*, 726 F.2d 1505 (11th Cir.), *cert. denied*, 469 U.S. 869 (1984).
230. Whose execution required three jolts of electricity and took fourteen minutes: HOFFMAN, *supra* note 47, at p. 1056.
231. *Id.*, at p. 1051.
232. *Ritter* v. *Smith*, *supra* note 229.
233. Affidavit of Russell F. Canan (June 22, 1983), filed in support of application for certiorari, quoted by Justice Brennan in *Glass* v. *Louisiana, supra* note 8, at pp. 1091–92 (U.S.) (Brennan, J., dissenting from denial of certiorari).
234. *Id.*, at p. 1093 (U.S.) (Brennan, J., dissenting from denial of certiorari).
235. *Hamblen* v. *Dugger, supra* note 50, at p. 1051.
236. HOFFMAN, *supra* note 47, at p. 1052.
237. *Buenoano* v. *State*, 656 So.2d 309, 311 (Fla.1990).
238. *Id.*, at p. 312 (Fla.1990) (Barkett, J., dissenting).
239. *Id.*, at p. 314 (Fla.1990) (Kogan, J., dissenting).
240. *Id.*, at pp. 313–14 (Fla.1990) (Kogan, J., dissenting).
241. *Id.*, at p. 314 (Fla.1990) (Kogan, J., dissenting).
242. *Id.*
243. *Id.*
244. *Id.*, at p. 315 (Fla.1990) (Kogan, J., dissenting).
245. *Hamblen* v. *State*, 565 So.2d 320 (Fla.1990); *Squires* v. *State*, 565 So.2d 318 (Fla.1990); *Bertolotti* v. *State*, 565 So.2d 1343 (Fla.1990).
246. *Hamblen* v. *Dugger, supra* note 50, at p. 1504.
247. UNITED KINGDOM, *supra* note 30, at p. 255.
248. *State* v. *Gee Jon*, 46 Nev. 418, 211 P. 676 (1923).
249. *Id.*, at p. 682.
250. *Hernandez.* v. *Arizona*, 43 Ariz. 424, 32 P.2d 18 (1934); *State* v. *Brice*, 214 N.C. 34, 197 S.E. 690 (1938); *People* v. *Daugherty*, 40 Cal.2d 876, 256 P.2d 911 (1953), *cert. denied*, 346 U.S. 827 (1953); *In re Anderson*, 69 Cal.2d 63, 73 Cal.Rptr. 21, 447 P.2d 117 (1968), *cert. denied*, 406 U.S. 971, 92 S.Ct. 2415, 32 L.Ed.2d 671 (1972). For scholarly writing on the subject at the time the gas chamber was introduced, see Robert A. MAURER, "Death by lethal gas," (1921) 9 *Geo. L.J.* 50; Raymond HARTMANN, "The use of lethal gas in Nevada executions," (1923) 8 *St. Louis U. L. Rev.* 167.
251. *People* v. *Daugherty, supra* note 250, at p. 922 (P.2d).
252. *Id.*; *Gray* v. *Lucas*, 710 F.2d 1048 (5th Cir.1983), *cert. denied*, 463 U.S. 1237, 104 S.Ct. 211, 77 L.Ed.2d (1983); *Gomez* v. *U.S. Dist. Court for N.D. of Cal.*, 112 S.Ct. 1652, 1653 (1992).
253. Cal. Penal code §3604; N.C. Gen. Stat. §15-187; Md. Ann. Code art. 27, §71.
254. Miss. Code Ann. §99-19-51; Ariz. Rev. Stat. Ann., Ariz. Const. Art. 22 §22.
255. *Fierro* v. *Gomez*, 865 F.Supp. 1387, 1406 (N.D.Cal.1994). The United States Court of Appeals, Fourth Circuit, refused to follow *Fierro: Hunt* v. *Nuth, supra* note 80, at p. 1337.
256. *State* v. *Gee Jon, supra* note 248, at p. 681 (P.).
257. "The average person looks upon the use of gas with horror, because of the experiences incident to the last war." *Id.*
258. TROMBLEY, *supra* note 57, at pp. 84–91.
259. See, for example, *Re Canadian Human Rights Commission and Canadian Liberty Net et al.*, (1992) 90 D.L.R. (4th) 190 (F.C.T.D.), at p. 194.
260. *Fierro* v. *Gomez, supra* note 255, at p. 1391.
261. *Id.*, at pp. 1391–92.
262. UNITED KINGDOM, *supra* note 30, at p. 252.
263. *Id.*, at p. 254.

264. *Id.*, at p. 252.
265. *Id.*, at p. 256.
266. *Fierro* v. *Gomez, supra* note 255, at p. 1391.
267. HILLMAN, *supra* note 174, at p. 748.
268. *Fierro* v. *Gomez, supra* note 255, at p. 1387.
269. *Id.*
270. *Id.*
271. *Kindler* v. *Canada, supra* note 205, at p. 817 (S.C.R.) (*per* Cory, J. dissenting).
272. *Fierro* v. *Gomez, supra* note 255, at p. 1397.
273. *Id.*, at p. 1400, references omitted.
274. *Id.*, at p. 1404, references omitted.
275. *Gray* v. *Lucas, supra* note 252.
276. *Id.*, at p. 1061.
277. *Id.*
278. *Gray* v. *Lucas*, 463 U.S. 1237, 1239, 104 S.Ct. 211, 77 L.Ed.2d (1983) (Burger, C.J., concurring).
279. *Id.*, at p. 1245 (U.S.) (Marshall, J., dissenting).
280. *Id.*, at p. 1246 (U.S.) (Marshall, J., dissenting).
281. *Id.*, at pp. 1246–47 (U.S.) (Marshall, J., dissenting).
282. *Calhoun* v. *State*, 297 Md. 563, 468 A.2d 45 (1983), *cert. denied*, 466 U.S. 993, 104 S.Ct. 2374, 80 L.Ed.2d 846 (1984), *reh'g. denied*, 467 U.S. 1268, 104 S.Ct. 3564; *Billiot* v. *State*, 454 S.2d 445, 464 (Miss. 1984), *cert. denied*, 469 U.S. 1230, 105 S.Ct. 1232, 84 L.Ed.2d 369 (1985), *reh'g denied*, 470 U.S. 1089, 105 S.Ct. 1858 (1985); *State* v. *Lopez*, 175 Ariz. 407, 857 P.2d 1261, 1271 (1993), *cert. denied*, 114 S.Ct. 1578, 128 L.Ed.2d 221 (1994)
283. *Fierro* v. *Gomez, supra* note 16, at p. 970 (Patel, J.).
284. *Id.*, at p. 971 (Patel, J.).
285. See: Stephen REINHARDT, "The Supreme Court, the death penalty, and the *Harris* case," (1992) 102 *Yale L.J.* 205.
286. *Gomez* v. *U.S. Dist. Court for N.D. of Cal., supra* note 252, at p. 1653. On the Harris case, see: Daniel E. LUNGREN, Mark L. KROTOSKI, "Public policy lessons from the Robert Alton Harris case," (1992) 40 *UCLA L. Rev.* 295; Janice Rogers BROWN, "The quality of mercy," (1992) 40 *UCLA L. Rev.* 327; Charles M. SEVILLA, Michael LAURENCE, "Thoughts on the cause of the present discontents: The death penalty case of Robert Alton Harris," (1992) 40 *UCLA L. Rev.* 345; REINHARDT, *id.*; Evan CAMINKER, Erwin CHERMINSKY, "The lawless execution of Robert Alton Harris," (1992) 102 *Yale L.J.* 225; Steven G. CALABRESI, Gary LAWSON, "Equity and hierarchy: Reflections on the Harris execution," (1992) 102 *Yale L.J.* 255.
287. *Gomez* v. *U.S. Dist. Court for N.D. of Cal., supra* note 252, at p. 1683 (Stevens, J., dissenting).
288. *Id.*, at p. 1655 n. 10 (Stevens, J., dissenting).
289. *Id.*, at p. 1654 (Stevens, J., dissenting).
290. *Id.*, quoting the declaration of Dr. Terence B. Allen, filed as an exhibit.
291. *Id.*, at p. 1655 (Stevens, J., dissenting).
292. *Id.*
293. *Id.*, at p. 1686 (Stevens, J., dissenting).
294. *Campbell* v. *Wood, supra* note 9.
295. *Fierro* v. *Gomez, supra* note 255, at pp. 1409–10.
296. *Id.*, at p. 1410–11.
297. *Id.*, at p. 1414: "Were the evidence to demonstrate conclusively that inmates executed in San Quentin experience the agonizing pain of cellular suffocation, acidosis, and tetany for minutes on end, the court would have no trouble finding the method of execution contrary to contemporary standards of decency. Conversely, were the evidence of pain to show that inmates suffer pain for only a matter of seconds, the court would be bound by Campbell and other

precedent to find the administration of lethal gas constitutionally acceptable. This case falls somewhere in between."

298. *Id.,* at p. 1414.

299. *Supra* note 19.

300. *Ng* v. *Canada, supra* note 28, §§16.3–16.5.

301. *Id.,* at p. 159 *(H.R.L.J.).*

302. *Id.,* at p. 158 *(H.R.L.J.).*

303. *Id.,* at p. 160 *(H.R.L.J.).*

304. *Id.*

305. *Id.,* at p. 158 *(H.R.L.J.).*

306. *Id.,* at p. 162 *(H.R.L.J.).*

307. *Makwanyane and Mchunu* v. *The State, supra* note 22, at p. 165 *(per* Chaskalson, P.).

308. HILLMAN, *supra* note 174, at p. 748.

309. *Callins* v. *Collins, cert. denied,* 114 S.Ct. 1127, 1128, 127 L.Ed.435 (1994) (Scalia, J.).

310. *Hill* v. *Lockhart,* 791 F.Supp. 1388, 1394 (E.D.Ark.1992).

311. *State* v. *Deputy,* 644 A.2d 411 (Del.1994).

312. UNITED KINGDOM, *supra* note 30, at p. 258. See: W. CASSCELLES, W. J. CURRAN, "The ethics of medical participation in capital punishment by intravenous drug injection," (1980) 302 *New Eng. J. Med.* 226; W. CASSCELLES, W. J. CURRAN, "Doctors, the death penalty and lethal injections," (1982) *New Eng. J. Med.* 1532; Thomas O. FINKS, "Lethal injection: An uneasy alliance of law and medicine," (1983) 4 *J. Legal Med.* 383; G. R. M. JONES, "Judicial execution and the prison doctor," (1990) 335 *Lancet* 713.

313. UNITED KINGDOM, *supra* note 30, at p. 258.

314. AI Index: AMR 51/16/92, January 29, 1992; AI Index: AMR 51/57/92, April 2, 1992.

315. *State* v. *Ross, supra* note 46, at pp. 1378–79 (Berdon, A.J., dissenting in part). See also: *Chaney* v. *Heckler,* 718 F.2d 1174, 1177–78 (D.C.Cir.1983), *rev'd on other grounds,* 470 U.S. 821, 105 S.Ct. 1649, 84 L.Ed.2d 714 (1985).

316. "A civilized way to die," *Newsweek,* April 9, 1984, p. 106.

317. *Glass* v. *Louisiana, supra* note 8, at pp. 1093–94 (U.S.) (Brennan, J., dissenting from denial of certiorari).

318. UNITED KINGDOM, *supra* note 30, at p. 260. See also: *Deena* v. *Union of India, supra* note 17, at pp. 1184–85 (A.I.R.) *(per* Chandrachud, C.J.).

319. *O'Bryan* v. *McKaskle,* 729 F.2d 991, 992–93 (5th Cir.1984); *Hunt* v. *Nuth, supra* note 80, at p. 1338.

320. *Supra* note 19.

321. *Kindler* v. *Canada, supra* note 20.

322. *Cox* v. *Canada* (No. 539/1993), (1995) 15 *H.R.L.J.* 410.

323. The affidavit is on file with the Human Rights Committee and the Government of Canada.

324. *Ng* v. *Canada, supra* note 28, p. 158 *(H.R.L.J.).*

325. But note the comments of the Ninth Circuit Court of Appeals: "The number of states using hanging is evidence of public perception, but sheds no light on the actual pain that may or may not attend the practice. We cannot conclude that judicial hanging is incompatible with evolving standards of decency simply because few states continue the practice." *Campbell* v. *Wood, supra* note 9, at p. 682 (Beezer, J.).

326. CAMUS, *supra* note 178, at p. 179.

CONCLUSION

1. *In re Kemmler,* 136 U.S. 436, 447, 10 S.Ct. 930, 34 L.Ed. 519 (1890).

2. *Weems* v. *United States,* 217 U.S. 349, 373 (1910).

BIBLIOGRAPHY

ACKER, J., E. WALSH, "Challenging the death penalty under state constitutions," (1989) 42 *Vand. I. Rev.*

ACKERMAN, Steven, "Torture and other forms of cruel and unusual punishment in international law," (1978) 11 *Vand. J. Int'l L.* 653.

AHANHANZO, M. G., "Introduction à la Charte africaine des droits de l'Homme et des Peuples," in *Mélanges Colliard,* Paris: Pedone, 1984, at p. 511.

ALEXIS, J., M. DE MERIEUX, "Inordinately delayed hanging: Whether an inhuman punishment," (1987) 29 *J. Indian L. Inst.* 356.

AMNESTY INTERNATIONAL, *When the State Kills . . . , The Death Penalty: A Human Rights Issue,* New York: Amnesty International, 1989.

AN-NA'IM, Abdullahi Ahmed, "The meaning of cruel, inhuman or degrading treatment or punishment," in Abdullahi Ahmed AN-NA'IM, ed., *Human Rights in Cross-Cultural Perspectives: A Quest for Consensus,* Philadelphia: University of Pennsylvania Press, 1992, pp. 19–43.

———, "Problems and prospects of universal cultural legitimacy for human rights," in Abdullahi Ahmed AN-NA'IM, Francis DENG, eds., *Human Rights in Africa: Cross-cultural Perspectives,* Washington: Brookings Institution, 1990, pp. 31–67.

ANCEL, Marc, "Le crime politique et le droit pénal au XXᵉ siècle," [1983] *Revue d'histoire politique et constitutionnele* 87.

ANGUS, Laurel, "Delay before execution: Is it inhuman and degrading treatment," (1993) 9 *South African J. Hum. Rts.* 432.

ARASSE, Daniel, *La Guillotine et l'imaginaire de la terreur,* Paris: Flammarion, 1987.

AVIO, K. L., "Capital punishment in Canada: A time-series analysis of the deterrent hypothesis," (1979) 12 *Can. J. Econ.* 647.

BADINTER, Robert, "Beccaria, l'abolition de la peine de mort et la révolution française," [1989] *Revue de science criminelle et de droit pénal comparé* 245.

BAILEY, W. C., "Murder, capital punishment, and television: Execution publicity and homicide rates," (1990) 55 *Am. Soc. Rev.* 628.

———, "Imprisonment v. the death penalty as a deterrent for murder," (1977) 1 *Law and Hum. Behav.* 239.

BALDUS, D. C., J. COLE, "A comparison of the work of Thorsten Sellin and Isaac Ehrlich on the deterrent effect of capital punishment," (1975) 85 *Yale L.J.* 170.

BECCARIA, Cesare, *On Crimes and Punishments,* trans. Henry Paolucci, Indianapolis: Bobbs-Merrill, 1963.

BECKMAN, Albert, Michael BOTHE, "General report on the theory of limitations on human rights," in Armand DE MESTRAL et al., eds., *The Limitations of Human Rights in Comparative Constitutional Law,* Cowansville, Qué.: Éditions Yvon Blais, 1986, at pp. 105–12.

BEDAU, Hugo Adam, *The Courts, the Constitution and Capital Punishment,* Lexington, Mass.: Lexington Books, 1977.

———, "The question of deterrence," in Hugo Adam BEDAU, ed., *The Death Penalty in America,* Garden City, N.Y.: Aldine, 1964, pp. 258–332.

———, "Thinking of the death penalty as cruel and unusual punishment," (1985) 18 *U.C. Davis L. Rev.* 873.

———, ed., *The Death Penalty in America,* Garden City, N.Y.: Aldine, 1964.

BERGER, Vincent, *Jurisprudence de la Cour européenne des droits de l'homme,* 4th ed., Paris: Sirey, 1994.

BERKSON, Larry Charles, *The Concept of Cruel and Unusual Punishment,* Lexington, Mass.: D. C. Heath, 1975.

BLACKSTONE, Sir William, *Commentaries on the Laws of England,* book 4, 9th ed., London: Strahen, Cadell and Prince, 1783 (rpt, London and New York: Garland, 1978).

BLUESTONE, H., C. L. McGAHEE, "Reaction to extreme stress: Impending death by execution," (1962) 119 *Am. J. Psychiatry* 393.

BOWERS, John L. Jr., J. L. BUREN Jr., "The constitutional prohibition against cruel and unusual punishment—its present significance," (1950–51) 4 *Vand. L. Rev.* 680.

BOWERS, William J., "The effect of executions is brutalization, not deterrence," in Kenneth A. HAAS, James A. INCIARDI, eds., *Challenging Capital Punishment: Legal and Social Science Approaches,* Beverly Hills, Cal.: Sage Publications, 1988, pp. 49–89.

BOWERS, William J., Glenn L. PIERCE, "Deterrence or brutalization: What is the effect of executions?" (1980) 26 *Crime & Delinq.* 453.

———, "The illusion of deterrence in Isaac Ehrlich's research on capital punishment," (1975) 85 *Yale L.J.* 187.

BOWERS, William J., et al., "A new look at public opinion on capital punishment: What citizens and legislators prefer," (1994) 22 *Am. J. Crim. L.* 77.

BRANT, Irving, *The Bill of Rights, Its Origin and Meaning*, Indianapolis: Bobbs-Merrill, 1965.

BREITENMOSER, S., G. E. WILMS, "Human rights v. extradition: The Soering case," (1990) 11 *Mich. J. Int'l L.* 845.

BRIGHT, Stephen, "Counsel for the poor: The death sentence not for the worst crime but for the worst lawyer," (1994) 103 *Yale L.J.* 1835.

BROWN, Janice Rogers, "The quality of mercy," (1992) 40 *UCLA L. Rev.* 327.

BURGERS, J. H., H. DANELIUS, *The United Nations Convention against Torture—A Handbook*, Dordrecht, London, and Boston: Martinus Nijhoff, 1988.

CALABRESI, Steven G., Gary LAWSON, "Equity and hierarchy: Reflections on the Harris execution," (1992) 102 *Yale L.J.* 255.

CAMINKER, Evan, Erwin CHERMINSKY, "The lawless execution of Robert Alton Harris," (1992) 102 *Yale L.J.* 225.

CAMUS, Albert, "Réflexions sur la guillotine," in Albert CAMUS, Arthur KOESTLER, *Réflexions sur la peine capitale*, Paris: Clamann-Lévy, 1957.

CANÇADO TRINDADE, A. A., "Co-existence and co-ordination of mechanisms of international protection of human rights (at global and regional levels)," (1987) 202 *R.C.A.D.I.* 9.

CASSCELLES, W., W. J. CURRAN, "Doctors, the death penalty and lethal injections," (1982) *New Eng. J. Med.* 1532.

———, "The ethics of medical participation in capital punishment by intravenous drug injection," (1980) 302 *New Eng. J. Med.* 226.

CASSESE, Antonio, "Prohibition of torture and inhuman or degrading treatment or punishment," in R. St. J. MACDONALD et al., eds., *The European System for the Protection of Human Rights*, Dordrecht, London, and Boston: Martinus Nijhoff, 1993, pp. 225–61.

CAVERIVIÈRE, Monique, "Article 8," in Gérard CONAC et al., eds., *La déclaration des droits de l'homme et du citoyen de 1789*, Paris: Economica, 1993, pp. 173–86.

CENTRE DES ÉTUDES DE SÉCURITÉ (ARABIE SAOUDITE), "L'égalité et commodité de la peine de mort en droit musulman," (1987) 58 *Revue internationale de droit pénal* 431.

CHOPKO, Mark E., Michael F. MOSES, "Assisted suicide: Still a wonderful life," (1995) 70 *Notre Dame L. Rev.* 519.

COHEN-JONATHAN, Gérard, *La Convention européenne des droits de l'homme*, Paris: Economica-PUAM, 1989.

COMMENT, "The death penalty cases," (1968) 56 *Cal. L. Rev.* 1270.

CONAC, Gérard, "L'élaboration de la déclaration des droits de l'homme et du citoyen," in Gérard CONAC et al., eds., *La déclaration des droits de l'homme et du citoyen de 1789*, Paris: Economica, 1993, pp. 7–52, at pp. 28–30.

COTTRELL, Jill, "The Supreme Court of India and the supreme penalty," [1985] *Lawasia* 75.

———, "Wrestling with the death penalty in India," (1991) 7 *South African J. Hum. Rts.* 185.

COUSSIRAT-COUSTÈRE, V., "Jurisprudence de la Cour européenne des droits de l'homme de 1989 à 1991," [1991] *A.F.D.I.* 583.

COUTTS, J. A., "Effect of long delay in execution," (1994) 58 *J. Crim. L.* 177.

COYNE, Randall, Lyn ENTZEROTH, *Capital Punishment and the Judicial Process*, Durham, N.C.: Carolina Academic Press, 1994.

CRAVEN, Matthew, *The International Covenant on Economic, Social and Cultural Rights*, Oxford: Clarendon Press, 1995.

DANELIUS, Hans, "Torture and cruel, inhuman or degrading treatment or punishment," (1989) 58 *Nordic J. Int'l L.* 172.

DARROW, Clarence, *Attorney for the Damned*, New York: Simon & Schuster, 1957.

DAVIS, Dennis, "Democracy—its influence upon the process of constitutional interpretation," (1994) 10 *South African J. Hum. Rts.* 103.

DAVIS, K., *Discretionary Justice*, Urbana: Univeristy of Illinois Press, 1976.

DAWLEY, Powell Mills, *John Whitgift and the English Reformation*, New York: Scribner's, 1954.

DELMAS-MARTY, Mireille, "La jurisprudence du Conseil constitutionnel et les principes fondamentaux du droit pénal proclamés par la Déclaration de 1789," in *La déclaration des droits de l'homme et du citoyen et la jurisprudence*, Paris: Presses Universitaires de France, 1989.

———, "Le rayonnement international de la pensée de Cesare Beccaria," [1989] *Revue de science criminelle et de droit pénal comparé* 252.

DENNO, Deborah W., "Is electrocution an unconstitutional method of execution? The engineering of death over the century," (1994) 35 *Wm. & Mary L. Rev.* 551.

DESCH, Thomas, "The concept and dimensions of the right to life—as defined in international standards and in international and comparative jurisprudence," (1985–86) 36 *Österreichische Zeitschrift für Offentliches Recht und Volkerrecht* 77.

DESTRÉE, A., "Opium et peine de mort en Iran," (1972) 52 *Revue de droit pénal et de criminologie* 568.

DINSTEIN, Yoram, "General report," (1991) 62 *Int'l Rev. Penal L.* 31.

———, "The right to life, physical integrity and liberty," in Louis HENKIN, ed., *The International Bill of Rights: The Covenant on Civil and Political Rights*, New York: Columbia University Press, 1981.

DiSALLE, Michael V., Lawrence G. BLOCHMAN, *The Power of Life or Death*, New York: Random House, 1965.

DONNELLY, Jack, "Human rights and human dignity: An analytical critique of non-Western conceptions of human rights," (1982) 76 *Am. Pol. Sci. Rev.* 303.

————, *Universal Human Rights in Theory and Practice*, Ithaca and London: Cornell University Press, 1989.

DOSWALD-BECK, Louise, "What does the prohibition of 'Torture or Inhuman or Degrading Treatment or Punishment' mean? The interpretation of the European Commission and Court of Human Rights," (1978) 25 *Neth. Int'l L. Rev.* 24.

DUFFY, Peter J., "Article 3 of the European Convention on Human Rights," (1983) 32 *I.C.L.Q.* 316.

DUNDAS, Ian, "Case comment: *Rodriguez* and assisted suicide in Canada," (1994) 32 *Alta. L. Rev.* 811.

EHRLICH, Isaac, "The deterrent effect of capital punishment: A question of life and death," (1975) 65 *Am. Econ. Rev.* 397.

ELDRED, Charles Kenneth, "The new federal death penalties," (1994) 22 *Am. J. Crim. L.* 293.

ELLIOT, Jonathan, *The Debates in the Several State Conventions on the Adoption of the Federal Constitution, as recommended by the General Convention at Philadelphia*, vol. 2, Washington: Taylor & Maury, 1854.

ELY, J. H., *Democracy and Distrust: A Theory of Judicial Review*, Cambridge: Harvard University Press, 1980.

FATTAH, Ezzat A., "The use of the death penalty for drug offences and for economic crimes—a discussion and a critique," (1987) 58 *Revue internationale de droit pénal* 723.

FAWCETT, J. E. S., *The Application of the European Convention on Human Rights*, 2d ed., Oxford: Clarendon Press, 1987.

FELTHAM, J. D., "The common law and the execution of insane criminals," (1964) 4 *Melb. U. L. Rev.* 434.

FINKS, Thomas O., "Lethal injection: An uneasy alliance of law and medicine," (1983) 4 *J. Legal Med.* 383.

FOHLEN, Claude, "La filiation américaine de la Déclaration des droits de l'homme," in Claude-Albert COLLIARD et al., eds., *La Déclaration des droits de l'homme et du citoyen de 1789, Ses Origines–Sa pérennité*, Paris: Documentation française, 1990, pp. 21–29.

FOUCAULT, Michel, *Discipline and Punish: The Birth of the Prison*, trans. Alan Sheridan, New York: Pantheon, 1979.

FOX, D. T., "Inter-American Commission on Human Rights finds United States in violation," (1988) 82 *A.J.I.L.* 601.

GALLEMORE, Johnnie L. Jr., James H. PANTON, "Inmate responses to lengthy death row confinement," (1972) 129 *Am. J. Psychiatry* 167.

GARDNER, Martin R., "Executions and indignities—An eighth amendment assessment of methods of inflicting capital punishment," (1978) 39 *Ohio State L.J.* 96.

GARNER, James W., "Infliction of the death penalty by electrocution," (1910) 1 *J. Crim. L. & Criminology* 626.

GETTINGER, Stephen M., *Sentenced to Die: The People, the Crimes and the Controversy*, New York: Macmillan, 1979.

GILMOUR, Joan M., "Withholding and withdrawing life support from adults at common law," (1993) 31 *Osgoode Hall L.J.* 473.

GOLDBERG, Arthur, Allen DERSHOWITZ, "Declaring the death penalty unconstitutional," (1970) 83 *Harv. L. Rev.* 1773.

GOULET, Jacques, *Robespierre, la peine de mort et la terreur*, Paris: Les Castor Astral, 1983.

GRANUCCI, Anthony F., " 'Nor cruel and unusual punishments inflicted': The orginal meaning," (1969) 57 *Cal. L. Rev.* 839.

GRAVES, William F., "The deterrent effect of capital punishment in California," in Hugo Adam BEDAU, ed., *The Death Penalty in America*, Garden City, N.Y.: Aldine, 1964, pp. 322–32.

GREGORY, N. G., S. B. WOOTON, "Sheep slaughtering procedures: Time to loss of brain responsiveness after exsanguination or cardiac arrest," (1984) 140 *Brit. Veterinary J.* 354.

GROVER, George G., "Execution of insane persons," (1950) 23 *S. Cal. L. Rev.* 246.

HANG, H., "Efforts to eliminate torture through international law," (1989) 29 *Int'l Rev. Red Cross* 9.

HARRING, S. L., "Death, drugs and development: Malaysia's mandatory death penalty for traffickers and the international war on drugs," (1991) 29 *Colum. J. Transnat'l L.* 364.

HARTMANN, Raymond, "The use of lethal gas in Nevada executions," (1923) 3 *St. Louis U. L. Rev.* 167.

HATCHARD, John, "Capital punishment in southern Africa: Some recent developments," (1994) 43 *I.C.L.Q.* 923.

HAY, D., "Property, authority and the criminal law," in D. HAY et al., *Albion's*

Fatal Tree: Crime and Society in Eighteenth-Century England, London: Allen Lane, 1975, p. 17.

HAZARD, Geoffrey C., Jr., David W. LOUISELL, "Death, the state, and the insane: Stay of execution," (1962) 9 *UCLA L. Rev.* 381.

HIGGINS, Rosalyn, "Derogations under human rights treaties," (1976–77) 48 *B.Y.I.L.* 281.

HILLMAN, Harold, "The possible pain experienced during execution by different methods," (1993) 22 *Perception* 745.

HOFFMAN, Lonny J., "The madness of the method: The use of electrocution and the death penalty," (1992) 70 *Tex. L. Rev.* 1039.

HOLLAND, Nancy, "Death row conditions: Progression toward constitutional protections," (1985) 2 *Akron L. Rev.* 293.

HOOD, Gary E., "*Campbell* v. *Wood:* The death penalty in Washington State: 'Hanging' on to a method of execution." (1994–95) 30 *Gonz. L. Rev.* 163.

HOOD, Roger, *The Death Penalty: A Worldwide Perspective,* Oxford: Clarendon Press, 1989.

HORVATH, Tibor, "L'abolition de la peine de mort en Hongrie," [1992] 2 *Revue internationale de criminologie et de police technique* 167.

HOSNI, N., "La peine de mort en droit égyptien et en droit islamique," (1987) 58 *Revue internationale de droit pénal* 407.

HUMPHREY, John P., "The Universal Declaration of Human Rights: Its history, impact and judicial character," in B. G. RAMCHARAN, ed., *Human Rights: Thirty Years After the Universal Declaration,* The Hague: Martinus Nijhoff, 1984.

IKHARIALE, Mike, "Death penalty in Nigeria: A constitutional aberration," (1991) 1 *J. Hum. Rts. L. Prac.* 40.

IMBERT, Jean, *La peine de mort,* Paris: Presses Universitaires de France, 1989.

ITOH, Hiroshi, Lawrence Ward BEER, eds., *The Constitutional Case Law of Japan: Selected Supreme Court Decisions 1961–70,* Seattle: University of Washington Press, 1978.

JACKSON, Bruce, Diane CHRISTIAN, *Death Row,* Boston: Beacon Press, 1980.

JACOBS, Francis G., *The European Convention on Human Rights,* Oxford: Clarendon Press, 1975.

JAMES, Ryk, Rachel NASMYTH-JONES, "The occurrence of cervical fractures in victims of judicial hanging," (1992) 54 *Forensic Sci. Int'l* 81.

JAWSAL, Nishtha, *Role of the Supreme Court with Regard to the Right to Life and Personal Liberty,* New Delhi: Ashish Publishing House, 1990.

JEFFERSON, Thomas, *The Papers of Thomas Jefferson,* ed. Julian P. BOYD, Princeton: Princeton University Press, 1958, vols. 14, 15.

JOHNSON, Kathleen L., "The death row right to die: Suicide or intimate decision," (1981) 54 *S. Cal. L. Rev.* 575.

JOHNSON, Robert, *Condemned to Die: Life Under Sentence of Death*, New York: Elsevier, 1981.

————, *Death Work: A Study of the Modern Execution Process*, Pacific Grove, Cal.: Brooks/Cole, 1990.

————, "Under sentence of death: The psychology of death row confinement," (1979) 5 *Law Psychol. Rev.* 141.

JONES, G. R. M., "Judicial execution and the prison doctor," (1990) 335 *Lancet* 713.

JOSEPH, Philip, "Towards abolition of Privy Council appeals: The Judicial Committee and the Bill of Rights," (1985) 2 *Canterbury L. Rev.* 273.

KAINE, Tim, "Capital punishment and the waiver of sentence review," (1983) 18 *Harv. C.R.-C.L. L. Rev.* 483.

KEETON, George William, *Lord Chancellor Jeffreys and the Stuart Cause*, London: Macdonald, 1965, at pp. 301–31.

KENNER, William D., "Competency on death row," (1986) 8 *Int'l J. L. Psychiatry* 253.

KLAYMAN, Barry, "The definition of torture in international law," (1978) 51 *Temple L.Q.* 460.

KLEIN, S. P., "Capital punishment in the electric chair," (1914) 49 *N.Y. Med. J.* 1089.

KODJO, E., "La Charte africaine des droits de l'homme et des peuples," (1989) 1 *R.U.D.H.* 29.

LABAYLE, Henri, "Droits de l'homme, traitement inhumain et peine capitale: Réflexions sur l'édification d'un ordre public européen en matière d'extradition par la Cour européenne des droits de l'homme, (1990) 64 *Semaine juridique* 3452.

LAMARCHE, Lucie, *Perspectives occidentales du droit international des droits économiques de la personne*, Brussels: Éditions Bruylant, 1995.

LANDERER, Lilly E., "Capital punishment as a human rights issue before the United Nations," (1971) 4 *H.R.J.* 511.

LAURENCE, John, *A History of Capital Punishment*, New York: Citadel Press, 1960.

LAUTERPACHT, Hersh, *An International Bill of the Rights of Man*, New York: Columbia University Press, 1945.

LAWES, Lewis Edward, *Life and Death in Sing Sing*, New York: Doubleday, 1928.

LEPOINTE, Gabriel, *Histoire des institutions du droit public français*, Paris: Éditions Domat Montchrestien, 1953.

LEPP, Alan W., "Note: The death penalty in late-imperial, modern and post-Tiananmen China," (1990) 11 *Mich. J. Int'l L.* 987.

LEVASSEUR, Georges, "Les grands principes de la Déclaration des droits de l'homme et le droit répressif français," in Claude-Albert COLLIARD et al., eds., *La Déclaration des droits de l'homme et du citoyen de 1789, Ses Origines—Sa pérennité*, Paris: Documentation française, 1990, pp. 233–45.

LEWIS, Peter W., "Killing the killers: A post-*Furman* profile of Florida's condemned," (1975) 25 *Crime & Delinq.* 200.

LILLICH, Richard B., "The *Soering* case," (1991) 85 *A.J.I.L.* 128.

LUNGREN, Daniel E., Mark L. KROTOSKI, "Public policy lessons from the Robert Alton Harris case," (1992) 40 *UCLA L. Rev.* 295.

LYNN, Steven, "Locke and Beccaria: Faculty psychology and capital punishment," in William B. THESING, *Executions and the British Experience from the 17th to the 20th Century: A Collection of Essays*, Jefferson, N.C.: McFarland, 1990.

MACDONALD, Carlos F., "The infliction of the death penalty by means of electricity: Being a report of seven cases," (1892) *Transactions of the Medical Society of New York* 400.

MACDONALD, R. St., J., "The margin of appreciation," in R. St. J. MACDONALD et al., eds., *The European System for the Protection of Human Rights*, Dordrecht, London, and Boston: Martinus Nijhoff, 1993, pp. 83–124.

MACDONALD, R. St. J., et al., eds., *The European System for the Protection of Human Rights*, Dordrecht, London, and Boston: Martinus Nijhoff, 1993.

MADHUKU, Lovemore, "Delay before execution: More on it being inhuman and degrading," (1994) 10 *South African J. Hum. Rts.* 276.

MAESTRO, Marcello, *Cesare Beccaria and the Origins of Penal Reform*, Philadelphia: Temple University Press, 1972.

MAKI, John M., ed., *Court and Constitution in Japan: Selected Supreme Court Decisions 1948–60*, Seattle: University of Washington Press, 1964.

MARCAGGI, V., *Les origines de la Déclaration des droits de l'homme de 1789*, Paris: Fontemoing, 1912.

MARIE, Jean-Bernard, "International Human Rights Instruments: Ratifications as of January 1, 1995," (1995) 15 *H.R.L.J.* 75.

MARKS, Susan, "Yes, Virginia, extradition may breach the European Convention on Human Rights," (1990) 49 *Cambridge L.J.* 194.

MAURER, Robert A., "Death by lethal gas," (1921) 9 *Geo. L.J.* 50.

MBAYA, Etienne-Richard, "À la recherche du noyau intangible dans la Charte africaine," in *Le noyau intangible des droits de l'homme*, Fribourg: Éditions Universitaires Fribourg Suisse, 1991, pp. 207–26.

MBAYE, Keba, *Les droits de l'homme en Afrique*, Paris: Pedone, 1992.

McCLELLAN, Jane L., "Stopping the rush to the death house: Third-party standing in death-row volunteer cases," (1994) 26 *Ariz. St. L.J.* 201.

McGOLDRICK, Dominic, *The Human Rights Committee*, Oxford: Clarendon Press, 1991.

McLANE, B. W., "Juror attitudes toward local disorder: The evidence of the 1328 Lincolnshire Trailbaston proceedings," in J. S. COCKBURN, T. A. GREEN, eds., *Twelve Good Men and True: The Criminal Trial Jury in England, 1200–1800*, Princeton: Princeton University Press, 1988, p. 36.

MERON, Theodor, *Human Rights and Humanitarian Norms as Customary International Law*, Oxford: Clarendon Press, 1986.

MIDGLEY, J., "Public opinion and the death penalty in South Africa," (1974) 14 *Brit. J. Criminology* 347.

MIHALIK, Janos, "The death penalty in Bophuthatswana: A new deal for condemned prisoners?" (1990) 107 *South African L.J.* 465.

MILLER, Arthur, S., Jeffrey H. BOWMAN, *Death by Installments: The Ordeal of Willie Francis*, Westport (Conn.), New York, and London: Greenwood Press, 1988.

MILLER, Edward, "Executing minors and the mentally retarded: The retribution and deterrence rationales," (1990) 43 *Rutgers L. Rev.* 15.

MOREL, André, "La réception du droit criminal anglais au Québec (1760–1892)," (1978) 13 *Revue juridique Thémis* 449.

MORSBACH H., G. MORSBACH, "Attitudes towards capital punishment in South Africa," (1967) 7 *Brit. J. Crim. Just.* 402.

NASH (LEICH), Marian, "U.S. presentation before Human Rights Committee (1995)," (1995) 89 *A.J.I.L.* 589.

NORRIS, Linda J., "Constitutional law: The death penalty as punishment for murder does not violate the eighth amendment," (1976) 8 *Tex. Tech. L. Rev.* 515.

NORRIS, Robert, "The individual petition procedure of the inter-American system for the protection of human rights," in Hurst HANNUM, ed., *Guide to International Human Rights Law Practice*, Philadelphia: University of Pennsylvania Press, 1984, at p. 104.

NOTE, (1890–91) *Harv. L. Rev.* 287.

NOTE, "The Caryl Chessman case: A legal analysis," (1960) 44 *Minn. L. Rev.* 941.

NOTE, "The death penalty cases," (1968) 56 *Cal. L. Rev.* 1270.

NOTE, "The death penalty in Massachusetts," (1974) 8 *Suffolk U.L. Rev.* 632.

NOTE, "The Eighth Amendment and our evolving standards of decency: A time for re-evaluation," (1969) 3 *Suffolk U. L. Rev.* 616.

NOTE, "European Court of Human Rights—extradition—inhuman or degrading treatment or punishment, Soering Case," (1990) 20 *Ga. J. Int'l & Comp. L.* 463.

NOTE, "Mental suffering under sentence of death: A cruel and unusual punishment," (1972) 57 *Iowa L. Rev.* 814.

NOTE, "What is cruel and unusual punishment," (1910) 24 *Harv. L. Rev.* 54.

NOWAK, Manfred, *CCPR Commentary*, Kehl, Germany: Engel, 1993.

NSEREKO, Daniel D., "Arbitrary deprivation of life: Controls on permissible deprivations," in B. G. RAMCHARAN, ed., *The Right to Life in International Law*, Boston: Martinus Nijhoff, 1985, pp. 245–83.

O'BOYLE, Michael, "Extradition and expulsion under the European Convention on Human Rights: Reflections on the *Soering* case," in James O'REILLY, ed., *Human Rights and Constitutional Law: Essays in Honour of Brian Walsh*, Dublin: Round Hall Press, 1992, p. 93.

OUGUERGOUZ, Fatsah, *La Charte africaine des droits de l'homme et des peuples*, Geneva: Presses Universitaires de France, 1993.

PAINE, Thomas, "Preserving the Life of Louis Capet," in Michael FOOT, Isaac KRAMNICK, eds., *The Thomas Paine Reader*, London: Penguin, 1987, pp. 394–98.

PAK, John, "Canadian extradition and the death penalty: Seeking a constitutional assurance of life," (1993) 26 *Cornell Int'l L.J.* 239.

PALAZZO, F. C., "La pena di morte dinanzi alla Corte europea di Strasburgo," [1990] *Rivista italiana di diritto e procedura penale* 367.

PANNICK, David, *Judicial Review of the Death Penalty*, London: Duckworth, 1983.

PASSELL, P., "The deterrent effect of the death penalty: A statistical test," (1975) 28 *Stan. L. Rev.* 61.

PECK, John K., 'The deterrent effect of capital punishment: Ehrlich and his critics," (1976) 85 *Yale L.J.* 359.

PERRY, Richard L., John C. COOPER, *Sources of Our Liberties*, Washington: American Bar Association, 1952.

PETTITI, L.-E., "Arrêt Soering c./Grande-Bretagne du 8 juillet 1989," [1989] *Revue de science criminelle et de droit pénal comparé* 786.

PETTITI L.-E., et al., eds., *La Convention européenne des droits de l'homme, Commentaire article par article*, Paris: Economica, 1995.

PHILLIPS, Barry, "Pratt and Morgan v. Attorney-General for Jamaica," (1994) 88 *A.J.I.L.* 775.

PHILLIPS, David P., "The deterrent effect of capital punishment: New evidence on an old controversy," (1980) 86 *Am. J. Soc.* 139.

PIERCE, G., M. RADELET, "The role and consequences of the death penalty in American politics," (1990–91) 18 *N.Y.U. Rev. L. & Soc. Change* 711.

PIRAGOFF, Donald K., Marcia V. J. KRAN, "The impact of human rights principles on extradition from Canada and the United States: The role of national courts," (1992) 3 *Crim. L.F.* 191.

POLLOCK, Frederick, Frederic William MAITLAND, *The History of English Law,* 2d ed., Cambridge: Cambridge University Press, 1952.

PREJEAN, Helen, *Dead Man Walking,* New York: Random House, 1993.

PRÉMONT, Daniel, ed., *Essais sur le concept de "droit de vivre" en mémoire de Yougindra Khushalani,* Brussels: Bruylant, 1988.

QUIGLEY, J., J. SHANK, "Death row as a violation of human rights: Is it illegal to extradite to Virginia?" (1989) 30 *Va. J. Int'l L.* 251.

RADZINOWICZ, Leon, *A History of English Criminal Law and Its Administration from 1750,* vol. 1, London: Stevens and Sons, 1948.

RAMCHARAN, B. G., ed., *The Right to Life in International Law,* Boston: Martinus Nijhoff, 1985.

"Recent Cases," (1950) 34 *Minn. L. Rev.* 134.

REEVES, J. S., "Extradition treaties and the death penalty," (1924) 18 *A.J.I.L.* 290.

REINHARDT, Stephen, "The Supreme Court, the death penalty, and the *Harris* case," (1992) 102 *Yale L.J.* 205.

RIALS, Stéphane, *La déclaration des droits de l'homme et du citoyen,* Paris: Hachette, 1988.

RICHARDS, Jef I., R. Bruce EASTER, "Televising executions: The high-tech alternative to public hangings," (1992) 40 *UCLA L. Rev.* 381.

RIDDELL, W. R., "The first British courts in Canada," (1923–24) 33 *Yale L.J.* 577.

RIESENFELD, Stefan A., "Law-making and legislative precedent in American legal history," (1949) 33 *Minn. L. Rev.* 103.

ROBERTS, T. D. M., "Cortical activity in electrocuted dogs," (1954) 66 *Veterinary Rec.* 561.

ROBESPIERRE, Maximilien, *Œuvres,* Paris: Presses Universitaires de France, 1952.

RODLEY, Nigel, *The Treatment of Prisoners Under International Law,* Paris: Unesco, Oxford: Clarendon Press, 1987.

ROLLAND, P., P. TAVERNIER, "Chronique de jurisprudence de la Cour européenne des droits de l'homme, [1990] *J.D.I.* 734.

RUTLAND, Robert Allen, *The Birth of the Bill of Rights, 1776–1791,* Chapel Hill: University of North Carolina Press, 1955.

SARAT, Austin, Neil VIDMAR, "Public opinion, the death penalty and the Eighth Amendment: Testing the Marshall hypothesis," (1976) 1 *Wisc. L. Rev.* 171.

SAVEY-CASARD, Paul, *La peine de mort: Esquisse historique et juridique*, Geneva: Droz, 1968, at pp. 70–75.

SAVITZ, Leonard D., "The deterrent effect on capital punishment in Philadelphia," in Hugo Adam BEDAU, ed., *The Death Penalty in America*, Garden City, N.Y.: Aldine, 1964, pp. 315–21.

SCHABAS, William A., *The Abolition of the Death Penalty in International Law*, Cambridge: Cambridge University Press (Grotius Publications), 1993.

———, "Canada and the American Convention on Human Rights: Will we ever ratify?" in *A New Policy for a Changing Hemisphere*, Ottawa: Carleton University Press, 1996 (forthcoming).

———, "Case Comment: Pratt and Morgan v. Jamaica," (1994) 5 *Crim. L.F.* 180.

———, "The death penalty for crimes committed by persons under eighteen years of age," in E. VERHELLEN, ed., *Monitoring Children's Rights*, Dordrecht, London, and Boston: Martinus Nijhoff, 1995, at pp. 603–9.

———, "Extradition et la peine de mort: Le Canada renvoie deux fugitifs au couloir de la mort," (1992) 4 *R.U.D.H.* 65.

———, *International Human Rights Law and the Canadian Charter*, Toronto: Carswell, 1991.

———, "International norms on execution of the insane and the mentally retarded," (1993) 4 *Crim. L.F.* 95.

———, "Invalid reservations to the International Convenant on Civil and Political Rights: Is the United States still a party?" (1995) 21 *Brook. J. Int'l L.* 277.

———, "Kindler and Ng: Our supreme magistrates take a frightening step into the court of public opinion," (1991) 51 *Revue de Barreau* 673.

———, "Soering's legacy: The Human Rights Committee and the Judicial Committee of the Privy Council take a walk down death row," (1994) 43 *I.C.L.Q.* 913.

———, "South Africa's Constitutional Court outlaws the death penalty," (1995) 16 *H.R.L.J.* 133.

SELLIN, Thorsten, "Homicides in retentionist and abolitionist states," in T. SELLIN, ed., *Capital Punishment*, New York: Harper and Row, 1967, pp. 135–37.

SEPARAVIC, Z. P., "Political crimes and the death penalty," (1987) 58 *Revue internationale de droit pénal* 755.

SEVILLA, Charles M., Michael LAURENCE, "Thoughts on the cause of the present discontents: The death penalty case of Robert Alton Harris," (1992) 40 *UCLA L. Rev.* 345.

SHARVIT, Pnina Baruh, "The definition of torture in the United Nations Convention Against Torture and Other Cruel, Inhuman and Degrading Treatment or Punishment," (1993) 23 *Israel Yearbook on Human Rights* 147.

SHEA, Michael, "Expanding judicial scrutiny of human rights in extradition cases after *Soering*," (1992) 17 *Yale L.J.* 110.

SHERLOCK, Ann, "Extradition, death row and the Convention," (1990) 15 *European L. Rev.* 87.

SINGER, Richard G., "Confining solitary confinement: Constitutional arguments for a new penology," (1971) 56 *Iowa L. Rev.* 1251.

SMITH, Keith I., "The penalty of death: Public attitudes in South Africa," (1989) 2 *South African J. Crim. Just.* 256.

SOHN, Louis B., "How American international lawyers prepared for the San Francisco bill of rights," (1995) 89 *A.J.I.L.* 540.

SPIELMAN, Alphonse, "La Convention européenne des droits de l'homme et la peine de mort," in *Présence du droit public et les droits de l'homme, Mélanges offerts à Jacques Vélu*, Brussels: Bruylant, 1992, p. 1503.

SPIZKA, E. A., H. E. RADASCH, "The brain lesions produced by electricity as observed after legal execution," (1912) 44 *Am. J. Med. Sci.* 341.

STACK, Steven, "The impact of publicized executions on homicide," (1995) 22 *Crim. Just. & Behav.* 172.

———, "Publicized executions and homicide, 1950–1980," (1987) 52 *Am. Soc. Rev.* 532.

STEPHEN, Sir James Fitzjames, *History of the Criminal Law in England*, vol. 1, London: Macmillan, 1883.

STRAFER, G. Richard, "Volunteering for execution: Competency, voluntariness and the propriety of the third party intervention," (1983) 74 *J. Crim. L. & Criminology* 860.

STREIB, Victor L., "Capital punishment for children in Ohio," (1984) 18 *Akron L. Rev.* 51.

———, "Death penalty for children: The American experience with capital punishment for crimes committed while under age eighteen," (1983) 36 *Okla. L. Rev.* 613.

———, *Death Penalty for Juveniles*, Bloomington and Indianapolis: Indiana University Press, 1987.

STRYPE, John, *The Life and Acts of John Whitgift*, Oxford: Clarendon Press, 1822.

SUDRE, Frédéric, "Article 3," in L.-E. PETTITI et al., eds., *La Convention européenne des droits de l'homme, Commentaire article par article*, Paris: Economica, 1995, pp. 155–75.

———, *La Convention européenne des droits de l'homme*, Paris: Presses Universitaires de France, 1990.

————, *Droit international et européen des droits de l'homme,* Paris: Presses Universitaires de France, 1989.

————, "Extradition et peine de mort—Arrêt Soering de la Cour européenne des droits de l'homme du 7 juillet 1989," (1990) *Revue générale de droit international public* 103.

————, "La notion de 'peines et traitements inhumains ou dégradants' dans la jurisprudence de la Commission et de la Cour européennes des droits de l'homme," (1984) 88 *R.G.D.I.P.* 825.

SUNDBY, Scott E., "The *Lockett* paradox: Reconciling guided discretion and unguided mitigation in capital sentencing," (1991) 38 *UCLA L. Rev.* 1147.

TARDU, M., "The Protocol to the United Nations Covenant on Civil and Political Rights and the Inter-American system: A study of coexisting petition procedures," (1976) 70 *A.J.I.L.* 778.

TAYLOR, Telford, *The Anatomy of the Nuremberg Trials,* New York: Alfred A. Knopf, 1992.

TEETERS, Negley K., Jack H. HEDBLOM, *". . . Hang by the Neck . . .": The Legal Use of Scaffold and Noose, Gibbet, Stake, and Firing Squad from Colonial Times to the Present,* Springfield, Ill.: Charles C. Thomas, 1967.

THESING, William B., *Executions and the British Experience from the 17th to the 20th Century: A Collection of Essays,* Jefferson, N.C.: McFarland, 1990.

TROMBLEY, Stephen, *The Execution Protocol,* New York: Random House, 1992.

UNITED KINGDOM, *Royal Commission on Capital Punishment, 1949–1953, Report,* London: Her Majesty's Stationery Office, 1953.

UROFSKY, Melvin I., *Letting Go: Death, Dying and the Law,* New York: Charles Scribner's Sons, 1993.

————, "A right to die: Termination of appeal for condemned prisoners," (1984) 75 *J. Crim. L. & Criminology* 553.

VAN DEN WYNGAERT, Christine, "Applying the European Convention on Human Rights to extradition: Opening Pandora's box?" (1990) 39 *I.C.L.Q.* 757.

VAN DER MEERSCH, W. Ganshof, "L'extradition et la Convention européenne des droits de l'homme: L'affaire Soering," (1990) *Revue trimestrielle des droits de l'homme* 5.

VAN DIJK, P., G. J. H. VAN HOOF, *Theory and Practice of the European Convention on Human Rights,* Deventer: Kluwer, 1984.

VAN DIJK, Pieter, "A common standard of achievement: About universal validity and uniform interpretation of international human rights norms," (1995) 13 *N.Q.H.R.* 105.

VAN NIEKERK, Barend, "Hanged by the neck until you are dead: The death penalty in South Africa," (1969) 86 *S.A.L.J.* 457, (1970) 87 *S.A.L.J.* 60.

VEIT, Helen E., et al., *Creating the Bill of Rights*, Baltimore: Johns Hopkins University Press, 1991.

VELU, Jacques, Rusen ERGEC, *La Convention européenne des droits de l'homme*, Brussels: Bruylant, 1990.

VERDOODT, Albert, *Naissance et signification de la Déclaration universelle des droits de l'homme*, Louvain and Paris: Éditions Nauwelaerts, 1963.

VOGELMAN, Lloyd, "The living dead: Living on death row," (1989) 5 *South African J. Hum. Rts.* 183.

WARBRICK, C., "Coherence and the European Court of Human Rights: The adjudicative background to the Soering case," (1990) 11 *Mich. J. Int'l L.* 1073.

WATTENDORFF, H., E. du PERRON, "Human Rights v. Extradition: The *Soering* case," (1990) 11 *Mich. J. Int'l L.* 845.

WAZIR, A., "Quelques aspects de la peine de mort en droit pénal islamique," (1987) 58 *Revue internationale de droit pénal* 421.

WHITE, Welsh S., *The Death Penalty in the Nineties: An Examination of the Modern System of Capital Punishment*, Ann Arbor: University of Michigan Press, 1991.

———, "Defendants who elect execution," (1987) 48 *U. Pitt. L. Rev.* 853.

WILLIAMS, Sharon A., "Extradition and the death penalty exception in Canada: Resolving the Ng and Kindler cases," (1991) 13 *Loy. L.A. Int'l & Comp. L.J.* 799.

———, "Extradition to a state that imposes the death penalty," [1990] C.Y.I.L. 117.

———, "Human rights safeguards and international cooperation in extradition: Striking the balance," (1992) 3 *Crim. L.F.* 191.

———, "Nationality, double jeopardy, prescription and the death sentence as bases for refusing extradition," (1991) 62 *Int'l Rev. Penal L.* 259.

WIRIN, A. L., Paul M. POSNER, "A decade of appeals," (1961) 8 *UCLA L. Rev.* 768.

ZALLER, Robert, "The debate on capital punishment during the English Revolution," (1987) 31 *Am. J. Legal Hist.* 126.

ZEISEL, Hans, "The deterrent effects of the death penalty: Facts v. faith," (1976) *Sup. Ct. Rev.* 317.

INDEX